ORGANIZATIONAL

PSYCHOLOGY

Bernard M. Bass

PROFESSOR, GRADUATE SCHOOL OF BUSINESS
DEPARTMENT OF PSYCHOLOGY AND
ADMINISTRATIVE SCIENCE CENTER

UNIVERSITY OF PITTSBURGH

Boston   ALLYN AND BACON, INC.   *1965*

Library of Congress Catalog Card Number 65 – 15299

Printed in the United States of America

First Printing . . January, 1965

Second Printing . . . June, 1966

To those administrators in government, education,
and industry who made this book possible

PREFACE

In a major address at the Walter Van Dyke Bingham lectures at the Carnegie Institute of Technology in 1961, Harold J. Leavitt (1962) called for the recognition of a new field of scientific inquiry, organizational psychology. The field grew directly out of the major interest of industrial psychologists with social processes in industry. By 1963, approximately 500 industrial psychologists in the United States revealed in a survey that from 34 to 43 percent of them were primarily interested in such areas as organizational theory, opinion and morale, organizational planning, and interpersonal relations. However, the study of organizational behavior is multidisciplinary. Engineers, economists, mathematicians, sociologists, and management theorists have also contributed to the growth of the study. While social psychologists in industry have focused on motivation and interpersonal interaction, economists have renewed the vigor of inquiry into the rational aspects of decision processes. Engineers and mathematicians have introduced a "systems" orientation showing how the complete study of organizational behavior must include both production processes and information technology as well as investigation of the men operating the system.

The approach of the economist, engineer, or mathematician will appear in this text only to the extent that we discuss the impact of technology and task on the behavior of management and worker.

This introduction to organizational psychology will begin with a consideration of the role of industry in American society and changing attitudes about its goals and purposes. This will lead us into looking at what motivates men to work and the role of their supervisor and their work group in developing and maintaining such motivation. We will conclude with a detailed inquiry into the nature of the large formal organization and some of what we know about its structure, its communications and its conflicts. A last chapter will consider executive decision-making where rationality is intended but is limited.

Space limitations will restrict inclusion of a variety of issues which might round out the study of organizations, such as creativity and management development. Discussion of these will have to await a volume focused more fully on the psychology of business personnel in which there is sufficient opportunity to examine the theory of individual differences prior to exploring its application to the industrial scene.

In the past few years, I have had an opportunity to consult with industrial managements on a variety of problems. One of the criteria I have used in deciding what to include in this text is based on the following question: Had this management had a course in organizational psychology, what about it would have been most significant to them? Strangely, I did not feel it was only "well-digested" generalities which were needed. Often, what seemed needed was understanding about the likelihood of multiple causation in human behavior, that no single factor was likely to ever account for a majority of one's performance in any single situation. There was need to think in terms of organizational systems.

Past books about social processes in industry often have concentrated on the line-production worker and his problems. While this text will not ignore the psychology of the production worker, it will increase coverage about studies of the skilled technician, the scientist, and the administrator.

This is a book in organizational psychology, primarily a basic discipline. We will deal with issues by trying to determine the fundamentals necessary to understand what affects the issues under study, not by reviewing current practices in industry. For instance, we will discuss the distortions due to attitudes that may occur when a manager relays a message to a subordinate. On the other hand, we will avoid intensive listing of what companies say they are doing to improve communications in their organizations, unless what they say has some generality.

Whenever possible, I have made an effort to restrict generalizations about human behavior and work to what has been demonstrated in actual business and industrial situations. Next, priority has been given to studies carried out in a more controlled but less realistic laboratories. I have been least prone to include material based on work in other organizational settings: military, educational, and institutional. Such material appears mainly when appropriate industrial studies were not found to cover the same points adequately. The text is about organizational psychology. The concepts derive from psychology, but at least half the cited references are from sociological, anthropological, or management sources. No effort was made to exclude phenomena of interest which were originally discussed in terms of disciplinary approaches other than psychology.

I have made a number of assumptions about the student reader.

First, I address this book to an upper undergraduate or graduate student whom I assume has had an introductory course in one of the behavioral sciences such as psychology or sociology, or else can read an elementary book in the subject and learn enough to be able to read this one.

Second, I assume that these students read other books, papers and magazines and know a good deal about all kinds of matters — and when they don't know, they can find out. In fact, I hope that this book raises more questions with students than it answers. As a basic text, I hope it forces the student reader to ask questions of the instructor; I hope it forces the student to ask questions of himself as he reads.

Third, I assume that the body of understanding which the student has at the end of the course is greater for having delved deeper at the expense of not comprehending every point than if the material had been sufficiently easy so that there had been little challenge in its reading.

Fourth, I hope to concentrate on meaning and understanding, rather than facts and figures. There are plenty of facts and figures in the book, but these are included to buttress general areas, to make a point, to focus attention, or to illustrate a trend.

Fifth, I have tried to provide the student with a framework for putting together in an integrated whole the important concepts, principles, and methods of organizational psychology. This has been done by conceiving the criterion problem in larger-than-usual scope, in terms of an industrial organization as a system, a system for which we seek satisfactory outcomes for all involved with the system: stockholders, management, workers and customers.

Sixth, the book is intended for students in business and industrial administration curricula as well as those more directly oriented toward psychology as a career. Some of the discussion may seem parochial to the nonpsychologist, yet it is important that the psychology being presented to the student of business and industry be the "real thing," not a highly modified, popular rendition for laymen, the cream without the milk.

The newer programs at schools of business and industrial organization are building upon bases in mathematics, economics, and psychology. It is important that the material from these disciplines be presented in these curricula without being changed over into the amalgam of business wisdom which formed the substance of older curricula in these schools. Out of these disciplines a new synthesis will arise, it is hoped, which will substitute in the business professional of the future the use of full and formal analysis with both inductive and deductive techniques in place of hunch and intuition.

Current developments in the behavioral sciences, as one reviewer has recently acknowledged, "challenges all who have managerial responsibility to take a long and objective look at what the behavioral scientists are discovering through research".[131] Management must become "an intelligent consumer" of what psychology has to offer. It must no longer remain the dupe of pseudopsychologists. While it does not seem necessary anymore* (as used to be the case with early books in industrial psychology) to warn against the practices of *phrenologists* who offer to select personnel by reading the bumps on the heads of the applicants, or against the *physiognomists* who make much of the facial characteristics judged from photographs, or against *astrologers* and what they can offer management, quackery of the following sort is still very much with us.

A salesman of personality tests may argue convincingly that "statistics can prove anything. Let's have a real demonstration. You take this test that I am selling, and I will give you a report based on your scores. If you don't agree that it's amazingly accurate, I won't try to sell the test to you."[634] Simulating these conditions, 68 personnel managers took a personality test, and all 68 were handed back the underlined *identical* report filled with glittering generalities like: you have a great need for other people to like and admire you, or you have a tendency to be critical of yourself, or security is one of your major goals in life, or you prefer a certain amount of change. Of the 68 managers, 50 percent marked the description as amazingly accurate about themselves while 40 percent marked the description as rather good! Presumably, these managers were ready to buy.

The student of management needs to become a great deal more sophisticated about behavioral science and its applications than those practicing personnel managers just mentioned. The hope is that this book will be of some assistance to the student in this endeavor.

BERNARD M. BASS
Pittsburgh, Pennsylvania

---

*Since writing this, I was informed by the middle management of a large industrial complex that the general manager carefully pursues a management development and promotion program based on the day of the year each manager was born!

ACKNOWLEDGMENTS

I wish to thank James Vaughan for his helpful reviews of the early chapters and Louis Pondy and Wilbur Steger for contributions to Chapter 10. I am particularly grateful for the secretarial help rendered by Mrs. Audrey Silver in the completion of the various drafts of the manuscript and by Miss Cynthia Lanza in the completion of the indexes.

CONTENTS

Chapter 8

Communications in Industrial Organizations   284

Chapter 9

Conflict in Industrial Organizations   318

Chapter 10

Psychological Aspects of Executive Decision-Making   364

ORGANIZATIONAL PSYCHOLOGY

In Brief

ORGANIZATIONAL PSYCHOLOGY IS THE STUDY OF THE INTERPLAY OF MEN and organizations. It employs psychological concepts such as withdrawal to promote understanding of behavior of men in industry as diverse as apathy, daydreaming, absence, lateness, and quitting work. It intends to be a science of verifiable principles rather than an applied art of techniques.

Organizational psychology grew out of industrial psychology. It has strong connections with the other social sciences. It is concerned with many of the major effects on individuals, management, and workers generated by our rapidly changing economy. It considers the effects of automation, information technology, and industrial research and development programs. Likewise, it looks at how the potential impact on industry of our many social and economic values has led to a more sophisticated level of psychological research in industry.

The organization is seen as a system of human, material, and monetary inputs and outputs. In turn, organizational psychology focuses on the way management, workers, owners, and the public reach a balance in their respective objectives which are manifold and diverse, not solely economic, social, or psychological.

Chapter 1

INTRODUCTION TO

ORGANIZATIONAL PSYCHOLOGY

ANY SCIENCE, BE IT PSYCHOLOGY OR PHYSICS, AIMS TO UNDERSTAND selected processes, products, and events. Understanding is checked by investigating the accuracy of predictions based on the understanding. Control of the processes, products, and events can be a result.

The science of organizational psychology deals with the products and process of business—the interaction of men with money and materials. Business, a social institution, is "too important to be studied only by economists."[277] To illustrate the importance of man in the mix of men, money, and materials, consider, for example, the amount of money and materials invested for *each* worker in the petroleum industry. In 1959, the amount was $62,000; this compared to an average investment per worker of $37,000 in the same industry in 1951. Comparable figures for other industries are shown in Table 1.1. Although the amounts are far less in such industries as food products, there are similar upward trends.

TABLE 1.1   AVERAGE INVESTMENT PER WORKER BY INDUSTRY*

Industry	1959 (thousands)	1951 (thousands)	Percent Change 1951–1959
Petroleum	$62	$37	+ 68
Distilling	53	40	+ 33
Tobacco	51	50	+ 2
Nonferrous Metals	28	15	+ 87
Chemicals	25	17	+ 47
Iron & Steel	21	11	+ 91
Autos & Trucks	15	7	+114
Food Products	11	7	+ 57

*From Forbes, October 15, 1962

Today, it is hard to realize how little attention was paid to the human factor in industry. In the early 1930's, it was possible to write the following:

So dominant has been the regard for the machine that until very recently the insignificant man placed in an obscure corner of industrial portraits has been assigned to a very minor role in the evaluation of factors responsible for the development of modern industry and for the success of our industrial civilization.[704, p.3]

There has been a drastic change in concern for the human factor in industry in the past three decades. We hope to document fully this revised view of the organizational mix of men working in collaboration to extract, create, or distribute materials, commodities, or services.

Conceptual Level of Study

Business, industry, and other social institutions, public or private, profit or nonprofit, engaged in processing goods or services, can only be described by an organizational psychology which is comprehensive, and not merely a collection of specialized techniques. As a scientific discipline dedicated to the formulation of principles for understanding the interaction of men on the one hand, with money and materials on the other, organizational psychology's methods are its means for promoting understanding. The methods are not ends in themselves.

We move from an applied technology to a distinct science of organizational psychology by using concepts from general psychology. Thus we examine psychological factors such as *withdrawal*, which in industry appears as apathy, fantasy, quitting, absence, and tardiness. We do this rather than center attention on a particular personnel symptom such as *avoidable turnover*. That is to say, we treat avoidable turnover as a manifestation of withdrawal, as part of a more general set of dynamics involving what attracts a worker and what holds him to his job. Again, instead of focusing on the economic or legal aspects of labor-management relations and what general principles of psychology might be applicable, we consider labor-management relations part of the larger issue of resolving intergroup conflict. Many of the same psychological phenomena of intergroup rivalry are seen whether two departments in the same company are competing, whether the company and unions are in conflict, or whether the staff and line are locked in a struggle for control of the organization. Instead of discussing specifics, such as how to set up and maintain a suggestion system, we focus on larger social-psychological issues, such as how to foster more efficient communication feedback to management. These examples illustrate how, wherever possible, we try to translate industrial events of a social character into psychologically meaningful terms.

BACKGROUND OF ORGANIZATIONAL PSYCHOLOGY

Management involves the control of men, money, and materials for the extraction, production, and distribution of goods. Like other sciences of importance to modern management, psychology develops principles—and methods of prediction to check those principles—to provide ways to increase control of the systems to be managed.

Organizational psychology is one among many scientific disciplines required for the full objective examination of the world of work. It has many connections to other disciplines, particularly economics, physical sciences, and various behavioral sciences. For instance, wages are both an economic and a psychological issue. On the other hand, resistance to change has engineering as well as psychological ramifications. Figure 1.1 displays some of the connections between organizational psychology and the physical and other behavioral sciences.

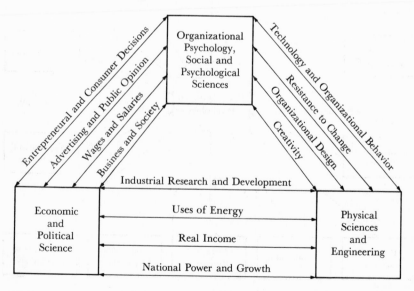

Figure 1.1: Some of the Interdisciplinary Connections Between Organizational Psychology and Related Social, Economic, Political, and Physical Sciences.

Organizational psychology itself is rooted in many disciplines, the most important of which are displayed in Figure 1.2. Significant traces of all the disciplines noted in Figure 1.2 can be seen. Some of these, like the industrial engineering of Fredrick W. Taylor, have made their mark and passed on; others, like the social psychology of Kurt Lewin, are directly influencing the course of events in the field today.

Organizational psychology may draw heavily on the techniques and concepts of *social psychology* when, for instance, the study concerns the contrasts in the way workers and managers perceive the union movement. From *educational psychology* come principles of communication, training, and change. *Clinical psychology* offers knowledge about adjustment and reaction to conflict. *Psychometrics* describes individual differences and techniques for evaluating the measurements used to assess attitude, opinion, and belief. *Experimental psychology* furnishes organizational psychology with a variety of methods for testing hypotheses about supervision, communications, and organizational designs. To *engineering psychology* and to *industrial engineering* we are indebted for formal tech-

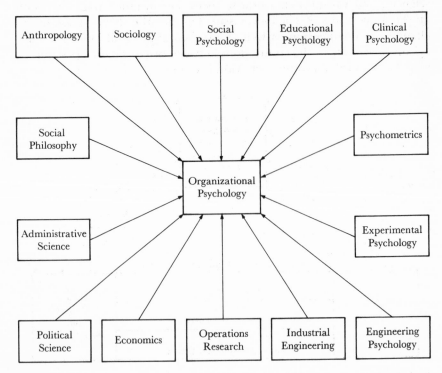

Figure 1.2: Disciplines Contributing to the Study of Organizational Psychology.

niques to describe and analyze work and systems of work. *Operations research* has contributed logical and mathematical techniques for analyses of the flow of work and information in large organizations. *Economics* provides a body of knowledge about decision-making and bargaining and offers a systematic account of the problem of labor-management relations. From the study of *management and administration* comes classical organization theory compounded of a traditional understanding of manager-worker relations, management experience and wisdom. From *political science* comes a philosophy about formal organizations, particularly the rules to which men ought to be committed. The study of organizational goals and values stems from *social philosophy*. An account of how work gets done in primitive societies is one contribution of *anthropology*; another is the description of consistent patterns of contact of men working in modern industry. Like social psychology, *sociology* is a particularly fertile source for organizational psychology. Sociological treatises on the subject of bureaucracy, as well as on the informal work group, pioneered in changing the method of study of formal organizations. This method was revised from a purely rational exposition grounded in ancient military tactics to one based more closely on the realities of human behavior.

Industrial psychology is the parent discipline which spawned organizational psychology as well as *engineering psychology, vocational psychology,* and *consumer psychology.*

Organizational Psychology: Past, Present, Future

Until the 1930's, psychology in industry was applied primarily as a technology to deal with vocational or personnel problems and secondarily with differences in individual aptitudes and proficiency, and the physical factors of work. Only modest interest was displayed in the social elements in industry. But from these modest beginnings has grown the full-fledged study of the individual as a member of a large, formal industrial organization and as a member of a work group within that organization (Figure 1.3). Now, not only are we interested in his working associates and physical arrangements, but also in the peculiarities of the communication networks in which the worker finds himself, as well as the effects of the historical and prescribed rules surrounding the workplace.

Since the 1920's, psychology in industry has shifted its main attention from the manual worker and problems associated with repetitive

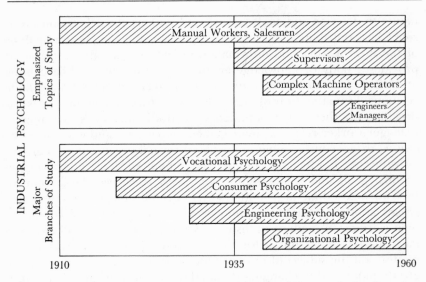

Figure 1.3: *The Development of Organizational Psychology and other Branches of Industrial Psychology.*

work and physical deterrents like poor lighting to the technician and administrator and the social, organizational, and technological impediments in his working environment. This shift, of course, parallels the changing nature of work in the United States, the reduction of the proportion of manual workers, and the increase in the proportion of service, technical, and administrative workers in the total American work force.

The Great Depression of the 1930's resulted in an upsurge of concern for counseling the unemployed. Massive concern for the unemployed re-occurred in the late 1950's as jobs disappeared for those with less education and skill. Such interest stimulated work on occupational information and aptitude testing. The growth of labor unions, as a consequence of the Depression and New Deal legislation, was seen by students of the union movement to have aroused in management much more of a desire for better human relations in industry. They viewed this concern for human relations as a search by management for an alternative to accepting collective bargaining and unionism.[248] And in some instances they may have been right. But the fact that the rise of the union, particularly the industrial union, occurred during the same period as the sponsorship by management of studies of employe morale does not necessarily mean that one was a consequence of the other. In fact, one observer who "lived through this era, knew management sponsors of research and something of their thinking" feels today that the threat of unionization was rarely an important factor in the promotion by management of research in psychology in industry at that time. He argues that:

Mostly such studies were sponsored because managements were genuinely interested in getting a better understanding of their own organizations and organization and personnel problems. Also, after the passage of the Wagner Act, it was illegal to interfere with unionization, and the forward-looking managements that sponsored research in their organizations tended to be ones that were not about to engage in illegal activities.*

It is interesting to note, in this connection, that during the deliberations before the passage of the Wagner Labor Relations Act in 1937, it was argued that the act would not help the union movement because management would simply disobey the law, fight unionization illegally and unfairly, and engage in court battles taking many years to settle, which, in effect, would effectively block unionization. After passage of the act, purely self-seeking, ruthless, and rational management might have adopted such delaying tactics (as some actually did—and quite successfully). But most managements actually obeyed the law, even if it was not in their self-interest to do so. That is, most set higher value in obeying the law of the land than in maintaining a possibly stronger bargaining position with their employes gained through illegal means.

The point is that the typical American manager in the late 1930's was simply not the robber baron of the 1890's. He had developed more of a sense of responsibility as a citizen and community member. For instance, Myron C. Taylor of U.S. Steel is said to have accepted collective bargaining with the United Steel Workers to avoid bloodshed, even though he could probably have successfully kept the union out of U.S. Steel if he had elected to fight.

The manager had changed in other ways between World War I and World War II. Now he preferred to be liked rather than disliked by his employes. He certainly saw the importance of being liked by the public. He was interested in learning how he could be viewed more favorably by his employes. And he generally felt that better employe relations meant higher production and profits (although we shall see in Chapter 2 that sometimes he may have been mistaken about this).

This change in the 1920's and 1930's in what was valued by management, therefore, created a climate conducive to psychological research in industry.

It may also have been that the popularization of Freud's ideas about unconscious motivation in the 1920's and 1930's stimulated enlightened managers to ask more sophisticated questions about worker needs and

*Personal communication from F. R. Wickert, October 9, 1963.

drives. In the same way a revolution was occurring in American child-rearing practices stimulated by national press and radio. This, in turn, paralleled the changes taking place in our schools where much more attention was being focused on the socioemotional aspects of learning and development. The manager, looking around him, seeing all these developments, surely must have been set to wondering about the implications to worker-management relations of social needs, frustration and aggression, shared decision-making, or learning-by-doing.

World War II focused attention on operating complex, high-speed equipment, generating the vast increase in engineering psychology. Aptitude testing for military assignments became standard operating procedure, further speeding the application of such testing in industry.

Following World War II there was an acceleration in the shift of workers from direct production to sales, clerical, and technical service. Now more Americans are working in service-oriented occupations than in production, and the shift away from production towards service continues. Indeed if the trends continue into the 1970's and onward, as shown in Figure 1.4 for the period 1947 to 1962, there will be a further proportionate reduction in the number of blue-collar workers required in production, and more will gravitate to white-collar activities. At the same time the material return in average weekly earnings will continue to climb faster than the cost of living (Figure 1.5). Each worker will

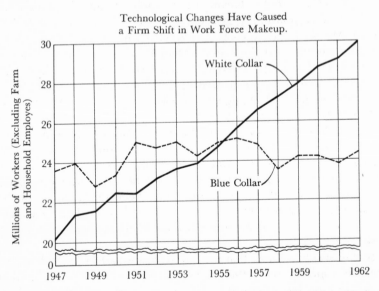

Figure 1.4: Shift in U.S. Work Force (1947–1962). (The New York Times, July 14, 1963, Sec. 4, p. 3E)

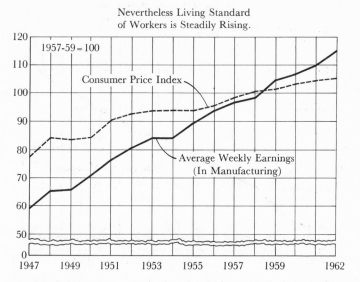

Figure 1.5: Rise in U.S. Worker Productivity (1947–1962).
(The New York Times, *July 14, 1963, Sec. 4, p. 3E)*

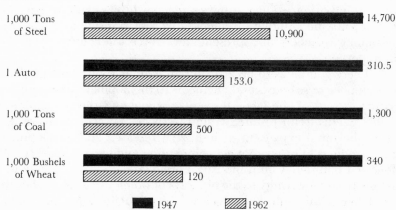

Figure 1.6: Reduction in Numbers of U.S. Production Workers (1947–1962).
(The New York Times, *July 14, 1963, Sec. 4, p. 3E)*

The Use of New Machinery Has
Increased Workers' Productivity.

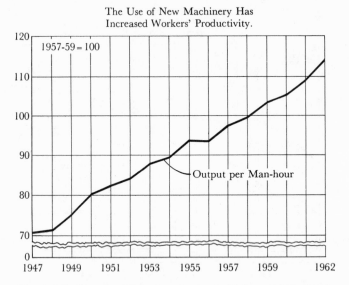

Figure 1.7: Rise in U.S. Standard of Living (1947–1962).
(The New York Times, July 14, 1963, Sec. 4, p. 3E)

earn more, yet produce more at an even greater rate as a consequence of
automation and other substitutions of equipment for manpower (Figures 1.6 and 1.7).

The individual member of an organization will be less mobile because of the benefits of seniority. This will place a further premium on
accurate selection practices as management becomes increasingly aware
of their importance. Once admitted the new hire is likely to remain with
the organization until retirement. Likewise transfer and training or
retraining members of a present work force will continue to increase
in importance.

There continues to be a steady growth, as shown in Figure 1.8 in
the number of scientists and engineers in the population in comparison
to the growth of the labor force as a whole and the population as a
whole.[82] This trend resulted from the space and armaments race, and
from the rapid expansion of industrial research and development of
new products in order to meet competition and expand markets. What
followed naturally within industrial organizations was a change in emphasis from conformity to the old ways of doing things to establishing a
creative environment, one which would stimulate rather than stifle innovation, flexibility, and change. The management of large laboratories
of scientists and engineers required considerable rethinking of the or-

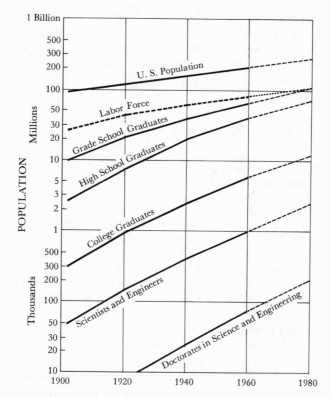

Figure 1.8: Growth of the Proportion of Scientists and Engineers in the U.S. (1900–1980). (After Brode, 1962, p. 4)

ganizational strategies of the past demanding emphasis on chains of command, specification of duties, and decisions by authority.

Looking Ahead. Organizational psychology will increase its attention to scientific and technical productivity and to the revolutionary advances that have occurred in information technology. Men at work will be observed in the context of the automated methods available for registering, transmitting, storing, calculating, deciding, and distributing results of decisions in the large organization.

The automation of our factories has been paralleled by the growth of information technology, of high-speed data processing, of statistical and mathematical methods of decision-making, and of mathematical programming and the simulation of higher-order thinking by computers. These developments suggest certain consequences for the organization of the future. Planning responsibilities will probably be shifted from middle management to higher-level specialists (including behavioral scientists) who will serve as staff aides to top management. More of middle management's decisions will be programmed — and therefore relegated to computer decisions. Innovation and creativity will continue to increase in importance as programmers move to the staffs of top management:

a search-and-research-oriented management, increasingly concerned with abstract rather than practical considerations. The increasing specialization, calling for more of an interchange among executives, programmers, innovators, and creators, will put a further emphasis on the study of the group approach to solving problems and the study of how to increase group effectiveness. These specialists will enter the organization at all levels requiring more accurate, highly refined psychological selection procedures for such high-level personnel. Their training will more likely be at universities, rather than on-the-job in specialized disciplines rather than in general management, as such.[397]

Organizational psychology may become more concerned eventually with studying the interaction of automated data, expert mathematicians, economists, psychologists, and operators of a productive system than with the interaction of general administrators and those in the hierarchy below them operating the system.

Organizational psychology will increase its cross-cultural interest sparked by the growth of interdependence among nations as well as by the growth of the international corporation with world-wide interests. Much of the early psychological research in industry was European. However, beginning with World War I, there has been an ever-increasing contribution by American psychologists to the field. American values heavily influence a psychology of American workers and management developed by American psychologists. It is doubtful that generalities based on American research about the social psychology of management and workers necessarily will have global applicability. Fortunately, we are beginning to discern large cross-cultural studies in organizational psychology. For example, a massive questionnaire survey of 200 executives in each of 18 selected countries has recently been completed pointing to a variety of consistent differences between managers in northern European, southern European, and newly industrialized countries in needs, goals, and satisfactions.[534]

Changes in Understanding of Motivation to Work

The increased sophistication and breadth in psychology in the business world is seen in the increasing understanding of motivation to work. Just one generation separates us from the pioneering studies of Elton Mayo and his associates who prior to the advent of World War II made popular with management the notion that workers are human.[562]

The Committee on Industrial Illumination was formed in 1924 by the National Research Council under the honorary chairmanship of Thomas A. Edison. Represented on this committee to demonstrate experimentally the effects of improved factory lighting on production were many prominent physicists, physiologists, ophthalmologists, and electrical engineers.

A series of pilot experiments were designed and carried out. Everything went according to plan at first. When illumination was made stronger for a test group at the Hawthorne Works of the Western Electric Company, production increased. The surprise came when illumination was lowered to its original strength: instead of dropping back, production continued to climb. When two groups were used in the test and only one was given the benefit of increased illumination, the production of both groups continued to climb. The same continued increase by a relay assembly group was observed with the introduction *and the later removal* of rest pauses. Control groups for which no changes were made in hours of work, illumination and rest showed production increases also.

Production continued to climb despite adverse physical conditions. Employes had developed a great deal of satisfaction from being able to communicate their ideas to management in the course of the experiments. They had developed the feeling that they had a voice in decisions concerning themselves.[41, pp.7-9]

Mayo's team concluded that industrial conflict was a function of irrational motives, that the informal organization was paramount to determining production and personnel problems, and that the primary work group was a closed system whose increased effectiveness was the means to increased industrial productivity. The conclusions were not actually completely warranted by the data, and while today it is generally conceded that industrial conflict partly may be a function of the needs for aggression arising from psychological tensions it is also understood that the conflict may be rational, economic behavior. Today, we also feel that the formal organization and what management wants may strongly affect productive efforts; and while the primary work group does exert influence on productivity, we can only account for worker performance if we understand the prevailing economic conditions, individual values and personality, union policies, and many other aspects of the open society in which the work group is embedded.[371]

The "human relationists" of the 1930's equated good management with authoritative but benevolent administration and ignored the functions and purposes of unions. Current behavioral scientists evaluate highly management that enhances the importance of an individual's rights and needs for self-determination and recognizes the positive significance of unions in successful relations. The problem in the 1930's was adjustment of man to machines; today it is the discovery of the

mode of organization, leadership, and values that will enhance the
mental health of worker and management alike. The human relationists
of the 1930's made popular the case as *the* method for training administrators in the "art" of human relations. Today, many more sophisticated, psychologically oriented methods are employed. For instance,
there is now considerable use of sensitivity training, psychodrama, and
business gaming. These contrived situations help the trainee to discover
his own strong and weak points. He thereby is brought to understand
better how groups actually work by focusing on his own behavior as he
tries to solve specific problems which develop as he works with others.

Changes in Psychological Research in Industry

Gradually psychological research in industry is beginning to grapple
with basic issues instead of continuing to study only applied problems,
problems usually of immediate concern to management but with relatively little generality. Basic behavioral research units have been established by such companies as General Electric and Bell Laboratories.
These formal units, with sufficient freedom to undertake long-range
programs in the behavioral sciences, have counterparts in at least a
dozen additional industrial research groups who are doing research
beyond simply "serving management." Such groups are to be found at
Prudential Life Insurance; Pillsbury Mills; Sears, Roebuck; Standard
Oil of New Jersey; Procter & Gamble; and A.T.&.T.[182]
Organizational psychology still relies heavily on R–R studies,
studies in which two or more sets of responses are examined simultaneously in a search for consistent relations between the behaviors.
For instance, the productivity of each of 28 departments will be obtained
for a given period. Then, each department supervisor will be asked to
indicate his concern for the welfare of his subordinates. Each supervisor's score will be plotted against his department's productivity as in
Figure 1.9. The correlation coefficient indicates how close all the plotted
points are to the best-fitting straight line. If the correlation were +1.0,
all the points would fall on the line. One could perfectly state a department's productivity just by knowing the supervisor's concern for his
subordinates. The correlation would be 0 if the points were scattered
helter-skelter all over the chart. A negative correlation would merely
indicate that the relation was reversed, that high productivity occurred
when supervisors lacked concern for subordinates.
When the results shown in Figure 1.9 are obtained, investigators
jump to the conclusion that supervisors who show consideration for

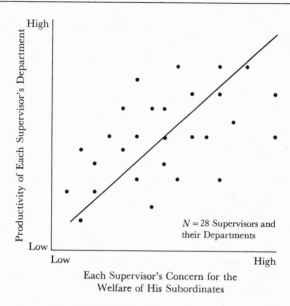

Figure 1.9: Hypothetical Illustration of an R-R Study.

their subordinates make them into a more productive department. But this R – R result, this correlation of two sets of responses, could equally suggest that a supervisor can afford to show more consideration for his subordinates only when his department is productive. An S – R experiment is needed to settle the matter. Here the investigator systematically alters the stimulating conditions, then notes how the responses of his subjects are changed as a consequence. For example, the researcher might test the hypothesis that when departments are productive, the supervisor feels he can afford to be more considerate of his subordinates. The researcher can do this by setting up, say, three kinds of departments to be supervised. In the first department the task is made so easy that the workers cannot help but reach maximum production levels. In the second department the task is moderately difficult; and in the third it is so difficult that workers are relatively unproductive. After the supervisors, who are unaware that the source of productivity differences are due to the different tasks assigned by the experimenter, have seen production reports, their attitudes are assessed concerning how considerate they ought to be of their subordinates.

Because it is so difficult and expensive to run such S – R experiments on the job, laboratory simulations of the workplace are likely to be used by the future behavioral science advisor to top management. He may become more like the operations-research scientist in proposing systems-modifications, then checking with his simulations to see if his forecasts about the effects of his modifications indeed occur as expected.

For these experiments the stimulating conditions may be physical, social, or psychological, as long as the experimenter can specify how he brought them about. The responses to the varying stimulus conditions may be objective or subjective. The quantity of items produced, the number of errors made, the number of times late, the volume of sales, or the amount of correct answers to a test of information are all examples of objective behavior. Statements by the subjects about how they feel, what they believe, what they think they see, or what they expect, illustrate subjective responses. The experimenter will need to show the *relevance* and the *reliability* of the responses he employs. He may argue that the responses to a job-knowledge test for electricians, for example, are *relevant* or *valid* to measure knowledge of that job because the *contents* of the test were developed and approved by a group of subject-matter experts. Or he may cite, as evidence of the *concurrent* validity of the test scores, the higher scores of electricians than non-electricians who took the test. He may point to the *predictive* validity of the test by showing that high-scoring apprentices were rated as better electricians six months later by their supervisors than low-scoring electricians. Or he may try to prove the *construct* validity of the test by showing that logical expectations about what one should be able to do with electrical knowledge displayed on the test were confirmed when subjects were confronted with new problems whose solutions required such knowledge.

The *reliability* of the response measurements would be demonstrated if the subjects earned the same relative scores repeatedly.*

Some Typical Problems

Management asks such questions of organizational psychology:

What can we do to get people in an organization to say what they think instead of merely saying what they think their bosses want to hear? How can the full range of ideas available in a group be brought to the surface? How do interpersonal relationships either facilitate or inhibit problem-solving effectiveness in business? How may the facilitating effects of group and personal

*A thorough treatment of the subject of measurement validity and reliability is not intended here; we merely wish to state here that measurements of human behavior require careful evaluation. For such treatment the reader is referred to textbooks on the measurement of individual differences such as L. J. Cronbach, *Essentials of Psychological Testing*. New York: Harper, 1960.

interactions be capitalized upon to maximize organizational problem-solving effectiveness?

How do we use our computer facilities to increase feedback to employes? What kinds of information will contribute positively to the motivation of employes? What measures of results may be developed to enhance the learning and/ or continued productive efforts on the part of all employes-managerial as well as rank and file? May the measures be "computerized"? In what form may information be presented most effectively to employes?

Should our diversification of organization be along product, process, or geographical lines? What are the significant human factors to be considered here as they interact with purely economic and engineering issues? What is the type of diversification likely to do for management development and organizational flexibility?

What are the effects of budgetary controls on executive behavior? What are the effects of group identification on negotiators? How is a decision-making team affected by the introduction of computer decisions into its deliberations?

What effects may be expected from flattening the structure of our organizational hierarchy? What new managerial skills may be required? How will they be developed? What new controls may be necessary that are not required in a more vertically organized company? How will these be developed and implemented?[183]

The frequent occurrence of these many fundamental problems in the typical large firm has led to the suggestion by the head of an international management program that companies should seriously consider creating a position of Vice President for the Behavioral Sciences comparable in rank and position to a Vice President in charge of Research and Development. One wonders how much more concern and awareness of these kinds of problems would occur in a company if one of its six vice presidents were a behavioral scientist and assigned to such a position?

To appreciate how organizational psychology proposes to attack such problems, we must turn to what it sees as its aims and how its purposes are dependent on a variety of value judgments.

THE AIMS OF PSYCHOLOGY
IN INDUSTRY

When psychology was involved primarily with improving techniques for selecting workers or developing principles about a better workplace, the utility of these efforts was assumed to be measured by such criteria as increased quality and quantity of worker output, reduced accident rates, and reduced energy expenditure. A criterion was considered particularly relevant if it could be directly related to money and increased profits. Increased worker satisfaction also was seen as a potential criterion of the success of a psychological program, for it was argued (erroneously) that more satisfied workers were necessarily more productive workers.

This approach to setting goals and measuring success of the psychologist's program had basic inherent difficulties. Relevant measures of worker output often depended on a complexity of factors, many of which were out of the worker's control. For example, a salesman's objective volume of sales might depend upon how much local and national advertising appeared in his territory during the sales period, local and national marketing trends, what his fellow company sales and service representatives were doing, the kind of pricing practices his company permitted him to use, and what his competitors were offering during this period.

A worker's success on the job was, and is, most often based on his supervisor's appraisal of how much of what he is doing is of worth to the company. But this evaluation of worth to the company requires someone else to determine just what is of worth to the company.[210] Is the good salesman one who gets as many new customers as possible without much repeat business? Is the good salesman one who builds up the company image in an area making it easier for his fellow salesman to work effectively? Is the good salesman one whose daily reports are most accurate and complete? Or, what? To determine what is of worth to the company, we must determine the company's objectives. To assume that there is a single ultimate objective—to make as much money as possible for the stockholders—is an erroneous oversimplification. Success in reaching the various ultimate objectives of a company is measured by a complex, interacting system of variables. To understand these complex objectives, we must enlarge the scope of our investigations and be ready to examine the interaction among those variables, for the interaction of man, economics, and technology is complex. "Attention is turning from simple cause and effect relationships between variables to . . . the fact that changes at one point in the system may bring about related changes in many variables throughout the system."[708, p.415] For example, Procter & Gamble decided to increase its effort to provide steady employment for its personnel. To do this led to a whole series of moves each contributing directly or indirectly to the goal of stabilizing jobs. And as a consequence, any research program or managerial action had to be evaluated in terms of how it facilitated these various organizational moves.

First, in order to provide steady jobs, sales and production had to be stabilized. More selling had to be done in off-seasons to have steady sales. This required an aggressive sales force, sound and flexible pricing policies, as well as efficient advertising. But the vagaries of the market place are such that sales still fluctuated a good deal; therefore to maintain steady production, there had to be more production for stock. This, in turn, demanded better inventory control, accurate sales forecasts, sound financing, and, of course, a product which is durable or storable. Above and beyond these technical considerations , employes had to be both willing and able to transfer from one assignment to another.

At the same time, stockholders and management had to be willing and able to support the research needed to develop new products, to diversify the production line, and to dovetail with the off-season market for older products.[238]

The Organization as a System

The organizational mix of men, money, and materials is a system of inputs, outputs, and waste as shown in Figure 1.10. Inputs of human effort, monetary and material expenditures produce psychic rewards, money, and products and services. Along with these outputs are outputs of satisfaction to employes, to management, and to the sponsor of the organization, its stockholders, as well as the outputs of value to the community and to society.[34]

System Inputs. While the costs in money and material are salient to the industrial observer, less attention is usually paid to the human costs of industrial enterprise. And just as it is important to work towards reducing the financial and material costs for a given output of goods and values, so it is important to work towards reductions in such matters as training time to reach proficient performance.

System Outputs. It would be unrealistic and superficial to reduce the evaluation of outputs to profits alone. First, there are too many forms of enterprise such as airlines, operating at a loss, whose existence is maintained in the public interest by public subsidies. Second, whether or not a particular organization is making a profit often may be a paper maneuver. The refinery may show a loss year after year, yet its parent holding company may be buying from it at a price resulting in the continued loss. In the overall scheme of things, the "unprofitable" refinery may still be regarded as an asset to the parent organization. Third, it may often be impossible to relate particular management decisions to the profit-and-loss statement. For example, how often has it been shown that a management training program brings about increased profits?

As some stock market investors have discovered to their chagrin, current high net profits actually may be an unhealthy sign indicating that a particularly efficient part of the organization has been sold at

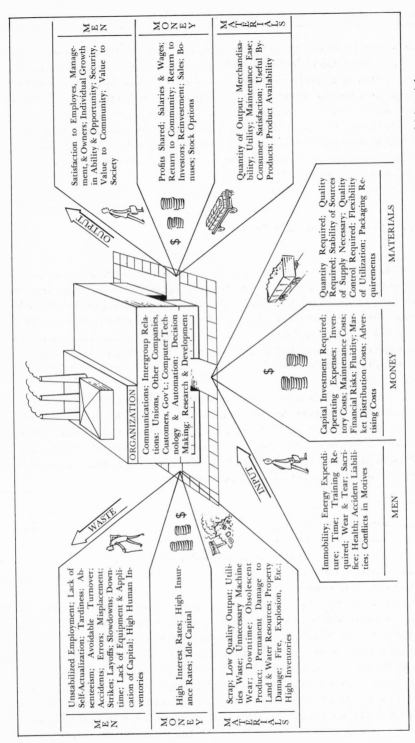

MEN

Satisfaction to Employes, Management, & Owners; Individual Growth in Ability & Opportunity; Security; Value to Community; Value to Society

MONEY

Profits Shared; Salaries & Wages; Return to Community; Return to Investors; Reinvestment; Sales; Bonuses; Stock Options

MATERIALS

Quantity of Output; Merchandisability; Utility; Maintenance Ease; Consumer Satisfaction; Useful By-Products; Product Availability

OUTPUT

ORGANIZATION

Communications; Intergroup Relations; Unions, Other Companies, Customers, Gov't.; Computer Technology & Automation; Decision Making; Research & Development

INPUT

MEN

Immobility; Energy Expenditure; Time; Training Required; Wear & Tear; Sacrifice; Health; Accident Liabilities; Conflicts in Motives

MONEY

Capital Investment Required; Operating Expenses; Inventory Costs; Maintenance Costs; Financial Risks; Fluidity; Market Distribution Costs; Advertising Costs

MATERIALS

Quantity Required; Quality Required; Stability of Sources of Supply Necessary; Quality Control Required; Flexibility of Utilization; Packaging Requirements

WASTE

MEN

Unstabilized Employment; Lack of Self-Actualization; Tardiness; Absenteeism; Avoidable Turnover; Accidents; Errors; Misplacement; Strikes; Layoffs; Slowdowns; Downtime; Lack of Equipment & Application of Capital; High Human Inventories

MONEY

High Interest Rates; High Insurance Rates; Idle Capital

MATERIALS

Scrap; Low Quality Output; Utilities Waste; Unnecessary Machine Wear; Downtime; Obsolescent Product; Permanent Damage to Land & Water Resources; Property Damage: Fire, Explosion, Etc.; High Inventories

Figure 1.10: *The Business Organization as a System of Inputs, Outputs, and Waste of Men, Money, and Materials.*

a good price, but that future earnings will be lower as a consequence of the sale of the property. In the same way a low net profit may be a sign of health due to a fast depreciation of capital equipment to reduce profits and current taxes, as well as to increase funds available for reinvestment in new plants.

Net worth would seem to be an objective accounting of the state of health of a firm, yet its calculation often involves many subjective judgments ranging from estimates of the value of as-yet-unsold stock in inventory to the good will of the firm.

Large numbers of executives, when observed in setting objectives for a simulated firm in a business game, usually set as their target some rate of growth for their firms. Again, it is sometimes difficult to evaluate the actual growth that occurs and what will follow afterwards, but it is likely that attainment of a desired growth rate comes closer than any other criterion to evaluating the success of a firm. Yet, here is a completely relative outcome.

For example, one set of executives elects to work for a 5 percent annual growth, returning a good portion of earnings to their investors annually. Another set elects to strive for a 15 percent rate, plowing back into the business each year all they have earned. Cash flows differently in the different firms, yet each may be equally successful in meeting the stated objectives of the firm's managers.

A large proportion of decisions within an organization are a consequence of many other goals, not necessarily related to profits. The output objectives, the goals of management, are multiple and include such aims as public service, high quality products, prestige for the company, continued growth of the organization, even though each of these objectives may not contribute to profits. Indeed, some of these objectives may even conflict with maximizing profits.

System Wastes. Waste is usually defined in terms of money and materials. Yet, we have reached a point in our industrial society where we must regard the inadequate use of our available human resources as a waste and an inhibition of progress. Layoffs and strikes are examples of such waste. In the same way the hoarding of engineering talent, using five engineers where one engineer and four clerks could do the same job, is another kind of extravagance our society, as well as the company in question, can ill afford. In the same way, when employes are misassigned to jobs too big for them, the $11,000 to $62,000 invested in capital for each employe (Table 1.1) makes this mismatching of employe and job a financial drain as well as a source of human frustration.

Affecting the influence of the inputs on the outputs are ways in which decisions are made within the organization, with other groups, such as unions, trade associations, other companies, customers, and government, and communication patterns within the organization. Coloring all this is the society in which the organization finds itself and the prevailing values of that society. More will be said about this shortly.

The Aim: To Optimize the System.   A most important point discerned by viewing organization as a system of many mutually influencing inputs and outputs is this: We cannot maximize any single output for a given amount of input without reducing one or more other outputs. In the same way, for a given output we cannot minimize a particular input without increasing some other input or inputs.[180] Thus if we demand immediate profits as high as possible, we only may obtain these profits by, say, reducing consumer satisfaction in the short run and producing a less merchandisable product in the long run. Or if we reduce the training time required to a basic minimum, we may increase the cost of materials by producing an increased waste of materials. ". . . any attempt to maximize some organizational output or to minimize some organizational input or waste is bound to end in less than desired outcomes somewhere else in the system. One can't have his cake and eat it too . . ."[183] The problem, thus, is not *how* do we maximize profits; rather, it is *what* are we trying to optimize? What is it we want to make as good as possible with the constraints and limitations in which our organization must operate? The answer is a relative one; for what we are trying to optimize depends on the *values* of the society within which we operate, particularly on the values of those who manage our business enterprises. Differences among organizations in different countries are likely to be due to a considerable degree to differences in the predominant values of the different countries.

IMPORTANCE OF VALUES

Predominant Values in American Society

Values characterizing American society include activitism, optimism, equalitarianism, abundance, and pragmatism. Our activistic, optimistic, and pragmatic society considers it better to act than to think, better to achieve than to be, and better to do than to contemplate.

Each of these values plays a considerable role when managers make efforts to optimize the system they must operate, when they review budgets, set objectives, or evaluate performance. Let us cite a hypothesis about how each value would color a judgment by the typical manager to illustrate the possible significance of each of these values.

Activism. The Protestant ethic is accepted that work is good; idleness is bad.[446] The system optimizer will put more weight on doing than on planning and thinking. An idle supervisor is likely to be downgraded by his boss, yet he may be making long-range plans, and he has this time to think because he has done such a good job planning in the past. Busy work must be found for temporarily unoccupied workers. For them to sit and do nothing is intolerable.

Optimism. We tend to believe that tomorrow will be better than today, and the new model will be better than the old one. Generally, organization leaders assume business and their share of the business will grow, not decline. They work to make it so. The economy would be extremely different if entrepreneurs and consumers were pessimists, who, for example, refused to ever go into debt for fear that their future income would be reduced.

Equalitarianism. Equalitarian attitudes and the openness of our society make it easier for all concerned to see that investors, management, and workers share a common interest in the success of their firm. Undoubtedly it would be more difficult in a society with rigid class lines for management to think in terms of an equitable balance of returns to all interests. At the same time the relation of American worker and manager is strongly influenced by their membership in an open society. It has been said that, while the typical class-conscious worker in less-open societies would like to destroy the upper classes, the American worker seems more interested in trying to emulate or to join the upper class. The British worker, for example, feels a sharp class distinction from management, coupled with a strong loyalty to fellow workers. However, according to a review of several hundred reports of British productivity teams in the United States, the American worker-management struggle is not like the European effort. The American worker is seen as fighting to gain power and benefits in the system, but he subscribes to the system and wants to maintain it. Despite the fact that union and government protect him, reducing his feelings of insecurity and his need for self-reliance, American workers are seen by British observers as remaining "productivity-minded" with a sense of "adventurous urgency in both management and men."[627] Yet, more open conflict is possible in the United States for those in less favored positions, such as the Negro or the worker in an old-fashioned sweatshop. They can aspire and legitimately fight to achieve real equality

when the society subscribes to equalitarian values and to open movement and communication but does not practice them fully. (As we shall
see in Chapter 9, there are decided differences between American
labor-management conflict and that in other industrialized societies.)

Abundance. Abundance has particular relevance. Consumers and
entrepreneurs alike accept and maintain a system of high cost, high
waste, and high output, purchasing new automobiles or plant equipment every few years and junking rather than trying to maintain older
hard goods. The attitude towards abundance makes the whole scheme
economically feasible, for the mass demand for the new material makes
the cost of production low enough so that it is cheaper to replace than
repair equipment. This, in turn, increases our belief in the goodness
of a sense of abundance. Whether our society is benefited as much by
the accelerated production-consumption cycle is another matter, for
there is an enormous cost in human and natural resources which might
be better spent in other ways.

Pragmatism. While some managers of firms might be willing to try
out new ideas because they follow accepted principles or because author-
ities have recommended them, the typical American executive is more
likely to base his decision on his guess about "will it work?" When choosing between different programs, the one which intuitively seems most
likely to work will be selected.

Again, each of these values may strongly influence what is seen by
management as satisfactory levels of output, input, and waste.

The manager must optimize the system for which he is responsible
in the absence of complete information about what will come into the
system, what will be produced, and with what waste. Even if his decisions
about his objectives involved less risk and uncertainty, they would be
still influenced by his values. Particularly because of the many uncertainties and ambiguities facing him when he makes judgments about
optimizing the mix of men, money, and materials, he becomes strongly
influenced by his own values. These, however, may contribute nothing
to a firm's net worth or to its profit-and-loss statement, but make matters more satisfying to the manager. In addition to the pervasive values
already mentioned, there are values about organizational life which
strongly affect a manager's decisions and objectives. Consider the
following:

1. *Size.* A bigger organization is a better one. Larger budgets are better
than smaller ones.

2. *Achievement.* It is better to accomplish, to get somewhere, to show progress.

3. *Rate.* It is better to be fast than slow. To reach a decision in one hour is better than to do it in two hours.

4. *Quality.* Higher quality is better than lower quality. It is better to give a high quality service than a lesser one.

5. *Effort.* Effort for its own sake is good. It is good to try.

6. *Satisfaction.* It is better to be happy than unhappy. The play that ends happily is the better one.

7. *Efficiency.* The more efficient organization is the better one.

8. *Security.* It is better for an individual or an organization to be secure in its existence.

9. *Newness.* New ideas and things are better than older ones.

10. *Changefulness.* Frequent changes are better than infrequent ones.

11. *Independence.* It is better to be self-sufficient and independent than dependent. To be able to go it alone is necessarily good.[601]

We do not wish to imply that the influence of these values on management decisions is good or bad. We are simply calling attention to the fact that these values must be taken into account if we want to understand management's objectives in modern American industry. Again, we do not wish to imply that all managers hold these values to the same high degree. On the contrary, we expect that individual managers will differ widely from each other in the extent they prize each of these values. Indeed, the managers of marketing, accounting, production, and engineering are likely to vary systematically from each other in attitudes toward size, quality, newness, and so forth.

Some Evidence

Evidence is accumulating that top management is setting multiple goals for itself along lines just discussed. For instance, chief executives of 145 businesses (or their deputies) were asked: "What are the aims of top management in your company?" Three-fourths of the managers mentioned more than one goal. One-sixth mentioned more than three goals. Consistent with our earlier comments about profits as a goal, only 36 percent of these top executives mentioned as their first aim "to make money, profits, or a living"; and only 52 percent mentioned these financial goals at all.[162]

At first glance one might regard these results skeptically. Yet, the respondents were drawn on a probability basis from all types of industry and all size groupings greater than 50 employes in five communities: Bridgeport (Connecticut), Philadelphia, Cleveland, Houston, and San Francisco. The managers were talking "off the record" in confidential interviews. They were not making public speeches (at which they typically underplay the profit motive). Instead of concentrating on profits alone, they expressed interest in growth, in public service, in employe welfare, and in good products. These varied aims can be understood if we consider the current manager as a professional, interested in "striking a fair balance between the claims of customers, stockholders, and employes. Most observers feel that the professional manager is more concerned with volume of production, with service, and with social responsibilities. He is less concerned with maximizing profits (although he is concerned that profits be satisfactory)."[162, p. 374]

While profits may be the symbol of success, it has been noted that the manager's salary is more closely related to the size of the business than to its profits. Above and beyond material considerations we hazard the guess that American management's goals are strongly affected by the value attached by Americans to bigness, growth, progress, and newness. For, we see a considerably different pattern of concerns among

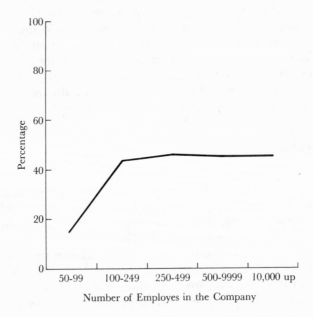

Number of Employes in the Company

Figure 1.11: Percentage of Managers Subscribing to the Goal of Good Products and Public Service as a Function of the Size of Their Companies. (After Dent, 1959, p. 378)

European managers. Their goals tend to be much less broad than those expressed by their American counterparts. For example, in a medium-sized European firm greatest importance was attached by management to financial security and guaranteeing a 6 percent return to investors. Almost as important was maintaining management security and the security of key personnel within the organization. Given considerably less weight were such aims as maintaining labor stability and gaining technological leadership.[115]

American Management's Aims Depend on Company Characteristics. The 145 American executives, confidentially interviewed, expressed aims which were strongly influenced by the size and growth of the companies they ran, as well as by whether their employes were skilled and unionized.

From 43 to 46 percent who ran organizations of 100 or more employes mentioned "good products or public service" as one of their aims, but only 14 percent of chiefs of smaller firms were interested in this goal (Figure 1.11).

Figure 1.12 shows that subscription to the goal of "employe welfare" depended both on the size of the company managed, as well

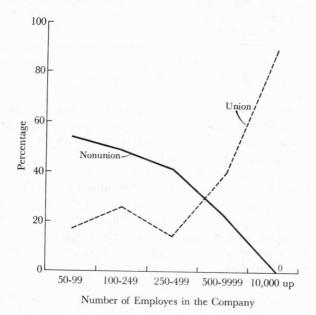

Figure 1.12: Percentage of Managers Subscribing to the Goal of Employe Welfare as a Function of the Size of Their Companies. (After Dent, 1959, p. 380)

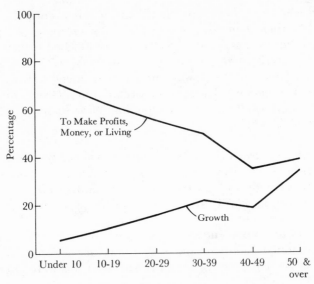

Figure 1.13: Percentage of Managers Subscribing to the Goals
of Growth and Profits as a Function of the Types of Employes
in Their Companies. (After Dent, 1959, p. 383)

as whether it was unionized. Managers expressed more concern for
employe welfare in the small nonunion shop and in the very large unionized company.

As shown in Figure 1.13 there was a proportionate increased interest in "growth" by management in companies with larger proportions
of white-collar, professional, or supervisory employes, paralleled by
decreasing concern for profits and money as such.

Figures 1.14 and 1.15 indicate that the managers of growing companies showed more concern for good products and public service, as
well as concern to meet and stay ahead of competitors, than did managers of stable companies or those declining in average annual percentage of employment during the past eight years. On the other hand,
companies declining in size had chief executives most likely to be concerned about satisfactory operations or "developing the organization."[162]

We conclude that most firms have many objectives. The selection
of these objectives depends on various characteristics of a particular
firm. Its manager has to balance his organization's efforts to attain these
several objectives. In doing so, he is influenced considerably by his own
manifold values.

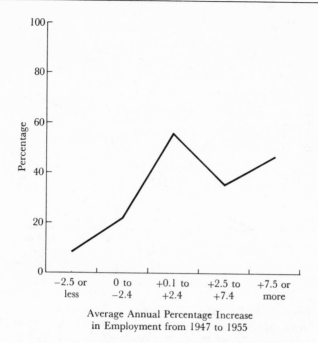

Figure 1.14: Percentage of Managers Subscribing to the Goals of Good Products and Public Service, as a Function of the Growth of Their Companies (1947– 1955). (After Dent, 1959, p. 388)

The Plan of This Book

After reviewing briefly the background of organizational psychology and the orientation of those who contributed to its development, we looked at the values sought by the managers of men at work. It would have been considerably easier to start by assuming that men manage firms or run drilling machines to earn a living or to make money. Assuredly such material income is important, sometimes all important; and we will concentrate on this in Chapter 3. Yet in our society, men at work seek many other values such as achievement, recognition, security, independence, change, comfort, and affection. Just keeping busy is so valued that many Americans on vacation, when completely free to do as they please, often work harder at their so-called leisure activities than on their regular jobs.

From these many values stem the multiple goals of American management and workers. If a firm puts all its emphasis on any one of these goals—say maximum immediate profits—then some other goals

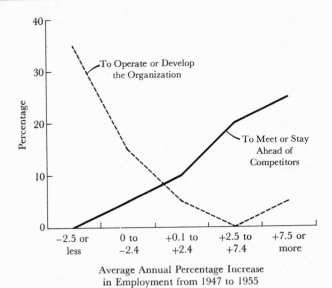

Figure 1.15: Percentage of Managers Subscribing to the Goals of Meeting Competition and Developing the Organization as a Function of the Growth of Their Companies (1947–1965). (After Dent, 1959, p. 389)

such as security or long-range growth will become unobtainable. Some optimum balance is to be sought so that the firm is of value to all its constituents: investors, managers, workers, consumers, and the general public.

In Chapter 2 we shall consider what attracts a worker to his job and keeps him working. A man's attitudes and expectations will be shown to be of critical importance in determining how hard he will work and whether he will stay with a job. In Chapters 3 and 4 particular attention will be devoted to the rewarding elements of the workplace, as well as to the ways individual workers react differently to these various rewards.

Next, in Chapter 5 the role of the immediate supervisor will be considered. This will lead naturally into a review of some of what we know about effective work groups in Chapter 6. Classical and modern ideas about formally organizing men and groups to operate effectively form the substance of Chapter 7, with special attention to the way technological processes of the firm affect arrangements. Special attention will be devoted to communications among men at work in Chapter 8; while Chapter 9 will examine the conflicts that arise as a consequence of communication failures and other reasons. Finally, in Chapter 10 we shall look at how the executive goes about trying to solve these and other problems generated by the system.

* * * * *

To sum up, organizational psychology is seen as the study of how men at work are affected by the system of men, money, and materials within which they work. Also, it deals with with how they, in turn, exert influence on the conversion of the inputs of human energy, money, and materials on the system's manifold outputs of wealth, goods, and satisfactions.

The system is one with many diverse goals and constraints. The desire for growth, service, and satisfying work vie with concern for immediate profits. Three or four decades ago, the industrial process was viewed primarily as a matter of money and materials and interchangeable uniform workers. Today the interplay of worker and manager as individuals and groups with the money and materials is considered of paramount importance in understanding, predicting, and controlling the industrial process.

We shall now examine how the attitudes toward work of the individual worker and manager interact with the workplace, colleagues, and system in which they work.

In Brief

JOB SATISFACTION MAY BE ONE OBJECTIVE OF MANAGEMENT AND WORKERS; high productivity may be another. Unfortunately one is not necessarily the consequence of the other. We are satisfied with our job if the rewards are commensurate with the expectations and aspirations that attracted us to it. Our productivity, however, may depend upon many factors other than our satisfaction. These include the extent we have the ability to do the work, the extent the rewards are contingent on our performance, the extent we have control over our success, the extent we are interested and involved in our success, the extent our work group is cohesive and shares a norm for high productivity, the extent management is trusted by workers, and the extent workers feel secure. Although job satisfaction may not lead to high productivity, most employes are likely to be satisfied if they are productive and if the psychic and material rewards they receive fit with what they have produced and what they expected for what they produced.

Employe attitudes can be assessed in many ways: by interviews, polls, attitude scales, and disguised, projective, and objective procedures. Regardless of technique, analyses suggest that a small set of factors account for the differences between employes in how satisfied they report themselves to be. These include satisfaction with supervision, working conditions, opportunities for personal development, material benefits, and the organization as a whole.

Chapter 2

ATTITUDES

TOWARD WORK

IN CHAPTER 1 WE CONCEIVED AN ORGANIZATION AS A SYSTEM OF MULTIPLE inputs, outputs, and goals. To understand the total outputs of satisfaction and productivity or inputs of human energy of the firm, it is useful to look first at the individual employe as a subsystem with his multiple inputs, outputs, and goals. The individual employe's values and aspirations set limits for him; but within these restrictions he is attracted to the workplace by expectations of various potential rewards. Like the system as a whole which, say, can only produce a limited array of merchandise, the individual employe must accept certain constraints. For example, if he is not a college graduate he can be attracted to a job with more modest incentives. A college graduate will find the same inducements less appealing. Dissatisfaction depends on the discrepancies between aspirations and opportunities as well as discrepancies between expectations and attainments. Dissatisfaction, in turn, will affect behavior to the degree that the employe has freedom to act on various alternatives to continuing to work. The dissatisfied housewife who is supplementing her family income may be less hesitant about quitting a dissatisfying job and risking a period of unemployment as she tries her luck elsewhere. The family breadwinner may feel that quitting is too risky. He may not find another job as good and cannot afford to be out of work for any length of time. In the same way the college graduate may quit if he finds his work dull because he has prospects of more interesting work elsewhere. The unskilled laborer may have no choice in the matter; and although he is as dissatisfied as the college graduate, he stays put and continues to be productive on the dissatisfying job for fear of losing it.

In Chapters 2, 3, and 4 we will concentrate on this individual subsystem within the larger organization, particularly focusing on the interrelations between what attracts us as individuals to work, what holds us to it, what makes it satisfying, and what increases our effort to perform well. The relations are by no means simple. The same outcomes will be satisfying or dissatisfying depending on what was expected and what was ventured. Consider the chagrin of a student who received a "C" grade if he had been attracted to a course because the instructor supposedly awarded only "A's." Consider how a hard-working student who expected an "A" for his effort felt if he earned a "C." In contrast consider the elation of a grade-conscious student who expected a "C" and earned an "A."

These discrepancies between instructor and student evaluations of the same inputs and outcomes are paralleled in industry by the supervisor and his subordinate. While the supervisor and subordinate usually agree on the subordinate's duties, they less often agree (privately, in particular) about the obstacles and problems faced by the subordinate in performing his duties.[430] However, when both can agree on the subordinate's role, the subordinate is more likely to succeed on the job in question.[560] Thus, workers who can accurately predict what their supervisor expects of them are rated higher in job performance by their supervisors.[290] Moreover, such workers, whose expectations are likely to be borne out, are less likely to be frustrated as the student expecting an "A" who receives a "C." Let us examine more closely the relations among *attraction* to work, *expectations* about work, *satisfaction* with work, *effort* expended on the job, and *success in performing* the job.

SATISFACTION AND ATTRACTION TO WORK

What *attracts* us to one job compared to other jobs is our expectation of the material, social, or psychic rewards it may offer us. What holds us to the job — our *satisfaction* with it — is the extent the job is rewarding to us relative to how much better we might do elsewhere and what aspirations we have.

How motivated we are to perform — how hard we try — will depend on the amount of the expected rewards. How well we perform will depend on our ability and whether the expected rewards are contingent upon our performance. So it is quite possible for job efforts, job performance, job attractiveness, and job satisfaction to be completely independent of each other. Thus, reviews of many surveys of employe

attitudes suggest that an employe's attitude toward his job is not necessarily related to his performance on the job. Rather, we are likely
to find that negative attitudes towards a job will reveal themselves in
various forms of withdrawal by the worker from the job: absence, turnover, tardiness, and even illness and accidents.[80]

Forms of Withdrawal as a Consequence of Dissatisfaction

Accidents, Illness, and Dissatisfaction. Accidents may be sometimes a
form of withdrawal, and the fact that high accident rates occur in groups
with low morale partly may be interpreted as "absence in an acceptable
way."[302a] Thus, interview studies of the mood of workers found accident rates to coincide with mood swings. Production also deviated
with moods of happiness or unhappiness, but not to the same extent.[300]

In the same way, high rates of men on sick call may indicate dissatisfaction with military life, and not an increased incidence of physical
illness. But real illness, particularly a psychosomatic disorder, may be
a consequence of job dissatisfaction. Heart disease and peptic ulcers
often develop from the continued frustrations and conflicts at work.
Alcoholism, another form of withdrawal from the dissatisfactions of
the workplace, has been termed "a billion-dollar hangover" for industry.
In all, twice as many man hours of work are lost due to mental illness
as for the common cold and all other respiratory diseases.[301]

Absenteeism and Dissatisfaction. Illustrative of the relation between absenteeism and dissatisfaction are the data shown in Figure 2.1. Respondents who are absent more frequently during a six-month period
are less likely to say that "our crew is better than others at sticking together."[412] However, absenteeism as a symptom of withdrawal from a
dissatisfying job is more common in certain work groups. Job dissatisfaction is related to absenteeism particularly among lower-skilled
levels of employees, but not among women employees or among highly
skilled white-collar employes.[477] (Perhaps high-status white-collar
employes have more freedom to use other forms of withdrawal when
dissatisfied, like taking extra long coffee breaks or three-hour lunch
periods.)

Turnover and Dissatisfaction. The most obvious way to withdraw from
a dissatisfying job is to quit it. Table 2.1 compares the attitudes of 99
insurance salesmen who remained on the job as much as 30 years and

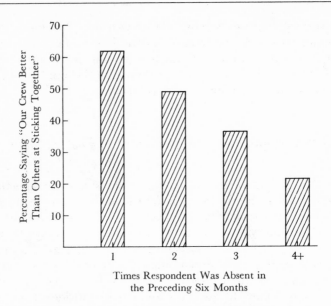

*Figure 2.1: Relation of Absenteeism to How Attracted a
Worker Is to His Group. (From Likert, 1961, p. 35)*

99 who terminated employment as insurance salesmen, mainly during
the first three years of employment. As can be seen those who quit
were much more dissatisfied than those who remained on the job.[731]

SATISFACTION AND PRODUCTIVITY

Until recently it was assumed that satisfied workers were more
productive than dissatisfied ones. But this assumption only holds true
when the expected rewards depend on the performance of the worker.
There are many reasons why such expected rewards may be independent of performance. Performance in various situations, therefore,
may be unrelated to job satisfaction.

First, productivity will depend upon many factors other than the
attitudes of the producers. Thus when two British firms differing in
productivity were compared, the highly productive company maintained its superior output because it employed younger workers, fewer
ex-miners (likely to be suspicious about management), better trained
employes, workers who lived closer to their jobs, and management which
made fewer mistakes.[448]

Second, a more productive worker may reveal more dissatisfaction

TABLE 2.1   HOW LIFE INSURANCE SALESMEN WHO SURVIVE
SIGNIFICANTLY DIFFER IN SATISFACTION FROM THOSE WHO QUIT*

	Survivors Checking N=99	Terminators Checking N=99
Part I—Satisfaction Items		
The freedom from supervision in my job.	56%	34%
Renewals as a source of deferred income.	63	42
The helpfulness of my supervision.	62	41
The way the home office shows its dependency on the individual agent.	37	20
The personal friendship I have with the manager.	70	53
The bulletins informing me of my work progress.	52	36
Prospecting.	36	23
Part II—Dissatisfaction Items		
The lack of special field training with the manager or supervisor.	7	23
The public's attitude toward life insurance agents.	25	45
The uncertainty while getting established.	27	47
Having my income or production figures made public.	0	8
Having to use pressure and subterfuge in order to get a person to buy.	4	15
Being expected to start producing on my own before completing training.	6	18
The training I received from the agency staff.	5	15
Not having paid vacation.	5	15
Not having a floor to my income.	8	19
The manager misrepresenting or failing to explain all the provisions of my contract.	6	16
The irregularity of the hours I have to work.	2	9
The amount of time the manager devotes to agents' problems.	4	12
The misrepresentation of my job and job possibilities by the manager during the hiring interview.	9	19
Having the emphasis placed on volume, rather than quality of sales.	9	19

*From Weitz & Nuckols, 1955, p. 297.

with certain conflicting aspects of his work as a consequence of his interest and involvement. For example, in one of two large departments of office workers, those most critical of placement and rating systems were the highly productive employees. These, in turn, were the most interested and informed members of the staff.[355]

Third, productivity of a group of workers may be strongly influenced by how the members, as a whole, feel about the group, whether or not there is absence of conflict, feelings of happiness, good personal adjustment, ego involvement in one's job, "we feeling," cohesiveness, and personal acceptance of the goals of the work group.[267] Yet in such a cohesive group productivity may be low if the cohesive group has established low standards. When employes are strongly attracted to their work group the group can set the standards or norms to be followed by its members. If the prevailing group standards call for high productivity and members are highly cohesive, or highly attracted to the work group, then the group's actual productivity is likely to be high. But if the established norms call for sluggish output, productivity will be low.

Thus, it was noted that while lack of attraction to the work group revealed itself in absenteeism, turnover, and malingering, positive attraction to one's work group did not necessarily yield performance desirable to management.[372] Favorable attitudes of members towards their work group might yield high work standards, ready acceptance of change, friendliness to other groups, cooperation with supervisors and minimum demands for conformity. Or the same high degree of group cohesion might yield lower than ordinary production standards, restriction in output, denial of membership to newcomers, and demands for conformity. A laboratory experiment demonstrating the point studied the productivity of subjects who perceived themselves to be either in highly cohesive work groups or in groups low in attraction to them. Notes, supposedly from fellow workers, requesting the speeding up of performance did speed up the performance of subjects who thought themselves in cohesive groups. Notes asking for a slowdown, likewise, succeeded in slowing the performance of workers in the more cohesive situation.[584]

When Attractive Groups Are Productive

Survey data has been gathered on the productivity and attractiveness of 228 factory groups varying in size from 5 to 50 involving 5,871 workers. Figure 2.2 pinpoints the conditions under which high group

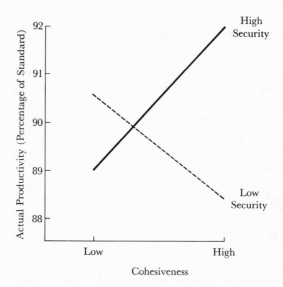

*Figure 2.2: Group Cohesiveness and Group Pro-
ductivity Standards for Groups Differing in
Security in Relation to the Company. (After
Seashore, 1954)*

cohesiveness yielded high productivity and where it yielded low productivity. Work groups were regarded as highly cohesive (or highly attractive) if, on a questionnaire, members tended to say they were really a
part of the group, they preferred to remain in the group rather than
to leave for a similar job in some other group, and they perceived their
group better than others with respect to mutual attraction among the
members. As seen in Figure 2.2, groups with lowest productivity were
highly cohesive ones who "felt insecure in relation to the company."
At the same time highest actual production was found among similarly
highly cohesive groups who also felt highly secure. Furthermore, the
cohesiveness of the group determined the extent to which group standards governed how much was produced by each worker. The objective
evidence for this was found by examining the variations in productivity
within the work groups and between the groups. There was relatively
little variation in the productivity of any worker who was a member of a
highly cohesive group. The workers in a group low in cohesion were
much more likely to vary in their productivity from others in their own
group. At the same time highly cohesive groups, as such, varied much
more in average productivity from other highly cohesive groups than
did groups which were low in cohesion.

Indirect Effects of Dissatisfaction on Productivity

Yet it would be an oversimplification to infer that productivity of workers has nothing to do with their attitudes. On the contrary the effects of dissatisfaction resulting in withdrawal may indirectly disturb production. Absent employes may affect detrimentally the productivity of their total department. The apathy of one employe may affect those around him, although his own particular efforts may not be noticed. Rapid turnover in a department may have deleterious effects on productivity in the long run because of the continued need to find and train replacements and because of temporary shortages of workers owing to the turnover. Finally, the profitability of production may be seriously reduced by the direct and indirect costs of turnover.

On the other hand, all turnover is not necessarily detrimental to an organization. In fact, a plan for increasing turnover was proposed in one sales company when it was found that merit ratings of performance were highly predictive of subsequent meritorious performance. Men in the bottom 10 percent of merit currently were almost always discharged for inadequate performance within the next six months. If future inadequacy were known currently, it was better for the man, as well as the company, for him to seek employment elsewhere now instead of waiting up to six months for the discharge.

Satisfaction and Maximum Profits

Except if we consider the possible indirect effects, happy workers do not necessarily mean increased profits. It is true that a contented worker is less likely to withdraw or to quit and that turnover generally is costly, but sometimes turnover per se may enhance profits, as noted.

If we choose to ignore worker satisfaction as an important goal of the industrial system we are trying to optimize, then it may be more financially profitable to keep turnover high so that few employees build up seniority rights, pension benefits, and secure positions preventing their replacement even if they are incapable of doing the work. On jobs requiring "a strong back and a weak mind," when productivity and satisfaction are unlikely to be related, a ruthless, authoritarian management may find its productivity highest when using coercion, force, and threats to cajole workers into maximum output at the expense of their contentment with the work. But this management probably will need a high degree of control over the workplace and will need to remain alert for hostile reactions from the work force.

However, we suggest that enlightened management does not choose to ignore worker satisfaction as one of its goals. Given the choice, maximum profits with dangerously disgruntled workers operating in slave-like conditions or satisfactory profits with happy, cooperative workers, modern management chooses the latter.

Effects of Productivity on Satisfaction

When several thousand students and employes are asked to express their relative concern in their work in comparison with concerns for themselves and how they interact, the average American respondent is almost always most concerned about his work, less about social interaction, and least about personal recognition for the work. This is more true if the respondent is a man rather than a woman, or an engineer rather than without technical training.[42] In our society, at least, we tend to value highly successful completion of tasks. High productivity may be an important source of job satisfaction, instead of vice versa. As noted in Chapter 1, we value success and optimistically expect it.

Enhancing Job Attractiveness With Success Experiences

When high departmental productivity has relevance or meaning to the worker, it should increase his satisfaction about what he is doing. Observing success of his group increases his expectations of subsequent reward. Naturally, if the success of the group does not yield the reward, the highly productive worker may also be the most disgruntled.[356] If one's work group is perceived as likely to achieve success, even if the task is a hard one, members may be highly motivated to belong to the group. Thus, employes in more productive work groups were found to have considerably higher "pride in their group."[130] On the other hand, if the worker regards himself as in a group lacking in capability, lacking in probability of success, he will be much less attracted to the group and will want less to remain on the job.[165]

This understanding of the effects of productivity and job success on subsequent desire to remain on the job can be used to reduce turnover by making suitable modifications in workers' expectations about the likelihood of their success on the job. Thus, turnover was decreased from 14 to 5 percent in one firm by de-emphasizing the final training standards and introducing easy progressive subgoals, so that workers could obtain numerous experiences of success and a sense of progress.[450]

Dissatisfaction and Imbalance of Expectations and Motivation

Analysis of dissatisfaction requires a more thorough examination of the imbalances of expectancies and motivation. The highly motivated, and therefore potentially productive, worker may quit the job because his expectations about the payment for what he regards as good performance may be violated. [Laboratory experiments show that under conditions raising their drive to perform well, subjects tend to over-value their own performance, expecting more as a consequence.][234]

The motivation to produce of 49 workers in a manufacturing plant was seen to relate strongly to matters of "distributive justice." The worker who was rewarded too highly for his output and skill was likely to feel guilty and to resent his own feelings of guilt. If the rewards for a worker's performance were lower than justified by his esteem among his associates and by his output, then his resentment was high and he felt he was being ill-used.[761]

The association of the imbalance with dissatisfaction was most clearly seen in a survey of the office staffs of a large oil company and its subsidiaries. High morale was determined by scoring the responses of all members of each department to 26 questionnaire items about job satisfaction.

In the high-morale departments, 43 percent of those who say they want a recommendation for a pay increase feel that they are likely to get such, while only 26 percent of those from the low-morale departments feel the same. . . . On recommendation for promotion, the high-morale departments are more confident by a margin of 35 percent to 21 percent. Achieving more responsibility is viewed as attainable by 47 percent of those who desire it in the high-morale departments but by only 33 percent of such persons in the low-morale departments. The possibility of training for a better job was viewed as likely by 34 percent of those interested if they were in the high-morale departments; but by the astonishing low percent of 3 if they were in the low-morale departments.[659]

Increasing Job Satisfaction by Reducing the Imbalance of Expectation and Subsequent Experience of Reward

A carefully controlled field experiment demonstrated that whether new life insurance salesmen remained on the job after six months was affected by their receiving a booklet at the time of employment describing the job, a booklet containing the admonition, "The company wants you to know in advance, insofar as it is possible, exactly the kind of work our agents do. Frankly, if this is not the kind of work you want to do, we want you to find it out now rather than later."[729, p.246] Of those 226 agents given booklets, only 19 percent terminated during the six-month period, while 27 percent of the 248 in the control group (not receiving the booklet) quit. Termination rates during comparable periods, prior to the start of the experiment, were 27 to 28 percent. The overall reduction of 30 percent in the quit rate was attributed to the introduction of the booklet at the time of hiring and providing new agents with a more realistic set of job expectations.

METHODS OF STUDYING EMPLOYE ATTITUDES TOWARD THE JOB

There are both direct and indirect methods for collecting information about the attractiveness of jobs and the satisfaction of employes. Among the direct methods are use of management estimates, interviews, polls, and attitude scales.

Management Estimation

We can ask management's opinion of employe attitudes. Although this might reveal management's insight, or lack of it, concerning employe attitudes as compared with the employes' own opinions, it would be quite erroneous to depend alone on management's views. Too many industrial leaders are still imbued with the notion of the worker as a "pure economic man." Generally, both management (and union leaders) tend to overweigh the importance of pay and fringe benefits in estimating employe attitudes. Likewise, they underestimate the importance to subordinates of job challenge, opportunities for advancement, job security, and so forth. For example, in open-ended interviews supervisors of research and development personnel argued that their subordinates were most in need of more pay and more material incentives. The R & D personnel, on the other hand, focused on the desire to see their education and experience put to better use, on permission to determine their own assignments, and on the need to be better oriented to the total operation.[25] Similar discrepancies between management and workers are found even in different cultural settings. For instance, interviews were held with a stratified sample of 800 Saudi Arabian employes of Aramco. These employes ranked opportunity for training and education as most important; future security, second; and opportunity for advancement, third; as shown in Table 2.2. Wages were seventh in importance. But when 301 American supervisors and technicians estimated the Arab employe rankings, they guessed that the Arabs would rank wages first.[384]

TABLE 2.2   COMPARISON OF THE RANKINGS OF IMPORTANCE OF 11 JOB SATISFACTION FACTORS BY 800 ARABS AND 301 AMERICAN SUPERVISORY PERSONNEL "SECOND GUESSING" THE ARAB EMPLOYE'S RESPONSES*

Ranking by Saudi Arabs	Ranking by Americans	Factor
1	3	Opportunity to obtain training and education
2	5	Future security
3	2	Opportunity for advancement
4	6	Opportunity to get work experience
5	7	The supervisor
6	4	Benefits
7	1	Wages
8	10	Importance of the work that you do for Aramco
9	11	People worked with at your own level
10	8	The company as a good place to work
11	9	Personnel policies (such as proper hiring, placement, grievance procedure)

*From Social Science Research Reports IV: Surveys and Inventories. Standard Oil of N. J., 1962

Managers and union leaders probably overemphasize the importance of pay because wages are the easiest thing for employes to discuss and request. Thus, when highly dissatisfied, dissatisfied enough to quit, workers seem most likely to mention inadequate pay as the reason for quitting[620], although pay seldom ranks first in importance when employed workers are asked to list items contributing to their satisfaction.

Interviews

We could resort to intensive interviews with employes. This is a frequent practice. But interviews are expensive and time consuming. Further, the employe may not feel free to "tell all."[58] Presumably, good interviewers can promote sufficient rapport with workers so the latter can feel free to talk. These interviews can be highly structured so that each follows the same pattern of questions by the interviewer, or the interview can be a free interchange where the interviewer asks few questions, but mainly uses nondirective techniques to keep the conversation flowing.

For example, instead of asking one direct question after another, once the conversation starts, the interviewer guides it by such devices as pauses, which permit the interviewee to continue further exploration of some idea he presented. Or, the interviewer clarifies or summarizes the employe's comments, often stimulating further elaboration by the employe of his feelings and attitudes.

The Exit Interview

Although it is usually too late to prevent an employe's quitting, the exit interview provides an opportunity to find out whether the separation could have been avoided or whether it was due to such unavoidable reasons as ill health, family relocation, desire to return to school, or better job offer.

If avoidable the important grievances resulting in quitting are likely to be mentioned, although the departing employe may still feel reluctant to express his real feelings if he must depend on a good recommendation from his old employer.

Twenty-two exit interviewers from a variety of cooperating companies estimated how often in five typical interviews, each of 16 topics was mentioned as a reason for leaving. Figure 2.3 shows a cluster analysis of the reasons given. Inadequate pay was the single most frequent dissatisfaction. It was mentioned 1.89 times per five representative interviews. When dissatisfaction with pay was expressed in an interview, poor housing or excessive rent, problems in promotion, and freedom to communicate with higher levels were also likely to be mentioned. On the other hand, grievances from this cluster were unlikely to appear in the same interviews when dissatisfaction with job security or working conditions were mentioned.

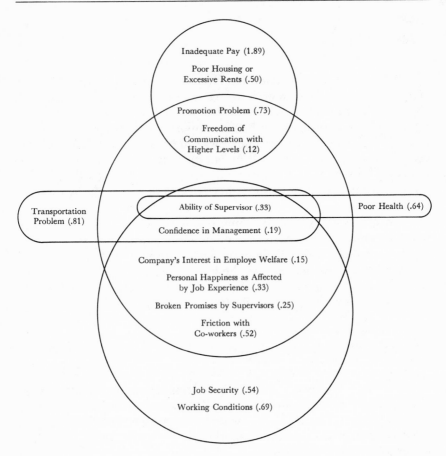

Figure 2.3: Exit Interview Content Patterns Showing the Number of Times an Item Was Mentioned Per Five Representative Interviews. (After Smith & Kerr, 1953, p. 353)

Polls

When we want a quantitative assessment of how a group of employes feels about a matter, we may ask a single question, merely noting the percentages of different kinds of response to the question.

A typical *yes-no* question is:

IS THIS A GOOD COMPANY TO WORK FOR?

☐ Yes   ☐ No   ☐ Don't know

In each department surveyed, the poll registers the percentage who respond "yes," "no," and "don't know."

A *cafeteria* or multiple-choice question is:

THIS COMPANY NEEDS MOST TO IMPROVE ITS:

☐ Benefit plans

☐ Supervisory practices

☐ Personnel policies

☐ Security for older workers

☐ Working conditions

The percentages choosing each alternative are reported. Or, respondents can be asked to rank alternatives in importance and the mean rank assigned each alternative is noted.

An *open-end* question like, "What can be done around here to improve management-employe relations?" will elicit a variety of free responses. After these are collected, their content is analyzed, categorized, and the percentages of responses in each category is reported.

Scales

In order to obtain a reasonably reliable answer, we usually must ask several questions. When doing so, we may combine all the answers of a single employe into a scale to be scored. This will permit us to scale employes along some continuum, from low to high in their attitude as reflected in their various answers to the several questions. Of the various scaling procedures, the most commonly employed is one developed by Likert.[409]

Figure 2.4 displays the last five questions of a scale about attitudes toward co-workers from the Sears Employe Attitude Research Survey.

146 . . . How do you generally feel about the employes you work with?
    A They are the best group I could ask for . . . .
    B I like them a great deal . . . .
    C I like them fairly well . . . .
    D I have no strong feeling one way or another . . . .
    E I don't particularly care for them . . . .

147 . . . How is your <u>overall attitude</u> toward your job influenced by the people you work with?
    A It is very favorably influenced . . . .
    B It is favorably influenced . . . .
    C It is not influenced one way or the other . . . .
    D It is unfavorably influenced . . . .
    E It is very unfavorably influenced . . . .

148 . . . The example my fellow employes set:
    A Greatly discourages hard work . . . .
    B Somewhat discourages hard work . . . .
    C Has little effect on me . . . .
    D Somewhat encourages hard work . . . .
    E Greatly encourages hard work . . . .

149 . . . How much does the way co-workers handle their jobs add to the success of your office?
    A It adds almost nothing . . . .
    B It adds very little . . . .
    C It adds only a little . . . .
    D It adds quite a bit . . . .
    E It adds a very great deal . . . .

150 . . . In this office, there is:
    A A very great deal of friction . . . .
    B Quite a bit of friction . . . .
    C Some friction . . . .
    D Little friction . . . .
    E Almost no friction . . . .

Figure 2.4: Five Items of the Sears Employe Attitude Research Survey All Correlating with Overall Attitudes of Employes Toward Co-workers.

Response to each favorable or positive question is scored +2, +1, 0, −1 and −2, depending on whether the response is A, B, C, D, or E. When the question is negative, like No. 150, then A is −2, B is −1, and so forth. Each question is pretested and is only included in the final scale if it relates with the total score obtained for that scale. That is to say, an employe who on the average is highly favorable toward fellow employes on all questions about them, also must be favorable towards them on each question that is to remain part of the scale. The scale becomes internally consistent when responses to each question of the scale correlate positively with the average response to all the questions. Responses to items 146 to 150 of the Sears Attitude Research Survey each correlate

	Agree	?	Disagree
73. When layoffs are necessary,			
they are handled fairly	☐	☐	☐
74. I am very much underpaid			
for the work that I do	☐	☐	☐
75. I'm really doing something			
worthwhile in my job	☐	☐	☐
76. I'm proud to work			
for this company	☐	☐	☐

Figure 2.5: Items 73–76 from the Science Research Associates Employee Attitude Survey. Copyright 1951 by the Industrial Relations Center of the University of Chicago.

to some extent with the total scores employes obtain based on all questions about attitudes toward co-workers.

Many variations of scaling technique have been tested, but often results tend to be similar regardless of the procedure employed. Thus, whether or not the 76 questions of the Science Research Associates Employee Inventory (four questions from which are shown in Figure 2.5) were asked in a random order, or grouped into their scoring categories, made little difference. Further, whether five choices were permitted (as in Figure 2.4) or just three (as in Figure 2.5) was also of no significance.[21]

Thurstone Scale. Attitude statements, say, about company policies, can be scaled according to how favorable or unfavorable they are judged to be by a sample of evaluators.[678] Thurstone scales are constructed by asking a large number of judges (any intelligent person can serve) to assign a large number of statements to each of 11 categories depending how favorable or unfavorable the statements (not the judges) are toward the company. Statements are discarded if the judges vary considerably in the category they place a particular statement. For statements to be retained judges have to be in close agreement on the category assignment. The median (or middle-most value) assigned by the judges becomes the scale value of each retained item. Fifteen to twenty such statements covering the range of scale values form the attitude scale. Figure 2.6 displays five statements from such an attitude scale constructed by Uhrbrock.[693]

An employe's attitude is given by the median value of all the fifteen to twenty statements presented to him that he agrees with. A high median would indicate the employe was favorable in attitude; a low, unfavorable.

Guttman Scale. Sometimes statements of attitude can be ordered so that endorsement of one of the statements makes it possible to predict

Statement	*Scale Value*
If I had to do it over again I'd still work for this company	9.5
A wage incentive plan offers a just reward for the faster worker	7.9
I believe accidents will happen no matter what you do about them	5.4
My boss gives all the breaks to his lodge and church friends	2.9
An honest man fails in this company	0.8

Figure 2.6: Five items from a Thurstone Attitude Scale Developed by Uhrbrock (1934).

that all others further down the scale will also be endorsed. Consider the following set of statements:

___A. Negroes should get preference over whites in job openings to make up for discrimination.

___B. There should be a quota system guaranteeing Negroes 10 percent of the jobs in the U.S.

___C. The law should guarantee Negroes equal rights to white people in job opportunities.

___D. Negroes and whites can work side by side.

___E. The law should guarantee Negroes the right to vote.

It is probable that a respondent who feels that Negroes should be given special preference (A), also will endorse all the other statements which are less extreme. If a person does not accept a quota system (B) but does favor equal job opportunities (C), he is most likely to reject also preferential treatment (A), and to accept working side by side (D) and guaranteed voting (E). If all respondents follow these consistent patterns, the scale is completely reproducible. Knowing that a person rejects A and B but accepts C makes it possible for us to reproduce his favorable responses to D and E.[270]

While Guttman scales are elegant they have had limited application in industry because of the narrowness of their content owing to the need for the response to the items to have such high interitem consistency. Yet, 40 such scales have been developed successfully in France for assessing workers' attitudes toward technical change, toward modernization, toward intergroup relations, and so forth.[27]

Indirect Projective Techniques

Various disguised techniques have been used to assess attitudes. For example, an ambiguous sketch of a group at work will be shown to an employe, and he will be asked to indicate what happened before the sketch was made, what is going on now, and what is going to happen. The themes of the stories generated by this *projective* technique are analyzed as assessments of the unconscious and subconscious needs of the respondent. These strivings, which are below the threshold of the employe's awareness, only reveal themselves when the fantasy life of the employe is stimulated by the ambiguous sketch.

In a somewhat more objectively scored procedure employes are asked to estimate the percentage of all workers in the office who like their jobs, their pay, their supervisor, and so forth. The assumption is made that employes again will project their own needs into their estimations. A satisfied worker will perceive that most other workers are satisfied; a disgruntled employe will estimate that a large percentage of other employes are likewise unhappy.

Error Choice. A more disguised variation is to have employes make estimates involving controversial topics.[285] "What is the annual salary of a vice-president of this company?" "How much does the union president earn?" Alternative answers are offered which are either erroneously low or erroneously high. The respondent is forced to err, but the expectation is that he will err in the direction of his biases and attitudes. Thus, a pro-management person is likely to underestimate the company vice-president's salary and to overestimate the union president's salary.

My Job Contest. "My Job Contest" was run by General Motors in 1946. Over half of the 300,000 employes of GM wrote essays on the topic "Why I Like My Job." The entries were separated according to the division of the company to which the contestants belonged, and the percentages of the various themes mentioned in the essays as making for job satisfaction were tabulated, division by division. Each division was able to compare itself with every other division. For example, as shown in Figure 2.7, the theme, medical service, was mentioned in essays much more frequently in some divisions than in others. Some divisions had a relatively large number of favorable themes on, say, opportunities for advancement. There emerged from the *content analysis* of the contest entries a relative profile of each division's strong points and weak points.[195] For example, as shown in Figure 2.8, Division 57 had many more favorable mentions about the cafeteria, publications, and steady work, while it was below average in favorable mentions of insurance plans. The management of Division 57 now had a profile of the more and less satisfying aspects of their division in comparison to all other divisions. Follow-up in six months indicates that the information from these profiles led to considerable remedial activities by the various division managements.

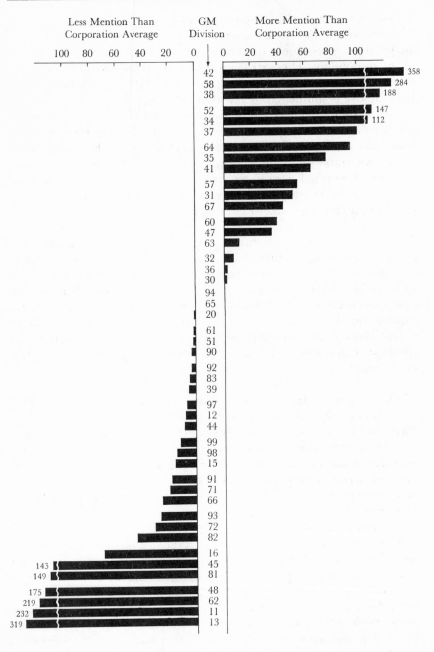

Figure 2.7: How 46 Divisions of General Motors Compared on "My Job Contest"
in the Extent Employe's Themes Were About the Adequacy of Medical Facilities.
(After Evans & Laseau, 1949, opp. p. 224)

Figure 2.8: *How a Single General Motors Division (#57) Compared with Corporation Average for All 46 Divisions in the Themes Mentioned in "My Job Contest." (After Evans & Laseau, 1949, opp. p. 225)*

Some Disadvantages. If we are interested in forecasting an employe's behavior, we probably are better off asking him open direct questions unless he has reasons to suspect our motives in asking the questions, and we have reasons to mistrust his answers. For, if we employ projective or disguised procedures, we are likely to assess the "Walter

Mitty" fantasies of the worker which may actually give few clues as to "here-and-now" behavior of the worker. The worker may have fantasies about being independent of supervision, but he has built up sufficient control of himself that such strivings for independence never actually reveal themselves on the job. He may have buried hostilities toward authority which appear only in projective fantasies. These subliminal feelings may have little or no effect on how he relates daily to his boss or about kinds of working relations with his boss he finds most comfortable.

Objective Approach

In an effort to obtain an inexpensive, easily repeatable, rapid check on morale, a mail-order concern with 25 departments correlated various objective, easily obtainable, periodic measures of departmental activity against a direct measure of attitude and morale obtained by surveying employees. From the results of this analysis it was possible for the company to construct an index accounting for 49 percent of all the variation among departments in morale for a period by adding together (appropriately weighing each added value to maximize the accuracy of the composite) each department's productivity, turnover, tardiness, and absenteeism for the given period.[239]

			Indicators								Background				
Work Group	No. Emp.	ERI	Absentees*	Disciplinary Suspensions†	Work Stoppages†	Plant Separations†	Initial Dispensary Visits*	Grievances†	Suggestions†	Insurance %	Continuous Service	Number of Dependents	% Male	Average Age	Shift
51-1	4	113	17	0	0	0	0	0	19	100	14	4	100	36	Midn.
51-2	10	103	7	0	0	0	2	0	8	100	11	4	90	39	Day
51-3	23	93	23	0	0	0	2	2	0	100	10	2	87	37	Day
51-4	23	124	9	0	0	0	1	0	34	100	10	3	83	46	Aftn.
71-2	19	85	21	8	0	0	2	0	25	100	8	1	32	39	Day
71-1	18	112	12	0	0	4	1	0	17	100	9	2	78	35	Day
71-3	20	103	8	0	0	0	5	2	19	100	9	3	90	38	Day
81-1	10	119	2	0	0	0	2	0	0	100	12	3	100	47	Mixed
83-1	19	96	21	0	0	4	10	0	4	100	6	3	100	41	Mixed
84-1	24	111	9	0	0	3	5	0	0	100	9	2	92	55	Day

*Expressed as per 100 employes per week.
†Expressed as per 1,000 employes per week.

Figure 2.9: Sample Employe Relations Index Report for 10 Work Groups at a General Electric Plant. (From Merrihue & Katzell, 1955)

A similar index—the Employe Relations Index—was constructed by General Electric. The ERI is constructed from the eight objective indicators shown in Figure 2.9.

An index value is calculated for each work group during any period. Although all eight objective indicators are considered, some indicators are actually likely to be less important than others in determining the different ERI values obtained for the work groups. Thus, the main sources of variation among the work groups shown in Figure 2.9 were absences, plant separations, and suggestions. On the other hand, in these groups, for this period, work stoppages contributed nothing to differentiating among the groups, for there were none in any of the groups.[474]

Errors in Assessing Attraction and Satisfaction

There are numerous possibilities for misjudging and mistaking job attractiveness and satisfaction. For example, analyses have shown that if, during a survey of employe attitudes, there is a threat to the employe's feelings of anonymity, there will be an increase in reports of attitudes favoring the company. This is particularly true on items threatening the employe if his identity is revealed. Threats of this sort also result in fewer, shorter, responses to open-end questions. Furthermore, it has been shown that when a company staff administers a survey, the results are more favorable to the company than when a university center or some other outside consulting service administers the same survey.[185]

Wording. Considerable error occurs as a consequence of improper wording of survey questions. The wording may be difficult, unclear, or ambiguous. Most workers have an attitude towards the Taft–Hartley Act, although they are generally unfamiliar with the provisions of this act. They may be against the act as a whole, yet in favor of a majority of its provisions. Thus, if we use Taft–Hartley in our wording, we automatically induce negative responses.

The alternatives to a question must be adequately and equally expressed. When the question was asked "Do you think most manufacturing companies that lay off workers during slack periods could arrange things to avoid layoffs and give steady work right through the year?" 63 percent of respondents said companies could avoid layoffs. When a carefully matched sample of respondents was asked the question with an alternative explicitly stated: "Do you think most manufacturing companies that lay off workers in slack periods could avoid layoffs and provide steady work right through the year, or do you think layoffs are unavoidable?" only 35 percent said companies could avoid layoffs.[515]

A question may be misleading because of unstated assumptions or unseen implications. The frame of reference for the question may be unclear or lacking in uniformity for all respondents. For example, a question such as "To which of these groups do you feel you belong — the white-collar, the working class, or some other class?" assumes that the person feels he belongs to a class based on occupation. One should first determine whether he feels any class identification and, if so, how he thinks of class.[595, p.563]

The wording of questions may be biased, emotionally loaded, or slanted toward a particular kind of answer. Addition of the italicized words in the following question would obviously increase the favorability of response: "Do you feel, *like most of the better and older workers around here*, that this company is a good place to work?"

Accuracy of responding will be considerably greater if objectionable questions are avoided. Thus, instead of asking an employe whether he was graduated from high school, the question can ask "In what grade were you when you left school?"[595, p.565]

Objective Error. Satisfaction indexes like ERI, based on objective records of turnover, suggestion, and so forth, can also suffer considerably in accuracy. For example, turnover can be distorted seriously by irrelevant conditions external to the company. Thus, it is probable that the turnover rate is strongly associated with the current level of employment. When jobs are easy to find, turnover is likely to be much higher than when jobs are scarce.[54] Also, it is often difficult to determine whether or not turnover was due to dissatisfaction and really avoidable, or whether it resulted from other reasons such as ill health, the desire of younger employees to return to school, or family matters, such as the spouse moving to another city. Also, what appears on the record as a "voluntary resignation" may have been an involuntary resignation and vice versa, depending upon the supervisor's understanding of the situation leading to an employe's leaving the job.

Importance of an Attitude

Complete understanding of employe attitudes requires assessing the importance of various sources of job dissatisfaction. For example, 1,171 insurance salesmen reported greatest dissatisfaction with the compensation plan. But, the item of dissatisfaction of greatest importance to them was the attitude of the public towards insurance salesmen. They were next most dissatisfied (according to three-point scales of satisfaction and dissatisfaction they completed) with the sales programs and procedures. Yet, on comparable scales of importance, the quality of clerical assistance was the next most important dissatisfier for these salesmen. Benefit plans were the third most dissatisfying aspect of the job, yet the third most important dissatisfier was having to work evenings.[758]

JOB SATISFACTION FACTORS

Job satisfaction is multidimensional. Workers may be satisfied with some aspects of their job and, at the same time, be highly dissatisfied with other phases of their work. The many factor analyses* of job satisfaction scales uniformly point to this multidimensionality.

A General Factor

Samples including 134 clerical and miscellaneous employes of a large merchandising firm, 163 clerical and factory employes of a large manufacturing firm, and 175 employes of a steel container company were administered the SRA Employee Inventory (sample items shown in Figure 2.5). The 76 items of this inventory yielded 14 scale scores for each respondent, indicating how satisfied he is with working conditions, pay, employe benefits, and so on. [18,22] All 14 scales tended to correlate positively, suggesting the existence of a *general factor* of job satisfaction. Some workers reported more satisfaction than others regardless of the scale to which they were responding. But, apart from this, a complex clustering of the scales appeared when factor analyses of the 76 items were completed independently for each sample.[738]

The Hierarchy

Figure 2.10 shows the complete hierarchy of job satisfaction scale scores following separate analyses of the responses of the different samples mentioned. Five group factors appear: satisfaction with supervisors, with working conditions, with confidence in management, with

*See Appendix C to this chapter for a brief description of factor analysis. Students without previous work in statistics should also read Appendix A and Appendix B as well.

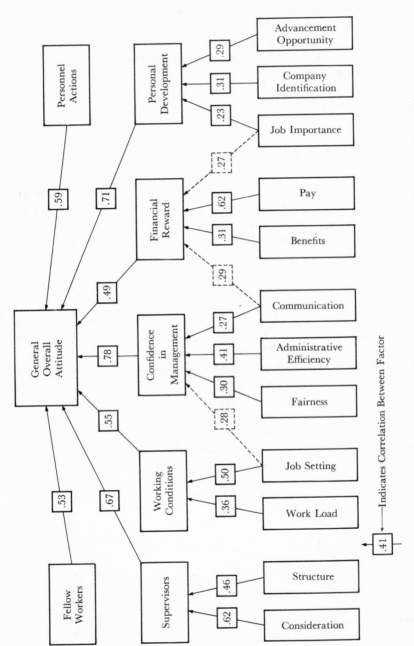

Figure 2.10: Factorial Structure of the Morale Survey (SRA). (After Wherry, 1958, p. 86)

financial rewards, and with personal development. Two other major factors also emerge: satisfaction with fellow workers, and satisfaction with personnel actions. Figure 2.10 shows how the sub-factors cluster within the group factors. For example, questionnaire items concerning work load correlate more with each other than they do with items about the job setting. But, items about load and setting correlate higher with all items dealing with working conditions, the group factor, than they do with items in other group factors such as confidence in management. That is, compared to a satisfied employe, a worker who reports himself satisfied with overtime conditions is also more likely to be satisfied with the place his job is located and with his working conditions in general. And, he is more likely to be more satisfied with his job in the overall, than dissatisfied.

Comparable Analyses

A similar pattern unfolded when responses were factor analyzed of 638 physically handicapped persons and 530 nonhandicapped individuals, broadly sampled by home interviews and telephone contacts in the Minneapolis and St. Paul area. Again, there emerged a general job satisfaction factor implying general adjustment and satisfaction with one's present job. There was also a factor associated with working conditions, one with supervision, one with compensation, and one with co-workers.[100] These results appeared in eight separate factor analyses of the handicapped and nonhandicapped workers and subgroups of skilled and unskilled, blue- and white-collar employes. These results can be compared with the cluster shown in Figure 2.10 as well as the earlier analysis shown in Figure 2.3 of the topics mentioned as reasons for leaving a job.

For two other samples of workers, using two different scoring methods and three separate factor analyses, five similar factors of satisfaction emerged: satisfaction with the job in general, with organization and management, with immediate supervision, with material rewards, and with fellow employes.[23]

Management Personnel. Even if the respondents are all supervisors and managers, results are not too different. For example, factor analysis of the responses of 226 Sears, Roebuck executives clustered again into a general attitude factor, and factors associated with satisfaction with compensation, with company concern for personal welfare, with supervision, with pride in job and company, and with effective cooperation in achieving organizational goals. Many subfactors emerged in this analysis similar to those shown in Figure 2.10. These included satisfaction with working conditions, communications, company benefits, job importance, and so on.[527]

Satisfaction Versus Dissatisfaction

These factors may not all display equivalent dynamics in attracting and repelling, particularly the technical or professional employe. A content analysis was completed of the responses in patterned interviews of 200 engineers and accountants from nine firms. Satisfied respondents tended to describe task-oriented factors, factors attracting them toward the task involved on their job such as the opportunity the job gave for achievement, for recognition, for responsibility and advancement, as well as for stimulation and interest. On the other hand, dissatisfied respondents tended to emphasize aspects surrounding the job which led to their being repelled by work. Such factors included company policy, administration, supervision, and working conditions. A satisfied respondent, thus, regarded his satisfaction as a consequence of his own behavior, his own needs for achievement and recognition that could be afforded by the job itself. The dissatisfied employe, externalized his complaints, noting that his dissatisfaction was a function of the inadequacies surrounding the job. Further, it was found that while improvement of the conditions surrounding the job might reduce job dissatisfaction, they would not necessarily promote job satisfaction among these accountants and engineers. For these personnel, satisfaction would only come if the task itself were intrinsically rewarding, if the task yielded opportunities for achievement, recognition, and a sense of challenge.[301]

*   *   *   *   *

To sum up, relatively few factors account for the responses of employes to questions on their liking of their jobs. First, some report more general overall satisfaction than others. Particularly among technical, better-educated employes, the work itself must be interesting and provide opportunity for advancement and achievement to be satisfying. To prevent dissatisfaction, compensation and other material benefits, working conditions, supervision, management, and co-workers must be favorable. The next four chapters will explore in detail these factors, how they relate to each other and to employe performance.

APPENDIX A

ANALYTIC STATISTICS

Surveys and experiments make use of samples. Analytic statistics are employed to estimate whether the results obtained with the samples can be generalized to the whole population from which the samples have been drawn. Particularly important is to calculate how much the values within the sample vary.

Suppose we obtained the days absent last year of ten employes of one shop, $A, B, C, D, \ldots J$, and arranged them according to absences as follows:

Employe:	A	B	C	D	E	F	G	H	I	J
Days Absent:	8	6	5	5	4	3	3	2	2	2

The *mean* of the array is its sum, 40, divided by 10, the number of values contributing to the sum. The mean is, therefore, 4.0 days.

The *variance* is a measure of how the array varies. It is also known as the *mean squared deviation* of the 10 absence figures from their own mean of 4.0. The mean of the array is 4.0, so the scores deviate from their mean as follows:

Employe:	A	B	C	D	E	F	G	H	I	J
Deviations:	+4	+2	+1	+1	0	−1	−1	−2	−2	−2

The squares of these deviations, therefore, are:

Squared Deviations:	+16	+4	+1	+1	0	+1	+1	+4	+4	+4

The sum of the squares is 36, so for the 10 values the mean squared deviation or variance is 3.6. The square root of the variance is the *standard deviation*. Here it equals approximately 1.9.

Within one standard deviation on either side of the mean lie approximately 68 percent of the scores if the distribution is random. Or, about two-thirds of the scores should lie between 4.0 ±1.9. Almost all the cases should lie within two standard deviations of the mean.

The variance has many applications. One of the simplest, for example, would be to use it to test whether the one-shop sample of 10 absence scores we have been describing was drawn from the same population of all such shops as another set of scores, taken from another shop, with a different variance in absence scores. The probability that our sample was drawn differently is a direct function of the F ratio, the ratio of the larger variance divided by the smaller. If the F ratio were close to 1, we would infer that there was no difference between the two shops in how the employes within the shops varied from each other in days absent. Only about 1 percent of the time would we expect an F of 5.35 if the shops were truly alike. Therefore, if F were this high, we would infer that the shops differed significantly. (Such an effect would occur if one of the shops, but not the other, were highly cohesive and set norms for absences which all its members accepted, restricting the variance in absenteeism.)

Testing Mean Differences

The F ratio most commonly is employed to test whether or not estimates of the *variance of means* of samples are the same.

Knowing that our array had a variance of 3.6 makes it possible for us to *estimate* how the *mean* of the array would vary if we were to collect the data again in other shops of the same size differing only randomly from our shop. An estimate is obtained by dividing the variance of 3.6 of our one shop sample by one less than the number of scores (10) contributing to it, as we estimate that the variance of the mean of 4.0 on a chance basis should vary (3.6/9) or 0.4 days. Suppose we sampled in five shops. Then from each of the five arrays of scores, we could obtain an estimate of how its mean should vary from the way each of the five arrays of scores varied *within* each of the five shops. But, we also could calculate how the five means, one for each shop, actually varied *between* shops to make possible an independent estimate of how these means would vary in an infinity of such shops (the population of shops). Now, if the "between" estimate were the same as the "within" estimate, the F ratio would be 1 and we could infer that the means of the five shops varied randomly from each other. But if the F ratio obtained by dividing the "between" estimate by the "within" estimate were 3.75 or higher, we would reject the randomness notion confident that only once in a hundred times would chance produce such a high rate. (The chances of obtaining different F ratios are known and tabled in any recent book of introductory statistics.) We would infer that some of the five shops had significantly higher mean absenteeism records than others. In this instance, the probabilities of obtaining an F as high as 2.57 would be 5 in 100. Such an F value would permit us to reject the randomness hypothesis *at the 5 percent level of confidence.*

If we were comparing two shops, the same *analysis of variance* could be employed to test whether the differences between means we found between the two shops could be accounted for by the variance we observed within each of the shops. Another ratio, t, which in this case of two shops is the square root of F is more frequently used (because of historical reasons), but the interpretation is similar.

In the remainder of this book, we will refer to many surveys and experiments whose results were *statistically significant*. Generally what we will mean is that the survey or experimental samples yielded nonrandom mean differences. The investigators, after subjecting the results to t or F tests, had to reject the hypothesis that the means differed only for chance reasons. The t or F values were so high that the investigators inferred that the means they obtained were not drawn from the same population of values.

APPENDIX B

CORRELATION

Consider again those deviations from the mean absence value in our shop last year:

Employe:	A	B	C	D	E	F	G	H	I	J
Deviations:	+4	+2	+1	+1	0	−1	−1	−2	−2	−2

And suppose the equivalent deviations for the same 10 workers this year were the following:

$$+4 \quad +2 \quad +1 \quad +1 \quad 0 \quad -1 \quad -1 \quad -2 \quad -2 \quad -2$$

Then, the *sum of the cross-products* of these deviations would be $(4 \times 4), + (2 \times 2) \ldots + (-2 \times -2)$ or 36. A *covariance* of 3.6 would be obtained by dividing the sum of these cross-products by 10, the number of cases contributing to the sum.

Suppose the workers were absent next year as follows:

A	B	C	D	E	F	G	H	I	J
0	2	3	3	4	5	5	6	6	6

Compare this to days absent this year:

$$8 \quad 6 \quad 5 \quad 5 \quad 4 \quad 3 \quad 3 \quad 2 \quad 2 \quad 2$$

Then next year the deviations for each of the workers would become as follows:

$$-4 \quad -2 \quad -1 \quad -1 \quad 0 \quad +1 \quad +1 \quad +2 \quad +2 \quad +2$$

Then the sum of the cross-products between deviations of this year and next year would be $(4 \times -4) + (2 \times -2) \ldots + (-2 \times 2) = -36$ and the covariance would be -3.6.

If the deviations next year each had been twice as large, the covariance would be -7.2. The covariance reflects the size of the relationship between the two arrays, the direction of the relations, but also the magnitude of the standard deviations of the arrays. To correct this, we divide the covariance by the product of the standard deviations to obtain the *correlation coefficient*—an index of covariance free of the effects of the variances of each array.

The correlation coefficient (r) between absences last year and this year is 3.6/(1.9)(1.9) or 1.0.

The correlation coefficient between absences this year and next is $-3.6/(1.9)(1.9)$ or -1.0.

Note how the scale of absolute values of either array does not matter for we correct r by dividing by the standard deviations of the arrays. The larger all the absolute values, the larger are the covariance and standard deviations, but the larger also is the correction. Note that the means do not matter either, because we deal only in deviations from the array mean which with our calculations is always set at 0.

These arrays are scatter-plotted in Figures 2.11 and 2.12. Note in these covarying arrays of perfect positive ($r = 1.0$) and perfect negative correlations ($r = -1.0$) that all plotted points fall on a straight line, *the line of best fit.* The *slope* of this line (how much change of score in one array, accompanies a given amount in the other) is the correlation coefficient when both arrays have the same standard deviations.

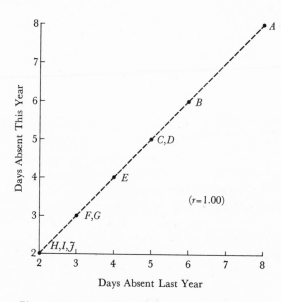

Figure 2.11: *Example of a Perfect Positive Correlation Between Days Absent This Year and Last
Year by Workers A Through J.*

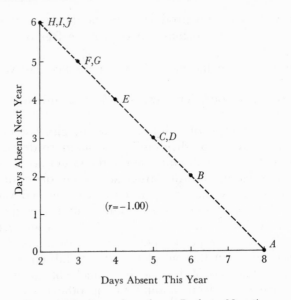

Figure 2.12: Example of a Perfect Negative Correlation (r = −1.00) Between Days Absent This Year and Last Year by Workers A Through J.

Suppose job dissatisfaction scores for these same 10 workers were the following:

A	B	C	D	E	F	G	H	I	J
6	6	6	3	6	0	7	4	2	5

This would yield a mean of 5.0 and deviations of:

$$+1 \quad +1 \quad +1 \quad -2 \quad +1 \quad 0 \quad +2 \quad -1 \quad -3 \quad 0$$

so that if we correlated job dissatisfaction scores and days absent last year, we would calculate the sums of the cross-products (4×1) + $(2 \times 1) \ldots + (-2 \times 0)$ giving a total sum of cross-products of 11 and a covariance of 1.1. The sum of the squares of the deviations of job satisfaction scores is 22, the variance, thus, is 2.2, and the standard deviation is approximately 1.5 for the 10 workers, so:

$$r = \frac{1.1}{(1.5)(1.9)} = .37$$

This correlation of .37 is shown in Figure 2.13. Note that despite the badly scattered values, only D and G are below their means in one

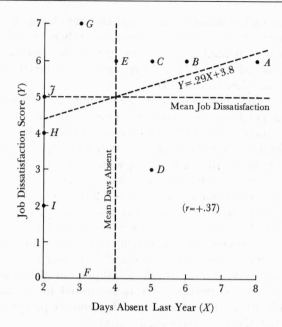

Figure 2.13: Example of a Positive, But Not Perfect, Correlation Between Job Dissatisfaction Scores and Days Absent of Workers A Through J.

variable, yet above on the other. The line of best fit, $Y = .29X + 3.8$, calculated from the obtained correlation and the means and standard deviation of the two arrays, passes through the intersection of the means. The vertical distance (squared) of the 10 plotted points from this particular line sum to a minimum. This is the *least squares* solution. The plotted points will depart further from any other straight line. The slope of the line is .29 which is the correlation coefficient, .37, corrected for the differences of the standard deviations of the two arrays:

$$.37\left(\frac{1.5}{1.9}\right) = .29$$

Meanings of Correlation

As mentioned earlier, as a corrected slope of the line of best fit the correlation coefficient shows how changes in one variable accompany changes in another. In Figure 2.13 we observe that every increase of one day in absenteeism is accompanied by an increase of .29 in job dissatisfaction. Note we did not say that absenteeism caused or was affected by job dissatisfaction, merely that change in absenteeism coincided with change in job dissatisfaction. When we observe a particular correlation, it might be due to one variable affecting another, or both might be influenced by a third variable, or the correlation might be a matter of other coincidences.

With the least squares solution, we minimize the error in predicting one variable (Y) from the other (X). The size of the correlation coefficient is an indicator of how much error remains. For example, when $r = 1.00$, there is no error. When $r = 0$, the error is 100 percent. That is, knowledge of X values coinciding with Y values is of no help in reducing the error in predicting Y values. When $r = .40$, the percent reduction in error from 100 percent is 8.3 percent; when $r = .80$, it is 40 percent. [Percent Reduction in Error $= (100 - 100\sqrt{1 - r^2})$.]

Probably the easiest way to interpret quantitatively the meaning of a correlation coefficient is to consider the actual variance of Y—the variable we are trying to predict—and how much of its variance is accounted for by X. If r is 1.00, then 100 percent of Y is accounted for by X. If $r = .80$, 64 percent of Y is accounted for by knowing X; if $r = .40$, only 16 percent is accounted for and 84 percent remains unaccounted for. (Percent Accounted $= 100 \, r^2$).

The correlation indicates the accuracy of forecasting one variable, knowing another. It says nothing about the utility of the information. A very low correlation of .20 may be useful if (1) the sample is large; or (2) the predictor can be added with other predictors to improve the accuracy of forecast; or (3) we are trying to make a crude forecast of, say, whether a case will be above or below average on Y, if it is extremely high or low on X; or (4) cases vary greatly on Y, and so forth. In the same way a large correlation of .80 may not mean very much obtained from a small sample, where we guess that the figure of .80 is not necessarily a true statement of the relation between X and Y.

APPENDIX C

FACTOR ANALYSIS

The Clustering of Multiple Measurements

Suppose we collect the attitudes of workers on each of eight different scales; satisfaction with pay, with bonuses, with vacation benefits, and so on. We can display their responses or scores on each scale in a score matrix as shown in Table 2.3.

TABLE 2.3 SCORE MATRIX

		Scales							
		1	2	3	4	5	6	7	8
Employe									
	A	4	7	1	3	6	5	9	8
	B	6	4	0	4	0	9	1	0
	C	8	0	0	0	4	1	3	2
	.	.	.	.	.	.	.	.	.
	:	:	:	:	:	:	:	:	:
	N	4	1	3	2	8	7	9	2

Then we can calculate the correlation coefficients among each of the eight scales or transform the score matrix into a correlation matrix (Table 2.4).

TABLE 2.4 CORRELATION MATRIX*

		Attitude Scale							
		1	2	3	4	5	6	7	8
	1	—	.20	.28	.36	−.09	.01	.06	.06
	2	.20	—	.00	.52	.36	−.04	.04	.04
	3	.28	.00	—	.04	−.36	.04	.04	.04
Attitude	4	.36	.52	.04	—	.66	−.02	.43	.39
Scale	5	−.09	.36	−.36	.66	—	−.06	.27	.24
	6	.01	−.04	.04	−.02	−.06	—	.09	.08
	7	.06	.04	.04	.43	.27	.09	—	.72
	8	.06	.04	.04	.39	.24	.08	.72	—

*From Cattell, 1952, p. 417

How much employes vary in scores on a particular scale, the total or 100 percent of the variance of the scale, can be subdivided into three types: *common, specific,* and *error* variance.

Error variance is the random variation of a scale score we obtain when we repeat the measurement of the same persons. The *reliable* variance of a scale is its total variance less its error. If the correlation between scale scores obtained this week and again next week were 1.00, the total variance of the scale would be reliable and the scale would contain no variance due to random error.

Some of the reliable variance is *specific,* uncorrelated with any of the other scales of Table 2.4. The remainder of the reliable variance is *common,* correlated with one or more of the other scales.

Factor analysis determines the common and specific variance in each scale. Beginning with the *matrix* of correlation coefficients of Table 2.4, it proceeds to identify a minimum number of factors which will account as simply as possible for all the *common* variance in the matrix. Table 2.4 is transformed and rotated mathematically into Table 2.5, a factor matrix showing how the same scales correlate with the common factors. The analysis may be performed so the factors will be *orthogonal* — uncorrelated with each other. Or an *oblique* set of factors can be obtained where the analysis permits correlated factors. Also factors yielding a *simple structure* are sought so that each scale correlates as highly as possible with one or more, and as low as possible with the other factors. For example, Scale 1 correlates $-.61$ with Factor II but only $-.05$ and $.10$ with Factors I and III. Almost all the common variance of Scale 1 is accounted for by Factor II. Thus, $100 \, (.61)^2$ or 37 percent of Scale 1

TABLE 2.5   ROTATED COMMON FACTOR MATRIX*

| | *Factor* | | | |
	I	II	III	*Common Variance*
Scale				
1	$-.05$	$-.61$	.10	.38
2	.46	$-.37$	$-.04$	.35
3	$-.38$	$-.47$	.13	.39
4	.75	$-.54$	.38	.98
5	.85	.08	.17	.76
6	$-.11$	.01	.14	.03
7	.12	.02	.89	.80
8	.10	.04	.80	.65

*From Cattell, 1952, p. 71

is accounted for by Factor II. Scale 2 is more complex for it correlates with Factors I and II. Factor I accounts for 21 percent, and Factor II accounts for almost 14 percent of the variance of Scale 2.

Factor Meaning. The scales correlating most highly with a factor help to name it. Thus Factor I appears to be one concerning Scales 4 and 5. Scale 5 is almost a pure measure of Factor I. In the same way Scales 7 and 8 define Factor III.

The sum of squares of the correlations of a scale with each factor is its total common variance (when the total variance is set equal to 1.00). For Scale 1, $(-.05)^2 + (-.61)^2 + (.10)^2 = .38$.

Since the common variance of Scale 1 is .38, when its reliable variance is, say .68, then its specific variance is .30 and its error variance is .32.

Set of Factors. Once the factors are known, it is possible to reconstruct the equivalent of any individual's eight scores on the original scales into scores in terms of the three common factors. Or we may now construct three new scales, one to measure each factor. Each is a pure or single measure, compared to most of the eight scales with which we began.

Once the factors are known it also becomes possible to reconstruct any correlation between the measurements in Table 2.4 in terms of the correlations of the measurements with the common factors. Thus the correlations between Scale 1 and Scale 2 of .20 can be formed by adding the products of the *factor loadings* (or the correlations of the Scales with the factors) from Table 2.5 of Scale 1 and 2: $(-.05 \times .46) + (-.61 \times -.37) + (.10 \times -.04) = .20$.

Certain aspects of factor analysis should be obvious. The more scales we start with and the more diverse issues they involve, the more factors we will obtain. If all eight scales concern material benefits, then we will probably emerge with several material-benefits factors. If no scale concerns material benefits, then no factor will either.

The factor structure may or may not be the same for different situations and persons. Thus factors found on the same scales for white-collar workers might differ somewhat when the scales are administered for blue-collar workers.

The factor structure will depend on the mathematical methods we employ. If we begin by assuming that a general factor exists with which all our attitude scales correlate, we may obtain a different structure than if we begin without this assumption. Fortunately there has been reasonable consistency in what factors have emerged in a host of analyses, although considerable variations have appeared depending on assumptions, scales used, and samples studied.

A Hierarchy of Factors

Suppose we have 12 assessments on each of 100 men. Three of the assessments concern height: actual, estimated, and self-estimated. A comparable three concern weight. Three concern attitudes toward supervisors and three measures concern attitudes towards co-workers.

Since the three height measures will correlate more highly with each other than with the weight or attitude measures they will form a "height" factor. A "weight" factor will also appear as will two attitude factors, one toward supervisors, the other toward co-workers. But in nature in general, and in our sample as well, height and weight are correlated to some extent, so that a group factor, "stature," also appears. A second group factor, "general attitude toward others" may also appear. Thus a measurement like estimated height relates most closely to other height measurements and clusters in a specific factor of height. But, it also is closer to weight measures than to attitude assessments so that it and other height assessments cluster in a group factor of stature.

Such a hierarchy has been found for factors of job satisfaction.

In Brief

WHILE MANAGEMENT AND ECONOMISTS HAVE OVERESTIMATED THE IMPORtance of pay, psychologists have underestimated it. Dissatisfaction with pay may be symptomatic of more deep-seated disgruntlement; but low pay in itself may spread in its disturbing effects to other issues.

The actual amount of one's pay is not as significant as how much a person believes he should be paid. This belief depends on with whom he compares himself.

Basically, an employe is paid wages either for the amount of work he finishes or the amount of time he puts in. Or he receives a salary for agreeing to be an employe. Since employe effort may be much more a matter of commitment to his organization than of immediate payment for each sale he makes, piece he completes, or hour he works, in some areas it may make more sense to shift employes who traditionally have worked for wages to straight salaries. However incentive plans for effort do work well in many kinds of activities depending on the nature of the plan, the work done, the amount of mutual trust which has developed between worker and management, the clarity of feedback of results of worker efforts, and the extent the work group is involved in the plan.

Numerous other matters affect the extent an employe feels he has a good job. Job security is one of the most significant of these. Opportunities for advancement are likewise of significance to many employes, particular younger, more able ones. Some jobs are more important than others for they give more status and satisfaction to the job holders. On the other hand, an employe is likely to be disgruntled, particularly if he is young and able, if he must cope with inadequate equipment or facilities, monotonous work, noise, and congestion at work. Inadequate housing and transportation also may be a problem.

Chapter 3

REWARDS

OF WORK

MATERIAL BENEFITS, GOOD WORKING CONDITIONS, AND CHALLENGING work number among the several independent factors contributing to job satisfaction. Conditions which increase or reduce their occurrence and potency will now be considered.

MATERIAL SATISFACTIONS

The need to work in order to survive no longer applies in an economy of abundance such as in the United States. If one is content with the bare-subsistence standard of living provided by relief agencies, he can remain permanently unemployed.

Why, then, do most of us work? And why are some jobs preferred to others? We work for at least three reasons: (1) because it is expected of us. In our society the adult hobo who deliberately does not work is an outcast, a pariah, and actually likely to be suffering from simple schizophrenia; (2) because work provides us with *extrinsic* rewards such as higher-than-subsistence wages; and/or (3) because the work itself is *intrinsically* rewarding—doing the work, in itself, is pleasing and satisfying.

If all work were intrinsically rewarding much of the problem of management control would disappear. Assuming the worker had the ability, work would become for him as recreational as play. He could be given a straight salary to provide him with his accustomed standard of living. How hard he worked would neither depend on his salary, nor affect it, nor would it be necessary. There would be little need to worry about whether he was doing his job to the best of his ability. For the closer he stuck to his task, the more satisfaction he would be receiving. Unfortunately much of work by its very nature has little intrinsic interest to those who must perform the work, so extrinsic rewards must be offered to attract men to particular jobs and keep them working hard at those jobs. Extrinsic rewards for work such as high pay, steady income, or congenial co-workers become essential. These extrinsic rewards of work such as the amount of money or the fringe benefits of a job can be quite independent of the work which is actually done on a job. The same monetary rewards might be earned for bookkeeping or building birdhouses. Pay is determined by factors not necessarily associated with the kind of work done.

Often men are faced with the choice of leaving a more intrinsically rewarding job, say as a high school teacher, for a more extrinsically rewarding job, say as a book salesman. Naturally, the best of all possible arrangements is when the teacher's income matches that of the book salesman and the selling job becomes as interesting and stimulating as the teaching job.

Management control problems become much greater when workers are motivated extrinsically. If pay, recognition, and advancement are earned for speedy performance but excellent work is also desired, the quality of output may suffer. Unless workers are craftsmen who find working at producing high quality products intrinsically gratifying, they will be likely to take shortcuts to earn their rewards for speed. Management must offer extrinsic rewards for quality and introduce quality-control inspection systems. For the craftsman whose work is also his play, such inspection is seldom needed.

In this chapter we shall concentrate on such extrinsic rewards as pay, security, advancement, and fringe benefits along with those aspects surrounding the job that can make the job itself more attractive. Then in the next chapter we shall look at what it takes to make a job, as such, more intrinsically rewarding. This will necessitate investigating how people differ in their interests, vocational motives, and goals. While supervisors, co-workers, and the organization will figure in our discussions in this and the next chapter, more detailed consideration of these factors will be delayed until Chapters 5, 6, and 7.

Let us be clear about our position. Just because we shall try to catalog all the important factors involved with job satisfaction does not mean that we undervalue what in the past was always regarded as the only really important factor — pay. Indeed, it is still argued by some behavioral scientists that pay is the single most important consideration:

Pay, in one form or another, is certainly one of the mainsprings of motivation in our society. The drive for private money gain — the profit motive — provides the main ideological cleavage in the world today. Deep down, everyone assumes that we mostly work for money. The most evangelical Human Relationist insists it is important, while protesting that other things are too (and are, perhaps, in his view, nobler). It would be unnecessary to belabor the point if it were not for a tendency for money drives to slip out of focus in a miasma of other values and other practices. As it is, it must be repeated: pay is the most important single motivator used in our organized society.[279]

Unfortunately little psychological research has been completed to date on the operation of pay and pay raises as incentives before and after they are earned. What kind of an increase does it take to have an effect? How much will more pay adequately substitute as a reward for other extrinsic benefits like prestige or intrinsically satisfying work? What is equitable pay? With whom do we compare ourselves in earnings? Yet, some evidence is accumulating to answer these psychological questions about compensation.

Importance of Pay

Indicative of the importance of compensation is a listing of the rewards desired by samples drawn from office staffs in the same company. Fifty-six percent wanted a recommendation for pay increase; 49 percent wanted a recommendation for promotion; 37 percent wanted more responsibility; 30 percent wanted training for a better job; 26 percent wanted sincere praise; 10 percent said they wanted more interesting work or a pat on the back; and only 2 percent felt they wanted any more privileges.[659]

While exiting employes give pay as the most frequent reason for quitting the job,[620] job applicants tend to say that security, the type of work, and opportunities for advancement are somewhat more important than the pay of the job for which they are applying, according to an analysis of 3,000 applicants for a position with a public utility.[346] Whether the applicants are men or women, the material fringe benefits associated with the job—vacations, insurance, and sick leave—are regarded as least important. Results are similar for employed samples. Pay is seldom, if ever, ranked first among a list of job satisfaction factors when employes are asked directly to rank their sources of satisfaction in order of importance. Pay rate was among the top five choices of over half of the 7,000 workers surveyed in Table 3.1, but only 7.2 percent listed pay as first in importance. Similarly, the average rank in importance assigned to pay was third when over 1,000 retail store executives ranked 14 items of significance (Table 3.2).

TABLE 3.1   RATINGS OF IMPORTANCE BY 7,000 WORKERS IN A NATION-
WIDE FIRM ON VARIOUS JOB FACTORS*

	Percent of 7000 Workers Including this Item in the First Five	Percent of 7000 Workers Including this Item as First Choice Only
A steady job	61.9	36.1
Pay rate	52.6	7.2
A chance to get ahead	41.9	6.9
A square boss	39.6	4.8
Working on the job you prefer	35.3	15.2
Credit for the job you do	29.6	2.2
Vacations and holidays	21.5	0.4
Friendly working companions	21.3	0.7
Medical and health facilities	20.8	0.6
Pension	9.7	7.1

*From Stagner, 1950, p. 6

TABLE 3.2   HOW 1,037 RETAIL STORE EXECUTIVES (SEARS, ROEBUCK)
RANK JOB SATISFIERS IN IMPORTANCE*

Order of Importance	Category Title
1	Opportunity for growth and advancement
2	Identification with the company
3	Pay
4	Status and recognition
5	Technical competence of supervision
6	Confidence in management
7	Interpersonal relations with supervisor
8	Security of job and work relations
9	Employe benefits
10	Effectiveness of administration
11	Adequacy of communication
12	Friendliness and cooperation of fellow employes
13	Job demands
14	Physical working conditions

*From Poduska, undated

A more decisive aspect of pay is starting salary. When 456 professional and technical candidates who accepted a job with Standard Oil
of New Jersey were compared with 56 who refused to accept jobs, those
who refused jobs said they liked the company, its reputation for tech-

nical achievement, its fairness to its employes, and its opportunities for self-development. But, they felt the company's starting salary was inadequate and this was a common reason why they refused to accept a job with the company.[659]

Starting salary is a key consideration in a program to upgrade a firm's sales or technical force. Whether the selection tests and training procedures have effects will depend upon the firm's ability to attract good recruits. No amount of accurate screening will work if the quality and quantity of applicants for positions with the firm remains low. Raising starting salaries is one way to increase the quality and quantity of applicants for the job.

The starting salary of a job is often of greatest importance in attracting us to it, but it becomes less important in holding us to the job once we accept it, in comparison to such factors as security or opportunity for advancement.[289]

Overestimated Importance of Pay

In studying labor-management relations, the significance of wages may be magnified erroneously. Inadequate pay is important, but is not the only, or even the most important, source of job dissatisfaction. However, it is easier to articulate dissatisfaction with salary and to make specific wage demands than to voice dissatisfaction with, say, supervisory behavior or lack of job interest, so it is not surprising that of 2,055 union demands analyzed for a three-year period (1942–44) 44 percent involved monetary issues[679] or that of all strikes in the United States in 1948, a majority involved higher wages as an issue.

[But] . . . how fallacious these figures are. In many cases the workers first get angry and go on strike, then look around for something to demand. Higher wages and shorter hours are simple, neat and easy to formulate. . . . The fallacy . . . that only money counts can be seen if we consider even a single strike which lasts for any considerable period of time. (The cost in wages to employes of the strike cannot be made up by them for many years. Likewise, the loss in profits by management cannot be made up, either.)[630, p.3]

Yet salary, particularly starting salary, is an important job attraction. As pointed out before although salary may not be what holds a man to a job once he accepts it, if pay is considered inadequate the worker is likely to be dissatisfied. If pay is adequate the worker may not necessarily be satisfied. But continued dissatisfaction despite adequacy of pay may be reflected in demands for more pay, although what is really missing from the job are such satisfiers as opportunities for advancement, recognition, and achievement.

Spread of Effects

Despite the fact that other factors may be more significant, material success spreads its effects and, again, is likely to be overestimated in importance as a consequence.

Pay is a symbol of success or failure. Workers may elect to receive unemployment compensation rather than to accept a new job at a pay level slightly below what they had been earning. According to home interviews with over 600 workers in an aircraft factory, if their beginning salaries with this company were lower than their previous ones, they were less favorable in attitude towards the company, more likely to quit, and earned lower merit ratings on their new job.[643]

The overall outlook of a highly paid person tends to be more optimistic than that of one whose pay is inadequate. He is more likely to agree that his children have good opportunities, that he likes his work, that his pay is fair, that he is well treated by his boss, that he is in no danger of losing his job, and that he has an opportunity to enjoy life and to get ahead.[107] Examining a large sample of executives on the same level—one group earning a greater salary than the other—the more highly paid managers felt more secure, free, and esteemed by their companies than did those earning less money.[385]

Observers and interpreters of the industrialization process taking place in underdeveloped countries suggest that workers are not fighting against industrialization or detribalization and the loss of the old culture. Rather, they are struggling for a greater share in the material benefits of industrialization. Through material gains they see hope for a better life than before.[363]

Variations in Satisfaction with Compensation

The importance of compensation certainly will vary from one work situation to another, with changes in the economy, with the particular employe and his needs for income, and so forth. Actual low pay may be more satisfying to a worker under certain conditions while much higher compensation might be dissatisfying to another if it failed to meet his expectations. It may not be the absolute pay differentials that produce greater dissatisfaction with compensation among white-collar compared to blue-collar respondents, but a sense that white-collar work, more satisfying in general and of higher status or value, should also be more rewarding financially as well. Also it is possible that all things being equal, the unorganized white-collar worker earns less relative to his education, skill, and responsibilities than a comparable blue-collar worker.

Figure 3.1 displays the results of 1,068 interviews in which the mean satisfaction of white-collar employes was found higher than that of blue-collar employes on most factors—such as working conditions, supervision, and co-workers—yet the white-collar workers reported greater dissatisfaction with their compensation than did blue-collar workers.[100]

Attitudes of Executives Towards Their Own Compensation. A survey of a 10 percent sample of the American Management Association uncovered a number of interesting patterns. As might be supposed, executives' expectations about the pay they should receive were related to their level in the management hierarchy. And the higher their pay, commensurate with their level in the organization, the more satisfied they were likely

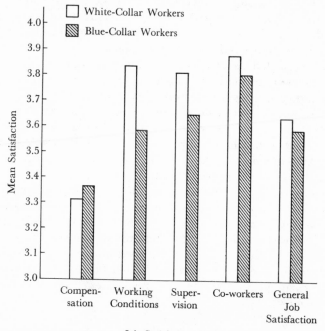

Figure 3.1: Comparison of White- and Blue-Collar Workers in Satisfaction with Compensation, Working Conditions, Supervision, Co-workers, and General Job Satisfaction. (Data from Carlson et al., 1962)

to be with their compensation. But regardless of their actual status or level in the organization, as might be expected, the less highly paid executives attached the most importance to executive compensation while the highly paid men were less concerned about salary.[385] Those deprived of pay see it as more important in governing their own behavior. But, deprivation is a relative matter.

Relative Deprivation and Dissatisfaction with Wages

A worker will regard himself as underpaid because he sees himself as personally equal in worth to someone who is being paid more. Or he may regard his job as important as that of someone earning more than him. He may also be dissatisfied because his own salary is failing to keep up with economic inflation or with the growth in income of his friends in the community, or his wife, or his fellow workers, or what he sees are the gains being made by other occupational groups.[379]

When 489 nonsupervisory refinery workers each chose two other persons with whom to compare earnings, 59 percent of the comparisons were with more highly paid workers. A worker was dissatisfied with his own pay if he compared himself with someone earning more money whom he regarded as equal or inferior in seniority, education, and family. Satisfied respondents who compared themselves with persons earning higher salaries could justify the differential in pay.

If a respondent rejected personal responsibility for his wages and regarded them as low, he would compare himself with someone earning more and would be dissatisfied with the unfavorable comparison with his own income. Again, a worker was more likely to be dissatisfied with his chosen comparison earning higher pay when he had no opportunity to advance. Workers with low pay who accepted personal responsibility for their condition, or who were in career advancement programs, were more likely to be satisfied with the lower pay. Thus, absolute pay was less significant in determining satisfaction with income than was pay relative to others considered similar in skill, type of work, age, education, and seniority, and whether blame was accepted for inadequate earnings and whether the respondent had opportunities for advancement.[513]

Reverse Consequences of Wage Inequities. Curiously, the need to feel that work and pay are in balance seems also to lead people to work harder if they have been made to feel they are earning more than is really equitable.

Twenty-two college men were hired through the regular placement referral service for temporary work as interviewers at a pay rate of $3.50 per hour for jobs that were supposed to last several months. Half of the men hired were led to believe that they lacked the qualifications for the job of open-end interviewing, that a mistake had been made by the referral agency, and that $3.50 was too much pay for them, but that they were to be paid at this rate anyway. The other 11 men were told they were completely qualified for the jobs as interviewers and that $3.50 was the standard for such work. In the first approximately 2.5 hours, each of the men who believed he was being overpaid interviewed approximately an average of 40 people. Each of the 11 men who were informed that their pay was consonant with their qualifications and the work to be done interviewed only 28 persons during the same period! It was inferred that the *cognitive dissonance* created by the feelings of being overpaid led to higher productivity. But it was also possible that the instructions caused the overpaid men to feel the need to work harder to keep their jobs. This latter economic explanation, however, failed to account for findings in a second experiment which offered piece rates of 30 cents per interview instead of the hourly $3.50 to half of 18 men given the dissonant instructions. In the same way, half of 18 men who were led to believe they were earning fair amounts were placed on piece rates and half on hourly amounts. Those on hourly wages handled about the same number of interviews as in the first experiment. But the men on piece rates who were told that they were being paid fairly interviewed more people (about 28 on the average) than those who were told they were overpaid. Those believing themselves to be overpaid per interview, interviewed only about an average of 22. It was inferred that overpaid piece workers could reduce the dissonance and earn less by interviewing fewer people—which they did. A third experiment suggested that the "overpaid" piece workers attempted to justify their earnings by greater attention to quality and a sacrifice in the speed with which they performed.

From this series of experiments it was concluded that seemingly overpaid workers with fixed hourly earnings restore cognitive balance by increasing their productivity. Ostensibly, overpaid workers on piece rates restore balance by lowering productivity to reduce their earnings per hour and increasing the quality of their performance. Thus, under some circumstances, "individuals behave so as to *earn less at the cost of greater effort.* This is clearly contrary to the usual assumption that workers behave so as to maximize their gains and minimize their effort."[3]

We still have much to learn about the psychological effects of pay and pay raises.

Compensation Plans and Their Effects

Actual dissatisfaction with pay may depend on how it is determined. For example, in three British factories, interviews with workers at different wage levels revealed that satisfaction of workers with wages depended to some extent on the simplicity of the group payment plan used. Where the group payment procedures were complicated, satisfaction with wages was less.[449]

Plans of Payment.   Compensation plans take three forms. A worker may be paid for each piece he produces. He may be paid for the hours he works. He may be paid a salary regardless of his production or his hours worked.

Piece rates, hourly wages, or salaries may be raised as a reward for length of service. Hourly wages or salaries can also be raised for merit. In the case of piece rates, special rate increases, bonuses, or premiums can be attached for attaining successively higher levels of output. For example, the rate may shift from 10 cents to 12 cents per item produced after the first 200 items have been produced during a day. Or a sales clerk working on straight 6 percent commission might be given an additional $100 bonus for sales over a specified quota during a month's business.

Most piece rate or commission plans provide a guaranteed hourly base wage so that the new worker or the salesman in a new territory can earn a living wage despite the fact that his production or sales is below what it will be once he has learned the job or opened the territory satisfactorily.

The higher the level of the work, the more likely is the employe to be salaried. Executives and technical or professional employes "exempt" from punching a time clock usually are paid a salary independent of immediate hours worked and immediate output. Bonuses and stock options are given depending on the overall success of a department or organization to which the salaried employe has contributed. In the same way piece rates and worker bonuses may be geared to group output or to the firm's productivity or profits.

Utility.   According to an American Management Association survey during World War II, 62 percent of "direct producers" were on incentives of some sort while even 17 percent of "indirect producers" were paid depending on their output. In "management theory," such incentive payments should produce 20 to 30 percent greater hourly output.[253] In practice, incentive payments may result mainly in increased costs of production rather than increased productivity. Incentive schemes are expensive to administer and employes may concentrate on tactics of making money with a minimum of effort so that the overhead costs of quality control and bookkeeping may be more than the gains of tying compensation directly to output.[577] Moreover, incentive systems create dissatisfaction and dissension. Sixty percent of British building workers opposed incentive plans although the plans would mean greater take home pay for them, for the plans were seen by them as likely to reduce harmony within the work group. Such group conflict is handled by uniform restrictions in output by the work group.[457] The fear by workers that management will raise standards and lower payment per piece (bust rates), leads to a general restriction of their output. If all workers produce the same informally accepted amount, then no one worker can be accused of being a rate buster by his colleagues. And so, in spite of an existing piece rate incentive plan, as much as three hours of an eight-hour work day was seen wasted in one American machine shop where workers informally enforced quota restrictions and goldbricking on each other.[576]

The production records of men in 228 work groups in a factory were analyzed according to the extent each group was high or low in cohesiveness. The cohesiveness of each group was determined by asking each of its members how attractive the group was to them, how much the group worked as a team, and so on. When employes of a work group were highly cohesive, as shown in Figure 3.2a, they tended to vary less

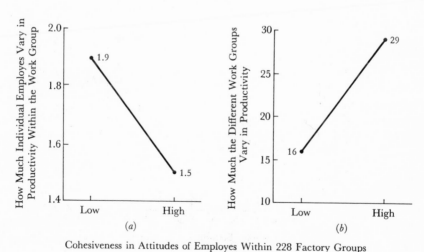

Cohesiveness in Attitudes of Employes Within 228 Factory Groups

Figure 3.2: Group Cohesiveness and Variance in Productivity Within and Between Groups. (After Seashore, 1954)

from each other in productivity than comparable employes in groups
low in cohesiveness. Conversely, cohesive employe groups differed more
from each other in output than did groups low in cohesiveness, as shown
in Figure 3.2*b*. Workers within a cohesive group conformed to whatever
output level was set by their own group. A highly cohesive group has
the potential to set high standards for all its members or to restrict
their output. The group, low in cohesiveness, is less important in determining what its members will produce. In such groups, individual differences are more significant in determining output.[593] Paradoxically,
output restriction by workers is likely to be greatest in cohesive groups
rather than in groups described as lacking in teamwork and "together-
ness."

Output restriction was directly revealed when an examination was
made of the productivity of 55 machine operators for one week, paid
by the hour, and given a standard against which to produce. Figure 3.3
shows how output here was never greater than the standard, but most
workers produced at or close to it. These operators were behaving perfectly sensibly, for the data were collected when business was poor and
men were being laid off.[575]

Plans in Conflict with Motivation.   Payment plans often are based on
a very simple and naive hypothesis that workers are purely mercenary in
their concerns. There are many examples of compensation programs
in conflict with motivation to conform, to be like others, to belong, to

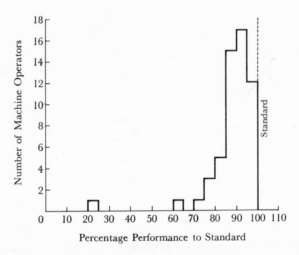

*Figure 3.3: Output Rates During One Week of 55
Machine Operators in a Shop. (After Rothe & Nye,
1961, p. 53)*

be liked by one's peers. A big earner may find himself branded as an apple polisher or a norm breaker; one who produces too little will be seen as a slacker by his fellow workers.[55]

Improving the Effectiveness of Compensation Plans

There is a "veil of secrecy" surrounding many wage and salary departments. Management often fails to describe adequately how compensation depends on one's contribution to the organization. Rather than improving wage and salary administration, there often is a complete rejection of money as a motivator. Compensation administrators adopt an accounting philosophy; they merely keep everything orderly.[182] But "when used in conjunction with, rather than in opposition to other men's needs, . . . compensation may . . . become an effective tool for motivating employees."[182, p. 301] And, there have been some remarkably successful plans. Lincoln Electric was able to double the prevailing wages in a competitive industry, yet had lower employment costs, no work stoppages, and lower turnover than competitors.[413] Productivity was raised in eight Australian firms after the introduction of incentive plans, particularly in those tied to individual payments for increased output rather than dependent on increased plant productivity.

The Scanlon Plan is a promising example in which employes are rewarded to the extent their greater efforts yield more output with the same overhead and labor costs.[401] Workers receive the benefit of any money saved in such operating costs. Management gains because it is better able to guarantee deliveries to customers (which affect its sales potentials). Customer complaints diminish about product defects. New employes are trained with enthusiasm by older men. There is no tendency or need for employes to restrict output. Capital investment is put to work more profitably. The Scanlon Plan is a particularly meaningful one for it gives employes rewards for success in what they have greatest control. Reward does not depend on external market conditions or company profits, yet it is tied to the success of company operations. Group influence can be used to foster cost reduction objectives. Naturally, the success of this kind of approach depends on the degree to which mutual trust develops between management and labor, on the degree to which the program is worked out collaboratively so all concerned are committed to the plan which finally takes shape. Issues to be discussed in Chapter 6, in particular, are relevant to understanding whether various plans that require sharing of profits or sharing of gains from reduced costs will work. But in addition to such social-psychological factors as the extent management and workers trust each other, success of a compensation plan also depends upon the nature of the task, the consistency and clarity of feedback of results to workers, and the extent the group is allowed to set its own standards. In all, both management and labor search for a sensible pattern of earnings and production, a pattern that is stable and that is satisfactory to both. Success depends on finding such a balance.[253]

Factors Affecting the Success of Incentive Plans: Nature of Task

When young women spent one day a week on each of five tasks paid hourly wages by piece rates or bonuses, as shown in Figure 3.4, output on some tasks such as wrapping was raised almost 300 percent by piece-rate incentive, while performance on other tasks such as unwrapping were hardly affected.[756]

A possible explanation of these results may be found in a laboratory study of the effects of incentives on performance of the complex task of tracking a target. When subjects were relaxed according to measure-

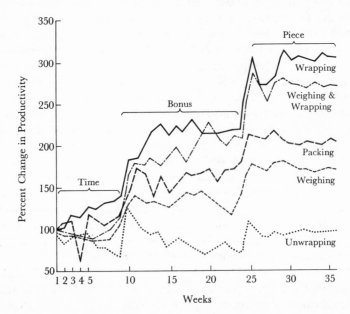

Figure 3.4: Effects of Different Incentive Plans on Different Kinds of Work. (Wyatt, 1934, p. 24)

ments of their muscle potentials (bioelectric currents associated with muscle arousal) and palmar skin conductance measuring their auto-nomic activity (lack of electrical resistance associated with palm sweat-ing), and when they were highly motivated, tracking errors were greater than when only moderate incentives were applied.[640]

When the task is complex, if motivation is already high, incentives may be a detriment to performance. There is an optimum level of moti-vation for performing each task best. This optimum is lower the more complex the task, and is higher the simpler the task. Increasing motiva-tion and stress speeded the performance and improved the accuracy of laboratory subjects working on easy tasks, but was deleterious when the task was made more difficult.[46]

Thus, we expect that incentives will be most effective when interest in the work is lacking and the work is simple. Incentives will be least effective when interest in the work is already high and the work is com-plex.

Often, with complex tasks in particular, extensive improvements in the methods of completing the job yield more gain in output than in-stalling incentive plans. For instance, at Westinghouse, important in-creases in productivity occurred when a better system of planning, measuring, and controlling was instituted, not by increasing employe effort. Paradoxically, incentive plans interfere with the opportunity to introduce improved work methods. Highly paid employes, in particular, are likely to resist changes in methods if they see such changes as reduc-ing what they earn for the amount of work they perform currently.[136] Even where their income and job security might remain the same and they could double output by using a new method, there might still be resistance. Accustomed to completing 50 units to earn $100, an employe might regard as unfair having to complete 100 units to earn the same money, although he could do so with the improved method with no increase in time or energy requirements.

Mutual Trust. If employes see incentives as a money-making game rather than as a plan to return more money to them for greater effort, or if after setting rates management revises piece rates downward be-cause it feels some employes are earning too much, or if other factors make for an unfavorable climate of employe-management relations, incentive plans may fail despite their intrinsic merit.

In many cases plans fail . . . because the basic employer-employe rela-tions were not such as to produce mutual confidence and good will. Indeed some observers point out that a profit-sharing plan (like other incentive pro-cedures) may produce more problems than it solves if injected into an organiza-tion having unsatisfactory employe relations.[189, p.161]

Consistency and Clarity of Feedback.   An effective incentive plan requires that the production goal of a worker be intelligible to him and that he be able to assess the degree to which the goal is attained.[423] Otherwise the worker becomes like an animal stimulated into neurotic behavior by experimental manipulation; that is, he is punished for his inability to discriminate the correct response. Discrimination is made difficult, if not impossible, by altering on a random or otherwise undetectable basis what response will be rewarded and which will be punished.

The lack of clarity and lack of consistency in industry is illustrated by one survey which revealed that 33 percent of respondents felt "they did not know the quality of work that would be passed or rejected by their inspectors." Furthermore, 47 percent believed that inspectors sometimes pass items that the workers would reject. Again, 29 percent said that the same inspectors varied in their requirements from day to day, and 32 percent believed that different inspectors had different standards. At the same time 62 percent of the inspectors in this one plant felt that occasionally they were uncertain as to whether an item or tray should be passed or rejected. The need in this plant to define and establish reliable standards for workers and inspectors was apparent if consistency and clarity of goals were to be obtained.[180]

Group Standard Setting.   Since the work group so often sets the standards of performance for its members regardless of the individual incentives available to them, management is only being realistic when it involves the work group in joint deliberation about standards, quotas, and goals.[423]

The need to reduce costs was explained to four groups of garment workers in the same plant. In one, the control group, a new piece rate was thoroughly explained by the time-study man, and employes' questions about the change were answered. Immediately after the change in rate was put into effect, marked expressions of aggression against management occurred. There was open conflict with the methods engineer, hostility against the supervisor, and deliberate curtailment of production. During the first 40 days of the new rate, 17 percent of the workers quit. Figure 3.5 shows the units produced per hour by this control group before and after the change in rate. There was a considerable drop in productivity of this group following the introduction of the new rate.

The first experimental group approved a plan presented by management to improve the design of the job to be performed. They elected several special operators to be trained in the correct methods. New piece rates were set by time studies on these specially trained operators. All operators then were trained in the new ways under the new rates. The elected special operators contributed suggestions in the design of the

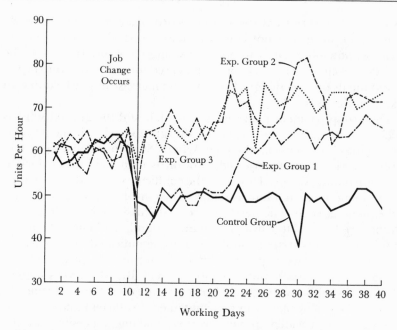

Figure 3.5: The Effect of Participation on Production. (After Coch & French, 1948, pp. 512–32)

revised job and also helped to train other operators later on the new job. Since experimental groups 2 and 3 were smaller it was possible for all members to be involved in the design of the new job, the retraining process, and the setting of new rates. During the first 40 days the experimental groups were cooperative and interested, and no member quit. As shown in Figure 3.5, there was an immediate increase in productivity of experimental groups 2 and 3 and a delayed increase in experimental group 1. To confirm the effects, the control group which had been underproducing was now given an opportunity to participate in decisions about rates and job redesign, following which it gradually achieved the higher levels of productivity already obtained by the experimental groups.[121]

Group Payment.   In addition to group standard setting, it has been found useful to shift to group payment plans. Salesclerks on a straight 6 percent commission basis found themselves in competition with each other. Morale was very low, and although individual sales were high many other duties were avoided such as taking care of stock and showing consideration for customers returning unwanted merchandise. A division of labor resulted when a group plan was innovated so that all sales clerks shared in the group sales record. Each man could now do the things he liked and not concern himself with direct competition. There was now no attempt to tie up customers nor any rush to be the first to greet a customer. Stock was better cared for, and the group began to discipline its own members. There was an increase in satisfaction with working in the group.[20]

The group payment plan seems to work best if the group itself has participated in setting standards for the group and if it has regular opportunities for discussing the plan. When 386 men and 402 women in British factories were interviewed, two-thirds expressed dissatisfaction with group bonus systems. However, the conflicts expressed were mainly social and emotional, not intellectual.[153] They involved group problems, not the plans, as such. The need for group discussions at which feelings could be aired and better insight and understanding obtained by members for such bonus systems would seem to be indicated. To the extent that group wage plans depend on mutual policing, the group may become too large for such mutual control.[167] Yet, British surveys suggest that even where the work group becomes extremely large, satisfaction with group payment plans can be maintained if sufficient knowledge of the results are provided to each worker, making it possible for the worker to understand the incentive pay plan as well as his own contribution to the group success.[97]

Interviews with random samples of 976 employes in British automobile plants and metal-rolling mills generally disclosed favorable attitudes toward group payment plans, particularly plantwide bonuses (adjusted to hours worked and base rate) and group piece rates. However, the acceptability of a group plan depended upon a number of other factors. Older men were more favorable to it than younger workers. Group payment was more favored in small groups (fewer than 10 men) rather than in groups containing more than 50 members. Comments were favorable when standard times and rates yielded a good and consistent income. Comments were unfavorable when earnings could be reduced by material or mechanical difficulties out of the worker's control.

It was inferred from these interviews that—

group incentive payment schemes were likely to yield the best results when:

(a) groups are small, compact, and stable.
(b) the members of a group are well matched and engaged in the same type of work.
(c) the form of payment is simple and the workers are able to translate output into earnings as work proceeds throughout the week.

(d) there are no anomalies in rates and standards within a group or between groups.

(e) output depends on the worker rather than on the machine.

(f) the operational cycle is fairly short and repetitive.

(g) variations in the quality and flow of material are reduced to a minimum.

(h) the group is able to earn a reasonable bonus. (It is generally recognized that the bonus should be about one-third of the time rate, but the optimum rate has never been determined and the main justification for the present figure is that it satisfies both management and workers.

(i) there is an atmosphere of mutual trust and understanding between management and workers.[757, p.107]

When the subgroups within a department have irregular or varied responsibilities, the incentive plan may be related to the total departmental output. Corrections will have to be made if the department's products vary from week to week. The same can be done if a plantwide bonus scheme is adopted,

. . . though the scheme will loose some of its incentive value as its remoteness from individual effort increases. On the other hand, a payment scheme based on the total output of a department or factory is less costly in administrative and clerical work than one based on the output of individuals or small groups. It also reduces or eliminates many sources of friction and facilitates the movement or interchange of workers.[757, p.107]

Group payment is likely to conform to the desire of most Americans to see that payment to all is sufficient to satisfy everyone's needs regardless of how much each individual contributes toward earning the group payment. Although we live in a society with norms which stress free enterprise and individual incentive, American college students typically elect to share rewards according to need rather than contribution. For instance, when students were given the opportunity to distribute course credit among themselves for success in group performance, they preferred to give more credit to students with low grades rather than to the students who contributed the most to the group's effort.[308] Consistent with this tendency was finding that American student trios who had to work cooperatively were less successful the more the three members were rewarded differentially.[482]

Supervision and the Success of Incentive Plans. Understanding of the pay scheme is particularly important and the communication problem most difficult under conditions where the work situation is constantly changing.[606] The supervisor may play a critical role in this communication. An American survey suggests that workers were more satisfied with their wage incentive system when they reported the supervisor did a very good job of explaining the reasons for changes in the system, when the supervisor gave reasons for changes in the standards, and when he told men ahead of time when changes were to occur. Satisfaction was also greater among these 3,500 factory and office workers when the time study engineers did a good job of communicating plans and changes.[425]

The immediate supervisor's involvement in the payment plan may be an important determinant of the effectiveness of money as an incentive. The supervisor has lost considerable power and control with the shift in decisions about wages from him to a wage and salary department.[182] When the Burroughs Corporation decentralized salary administration and permitted operating divisions to assign salaries and salary changes, there was an increase in understanding and acceptance of the program by supervision, and the time between a supervisor's recommendation and the consequent granting of a raise was greatly reduced.[370]

The extent to which a foreman can personally profit from the performance of his subordinates is also likely to make a difference in the extent to which money can be used as an incentive. Thus, in the Soviet Union, suggestion systems are increased in effectiveness by permitting the foreman to participate in the bonus awarded a worker for suggestions. In the United States, on the other hand, not only would this be unusual but foremen, as such, seldom are permitted to participate in suggestion systems on the same basis as the employes. Their suggestions are regarded as part of their job assignment for which they are already receiving sufficient pay.[253]

Salaries for All Workers?   If it is true that money attracts employes to a particular job and holds them to that job but does not necessarily affect how hard they work on the job nor how well they perform the job, a good case can be made for separating what an employe is paid directly and his immediate effort and success on the job. Placing an employe on salary, of course, still permits him to be given raises in pay commensurate with effort, seniority, and success, but it is not a day-to-day affair. An hourly paid employe shows up for work almost every day for many reasons, not only for fear of losing a day's pay if absent. He has some sense of responsibility. He recognizes that he could not keep the job if he were absent too frequently. He might want to loaf some days, but he is likely to be just as comfortable at the workplace as at home. (He now has plenty of leisure time available after working hours, on weekends, holidays, and vacations.) His friends are likely to be at work during the same hours. He would almost feel foolish wandering around in the community doing nothing when he could be at work. For these reasons a company sometimes stands to gain considerably by changing employes to straight salaries from incentive plans where pay is based on output or from hourly wages where pay is based on time served. It makes the job more attractive; therefore when employes have been shifted to straight salaries, for example, at IBM or Gillette Safety Razor, instead of this increasing absenteeism, there has been either no change or even decreases in such withdrawal tendencies. Like the white-collar worker and the executive, the blue-collar worker who no longer has to punch a time clock is given responsibility for checking and controlling himself. And, in companies with a relatively good history of management-employe relations, the expected effects are achieved if workers are seen as mature adults whose hour-to-hour efforts are not governed by money considerations alone. Noting that absenteeism was no different among its salaried white-collar employes and its hourly blue-collar men, Gillette shifted its blue-collar employes to salaries also. The cost of administering the payroll was reduced, yet absenteeism dropped slightly among blue-collar employes. IBM reported no change in absenteeism when it shifted to salaries, those one third of its employes who previously had been paid by the hour. The most controlled study involved the shifting of two divisions of the Cannon Electric Company of Los Angeles to straight salary. For over two years, the absenteeism, tardiness, and tendency to quit early were recorded for these thousand skilled and unskilled workers. In contrast to comparable divisions where workers remained on hourly rates, employes in the straight salary divisions were absent and late less and were less likely to leave work early.[352]

In addition to giving an employe an increased sense of personal worth, straight salary probably increases his sense of security. He can plan his family budget more easily. He need not be a clock watcher. Management has less need to see itself as a police agency continuously concerned with setting and maintaining standards.

As we move into an era dominated by technological innovation, incentive plans and hourly arrangements become increasingly awkward obstacles to change. For each new process, conflicts arise between individual job holders and departments as rates must be renegotiated. For the employe on piece work, innovation means a relearning period of high stress due to possibly reduced earnings, a condition likely to impede his speed and accuracy of learning. For hourly workers, times of change are fraught with dangers of temporary layoffs. For management, times of change may mean creation of new rates of payment in which employes earn too much as far as management is concerned. (If this happens, management is likely to reengineer jobs on which employes' earnings exceed management expectations.)[742] A firm with only salaried

employes can innovate without concern for labor costs, as long as the
current labor force can learn the new methods and processes. Salaried
employes can concentrate on such learning. And such a firm can minimize its errors in estimating labor costs as well as administering its
payroll. Clearly, when one takes a second look at shifting all employes
to straight salaries, the change often seems more sensible than if only
a casual examination is made of the possibility. Straight salaries, in the
long run, may be more rational than any highly rationalized piece-rate
incentive plan.

Job Security

Surveys of factory workers, both men and women, during the years
of the Great Depression showed job security to be the single most important factor contributing to job satisfaction.[299] While this concern may
have been reduced during the prosperous postwar era, particularly
among skilled secure employes, it still is of considerable importance to
all from the company sweeper to the chief executive. For example, in
the General Motors' employes' "My Job Contest" in the late 1940's it
appeared about midway in mention among the top themes,[195] and third
in a list of nine factors in surveys of employes of six firms during the
same period.[495]

One firm with nationwide operations received responses from almost 50 percent of 7,000 of their employes in 1947 on rankings of the
importance of 19 items. As Table 3.1 shows, "a steady job" was most
frequently first choice and most often among the top five items listed.[630]
But management personnel report much less concern with security. A
recent survey of Sears, Roebuck retail store executives and managers
found security ranked eighth among 14 factors they reported contributing to job satisfaction (Table 3.2).

More specific occupational analyses revealed that security was first
in concern among 10 factors of importance ranked by mechanical
workers, tied for second in importance among clerical workers, and only
fourth in importance among salesmen.[345]

Relative Importance.   Security, no doubt, is of paramount importance
to those who do not have it, and as long as a substantial block of workers
remain insecure, others more fortunate will continue to feel the value
of their more secure positions. Thus, during the 1930's, 93 percent of
nonunion workers regarded steady employment as one of the four most
important aspects of a job, while only 65 percent of unionized workers
reported this much concern.[299] In such countries with large labor sur-

pluses as Japan and Italy, those workers without reasonably guaranteed steady work certainly would consider security supremely important, as might workers in such states of the United States as West Virginia where unemployment of over 10 percent of the labor force seems endemic in the 1960's.

Sociopsychological Significance. In our society job security has considerable sociopsychological meaning. The material and economic penalties suffered by an unemployed breadwinner and his family may be accompanied by social disapproval and a sense of worthlessness by the man who cannot find work. Admissions of white men per year to the Louisiana State Penitentiary during the years 1940–55 were found to correlate .78 with total weeks unemployment by those seeking it in the state during the same years. For Negroes, the correlation was only .08. While economic needs may play some part in the contribution of unemployment to crime, the fact that it seems to affect whites only suggests that a strong social phenomenon is operating: that is, for whites, unemployment is seen as a disgrace, a sign of personal failure, and may be reacted to by hostile acts toward society, by criminal acts not necessarily economic in goal. For the Negro "last hired, first fired," unemployment is a commonplace among his peers, and unemployment is expected, or at least not likely to be as much of a source of personal conflict. Failure to hold a steady job may be interpreted as one more among the many penalties inflicted simply for being a Negro, a penalty shared by one's social peers.[170]

The desire for security as shown in Table 3.1 "foreshadows the union drive for security, expressed, however, in a demand for pensions and welfare funds."[630, p.7] While workers near retirement may tend to place pensions first on their list of satisfiers, the mass of employes want steady work. But what has been most sought and what has been granted so far are fringe benefits as substitutes. The guaranteed annual wage is still a rarity. Perhaps what is needed is an economic solution as proposed by Galbraith.[228] He suggests that our affluent society can provide for increased consumer demand during slack periods and periods of much unemployment by unemployment compensation that practically matches the regular income of the laid-off employe. During times of labor scarcity and full employment, compensation for those unemployed would be reduced to subsistence minimums since most unemployed workers should shortly be able to find new jobs. It is interesting to note that an *economist* suggests that most Americans would prefer employment to unemployment compensation, even if financial returns were the same. For many years now the fact that our farms produce more than can be consumed have resulted in payments to farmers not to produce as much as they might. The social implications need to be considered now of what will occur if some segments of our ever-more productive work force begin to be paid *not* to produce in order to maintain a balance of production and consumption!

Fringe Benefits

The take-home pay after taxes received weekly by an employe is considerably less than his total income. In 1959 almost 23 percent of an American employe's income was in the form of fringe benefits and security features. Over 7 percent was for pension and related funds, and another 7 percent was payment for vacations, sick leave, and so forth, while the remainder was for other compensation and security plans required legally or profit sharing and bonus schemes.[188] Some firms reported as much as 40 percent of the payroll as "hidden" in pensions, vacations, sick leave benefits, group insurance, stock plans, special services, profit sharing, and the like.

Despite the sizable proportion of total pay now in the form of fringe benefits, workers do not rank paid vacations, unemployment insurance, pension funds, sick leaves, and other material benefits as of paramount importance. Sales, clerical, and mechanical employes are in agreement in ranking such benefits as ninth or tenth in a list of 10 factors of importance.[345] These benefits, which emerged during World War II because wages were frozen and benefits could serve as substitutes in collective bargaining, are expected as part of the job; and their absence is likely to bring on pressure, particularly by unionized employes for gaining those not already in force because of state or federal laws. As seen in Table 3.1 hardly any of the 7,000 employes surveyed consider holidays and vacations primarily important. Pensions were important to 9.7 percent of these workers, and they were of first importance to 7.1 percent of these same men suggesting that there is a block of men, older employes nearing retirement, for whom pensions are of prime significance. At the same time most (90.3 percent) do not include pensions in the first five items of importance to them.

Yet, fringe benefits do take on more importance if we ask employes in what form they would prefer to receive *increments* to their current salaries. When 132 General Electric employes were asked how they would prefer to use a possible $190 increase in yearly compensation, they allocated over 30 percent to sick leave benefits, 22 percent to more days of vacation, 12 percent to immediate payment and to a pension plan, and lesser percentages to dental insurance, disability pay, medical care for the retired, and life insurance.

Figure 3.6 shows what would appear to be obvious. Among the four

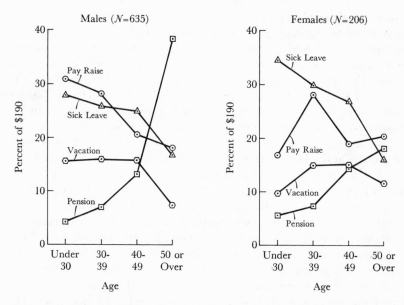

Figure 3.6: How 841 General Electric Employes Report They Would Prefer to Allocate a $190 Increase in Annual Earnings. (From Nealy, 1964, p. 24)

most popular benefits, pensions increase in favor as workers age according to a survey of an additional 841 GE employes. On the other hand, the decline with age in interest in sick leave is not so obvious, for the men at least. Pensions are also favored more by higher-income groups in lieu of immediate payment. While many other such differences in preference might be cited, it is most important to recognize that the differences do exist. An accurate fix on the attitudes toward fringe benefits rather than pay at an individual plant location requires a local survey of the kinds of employes involved and of the nature of the working situation.[497]

Advancement

Seniority rights and the danger of unemployment are of major importance in deterring workers from leaving one job for another, according to a review of eight studies. On the other hand, some workers, at least, are ready to change if they see greater long-range possibilities opening for them if they shift.[74]

The absence of a class struggle in American society is reflected in expectations and hopes of the middle and working classes, not of destroying those on top, but of moving up into the higher circles, or at least of seeing one's children move up. And our open society does make it possible through money, marriage, and free public education for many to move up each generation. For example, only 41.7 percent of the sons of unskilled workers, according to a recent survey, follow in their fathers' footsteps. Of the majority, 16.5 percent become semi-skilled; 13.7 percent skilled; 13.7 percent, clerks; 10.3 percent, propri-etors; and 4.1 percent become professionals.[252] This movement has been facilitated by the greater demand of each generation for more of what the sons could offer than their fathers before them.

We see our retail store executives of Table 3.2 prizing opportunity for growth and advancement as most important. And workers, in gen-eral, as shown in Table 3.1 also place "a chance to get ahead" high on their list. As can be seen in Table 2.2 concern about advancement also is great among newly industrializing workers, although their American supervisors seem to think they (Saudi Arabians) consider advancement even more important than they actually do. In general, men will be more interested in advancement opportunities than women; younger employes will be more interested than older employes[77]; highly skilled employes will be more interested than unskilled employes[76]; sales and clerical employes will be about equally interested as mechanical workers [345]; and supervisors will be more interested than those supervised in opportunities for advancement.

WORKING CONDITIONS

Often, working conditions are of little consequence to job satisfac-tion since they are generally comfortable and not an issue. As seen in Table 3.2 retail store executives rank physical working conditions and job demands at the bottom of a list of 14 factors affecting their satisfac-tion. On the other hand, under direct questioning retail grocery store workers mentioned working conditions relatively frequently among 13 reasons for liking their work. Similar responses occurred when pro-jective techniques were employed.[280]

But if we move from the store to the factory, working conditions become of more consequence.

Equipment Maintenance

"It really isn't a bad company," the girl assured the interviewer, "but the welding machine used to give me little shocks every once in awhile and made me jump. But they couldn't fix it, I guess, because I told the mechanic and he was always fooling with it. It got on my nerves so I quit."[502] p.195

This statement from an exit interview is not exceptional. Approximately 20 percent of workers leaving a manufacturing company because they didn't like the work mentioned specifically that the work was nerve-racking or ulcer-producing and marked by constant troubles owing to machine failure.[502] In the face of such conditions workers seem quite ready to change jobs.[74]

The extent that poor maintenance contributes to job dissatisfaction is clearly revealed in Table 3.3. As can be seen, where machine down time was high, employes were more dissatisfied, more likely to be absent, more likely to be late, to quit, to develop grievances, and to argue with other employees.

TABLE 3.3   COMPARATIVE MORALE STUDY OF OPERATORS ON WELL-MAINTAINED VERSUS POORLY MAINTAINED EQUIPMENT*

	Results on Ten Poorly Maintained Machines	Results on Ten Well-Maintained Machines
Percentages of down time due to machine jams, poor quality, breakdowns	40	12
Expressed employe job dissatisfaction	57	6
Absenteeism	22	3
Tardiness	16	1
Quit	2	0
Grievances	10	2
Observed arguments with other employes	13	2

*From Odiorne, 1955, p. 196

In another analysis, six workers rotating assignments to operate six different machines were found to develop strong dissatisfaction and grievances only when operating the one particular machine that was defective.

Here we are again faced with a significant interaction among the input, waste, and output of men, money, and materials.

In many instances a plant is forced to operate equipment at less than perfect maintenance. Heavy operating schedules may require seasonal periods when maintenance is delayed. Occasionally an old and quite unrepairable machine must be nursed along until the new item can be obtained. In still other instances it is obsolete and totally written off, but management decides that it is still profitable to squeeze a little more production out of it. In such cases, the circumstances may dictate that running a poorly maintained machine is necessary, but the hidden costs of doing so should not be overlooked.

In addition to the obvious costs of increased spoilage, higher operating costs, and customer complaints for poor products, there are the costs of lost production, turnover, and general employe dissatisfaction which can lead to eruptions that will wipe out any minor profit to be obtained from cutting corners on maintenance.

Poor morale, conflict, confusion, and a shop full of disgruntled workers is a high price to pay for the savings in the maintenance budget.[502, pp.199–200]

Monotonous Jobs

Monotonous jobs, jobs with little variety to them, are likely to produce feelings of boredom, weariness and tedium in workers who must continue to carry on the work. Particularly where jobs are semirepetitive, where the worker must continue to pay attention to the job, but where the same work is repeated in endless cycles, feelings of tiredness and boredom will be great and job satisfaction is likely to be low. When the work to be done is far below the abilities of the worker and is no challenge to him, it is likely to be boring and dissatisfying to him. And such boredom and dissatisfaction may often result in quitting the job. In the electronics industry, one of the few among 24 measures which consistently correlated with turnover was job monotony.[365]

Causes and Effects. Free response interviews with women working on 35 types of repetitive jobs concluded that monotony depended on the amount of attention demanded by the work, the amount of skill demanded, how diverse the work was, the surrounding physical conditions, as well as whether or not teamwork was required on the job.[133] Studies in a number of English motor car and rolling mill factories noted that feelings of boredom were greatest on assembly line jobs. Yet, 59 to 75 percent of workers in these jobs reported themselves as fairly satisfied or satisfied with their work.[714] These other British studies suggested that workers slow down, talk more, and exhibit more restlessness and variability as a consequence of boredom. But, interviews with two groups of eight American women power-machine operators doing light repetitive work, observed no such consistent relation. Feelings of boredom expressed in interviews were unrelated to how fast or variable workers were in their job productivity, the frequency of their rest periods, or their talkativeness on the job. Nor was any characteristic work curve found related to their feelings of boredom. Rather, these workers were affected by the approaching end of the day and would speed up or slow down in order to fulfill some standard of what they thought was a day's work. Production then depended on how much each worker thought should be produced or what was needed to fulfill expectations.[624]

Individual Differences.   Whether light repetitive work produces boredom seems to depend considerably on the individual. On the same jobs, the younger among 72 women workers reported more feelings of tedium. Those reporting themselves as restless in daily and leisure-time habits were also likely to report feelings of boredom at work. Again, those less satisfied with their home life, the plant, or personal living conditions in aspects not directly related to the repetitiveness of their job were most likely to report their job boring. Contrary to expectation, among these women workers, their ambitiousness, the extent they daydreamed, and their extraversion seemed unrelated to feelings of monotony. Those less susceptible to boredom were ones who preferred regularity in daily routines and preferred inactive leisure-time activities.[625]

In clerical jobs as a whole, a curvilinear relationship between intelligence and turnover has been observed. Turnover seems highest among those clerical employes who do not have the ability to cope with the tasks of the job; turnover seems equally high among the very bright workers who find the same jobs are not sufficiently challenging to them.[703] But how an intelligent employe will react depends on the complexity of his job. Among office workers in a large company on difficult or complex jobs the highest turnover occurred among workers of very low intelligence. Presumably these employes lacked the ability to do the work required. On the other hand, when jobs lacked much challenge and were simple and easy to perform, quitting was greatest among the most intelligent workers.[66] These intrinsic aspects of job dissatisfaction will be discussed in more detail in the next chapter.

Alleviation of Boredom.   Little experimental research has been completed on how to alleviate boredom. One proposal is to make work more interesting to the employe. It is suggested that the worker may be more interested in his job if he learns and understands the product he is making and the importance of his contribution to the larger productive effort. But it is difficult to see how such increased information could sustain unflagging worker interest over many years. Another suggestion is to improve the worker's leisure-time activities and interests.[92] A worker with interesting outside leisure activities may be able to remain more content with a routine job. Even managers who have found their path to further upward success blocked may shift the goals of their major concern from inside to outside the plant and become active in community chest drives, little theaters, or real estate speculation. In this way, they "serve their time" within the company, but in the overall remain relatively content with life.

Work rotation is another approach to alleviating tedium.[92] By shifting the worker from one machine to another so that, for example, he works one place during the morning and in another during the afternoon, feelings of boredom may be reduced. Or, the worker can stop periodically to go and get more materials. Rotational schemes appear to have improved the productivity of young women assembling bicycle chains or weighing and wrapping tobacco. But job rotation may come too frequently. Productivity may suffer if there is too much starting and stopping, too much warm-up time required for each new activity, and so on. Also, feelings of boredom may not be dissipated very much if the various tasks to which one shifts are similar to each other.[755]

Another technique is batching. Batches of work are provided the employe which he can complete within a particular amount of time. No new work is given him until he completes a batch. One analysis suggests that workers on time rates prefer a batch which can be finished in one to one and one-half hours.[134] A more carefully controlled study investigated women employed in filing operations who were accustomed to procuring their own work in tins of 3,100 pieces which took them approximately 4 hours to complete. During the time to finish a tin of 3,100 the mean number of voluntary rests were 11 per 105 minutes. When the tins were reduced to 620 and 310 pieces voluntary rests reduced to 9 per 105 minutes for batches of 610 pieces; and to 8 per 105 minutes for batches of 310 pieces. The desire to complete a task near its end tended to "pull along" a worker. Such completion was much more frequent with the small batches, so that the stops because of boredom were less with the smaller batches. However the workers' overall productivity was no different, and they preferred the customary larger batches.[626] Evidently these workers preferred to return to a more monotonous schedule, but one to which they were more accustomed.

Rest pauses or short coffee breaks may help to alleviate boredom for even where little physical fatigue is likely to occur, such as in light repetitive work, the introduction of rest pauses helps to increase productivity.[92] Changes in incentive conditions have also been proposed, for example, switching from hourly to piece rates. However the arousal of tensions as a result of introducing piece rates may lead to new morale problems.

In recent years there has been considerable effort to broaden the job in order to alleviate boredom. Not only is job enlargement seen as a means of reducing monotony and feelings of subjective fatigue, but it also may have positive effects on productivity. For example, job enlargement coupled with the reduction in job specialization has been found to reduce overtime in billing departments as well as to reduce billing costs per customer.[681]

But job enlargement may not be a panacea. No differences in attitude towards work were found between assembly operators on a single task and comparable assembly operators working on a wide variety of tasks.[361] It may be that if the variety of tasks do not comprise a meaningful whole and if the tasks are a group of unrelated activities, there may be little increase in satisfaction as a consequence of job enlargement. Moreover, workers at lower levels of intelligence who routinely can daydream on the job or who for other personality reasons are quite content to work on repetitive jobs requiring little of their attention may reject increases in job challenge brought about by job enlargement. On the other hand, increasing job responsibilities, increasing job variety, broadening the types of work and methods used, increasing the job challenges for the occupant may provide increasing satisfaction with work and reduced feelings of monotony for more intelligent employes, for higher level personnel in supervision, skilled, or technical work.

A most promising attack on boredom due to repetitive work or to work on the assembly line is to increase opportunities for the workers to socialize. This may mean breaking up the assembly line into a series of task forces, with each task force responsible for a certain part of the assembly process. Each work group develops a sense of group responsibility for its part in the total productive operation. Instead of feeling completely isolated as a man on the assembly line with no possibilities for social interchange with anyone else, a victim and slave of the assembly line pace, the worker now sees himself as a participating member of a group which has considerable responsibility for a particular segment of the total productive effort. This fracturing of the assembly line and its specialized and repetitive jobs requires profound changes in management thinking towards what is really efficient and what is not. The material and economic "logic" which led to the assembly line failed to take much account of the human operators in the circumstance, their feelings and attitudes and some of the consequences of the negative attitudes towards working on an assembly line.[713] One California company, Nonlinear Systems, an electronics firm, has reported noticeable success after changing from an assembly line production process to a series of six- or seven-person work groups, each responsible for a different segment of the total assembly process. However, this splintering of the assembly line has also been accompanied by the introduction of a number of other changes in policy, management, and organization to be discussed in Chapter 7, which may be intimately related to the increased productivity and satisfaction associated with the creation of these task forces.

Opportunities for Social Interaction

Apart from any questions of standard setting or any other aspects of group cohesiveness, when structural changes are made in the workplace so that workers have an opportunity to interact with each other rather than remain isolated as on an assembly line, there are marked increases in satisfaction with the new arrangement. Shoe fabricators who worked on one of six successive operations required to complete the shoes produced 9.6 percent more when they were permitted to work around a table than when they had to perform the same operations in isolation. The tempo of the whole group was faster than the mean tempo of the individual working alone. Part of the effect here was probably a consequence of the face-to-face opportunities afforded by being seated around a table and the opportunities for social interchange.[417] One of the few factors found to correlate positively with turnover in a wire and cable company was the amount of noise on the job. Where noise made communications difficult for skilled machine operators and they had less opportunity to contact each other socially or to become members of a group, absenteeism was greater and they were more likely to quit than where such noise was not present.[581]

In addition to its effects on blocking opportunities for social interaction, noise may be detrimental to satisfaction in other ways. It is probable that a complex relationship exists between noise, job satisfaction, and interpersonal behavior. There is a greater chance of misunderstanding directions and more difficulty in communicating in a noisy plant or office. Where the workers cannot adapt or become accustomed to the noise because it is erratic, they will expend more energy to perform the same amount of work. This may tend to decrease job satisfaction.

The irritating influences of noise are not necessarily related to its loudness. For example, the drip of a faucet at night may be far more irritating than the roar of an airplane flying overhead.[110]

Hours and Shifts

Earlier studies when hours of work were much longer than now showed a clear relation between the length of the work week and tendencies by the worker to withdraw or remain away from the job through absence and lateness. In a 1921 study, lost time was 6 percent among men and women working 62 hours per week while it was 4 percent for men working 54 hours a week and 3 percent for women working 44 hours per week.[701] While the work week has been reduced considerably since 1921 the continued need for two or three shifts during the 24-hour period has provided a source of dissatisfaction. During the years 1951 – 56, 12 percent of manufacturing workers in New York were on night work and 32 percent in Detroit were on night shifts. Workers neither like night work nor rotation to night work from day work on some periodic basis.[449] Higher pay rates for night work may attract some workers, yet, as many as 73 percent of nonsupervisory utility plant employes indicated their dislike of shift work. A major complaint of shift workers was the interruption of their normal physiological rhythm as a consequence of rotating shifts or of working out of phase with the normal sequence of community activities. Difficulties with sleep, appetite, and digestion were problems for a majority of workers in the two plants surveyed. One-fifth of the respondents said it took them four days or more to adjust to a new shift, yet many had to rotate shifts weekly. The majority of workers in both plants said that their families did not like their working shifts. Working shifts deprived the worker of intensive friendship relations. Shift workers visited friends less frequently than nonshift workers.[439]

Despite the dissatisfactions associated with shift work, the introduction of automation and the consequent increase in capital investment per employe, the relative reduction in power rates given by utility companies for use of power at night, and the percentage reduction in plant and overhead needed for the same total production has increased the utility of 24-hour-a-day operations of plant and equipment. Even the white-collar worker is now experiencing night work as a consequence of the introduction of electronic data processing equipment. Research and development will be needed on the relative desirability of permanent night shifts in comparison to rotating shifts, the periodicity of rotation, the expansion of recreational activities for night workers, the improvement of family and social relationships disturbed by night work, and the development of means to overcome the physiological disturbances to sleep and eating now resulting from night work.[439]

Organization

An organizational consideration is the size of the unit in which the worker finds himself as well as the size of the company for which he works. Both plant size and department size affect absenteeism rates, tardiness, accidents, and strikes.[552] Smaller units have better records. A survey in one community suggested that small plants under 500 permit more intimate personal contact resulting in more cohesiveness among workers and management and a more favorable atmosphere.[119]

Even after controlling for six other variables, in 11 organizational units of an airline ranging in size from 172 to 3,205 employes, absenteeism was found greater in the larger units and less in the smaller ones. The larger units were less attractive, more impersonal, and identification with the organization was much more diffuse.[52] Among 228 factory groups varying in size from 5 to 50, smaller ones were more cohesive.[593] Morale was also likely to be higher in smaller groups according to industrial surveys.[354]

Organizational arrangements and policies affecting the upward and downward flow of communications are paramount in employe satisfaction. These will be discussed in detail in Chapters 7 and 8.

Size of City. The size of the city in which an employe works seems related to job satisfaction. For example, a majority of factory workers of Evansville, Indiana, a city of 100,000, felt it was a good place in which to work, whereas less than a quarter said the same about Detroit with close to 2,000,000 in population. In a survey of 12 cities, satisfactory places in which to work emerged in the following order: Evansville (Indiana), Tulsa, Denver, Milwaukee, St. Louis, Houston, Kansas City (Missouri), San Francisco, Dallas, Chicago, Los Angeles, and Detroit. If Evansville and Tulsa are representative of small American cities, and Chicago, Los Angeles, and Detroit are representative of large ones, then city size as such probably makes for job satisfaction or dissatisfaction of workers in those cities. The agreement is by no means perfect between city size and worker satisfaction, but nevertheless the influence on job satisfaction of city size must be considered along with such conditions as greater distance to travel to and from work, more crowded transportation, and less private home dwellings.[639] As already noted in Figure 2.3, transportation and housing problems are frequently mentioned in exit interviews as reasons for quitting work and seeking a job elsewhere. But a study of 6,300 white-collar workers in 30 Swedish insurance companies found no association between commuting time and absenteeism.[297]

Regional Attractiveness. Another source of satisfaction or dissatisfaction is expressed in the continued migration of large numbers of workers to the West Coast and to Florida. In many cases, firms, particularly in research and development, have elected to move to places such as California for noneconomic reasons. California locations may make it

easier to attract technicians than a more economical location in North
Dakota or Arkansas. But weather appeared of no significance to absenteeism in the Swedish companies just mentioned. However weather does
seem to have an effect on tardiness. The time of arrival of 101 men and
31 women for 69 working days in an engineering research laboratory
depended on the brightness of the morning light. Workers were likely
to be late on sunny and beautiful days and likely to arrive early on dark
and dreary ones. Tardiness tended to increase towards the end of the
week from 20 to 23 percent.[492] If anything, good weather per se, in
California, probably contributes to less desire to go to work. But the
migration to it is for its leisure-time possibilities and potential good
living as a whole.

Music and Job Satisfaction

Cuban cigar makers and South American factory workers pay gui-
tarists out of their own meager wages, join them in singing, and use
music to counteract the dullness of work. Stevedores, laborers, seamen,
and cowboys make use of music to relieve the fatigue and tediousness
of their jobs.

A review of 58 articles on the effects of music on work including a
number of reports of controlled experiments in industry disclosed that
feelings of euphoria (happiness and elation) during periods of musical
stimulation have a physiological basis. Changes in blood pressure occur
when some subjects listen to music. These articles also examined how
attitudes and productivity on the job were affected by music. Experiments showed that men working in an architectual drafting room, motor
car employes, workers making table decorations, women radio tube
assemblers, and factory workers in other locations prefer working where
music is played rather than where it is not played. However not all
workers like music while they work. Approximately 1 to 10 percent are
annoyed by it.

A majority of workers prefer instrumental to vocal music during
working hours. Furthermore, preference for music at work decreases
with the age of the employe. But satisfaction with music on the job does
not necessarily result in increased productivity. Despite the generally
favorable reception of music by workers on all kinds of jobs, only when
employes are doing simple, repetitive, and monotonous tasks is their
output likely to be significantly stimulated by music. Older experienced
factory operators performing complex tasks do not exhibit such increases in productivity when music is played.[694]

CO-WORKERS AS A SOURCE OF SATISFACTION

We have already seen how the immediate work group is important, if not paramount, in determining the productivity level of all the members in the group. But individuals within the work group will vary in their relative satisfaction with each other and with the standards set by the group. For example, an employe will be satisfied with his job to the extent there is some consensus on the role this worker is supposed to play and the job he is supposed to do within the work group. If a worker is in considerable disagreement with his colleagues concerning what is expected of him, he is undoubtedly less likely to be satisfied with the working situation than if he feels he is meeting the expectations of the group in which he is a member.[708] Likewise, since persons tend to value more that which is harder to get, employes who have had more difficulty in joining the work group will tend to be more attracted to that group than workers who found it easy to be admitted to the group.[16]

Shared Attitudes

An employe will be more satisfied with his circumstances the more he finds his own attitudes and beliefs shared by his associates. In industry, workers tend to be attracted to those like themselves in age, seniority, marital status, education, and race.[525] This tendency to want to be among others similar to one's self and to reject those who are different may be a way one uses to enhance his own self-esteem.[41] By putting a premium on friendships with those who are seen as like ourselves, we give notice that we prefer our ownselves.

Esteem and Satisfaction

How satisfied we are with work seems to depend upon how valued we are or how esteemed we are by our co-workers. Observers classified 49 workers in a manufacturing plant as regulars, isolates, and deviants.

The regulars were the highly esteemed members, the dominant figures in the informal group, who produced in conformity to the group standards and were generally satisfied with circumstances. The isolates and deviants, on the other hand, were most dissatisfied and most likely to deviate from the group norms for production.[761] In another plant, highly esteemed workers were found to be more satisfied with their jobs in general as well as to have more favorable attitudes towards their company.[697] But this relationship seems conditioned by other factors. For example, the more esteemed of 46 professional workers in a child welfare agency were more satisfied with the agency. But this was not necessarily so for the 26 nonprofessional stenographers, typists, and janitors.[329]

JOB STATUS

Work differs in its perceived value and importance. Those performing seemingly more valuable work will be accorded more *status*. And, people with more status (regardless of their personal worth or *esteem*) are more satisfied with their work.

Work or tasks, when combined in the same way for several men in a firm, form a *job*. These jobs can be ordered in their importance to the firm, often by means of a formal *job evaluation*. When the same job is found in many firms it is an *occupation*. Occupations likewise vary in status. College students, both in 1925 and 1946, when considering 25 occupations ranked physician, banker, lawyer, school superintendent, and civil engineer as the first five in status, and truck driver, coal miner, janitor, hod carrier, and ditch digger as the last five in status among 25 to be ranked by them.[161] And miners ranking the same 25 occupations agreed completely with the college students on the five highest and five lowest status occupations.[732]

A complete consideration of the status of work also requires examining differences in the status of industries. Table 3.4 shows the rank order in prestige of 52 industries according to 360 college students.

Industry ratings seem consistent with occupational evaluations. Banking, medicine, and education are highly valued as industries and in occupational terms; coal mining, both as an industry and an occupation, is downgraded.[99] Extrapolating from the evidence to be presented below, we expect that generally both management and employes are likely to be more satisfied with their jobs in banking, medicine, and education than in say, meatpacking, laundries, or coal mining.

TABLE 3.4   RANK ORDER OF 52 INDUSTRIES BASED ON MEAN SCORES
OF PRESTIGE RATINGS BY 360 COLLEGE STUDENTS*

Industry	Rank	Mean Score	Industry	Rank	Mean Score
Medical services	1	92.2	Marines	27	63.0
Colleges and universities	2	90.1	Weapons mfg.	28	61.8
Research laboratories	3	88.5	Rubber products mfg.	29	61.7
Atomic energy plants	4	87.8	Local government	30	61.5
Banking	5	85.0	Department stores	31	60.0
Private schools (secondary)	6	79.4	Ceramic products mfg.	32	59.6
Commercial airlines	7	79.3	Motels	33	58.0
Television broadcasting	8	77.4	Furniture mfg.	34	57.7
Chemical products mfg.	9	77.0	Clothing mfg.	35	57.2
Aircraft mfg.	10	75.57	Restaurants	36	56.73
Motion picture industry	11	75.50	Tobacco mfg.	37	56.71
Federal government	12	75.2	Coast guard	38	56.5
Drug products mfg.	13	73.8	Building construction	39	56.2
Religious organizations	14	73.0	Drug stores	40	55.6
Publishing companies	15	72.7	Forestry	41	55.3
Insurance companies	16	70.3	Iron and steel mills	42	54.5
Petroleum refining	17	69.4	Railroads	43	54.1
Real estate companies	18	66.7	Interstate bus transportation	44	51.7
Automobile mfg.	19	66.6	Army	45	49.9
Air Force	20	66.4	Farming	46	47.8
Telephone companies	21	64.8	Grocery stores	47	47.0
Public schools (secondary)	22	64.7	Meatpacking	48	45.2
Hotels	23.5	64.4	Labor organizations	49	42.9
Navy	23.5	64.4	Laundries and dry cleaning	50	39.66
Ship and boat building	25	63.8	Local bus transportation	51	39.60
Electric power and light companies	26	63.7	Coal Mining	52	30.1

*From Campbell, 1960, p.3

Status and Satisfaction Within the Firm

In an insurance company 58 percent of those in high-level technical work reported themselves as satisfied with their jobs while only 23 percent of those in routine clerical work were satisfied.[349] Similarly, among Sears, Roebuck retail store executives, job satisfaction was found highly related to job status.[527] A considerable proportion of the variance in satisfaction of 1,242 Swedish bank employes depended upon their position in the bank.[549] The status-satisfaction correlation seemed to reveal itself among airline employees in the greater absenteeism among those lower in status.[52]

Status and Satisfaction Between Organizations

While 61 percent of factory labor in a 1938 Fortune Magazine survey stated they would choose some other work if they could, only 29 percent of professional people said they would change. Whereas 95 percent of teachers indicated satisfaction with their work (during the Depression), 98 percent of textile employes were dissatisfied.[312]

Corroborating an earlier finding that skilled workers were more satisfied than unskilled ones[660] when 1,168 handicapped and normal interviewees were compared, job satisfaction was associated more strongly with skill level of the interviewees than whether or not they were handicapped physically.[100]

Table 3.5 summarizes differences in proportions of respondents in professional occupations of higher status and working class occupations of lower status who would choose the same kind of work if they were to begin their careers again. Clearly, the professionals are much more satisfied with their positions.

TABLE 3.5   PERCENTAGE IN VARIOUS OCCUPATIONS WHO WOULD
CHOOSE SAME KIND OF WORK IF BEGINNING
CAREER AGAIN*

Professional Occupations	Percent	Working Class Occupations	Percent
Mathematicians	91	Skilled printers	52
Physicists	89	Paper workers	52
Biologists	89	Skilled automobile workers	41
Chemists	86	Skilled steelworkers	41
Lawyers	83	Textile workers	31
Journalists	82	Unskilled steelworkers	21
		Unskilled automobile workers	16

*Adapted from Blauner, 1960, p. 343

Status, Control, and Satisfaction

Generally, the higher one's status, the more he has control over his own fate at work. And it is this control over how time is spent, how physical movements must be made, how work will be paced that seems most significant in understanding why status and satisfaction correlate. In the same way, control over one's technical and social environment and freedom from supervision accompany higher status and contribute to job satisfaction.[72]

Assembly line work, especially in the automobile industry, with its accompanying machine-set pacing of the worker is among the most dissatisfying of occupations. Merely to be "off the line" was what most of 180 assembly line workers wanted. Turnover of assembly line workers is twice as great as for men in the same plant who were off the line.[713]

Yet, blue-collar work is quite satisfying when it affords the worker technical control over his environment and freedom from close supervision. For instance, railroad employes ranked just below professional men in satisfaction with their work.[312] The following is a typical comment from a happy railroader: "I wouldn't last three days working in a shop with a foreman breathing down my neck. Here I'm my own boss. When I run the trains, nobody tells me what to do."[607] Moreover, like truck drivers, railroad men such as engineers, switchmen, and brakemen derive a sense of power moving the heavy equipment with which they work.[72]

It should be apparent that merely changing an employe's job title, without a comparable change in the importance of the job or in the control of what happens on the job, is unlikely to affect an employe's satisfaction with a job. Indeed, it may arouse false expectations. When the expectations which attracted the employe to the retitled job cannot be fulfilled, frustration and dissatisfaction will result. Telling a sweeper or a janitor he is now to be known as a custodian or superintendent, without increasing his real importance or control, generally is unlikely to carry with it an increased satisfaction with the work.

*   *   *   *   *

In summary, we see that a host of conditions about work and the workplace make for more or less satisfaction with jobs. We see that the importance of pay acceptance and satisfaction may be obscured in surveys of employe attitudes by the fact that it is taken for granted in a society of abundance. For even fringe benefits begin to seem more important if we ask a worker what else he wants as an addition to his current income. But satisfaction with the exchange of material gains for work requires extensive psychological consideration in contrast to purely economic analysis. Satisfaction with pay and benefits will depend upon the worker's ideas of equity, his understanding of how and for what he is paid, with whom he compares himself, and so on. Moreover, concern about pay may merely be symptomatic of dissatisfaction with such sociopsychological factors as the security and status of one's job; it is easier to complain or bargain about pay than about prestige.

We have learned a considerable amount in the past 30 years about what workers say they want in a job. Yet we cannot write a prescription about how to make a job satisfying, for in the last analysis *chacun à son goût*; each man has his own tastes. Each organization must plan to survey its own members if it would wish to begin to understand what kinds of extrinsic and intrinsic rewards they prefer in exchange for their working in the organization. In this chapter we hope we have been able to point out what it may be important to ask them, mainly about the extrinsic material and related aspects of their work. In the next chapter we shall look at what differences to expect in response from one worker to the next, even in the same organization. We shall examine in particular the differences associated with a given job itself and the intrinsic satisfaction which some but not all may derive from working at the given job.

In Brief

PEOPLE DIFFER IN WHAT THEY EXPECT FROM THEIR JOBS AND WHAT THEY value as important. Some individuals are so frustrated by life in general that they report their jobs highly dissatisfying, although no change in their work would really make much difference in how they felt about it.

Men and women will differ in how satisfying they find the same type of work. Length of serivce will also make a difference. As tastes differ, so do interests. The advertising salesman with a home workshop who likes to work with his hands is likely to be as dissatisfied with his job as the carpenter who enjoys spending his spare time trying to influence others.

To be interesting and challenging the demands of the job should match the abilities of the jobholder. If demands are too great the worker will be frustrated by his failure to succeed; if demands are too light he will be bored by the lack of stimulation.

Motivation to work will depend strongly on the extent the individual worker is clear about his objectives in working. He is likely to be influenced by his own level of aspiration, and when faced with goallessness, negative goals, or conflicts in goals he will seek flight or fight, alternatives to productive or adaptive action.

Chapter 4

THE INDIVIDUAL AND HIS

MOTIVATION TO WORK

BEFORE DETAILED EXAMINATION OF THE EFFECTS OF SUPERVISION, GROUPS, and organization on motivation to work which will follow in subsequent chapters, it will be useful to pause here to see how individual employes differ in what they find rewarding about work, for whether the work-place is rewarding and satisfying will depend on the particular worker's age, sex, seniority, interests, abilities, and personality. Some workers find certain rewards pleasing; other will search for different sources of satisfaction; and still other workers will be dissatisfied no matter what rewards are available in the work situation.

Individual differences in personality will be considered first, followed by other attributes of the employe affecting what he wants from his job.

Personality and Job Satisfaction

Much of the "general factor" of overall satisfaction with work first mentioned in Chapter 2 may be part of an even more generalized attitude toward the total environment. In fact, a generalized "dissatisfaction with everyday life" scale was developed. Employes who were dissatisfied with such items as their homes, 8½-by-11-inch-size paper, politics, and so on, also were found likely to be dissatisfied with their jobs. Satisfied jobholders were also generally satisfied with home, politics, and many other matters.[728] Similar results were obtained with college students, unemployed workers, and city government employes, although much lower consistencies in satisfaction from job to life in general were found for female compared to male city employes.[81]

The generally satisfied worker describes himself on personality tests as more sociable, stable, and dominant.[737] An *acquiescent* response syndrome has been described that may be characteristic of the fellow who is satisfied with everything. The acquiescer seems to agree and accept whatever statements are presented to him, even conflicting and contradictory ones. He is less skeptical about all kinds of issues and somewhat more outgoing emotionally.[37] On the other hand, some persons are continually negative about almost everything. As a demonstration of this a class of 44 managers were asked to guess at the answers to questions which the lecturer had in mind but had not expressed.[39] The answer to the first question was "yes" or "no"; the answer to the second question was "reject" or "accept"; the answer to the third question was "support" or "oppose"; the answer to the fourth question was "deny" or "affirm"; and the answer to the fifth question was "true" or "false."

The procedure was repeated on a new sheet of paper but the "questions" were given in a different order as were the alternatives. The sixth question's answer was either "accept" or "reject," the seventh, "false" or "true," and so on.

All "yea-saying," acquiescent responses were scored as $+1$; all "nay-saying" responses were scored as 0. A score of 0 meant that a respondent gave the negative answer to every question. A score of 5 meant that the respondent had used an affirmative reply five times.

When scores on the first procedure were compared with scores on the second run, it was seen that behavior here was highly consistent. A 5 on the first round was most likely to score 4 or 5 on the second; a 0 scorer on the first was likely to earn 0 again. The correlation was approximately .60 between scores on the first and second rounds.

As the instructor was commenting on the significance of this demonstration, one manager exclaimed that he did not see the value of the exercise at all.

"Doesn't this show that such behavior is consistent," asked the instructor, "even on a two-minute test?"

"No!" was the strong reply.

"Doesn't this illustrate that employe responses to attitude questionaires may depend on their generalized tendency to acquiesce."

"Definitely, not!" argued the manager.

"By the way," asked the instructor, "what were your scores on this little test we just ran?"

"Zero-zero," replied the manager.

"Then, don't you see, that this brief test is consistent with what you are doing right now?" said the instructor.

"No, not at all," quoted the manager, maintaining his stance, even though the rest of the class was now in a riotous uproar.

General dissatisfaction with everything characterizes a disturbed, hostile personality. Most of us are familiar with the chronic "griper." As a result of a series of continuous conflicts giving rise to many frustrations, the griper develops a method of releasing his blocked motivation. He attacks verbally (and sometimes physically) all sorts of stimuli which have no direct bearing on his source of conflict. He displaces his aggression. Such a person will be angry with the company for which he works, the union to which he belongs, his foreman, his co-workers, the weather, the local mayor, his next-door neighbors, his automobile and the company that manufactured it. He also often will manifest prejudice against minority groups as well as foreigners. In short anything and anybody (but preferably one which cannot strike back) may be a target for his vitriolic attacks. Often such an individual creates a source of friction within the group. He may sell the group some of his ideas, since other members with conflicts may find release through group "griping" sessions, although these in themselves may serve a useful function in releasing tensions. However, in general, the "chronic griper" or "prejudiced personality" will be dissatisfied with his job and will probably increase job dissatisfaction and lower morale in the group with which he is associated.

Sex and Job Satisfaction

Apart from personality considerations the worker's sex seems to be an important conditioner of attitudes toward work. Whether an employe is a man or a woman appears to exert some influence on satisfaction with job conditions. Thirty-seven percent of women queried in one investigation said they would change their work if they could, whereas 45 percent of men said they would change, and three out of four other studies showed women to be more satisfied with their work than men.[289] Of 635 white-collar workers, 55 percent of the men and only 35 percent of the women were dissatisfied.[490] If these differences are representative and reliable, they may be due to the fact that women more often than men work voluntarily. Yet, some women may perceive themselves as being "forced" to work, whereas men take work as a matter of course. However, one survey of working women revealed that 74 percent said they would work even if they had inherited enough money to live comfortably without working.[241]

Education is a factor. According to a survey of college-educated married women, those who are gainfully employed are more satisfied with their marriages than those who are only homemakers.[717]

The nature of the work may determine whether the sexes will

differ in satisfaction. A series of studies suggests that women at all age levels are more *interaction-oriented* while men are more *task-oriented.*[42] As a whole, women prefer to work in groups, to converse, to have social opportunities; men are more likely to be enticed by the work itself and be more satisfied when they can have a sense of task completion, of overcoming obstacles, or of success in solving problems.

Although the personality similarities between men and women may be more important than the ways in which men and women differ as a whole from each other,[468] certain characteristic differences may partly help account for the fact that female employes are generally more satisfied with their work than are male workers. For instance, we have seen in Figure 3.6 in the last chapter how women differ from men at various ages in their preferred fringe benefits. Other surveys have shown that as a whole women tend to be less concerned than men about pay, job security, and opportunities to advance. On the other hand, they put a premium on cleanliness, pleasant surroundings, good supervision, and loyalty. Given the same work it takes less money to make a woman happy, provided the work place and organization are pleasing.[241] Also, women may be more content with routine work for women report they daydream more than men.

Length of Service

Several sources of evidence indicate that the newly hired employe is likely to be less satisfied and more likely to withdraw than the employe with longer service. Employes on the job longer are less likely to be absent,[52] just as they are less likely to quit.

But the data about job satisfaction are more complex. According to one *cross-sectional* survey, a survey made of all men working at a given time but with differing lengths of service, job satisfaction rises to a peak before the end of the first year, hits a low between the fifth and eighth years, and rises steadily until the twentieth year.[319a] Another cross-section analysis shows the same trough between five and nine years and a leveling off after the tenth year.[61]

These results are confounded with other factors affected by length of service. First, as shown in Figure 4.1 seriously dissatisfied workers are quitting at particularly high rates during the first few months and at sharply lower rates thereafter.[591] Most workers who quit will quit during the first six months. What is left in the cross-sectional sample, then, are only workers who have not quit. Second, at a given point in time the cohort of men who have worked 20 years have worked their first 10 years during a different decade than the cohort of men who now

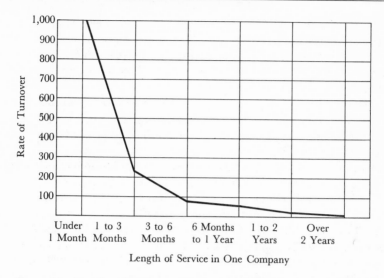

Figure 4.1: Length of Service and Turnover in a Company. (After Scott, Clothier et al., 1941, p. 501)

have completed 10 years of service. Satisfaction now may depend upon what job entry conditions were like. Those who began 20 years ago may have experienced a considerably different portion of the business cycle during their first 10 years than those who currently have worked only 10 years. Third, aging of the worker, regardless of his seniority, may affect his satisfaction. Overall satisfaction of employes appeared lowest among those between 20 and 29 and climbed thereafter according to one analysis.[61] Needed are *longitudinal* studies following the satisfaction of the same men throughout their careers. Some of our larger corporations are beginning to carry out such studies.

Interest in the Work

Without intrinsic interest in the work itself we have already seen that there can be little positive satisfaction with it, at least among higher level personnel such as accountants or engineers.[301]

College freshmen at Stanford University were administered Strong Vocational Interest Inventories. Ten years after they graduated from college, their occupational histories were studied. Men continuing in an occupation five to ten years after college showed more interest (as measured by the inventory) in that occupation than did other college freshmen of the same class. Men changing occupations showed lower interest in their old and new fields than men who remained in either of the fields. Of men who expressed dissatisfaction with their work 82 percent were in a field other than the one of the greatest measured interest, whereas only 57 percent of those in their field of major interest expressed some dissatisfaction.[655]

Work, intrinsically, can afford the opportunity to gratify interest in being of service to others, in manipulating things, in maintaining order, in being persuasive, in understanding man or nature, and so forth. Thus, if one has strong needs to be of service, doing service work itself will be a continuing source of reward. But if one has little interest in being of service, the same job will be a frustrating bore.

The same job will be interesting to one employe and uninteresting to the next depending on their individual preferences. But apart from such individual differences in interests there are certain conditions inherent in the work itself which are likely to stimulate and satisfy most employes. At the same time other facets intrinsic to the work are likely to produce lack of interest and dissatisfaction, particularly if the employes are reasonably educated (as most are becoming, these days). We have already described in the last chapter some of the consequences of repetitive and semirepetitive work on job satisfaction. At the other extreme, intrinsic motivation in work itself is likely to be aroused by jobs with variety, novelty, and challenge. But what is challenging to one man is child's play to another, so before we can examine in detail this issue we need to look at how differences in ability among employes color their attitudes toward work.

Ability and Satisfaction

Some men are dissatisfied because their jobs do not challenge their abilities; for others the challenge is too great. For instance, both extremely high and low, rather than average, scorers on seven aptitude tests were more likely to quit as taxicab drivers.[84] The highly capable drivers quit because they were too good for the work; the low scorers quit because they could not do the work well enough. This same pattern of results was found in studying turnover among clerks.[66]

But even more important to producing discontent with routine work than aptitudes and intelligence may be overall amount of education. While higher intelligence was predictive of turnover among female clerical workers, education and interests were even more predictive.[375] Again, education was higher among the 50 most dissatisfied compared to the 50 most satisfied of 1,242 Swedish bank employes.[550]

The intelligence, aptitude, skill, and education of an employe cannot be much less than the requirements of the job, or inability to perform the job tasks will lead to the employe's dissatisfaction as well as to those who depend on him and who are responsible for his efficiency. On the other hand, an employe may be too intelligent, too skilled, or have too much education for his job, in which case he will become dissatisfied because the job is below his level of aspiration and fails to challenge his abilities sufficiently. If applicants selected have abilities too far above the job requirements, high turnover will result.

Such a result was found not only for clerks, bank employes, and taxi drivers, but also for policemen.[677] New patrolmen of superior intelligence were more likely to quit after a few months for more attractive jobs elsewhere.

During times of labor surplus, firms are tempted to hire applicants with more talent than needed for the job. Unless provision is made for rapid advancement in salary and position of such capable applicants, high turnover rates are likely, particularly if the labor surplus disappears and job opportunities become plentiful again.

Ability and Differential Reward

What will be satisfying to a worker will depend on his ability, specifically his intelligence. Of 300 British war veterans in vocational counseling interviews, those with more intelligence were likely to be interested in long-range goals, in future prospects, in security, in jobs with variety, and in being members of efficient organizations. Men with less intelligence were more likely to be concerned about their workmates, vacations, hours of work, and compensation.[746]

One man's reward may be another man's punishment. The unskilled laborer given comfortable quarters and a simple repetitive job requiring fairly continuous attention but not much else, might be quite happy with the arrangement, whereas the same conditions would be punishing to a bright college graduate who can only be satisfied when what he is doing satisfies his need for achievement, recognition, exploration, creation, and variety.

But some people, apart from what they are capable of doing, prefer greater certainty of success in their efforts before they can be comfortable about their jobs. Others thrive on risk.

Risk Preference and Satisfying Jobs. Persons differ in how much challenge they want and in how likely they are to succeed; this variation is related to how strongly they are concerned about their achievement. Achievers seem to be stimulated most when the task is neither too difficult nor too easy and when the probability of success through their efforts is about 50 percent.[460]

Persons who prefer risk and greater rewards for success rather than certain but lesser reward, as a consequence, are more satisfied when salaries are based on their performance. They also favor periodic appraisals of themselves and feedback of results to them and are likely to take action as a result of such feedback.[479]

VOCATIONAL MOTIVATION

We have seen that a purely economic man driven solely by expectations of material benefits or by the desire to avoid the loss of economic security is a fiction which does not fit the facts. There is no question that material satisfaction and security are important, but particularly when these have been provided as has been done for a majority of workers in our affluent society, other rewards are necessary to satisfy the kinds of needs remaining.

New Understanding of Motivation

Our understanding of motivation and rewards needs revision in several ways. Incentive plans assumed that all work was dependent on external reinforcers, rewards, and punishments, and that economic reward was the most powerful reinforcer. But we have seen already that social and psychological rewards may at times outweigh economic effects. Second, we are beginning to learn that there are many forms of stimulation not ordinarily viewed as rewards or as capable of reducing workers' needs which in effect are gratifying.

Until recently it was generally held that behavior was driven by needs and tensions which could only be reduced by appropriate rewards or substitute rewards. A man searched for food if he was hungry. After he ate the food his hunger was satisfied. His need was reduced.

Yet, recent research indicates that there is much rewarding stimulation in our environment which we seek without any observable need for those rewards or any reduction in the need after the rewards are obtained. There is no necessary return to equilibrium after receipt of such gratification from the environment.[122]

Mild electrical stimulation in the limbic region adjacent to the hypothalamus in the brain seems more gratifying to a rat than the satisfaction of food and water after many hours without food or water. The hungry or thirsty rat will choose more electrical stimulation rather than food or water. "Perhaps a new model of motivation . . . will emerge from the study of the reticular formation, hypothalamic centers, and stimulation of the limbic system."[122,p.194] There is no known need to have one's limbic system stimulated, but such stimulation seems extremely rewarding.

Rats learn to prefer a goal box which achieves for them a morphine injection and euphoria. Saccharine sweetening, without any food value, will work as well as a reinforcer of animal behavior as sugar, yet no hunger need will be reduced by the saccharine.

There are built-in animal behaviors unrelated to other primary wants for food and water. Animals prefer novelty, spaciousness of the area surrounding them (for example, a big cage rather than a small one), stimulus complexity, certain temporal intervals, and so on. We need to catalog and research for humans those aspects of the job itself which are sources of desired stimulation to the worker. Satisfactions may accrue from the esthetics of the work place, from a sense of power over the environment, from opportunities to overcome challenges, from personal and financial risk-taking, and from unexpected novelties and complexities.

"Capacity is its own motivation."[501] What and how much activity can be energized and sustained depends as much upon the individual's capacity to perceive and learn as upon his survival requirements. An individual of borderline intelligence and restricted education is limited in what will challenge him, what will excite his curiosity, what will arouse his interests, and what will plunge him into feverish activity as a consequence of failure and sustain his persistence until a problem is solved. At the other extreme, giving educational advice to the gifted individual is often extremely difficult; for not only can he learn almost anything he wishes, he is also likely to be interested in almost anything he can learn.

Above and beyond the needs and drives of the worker, the external environment can be more or less stimulating and therefore more or less satisfying. Experiments with extremely restricted external environments demonstrate this point. These *sensory deprivation* experiences are punishing and disturbing to subjects although there is no known need for such stimulation for bodily survival. When a person is deprived of ordinary sights, sounds, temperature, and other sensations by being immersed in water of body temperature with eyes, ears, and nose blocked, he is likely to find this sensory deprivation most punishing, disorienting, and disturbing.

Animal research suggests that an *optimal* level of stimulation is sought. Blinded rats show more search for stimulation in open-field and Y mazes than seeing rats. Merely returning rats and monkeys from the dark to the light is rewarding. It is a prize for which they will work hard.[122]

Less extreme forms of such sensory deprivation occur in industry. The miner, for instance, works in semidarkness and in confined spaces. Assembly line operators may perform in a considerably restricted environment. Such workers are limited to very few variations and changes in much of customary stimulation during the workday. While narrow specialization and isolation of the worker is expected logically to increase the efficiency of his performance since all distracting influences are eliminated, removal of these "distractions" actually may punish the worker. Current motivational research points to a need to increase the amount of stimulation afforded such a worker if he is to be satisfied and productive.

As noted earlier in Chapter 3, somewhat analogous effects of deprived stimulation occur at the workplace as in the laboratory and that increasing the variety of stimulation promotes efficiency. Both satisfaction and productivity tend to increase as jobs are enlarged rather than made more specialized. Thus, office workers were more satisfied with their new jobs which were enlarged as a consequence of the introduction of electronic data processing equipment. They preferred the variety on their new jobs in contrast to the more routine requirements of their former assignments.[331] Job enlargement for maintenance repairmen and packaging crews led to reduced costs, greater quality, as well as better interpersonal relations.[151] Again, jobs on an assembly line were redesigned so that each individual girl alone completed all nine operations that had been done by different girls. Each girl now went for her own supplies and inspected her own work. Six days after the changeover, production was higher, the number of rejected assemblies had dropped by 25 percent, and satisfaction with work was much higher. Workers could now be employed more flexibly since everyone could perform every operation. Errors could be located and corrected more easily. The individual girl experienced more of a sense of accomplishment and required less direct supervision.[444] (More will be said in Chapter 7 about the social and psychological inadequacies of assembly line work.

Optimum Motivation.   Complicating matters is the fact that the rewards and expectancies of a job may be too great resulting in detriment, particularly to the accuracy and quality of performance. Witness the baseball pitcher who finds it increasingly difficult to throw the ball over the plate, who "blows the ball game" with wild pitches when the score is tied in the last inning of a critical game in a hotly contested pennant race.

When ROTC cadets were told that successful performance at a

verbal task under extremely noisy or quiet conditions could relieve them from extra marching duty earned for demerits, accuracy of performance was lowest under the following conditions: they had many demerits to "walk off"; the verbal task was complex rather than simple; and conditions were painfully noisy rather than quiet. Speed of performance was greater under noisy conditions and if the cadets could gain much from reduction in demerits when the task was simple.[46] Thus when the job is complex or the workers are not well trained, highly competitive incentive schemes may raise anxieties and tensions, not necessarily production. At the same time, if motivation is already high, increasing the complexity of the job may result in a deterioration, rather than an increase in performance.

Matching Reward to Effort.   Still another complication derives from our tendency to make work and reward match each other, either by reducing the amount of work or increasing the apparent value of the reward. While it is true that we work harder for greater reward, it also is true that the harder we work for a reward, the greater the reward will seem.[205] Fraternities are more valued by those who suffer hazing ceremonies before being admitted to them. Education seems more valuable if it has been hard to acquire.

Development of Vocational Motivation

Quite early the child learns to couple the bringers of reward with the bodily comforts they provide. Soon, the appearance of mother is comforting by itself. The child begins to desire the appearance of mother apart from the bodily contact, food, and other rewards she provides. The rudiments of social motivation are extended to include others in the family. To be with others is now rewarding; to be isolated is punishing. To be approved by others is rewarding; to be disapproved is punishing. Recognition for good work is now sought as one tries to raise his esteem in the eyes of others. Then, one begins performing to satisfy himself to maintain his own self-esteem. As maturity increases, self-direction becomes stronger. Satisfaction with outcomes depends on the independence with which we were able to select and achieve the outcomes. Finally, there is present in the mature, well-integrated personality the ability to be task-oriented, to find rewards mainly in accomplishment itself, in overcoming challenges, in planning, innovating, and creating.

The substitutability of cues for primary rewards is commonplace. Pay may serve as a stimulus representing task completion. Pay is not only a *secondary reinforcer*—capable of satisfying primary wants for food, shelter, and clothing—but it also may satisfy related secondary needs for status and esteem. Serving these needs by increasing income is an almost obvious chain of developments analogous to *higher-order conditioning*—the successive substitutions of one reinforcing stimulus of behavior for another. Pay increases, for instance, provide increased material comforts. But increased income also brings about increased spending and increased status. Gradually, this increased status due to one's increased spending comes to serve as a potential stimulus without the need to involve money, as such. A man learns to value the deference he receives because he has become rich. He now has more power over his environment than if he were poor. He has greater control over his own fate. Job success produces more income; more income leads to more spending; more spending produces more status; more status yields more power; more power results in more control of one's own condition. A *chain of conditioning* leads from job success to control of one's environment. Again, increased income may be an autonomous gratifying signal in itself. The man "who has everything" may find increments of salary still rewarding symbols of achievement. But other symbols of achievement might equally satisfy him, such as knighthood, political appointment, or honorary degrees.

Most important to the world of work is the satisfaction resulting from successful completion of tasks—with no necessary related rewards for doing so. The task-oriented person, in particular, seemingly derives great satisfaction from his accomplishments, big and small—completing a course, solving a mathematical problem, building a dam, or winning a game of solitaire.[42]

Mature Motivation Among Executives.   As mentioned earlier, material and social needs seems less important in energizing and directing the actions of the mature personality. Rather, the self-selected, self-generated task itself becomes the prime mover of the mature man. His main satisfaction accrues from a sense of accomplishment, from a sense of a job well done. Thus, the healthy person is seen to have a "constructive impulse." He does not seek equilibrium and rest, but rather, his motivation is a "forward thrust into the future."[6] Yet it is this "forward thrust," this desire for self-actualization that is least fulfilled according to one survey among 1,958 supervisors and executives. These men indicated the importance to them of a hierarchy of needs and the extent each motive was being satisfied on the job. The hierarchy was Maslow's[455] ascending order of needs: security, social, esteem, autonomy, and self-actualization. (Before a higher need in the hierarchy, say for autonomy, can be satisfied, a lower one, say for security, has to be). While this management sample as a whole felt its lower-order needs were fulfilled for material and social security and for esteem, its higher-order needs for autonomy and self-actualization were not satisfied. As might be expected, those of highest status, the presidents and vice presidents, were more likely to be satisfied in all respects, yet they too were most concerned for greater opportunities for self-actualization.[532]

Individual Differences. In this, as in all samples, there are consistent individual differences in the desire for autonomy and for opportunities for self-actualization. Several independent factor analyses of college students' attitudes toward work, toward occupations, and toward incentives reveal consistent clusters of preferences. Some students want freedom, independence, and autonomy at work, while others prefer more dependent relationships or ones in which they can control subordinates. Monetary and social rewards are a second cluster which some students reject in favor of opportunities for interesting work. Still another cluster revolves around how structured is the job assignment; some respondents preferring schedules, orders, and formality; others are more content to work without structure or system.[19,60,137]

Involvement and Job Satisfaction

How personally involved an employe feels with his work, how ego-involved he is with its success is strongly associated with his satisfaction with it. Six hundred telephone operators and service representatives at Michigan Bell Telephone were found more likely to remain with the company rather than quit if (1) they felt they had a chance to make decisions on the job, and (2) they felt they were making an important contribution to the success of the company. In this instance none of the usual turnover predictors, such as marital status or satisfaction with pay, had any effect on the tendency to remain or quit.[743]

In 48 sections of a large company 2,680 female skilled employes were asked such questions: How important is it to know how well you are doing? How important is it to be fully informed about the quality of your work? Matching procedures were used so that in samples of those workers who remained in comparison to 169 who quit, there were equal proportions of single and married "tentative" employes who were most likely going to quit for family, not job, reasons. The samples also contained equal proportions of careerists and long-time employes. Those who quit were no different from those who remained on the job in satisfaction with the quality of supervision they received, adequacy of on-the-job training or feeling that it was necessary to work. But, employes who quit were more likely to be dissatisfied with the recognition, achievement, and self-determination their work provided.[573]

Predicated on the theory that recall of interrupted tasks and tensions are greater for persons more ego-involved in the tasks, 94 supervisors, 305 nonsupervisory electronics employees, and 489 bluecollar refinery workers were asked, "If a problem comes up in your work and won't be settled by the time you go home, how likely is it that you will find yourself thinking about it after work?" Those who thought about after hours were much more likely to be satisfied with their jobs if the work offered them opportunity for self-expression. Such opportunities were less important to those who forgot about their jobs as soon as they went home. How well a worker performed depended on his ego-involvement particularly if he was in research rather than in manufacturing, that is where his work was such that "he felt free to set his own pace."[706] Such internalized motivation, such self-impulsion, is more likely if the job requires a great deal of skill and if the worker believes himself to have more opportunities for self-determination[616] as would be true in research compared with manufacturing departments.

PERFORMANCE GOALS

Subjective Expectancy Versus Objective Probability of Reward

Sixteen trios of airmen worked for rewards which actually could be obtained nine out of 10 times. Another 16 trios were in a situation where rewards were likely only once in 10 trials. Eight of each 16 were told they were likely to succeed and actually did experience reward immediately. Eight of each 16 were told they were incapable of succeeding, and it was arranged for them to fail at first. Those told of their likely success also received notes of optimism ostensibly from fellow members; those told of their likely failure were recipients of pessimistic notes. Objective reward ($9/10$ or $1/10$) had little effect on how attractive the situation was for members, but subjective expectation of reward attainment (optimism or pessimism) was influential.[164] Whether pay is actually good, bonuses are easy to obtain, and promotions come quickly are not as important in determining a worker's attitude toward the job and his performance as are his *expectations* about his goals of pay, bonuses, and promotions. Also important are the clarity of the goals, how close the worker is to them, and his level of aspiration about attaining the goals. Finally, the extent to which goals conflict with other goals affects the way the worker is attracted toward a particular rewarding situation or repelled from it.

The Importance of Clear Goals

A comparison of two large plants found workers much more satisfied in the one plant in which a great deal of attention was paid to explaining things that had to be done by workers when they were assigned tasks.[271]

If our goals are clear, we are surer about what we want and what we seek; we understand better the direction in which we are going and why we are going there. If our goals are clear, we are more satisfied with what we are doing, we put more energy into what we are doing, we pay more care and attention to the quality of our product, and we show better overall performance. To demonstrate some of the effects of having clear goals, laboratory subjects were asked to cut out as many paper forms as they could and to do so as accurately and as neatly as possible in a standard amount of time. Each was told that he was a member of a trio. The two other persons in his trio whom he did not meet were supposedly assembling and gluing together the forms that he was cutting out in order to build model paper houses. He saw himself as a member of a team building model houses of paper. Paper cutters under this condition were much more satisfied and proficient at their work than similar paper cutters in the laboratory who were asked to cut out the forms without being told their use. The goals of paper cutting were quite unclear to the latter subjects and their performance suffered.[546]

Positive Compared with Negative Goals

Positive goals and negative goals are not merely the opposite of each other in their effects on our behavior. If we are stimulated to work for positive goals such as money, achievement, or recognition, we learn readily how to make the appropriate responses to obtain these goals. We try out various ways of reaching them. Those responses which succeed are reinforced, fixated, and learned; those which fail tend to be eliminated from our repertoire. On the other hand, negative goals, goals to be avoided, such as physical injury, discharge, or rejection by others, serve to teach us what not to do, but they do not necessarily point out what we should be doing. If we live in a world of negative goals, we

learn how to avoid such goals; yet, we do not learn how to obtain rewards, how to perform proficiently, how to be accepted, or how to make
positive contributions to others around us.

Effects of Negative Goals.   If what is to be learned is *not* to do something,
punishment may be effective in teaching this. For example, consistently
enforced fines and penalties are probably an effective way to keep people
from smoking in a no-smoking zone of a petrochemical plant. Yet, punishments may lose their effect altogether when they are very severe. One
reason so many men continue to smoke in the face of the threat of lung
cancer and heart disease is that the threat is so severe that we tend to
block it out of mind rather than let it affect our behavior. We have this
same kind of reaction to many other extreme forms of threat and
danger, such as that from the possibilities of nuclear warfare. We
avoid thinking about the problem rather than trying to cope with the
problem to reduce the threat.

     To demonstrate this, strong, moderate, and mild fear-arousing
stimuli were used in dental hygiene propaganda. Mild fear provoca-
tion was most effective in helping school children resist counter-
propaganda.[334] Displaying horrible photographs of victims of venereal
disease, instead of encouraging the use of prophylaxis, led servicemen to
identify VD with prophylaxis; to avoid the anxieties associated with VD,
they avoided using prophylaxis!

     When punishment is severe, we sometimes fixate the very response
for which we are being punished. The severely shocked laboratory
animal may continue to respond in a way which will earn him more
shock instead of making an adjustment in his behavior to escape from
the shock.

     It even may be possible to create conditions where mild punish-
ment for a wrong response, signals that response, so that the ensuing
response is harder, rather than easier, to eliminate.

Closeness to Goals

     The closer a worker gets to his goals, the more they affect his behav-
ior. He speeds up his performance as his anticipation of successful
attainment increases. He is much more aroused as the goal comes into
sight. Just before the end of a work spell there may be an increase in
performance. Just before the end of a journey a driver may speed up.

     Mentioned earlier was *batching*, a procedure for breaking the work
load into smaller lots, so that goal attainment could be achieved more

quickly frequently—provided the worker establishes the smaller lot as his goal in comparison to the larger one to which he has been accustomed.

Storming is a specific illustration of this "goal gradient effect"—the observed speeding up of performance in Soviet manufacturing as the goal comes closer. Storming is the bunching up of production during the last ten days of each month to meet monthly quotas. It is accepted practice since it is thought that men work best under pressure of deadlines, of close goals. In 1950, 67 percent of the output of automatic machine tools in the USSR was completed during the last ten days of the month as was 54 percent of motorcycle assemblies and 78 percent of job shop production. The effects are multiplied since each department piles up work as it rests from the preceding month's storming and builds up to a maximum outburst again towards the end of the new month. Storming occurs in the U.S., but not to the same degree.[253]

The effects of being closer to goals is also a reason why *ad hoc* committees set up to do a specific job are often more effective than *standing* committees, committees in existence to take on any of a whole set of jobs likely to arise during the course of the committee's life. Standing committees are much more likely to suffer from lethargy, to fall apart, or do their work in a desultory fashion in comparison to *ad hoc* committees.

As mentioned earlier in discussing the goals of British war veterans, individuals differ as a consequence of their intelligence, skill, and maturity in the extent they are able to adopt long-range goals or remain responsive only to shorter-range ones.

Levels of Aspiration

The level of goal attainment we set seems to be a compromise between what realistically can be attained and what we want to attain. Expectations depend upon our past history of success, our self-confidence, our confidence in others with whom we must work, the experience of others in the same work situation, and how much help we expect to get from others in working toward our mutual goals. In addition to these rational and realistic factors which determine what we achieve, there are also emotional and unrealistic factors which affect our attainment. Among these emotional factors are (1) how strongly we want the goals in question; (2) how valuable they are to us; (3) our tendency to identify with some lucky individuals who happen to attain the goals; and (4) other wish-fulfilling tendencies on our part. We are likely to make more realistic judgments about our possibilities of winning $10 than $100,000 in a contest. The fantasies that come into play when we are talking about $100,000 interfere with our proper assessment of conditions in the situation.

Consistent with earlier comments about subjective expectations and objective realities, subjective aspirations are more important in determining what we do and how hard we try to obtain goals. We continue to play rigged slot machines. According to laboratory experiments people will continue to play "one-armed bandits" even when the payoff is practically eliminated as a possibility. If given four choices to play, individuals may choose one of the choices which never pays off, many hundreds of times. Why? Because they are reacting to their subjective expectancies of payoff rather than to the actual probabilities of payoff. They reason falsely that since the machine hasn't paid off so far, it is bound to do so soon. Players believe they have a fairly good chance of winning if they continue cranking the machine, although their chances are nonexistent.[407]

Goallessness

"The nearer man comes to complete mastery of the physical world, the more urgent it is for him to imagine further worthwhile goals. The alternative is spiritual stagnation, failure to find outlets for human energies and talents, and in the end, boredom and unhappiness."[179,p.5] It is easy to formulate goals when material needs must be met. Goals become increasingly fuzzy as the material, then social needs are fulfilled; thus we turn toward setting goals to satisfy higher-level needs for achievement and self-actualization. Many cannot rise above a torpor developed from the satiation of material wants. Such goallessness may be found in middle-aged housewives whose children are grown and who have not found new purposes for living. Feelings of being unwanted, psychosomatic complaints, and apathy may result.

The low morale of many otherwise "normal" young employes may be due to their failure to have developed any aims in life. They literally have no point in living. Again, the retired employe without plans or goals for the retirement years is likely to find his lot an unhappy one. Until goals can be discovered, members of groups will remain pessimistic, dissatisfied, and uncomfortable.

Groups that remain goalless suffer in performance. In a simulated survival study conducted by the Air Force, air crews "behind enemy lines" were much less able to "survive" when they were planless or goalless. Once a plan or a set of goals were formulated they were much more able to succeed in living off the land and eventually finding a way back home.

Group Versus Individual Goals

As will be stressed in Chapter 6, full understanding of the goals set and sought by the individual worker requires an appreciation of the group in which he works. A salient, successful, cohesive work group will exert considerable influence over the aspirations and the goal-determination of its individual members. So will the group in which sanctions are certain and swiftly applied, where the task requires cooperation, where activities of everyone are public, and where the attainment of the group's goals are relevant to the individual. He gains or loses as a consequence of the group's success or failure.

The influential group can increase the attractiveness of its goals and decrease outside interests of individual workers, or it can assure workers that group and individual objectives are identical. A group can make a member feel wanted so that contributions to the group effort earn him continued affection. In the same way, the group can avoid giving any support to an individual's private interests in conflict with group effort.[762]

Conflicts in Goals

Often an employe is faced with choices among many goals. Sometimes, if he works for one goal, he cannot work for another he considers equally desirable. He is confronted with a frustrating *approach-approach* conflict situation, a situation in which he wants "to have his cake and eat it too." Here he desires two competing positive goals but can only obtain one of them. The manager may wish to continue his advancement in the company requiring periodic relocation. At the same time, he may have as a positive goal remaining in the city in which he was born and reared because of the many strong family ties he has developed there. If he leaves the community he will lose many of these personal associations he values highly. On the other hand, he must leave in order to advance himself with his company. In such approach-approach circumstances most people tend to vacillate, first moving in one direction, then the other. But once they have made up their minds they usually move in one direction and give up the other without too much disturbance and difficulty. For example, if the manager finally decides to go

ahead and relocate, his subsequent behavior usually does not reflect too
much his loss of personal ties, as such. He makes appropriate adjustments, devoting any further thoughts on the matter to confirming the
correctness of the decision and finding new reasons for it.

Goal Avoidance Conflicts. Less easily resolved are avoidance conflicts.
Negative goals may compete in an *avoidance-avoidance* conflict. Only
one negative goal can be avoided, but both are noxious. An employe
may be unhappy with the work he is doing, but if he were to quit the
loss of income would make him still more unhappy. A strike often is
an avoidance-avoidance situation for labor and for management also.
The workers may stand to lose more in wages than they gain by striking,
and yet if they do not strike they may not be able to deal effectively
with a tough management. Management, unable to resolve its employe-
relations problems in a satisfactory manner, may lose more in profits
than it gains by forcing the strike, yet if it is now in such a win-or-lose
condition, and yields to union demands without a strike, it may have to
give up power it wishes to retain.

An employe may face an *approach-avoidance* conflict. In order to
start earning money as soon as possible, he wants to quit school. Yet,
he sees that further advancement requires more schooling and necessary delay in his desire for immediate financial independence.

When faced with these conflict situations we would rather avoid,
we commonly become defensive, either attacking or withdrawing from
the noxious conditions. It takes a mature individual to recognize that
he is confronted with such an avoidance conflict and to accept it realistically for what it is, without becoming defensive. For instance, when our
performance is criticized, our first reaction is to defend our performance
by attacking the critic, by excusing our failures, by explaining our actions, and so on. It is painful to listen even to helpful criticism, so we
attack it or withdraw from it. Yet, we would profit more by concentrating
on what was being said to us in order to ensure that we understood
the criticism and could evaluate more accurately both the critic and the
criticism. Then we would be in a better position to decide whether or
not to modify our performance. We would also be better able to know
how to change.

Defense in Fight

To protect himself against the frustration and discomfort of avoidance conflicts, the employe has available many psychological defenses.
Like primitive man, when attacked by noxious stimuli, the modern

worker can fight, or he can flee — but unlike primitive man, the modern employe has many more elaborate ways of fighting or withdrawing instead of coping with disturbing conditions realistically. An employe who finds himself unable to earn a promotion because of his lack of ability, instead of accepting his own limitations and living with them, seldom will fight *directly* against the source of his frustration — that is, he will not punch his boss in the nose, but he may fight by *displacing* his aggression against a weaker target. He may quarrel with his wife or beat his child.

He may fight against himself with a sense of guilt he develops over his failure. "I failed; it is my fault; I must be punished." The sense of conflict shifts to a sense of guilt. Strong feelings of worthlessness, uselessness, and other types of neurotic symptoms may develop. Instead of displacing his aggression and hostility on others he may turn it inward. If he is a "guts" responder he may end up with an ulcer. If he is a "lung" responder he may show characteristic difficulties in breathing or asthmatic attacks. A "circulatory responder" may find his cardiovascular system affected and may develop a false angina simulating some type of organic heart disorder. As primitive man's blood pressure went up in preparation for a fight with a dangerous adversary, so modern man's blood pressure also rises — only he seldom then can restore it to equilibrium in a physical melee.

Defense in Flight

Fleeing or withdrawing from the conflict may take several forms. When faced with uncomfortable conflicts some employes develop apathetic reactions. They display listlessness, emotional exhaustion, and indifference to what is going on about them.

Some men withdraw into the past. They regress to an earlier stage in their life when the conflicts did not exist and when they were successful. They may act quite immaturely on many matters displaying temper tantrums, dressing or behaving as an adolescent. "Well, I did not get promoted; but did I ever tell you about the time back in college when . . . "

Still another defense is by means of *identification*. Rather than develop means for uplifting himself educationally, economically, and socially (which may be difficult or almost impossible), a poor mill worker may get vicarious satisfaction by identifying with the famous, rich, successful movie star, adopting some of the movie star's mannerisms, values, and ways of talking.

All of us at times escape from our conflicts through daydreaming, through moving into a world of fantasy in which we are highly likely to be great successes and where our conflicts disappear. The unpromoted Walter Mitty dreams of his great adventures always as a bold, powerful, successful hero. Too many find too much alcohol necessary as an escape; others use the movies or television to a very great extent. If daydreaming does not vitiate effective coping with one's environment, it may be regarded as an aide to adjustment. No one can hope to be completely realistic about every conflict in his life, and the defense of fantasy acts as a safety valve. It becomes maladaptive when one begins daydreaming instead of adequately performing his job or maintaining a satisfactory educational, social, and personal life.

In the same way, everyone *rationalizes* about conflicts — finds socially acceptable excuses to explain them away. We "solve" our dilemma by describing ourselves as victims of general forces over which we have no control. Faced with the dilemma of a strike or giving in to union pressures, management may rationalize the situation by saying, that "outside agitators" have stirred the others into a strike; it is not management's fault. In turn, employes, faced with the reverse dilemma, may see as the cause of the strike reactionary, stubborn, and "stuck-up" management behaving in "typical" management fashion, not willing to deal fairly with the workers.

To rationalize about some of our conflicts seems to help us cope with the many others on which we may reach more realistic solutions. However if we are always like the fox and regard all grapes as sour that we could not reach, we eventually may find ourselves really hungry.

Elements of hostility and rationalization are to be found when a man defends himself by *projecting* his own feelings on another. "I am willing to compromise, but not the stubborn negotiator with whom I have to deal."

Many workers today express *dual loyalty* to both management and unions. They both share the goals of their management as well as the goals of their union, failing to see the conflicts existing in these mutually exclusive sets of goals.[540] These logic-tight compartments are seen elsewhere in our life. The sharp businessman who is a faithful churchgoer denies any conflict in the goals of his sharp business practices and the goals of his church. German soldiers gave unyielding support to Hitler, but at the same time most German soldiers thought it was all right to surrender to avoid being killed, although Hitler had ordered a fight to the death.[10]

While we all exhibit these various false solutions, it is only when these become our only approach to solving our dilemmas that such pseudosolutions really become handicapping, making us less effective and more maladjusted in the social world about us.

Adaptive Defense

One defense which seems most the adaptive is *compensation*. This occurs when we try even harder to cope with some frustrating problem facing us because of the existence of that problem and other conflicts. It may be a successful resolution of conflict for it may lead to an efficient dealing with our environment. A physically unattactive girl may work harder than other girls to make herself socially attractive. A physically handicapped worker may compensate for his handicap by working harder than the rest of those around him, by being on time more often and absent less often, and striving to show that he is as good as, if not better than, other workers around him. According to a 10-year follow-up of 151 post-poliomyelitic cases, despite serious physical aftereffects, the post-poliomyelitic has an employment record comparing favorably with normal workers.[723a]

* * * * *

If we wish to understand what attracts a man to work and sustains his efforts, we need to look carefully at what he is capable of doing, what he is interested in doing, how involved he is with his work, and the goals towards which he strives. These, in turn, will depend upon certain characteristics of the employe, such as his personality, length of service, and intelligence.

Jobs are being enlarged from routine, repetitive, simple assignments to provide variety and novelty. These are more likely to prove interesting and stimulating to the modern worker of the last half of the twentieth century whose education has reached a level demanding more challenging work. At the same time the nature of available work is keeping abreast of the increasing education of the worker for automation is eliminating many of the unskilled, routine jobs of the past.

Understanding an employe's motivation to work requires an analysis of how clearly he perceives his goals, whether they are positive or negative, how close or far he is from them, his level of aspiration, and the conflicts among these goals. Particularly important is how these goals are set. Here is where the supervisor enters the scene as a prime factor in affecting worker motivation.

In Brief

CONSIDERABLE EVIDENCE NOW SUPPORTS THE CONTENTION THAT THE supervisor plays an important role in the success of his department. Particularly important is the extent he is considerate of the welfare of his subordinates and the extent he initiates the structure of relations between men and work in his department. The supervisor, however, is considerate of his subordinates at the risk of displeasing his superiors. Likewise, he initiates structure at the risk of displeasing his subordinates. He is caught in a number of other such conflicting demands on his time and effort.

A supervisor must know what he is doing if he would persuade his subordinates. He must be valued by them if he is to be successful at persuading them. He can use his power either to coerce his subordinates or to permit them to share in the setting of goals and in the structuring of the work situation. Coercion is likely to yield overconformity, hostility, withdrawal, and various other dysfunctional effects. On the other hand, permissiveness is likely to yield commitment to the department's goals and to the execution of plans to reach those goals. However there are a number of instances where permissiveness is likely to be less efficacious than more authoritative supervision.

Chapter 5

SUPERVISORY

BEHAVIOR

A SUPERVISOR'S BEHAVIOR IS IMPORTANT TO HIS EMPLOYE'S GENERAL JOB
satisfaction. For instance, overall morale of 64 trades employees in civil
service was high if they said that their "supervisor lets them know how
they are doing."[437] Public utilities employes indicated that their overall
job satisfaction was high when their supervisor was more "personal"
in his dealings than "institutional," when he was more "downward" or
employe-oriented, and when he trained men for better jobs. Supervisors of high-morale groups differed from managers of low-morale
groups in that they reviewed their subordinates' work more frequently;
they welcomed discussion of mutual problems with subordinates; they
carried out group discussions; and they kept the men posted on new
information.[412]

Supervision and Satisfaction

As already noted in Chapter 2, while it contributes to general satisfaction with work, satisfaction with supervision may be independent of
contentment with other aspects of the job such as compensation. There
may be no correlation between the attitudes toward the material benefits
of work in a particular company and satisfaction with its supervision,
although workers favorable toward their supervision are likely to be
more satisfied with their jobs as a whole.

Where employes are often "on their own" or where they must deal
with many supervisors, the particular immediate boss may not be as

important to them as the general adequacy of their supervision. Thus, although the general job satisfaction of 715 railroad workers depended on their evaluation of the overall quality of supervision, it was relatively unaffected by how they felt about their immediate supervisor, for each of these workers was supervised by several men.[636]

Supervision, Turnover, and Grievances.   Attraction to work and satisfaction with it, evidenced by lack of turnover, absenteeism, and grievances, are affected by the supervisor. Fifty-seven production foremen each were described by three of their subordinates. (The three were selected randomly). How much each foreman exhibited each of 40 items of behavior indicated the extent he *initiated structure* for his subordinates and the extent he was *considerate* of them. A foreman who initiated structure a great deal would be described as a supervisor who maintains definite standards of performance, who assigns subordinates to particular tasks, and who specifies standard procedures to be followed. A highly considerate foreman is one who expresses appreciation for good work, makes subordinates feel at ease, and gets their approval on important matters before going ahead. Usually, consideration and initiation are independent of each other, but in this case the correlation was −.33. In this plant there was a slight tendency for initiators to be described as somewhat inconsiderate.[214]

Figures 5.1 through 5.4 show how initiation and consideration of

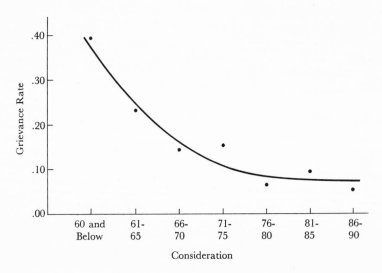

Figure 5.1: Relation Between Consideration and Grievance Rates.
(After Fleishman & Harris, 1962, p. 47)

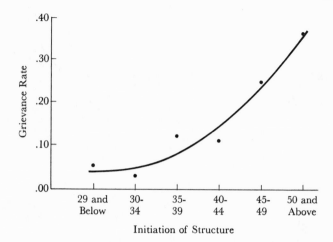

Figure 5.2: Relation Between Structure and Grievance Rates. (After Fleishman & Harris, 1962, p. 48)

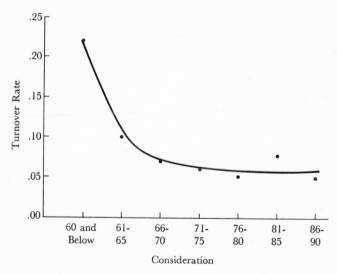

Figure 5.3: Relation Between Consideration and Turnover Rates. (After Fleishman & Harris, 1962, p. 51)

the 57 foremen related to grievance rates and turnover in the departments they supervised. Grievance rates and turnover within a department were particularly high for those supervisors described as least considerate and most prone to initiate structure.

In the same way, absences of white-collar workers were found di-

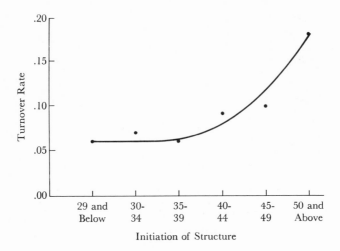

Figure 5.4: Relation Between Structure and Turnover Rates.
(After Fleishman & Harris, 1962, p. 51)

rectly related to how free they say they felt to discuss their job with their supervisor. Of men absent four or more times during a six-month period, only 29 percent said they felt very free to talk with their boss, while 57 to 69 percent of those absent less often said they felt very free to hold such discussions.[412]

Supervision and Productivity. Studies of leader behavior in a public utility company, an insurance office, an automobile plant, and in heavy industry suggest that productivity of a work group tends to be related to certain leadership practices. Groups are more productive where the supervisor does not perform the same functions as the rank and file worker but sticks to leadership roles and functions. Such supervisors spend more time trying to motivate their workers. Supervisors of groups low in productivity waste their time on routine activities which could be handled by the workers.[349] Supervisors whose groups have better production records are more likely to exhibit long-range planning and anticipate future problems rather than remain on a day-to-day operating basis. Highly productive groups have less close supervision from their foremen who in turn are less closely supervised by their superiors. Minor decision-making is allowed these supervisors and their workers.[355]

Supervisors of high-producing groups of skilled tradesmen were found to be more considerate of their subordinates than were supervisors of low-producing groups. They were also more consistent, more self-reliant, and displayed better judgment.[749] Even more significant than how supervisors motivated their subordinates was the ability of "high-producing" supervisors in the aircraft industry to plan well, to know their own jobs, and to communicate effectively.[128]

A Confirmatory Experiment. The survey evidence just enumerated was collected to support the argument that supervisory ability and attitude affect productivity, that the supervisor who is skillful and considerate brings about productive work groups. But the same data could support the reverse contention; that is, when groups are highly productive their supervisor can be and is considerate and skillful. Therefore, an experiment was conducted in a General Electric tube plant to demonstrate that supervisory behavior *causes* increases or decreases in productivity.

For three weeks, work groups of 5 to 11, on their regular assembly operations of parts assembling, fine welding, or soldering wires to leads, were either given favorable or unfavorable treatment by supervisory personnel. The groups were matched in age, productivity, seniority, and disciplinary records. *Favored* groups were praised on the high quality of their performance. Management went out of its way to be friendly and helpful. Deliberate efforts were made to avoid irritating incidents. *Unfavored* groups were threatened and subjected to repeated time and motion study. There were persistant attacks by supervision on the quality of their workmanship. Irritating incidents were contrived. For example, workers were forced to sort out washers from a dirty, greasy collection.

At the end of the third week minor changes in work were instituted. For instance, workers were shifted from assembling one type of vacuum tube to assembling a different type, put together somewhat differently. Once the changeover took place, the differential treatment of the favored and the unfavored groups ceased, so there would be no contamination of new incidents directly disturbing productivity.

Table 5.1 contrasts the quality of output of the favored and unfavored groups during the course of the experiment. It shows the percentage of assembled units requiring repair during each phase of the experiment. Note that when work is routine and relatively easy, as during the first three weeks when employes continued to work on old and familiar tasks, the unfavorable supervisory treatment had some, but not very drastic effects on the quality of performance. Yet when a changeover occurred and new work was introduced, work with which employes were less experienced, work which was therefore more difficult, unfavored workers had repair rates two to three times as great as the favored employes.[585]

These results are consistent with our earlier analysis of optimum

TABLE 5.1   QUALITY OF WORK BEFORE AND AFTER CHANGEOVER OF
WORK GROUPS SUBJECTED TO FAVORED AND UNFAVORED
SUPERVISORY TREATMENT*

Phase of Experiment	Percentage of Assembled Units Requiring Repair	
	Favored Group	Unfavored Group
During first week of contrived disturbance	10.6	11.8
During second two weeks of contrived disturbance	11.7	14.7
First week after changeover	21.1	31.4
Second week after changeover	13.8	28.0
Third and fourth weeks after	11.6	29.0

*From Schacter, Festinger, et al., 1962, p. 206

motivation and task complexity. When workers are experienced (or the job is easy for them) increased stress may primarily serve to speed performance, but when workers are inexperienced with the task (or the job is difficult) increased stress will seriously disturb accuracy. The real test of the adequacy of supervision comes when flexibility or change is required of the group supervised or when new problems arise. Good supervision is relatively less important when the work is completely machine dominated or otherwise out of the control of the worker, or when the work is easy. Here, stressing the worker mainly speeds his performance rather than reduces his accuracy.

BEHAVIOR OF SUPERVISORS

Distinguishing Supervisory from Nonsupervisory Behavior

What does the supervisor do that makes his job different from that of other personnel in nonsupervisory positions? Supervision consists in the changing of the behavior of subordinates in one of two ways: changing their motivation or the goals towards which they work, or initiating means making it possible for subordinates to do a better job.[41]

Motivating subordinates. Subordinates can be motivated either by threat of punishment or by promises of reward. A single factor describes how supervisors actually vary in their efforts to motivate. Some consistently emphasize threat; others consistently focus on promises of reward. The inconsiderate supervisor demands more than can be done, criticizes subordinates in front of others, treats them without considering their feelings, "rides" them for making mistakes and frequently deflates their self-esteem or threatens their security by acting without consulting them, refuses to accept suggestions or to explain action. At the other extreme is the highly considerate supervisor who emphasizes promises, rewards, and support. He sees that subordinates are rewarded for a job well done, keeps subordinates in good standing with those higher in authority, expresses appreciation for good work, stresses the importance of satisfaction among subordinates, maintains and strengthens the self-esteem of subordinates by treating them as equals, makes subordinates feel at ease when talking with him, remains easily approachable, puts subordinates' suggestions into operation, and gets approval of subordinates on important matters before going ahead.[212]

We have seen already that considerate supervisors are more likely to run work groups with lower absenteeism, turnover, and grievance rates. Consistent with these results is finding that absenteeism and turnover are lowest in those work centers of an aircraft factory where the lead man devotes most of his time to facilitating the work of others and attending to their personal problems. Such a lead man is willing to listen to the irritations and frustrations of the personal life of his subordinates and helps reduce tensions which probably detract from workers' productivity.[458] A summary of relevant research suggests that supervisors who have the most favorable and cooperative attitudes in their work groups are likely to be supportive, friendly, and helpful rather than hostile. They are kind, but firm, and never threatening. They are genuinely interested in the well-being of subordinates and strive to be sensitive to their subordinates. They are just, if not generous. They try to have the best interests of both their employes and their company in mind. They show confidence, rather than suspicion and distrust of their subordinates.[412]

Initiating Structure. Just as supervisors differ in how they motivate their subordinates, they also will differ in the extent they provide the cues and structure work for their subordinates. Supervisors who initiate a great deal are described as ones who insist on having things done in a standard way, who see that subordinates work to full capacity, who offer new approaches to problems, who emphasize the meeting of deadlines, and who decide in detail what will be done, how much will be done, and how it should be done.[212] While too much such initiation seems to increase the likelihood of grievances, absenteeism, and turnover,[214] a certain amount of pointing out of the "paths to successful effort" is characteristic of the effective supervisor. There seems to be an *optimum* amount of guidance by the supervisor which yields the greatest effectiveness and satisfaction in his work group. No doubt this optimum amount is greater when workers are untrained and/or unmotivated. Untrained personnel need more help; trained ones prefer less. Among higher-level executives such direction takes the form of time devoted to innovation and coordination. Among lower-level executives it concentrates on production.[83] Observations of 82 first-line blue-collar and clerical supervisors for 108 days and statements from 770 blue-collar supervisors suggest that they spend about one-third of their time reviewing the work of their subordinates and instructing and correcting their work. Somewhat less time is spent on scheduling.[437]

The supervisor has a teaching role.

> . . . the foreman should feel responsible for the education and training of those under him, the heads of departments should feel the same, and so all along up the line to the chief executive.[476, p.267]

Effective supervisors see that each subordinate is well trained for his particular job and is helped in his promotion by being trained for jobs at the next level. Relevant experience and coaching is given whenever the opportunity offers, particularly for assisting employes whose performance is below standard.

In addition to training subordinates, the effective supervisor plans and schedules the work to be done and provides adequate technical competence, particularly where work has not been highly standardized.[412] Yet this initiation must be accompanied by consideration.

> A supervisor who can plan his work well, who has good technical knowledge and who can install better production methods can raise production without necessarily increasing group satisfaction. On the other hand, a supervisor who can motivate his employes and keep them satisfied with his leadership can gain high production in spite of technical difficulties and environmental obstacles. . . . a combination of these two abilities results in the highest output . . . supervisors of high-producing units more often assume the management functions of planning, organizing and coordinating . . . the employe-centered supervisor does not ignore the need for production. In fact, it is important to him but he does not allow it to override his recognition of the need for maintaining group satisfaction.[9]

Much guidance by the supervisor is accomplished by his feeding back knowledge of results, by his checking and correcting efforts of his workers. Without feedback from the soles of our feet, our leg muscles, and the balancing mechanisms of our inner ear, we would find it difficult to walk. If we cannot hear our own speech, or even if we delay slightly in the feedback of our own speech to our ears, we may be disturbed in talking. Without such feedback, either from objective instruments or reports or from his supervisor or fellow workers, the employe would be at a loss as to whether he is currently performing well or how his performance can be improved.

High-speed data processing is beginning to make possible the feedback of objective data quickly and in amounts that can provide such feedback under certain circumstances. Instrumentation is also becoming of central importance to jobs requiring the operation of equipment or the control of processes.

But in most work it is the supervisor and his interpretations of the objective data and his subjective evaluations of an employe's performance that are the significant feedback for the average employe. Both the quality and quantity of feedback from the supervisor will be of central significance. A prime job for a good supervisor is reviewing his subordinates' work, correcting their performance, and instructing them in the appropriate methods for completing the job satisfactorily, but doing so with consideration.

Dimensions for Evaluating Supervisors

While two factors, consideration and initiation, seem sufficient to describe how supervisors differ in their overall behavior toward subordinates, there are many other way in which supervisors differ from each other in their contributions to the firm and how adequately they perform their respective jobs.

An analysis of 245 white-collar supervisors, evaluated on 328 items of behavior, found a factor structure as shown in Figure 5.5. In this particular study, consideration towards subordinates was subdivided into three clusters, open-mindedness, cheerfulness, and approachability. The general factor indicated that some supervisors were rated highly on all items while others were downgraded on all.[588]

The same general factor emerged in a factor analysis of superiors' ratings of insurance division managers. In this insurance study, other factors included skill in dealing with people, judgment, effectiveness in planning, effectiveness in supervision, and effectiveness in improving operating efficiency.[254] Thus there seem to be many independent dimensions upon which to evaluate the performance of supervisors.

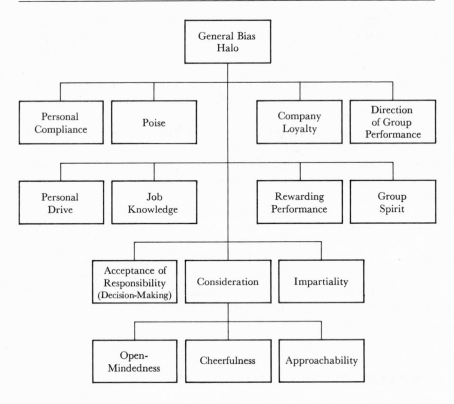

Figure 5.5: A Hierarchy of Supervisory Evaluation Factors. (After Roach, 1956, p. 489)

CONFLICTING SUPERVISORY JOB DEMANDS

The many bases upon which he is evaluated make it easy for the typical supervisor to find himself facing conflicts in demands for his time, conflicts of interests among those with whom he must work, and conflicts in his own needs and the requirements of his job. He sees serious discrepancies between how his boss treats him and how he is supposed to treat his workers. He complains that management fails to make its policies clear about supervisor-subordinate relations.[15]

Personal dependence upon the judgments and decisions of his superiors so characteristic of the subordinate-superior relation in modern industry makes the . . . situation basically insecure. . . . In some cases this preoccupation with what the boss thinks becomes so acute that it accounts for everything (said or done). . . [561, pp.285-95]

Men-in-the-middle in industry suffer anxiety from the ambiguities of their roles for it is seldom clear to them how they can satisfy both their bosses and their subordinates at the same time.[750] The foreman, in particular, may see himself in an impossible situation, especially where workers are unionized and top management deals directly with union officials to settle important matters. The least power in such circumstances is with the marginal man between workers and upper management.[754]

Time Demands

How much time executives say they spend in supervision correlates negatively with the amount of authority they say they have. However, reported supervisory time does not correlate with how much responsibility they feel they have or how much they delegate authority.[86] Perhaps because they feel production problems take precedence, they actually overestimate how much time they spend on production and underestimate how long they devote to personnel matters.[89] Higher-level executives seem to be able to spend more time in innovation, in attending to personnel relations, and in coordination according to a survey of 96 management personnel. But the first-line foreman usually must devote more of his attention to getting out production to be evaluated highly, particularly by his superiors. Yet, subordinates give greater weight in their evaluations to personal leadership.[83] However, only about 7 percent of the time of a large sample of blue-collar supervisors seems to be spent on personal matters.[437]

Some supervisors bury themselves or are buried in paperwork and have little time left for such important functions as motivating subordinates. In banks, in particular, executives may be kept busy with customers with consequent neglect of many supervisory activities.[13]

An unpublished study of the contact patterns of 80 members of management indicates that the executive heading a productive department is never extreme either one way or another in how he distributes his time. He avoids being tied up all day in meetings but spends more time in meetings than a supervisor of an unproductive department. Compared to ineffective supervisors the effective manager does not spend more time with one subordinate than another or with his superiors rather than his subordinates.

Conflicting Loyalties

While his superiors are likely to want him to demonstrate more initiation of structure, a supervisor's subordinates evaluate him more highly when he exhibits more consideration. The effective supervisor must be able to resolve the incompatibility of supervisors' and subordinates' interests. As a man-in-the-middle he must initiate structure requiring more energy expended by his subordinates but often with more rewards for his superiors if he succeeds. At the same time, he must be seen as considerate by his subordinates.

Some foremen, as well as those at higher levels, deal with the demands from above for production and the demands from below for consideration by giving both, by doing a successful balancing act.[563] In fact, some companies like Bell Telephone of Pennsylvania cultivate a program of such balanced objectives in their department heads. But it is probably more common to identify completely with superiors and organizational demands, disparaging any concern for subordinates.[333] Intimacy with subordinates is reduced to avoid any sense of guilt over lack of consideration for them, or a compromise is achieved by being friendly, but only "off the job."[303]

Among foremen, who usually come up through the rank and file, this involves a gradual transfer of loyalty. Only 4 percent of those in one survey on the job as foremen less than two years identified themselves as part of management, while 61 percent working as foremen between two and five years and 64 percent of those who had been foremen longer identified themselves as part of management.[106] Foremen who cannot make this transfer of loyalty are more likely to feel frustrated and dissatisfied with their jobs, particularly where workers are unionized.[282] (Here, the new foreman has left an organized, powerful group and moved into an unorganized in-between level without the power and security of the rank and file and without the status, prestige, and full identity as a manager.) Many cannot ever transfer loyalty; they remain identified completely with their subordinates, probably failing to carry out some of their responsibilities to their organization.[303]

This need to play the role of harmonizer and compromiser may help explain the differences in self-perception among managers at different echelons in a company; specifically, between 172 first-line supervisors and those 291 executives above or 320 operatives below them. Table 5.2 shows how these first-line supervisors and upper level management differed significantly in response to whether each of 64 paired adjectives applied to themselves. Similar differences between the supervisors and line workers are shown in Table 5.3.

TABLE 5.2 ITEMS DIFFERENTIATING UPPER-LEVEL MANAGEMENT PERSONNEL AND FIRST-LEVEL SUPERVISORS*

First-Level Supervisors	Upper-Level Management Personnel
See themselves as:	See themselves as:
Planful	Resourceful
Deliberate	Sharp-witted
Calm	Sincere
Fair-minded	Thoughtful
Steady	Sociable
Responsible	Reliable
Civilized	Dignified
Self-controlled	Imaginative
Logical	Adaptable
Patient	Sympathetic
Honest	Generous
Do not see themselves as:	Do not see themselves as:
Moody	Affected
Stubborn	Cold
Conceited	Infantile
Stingy	Shallow
Touchy	Defensive
Dreamy	Dependent
Nervous	Intolerant
Careless	Foolish
Egotistical	Apathetic
Evasive	Despondent
Selfish	Weak
Self-centered	Rude
Disorderly	Rattle-brained
Fussy	Submissive
Opinionated	Pessimistic
Excitable	Sly
Impatient	Irresponsible

*From Porter, L. W., 1959, p. 184

Compared to their superiors the supervisors see themselves as more conservative and cautious rather than resourceful and flexible, and compared to their subordinates they see themselves as more careful and restrained than free and open.[530]

These men-in-the-middle are conforming to demands as illustrated by the 100 top executives who said that their company should hire ag-

TABLE 5.3   ITEMS DIFFERENTIATING FIRST-LEVEL SUPERVISORS
AND LINE WORKERS*

First-Level Supervisors	Line Workers
See themselves as:	See themselves as:
Energetic	Ambitious
Practical	Industrious
Deliberate	Sharp-witted
Clear-thinking	Efficient
Fair-minded	Thoughtful
Steady	Sociable
Modest	Pleasant
Responsible	Reliable
Logical	Adaptable
Do not see themselves as:	Do not see themselves as:
Dreamy	Dependent
Rude	Self-centered
Rattle-brained	Disorderly
Submissive	Fussy
Cynical	Aggressive

*From Porter, L. W., 1959, p. 185.

gressive, energetic applicants for management jobs. Yet the same executives said they personally wanted their own immediate subordinate to be tactful and emotionally controlled rather than "only bright."[219] Top executives are more likely to see themselves as capable, determined, industrious, sharp-witted, and enterprising, while middle managers are more likely to describe themselves as discreet, practical, planful, deliberate, calm, steady, modest, patient, and self-controlled.[533] To maintain both satisfactory relations with his boss as well as his subordinates, the man-in-the-middle evidently must play a cautious game described as "the fine art of executive decision-making which consists in not deciding questions that are not now pertinent, in not deciding prematurely, in not making decisions that cannot be made effective, and in not making decisions that others should make."[30]

It has been suggested that the supervisor, caught in the middle, must be a good actor, yet avoid the taint of hypocrisy. He must remain objective yet considerate, masking his own feelings.[670] Perhaps this accounts for the greater prevalence of ulcer symptoms among supervisors than among workers of a large Midwestern plant or for the increasing incidence of ulcers at successively higher management levels in a large Dutch company.[222]

Some men-in-the middle employ a variety of power tactics which they at least believe may do more good for themselves than for their organization. They avoid seeking advice when they actually need it. They form cliques to obtain support on issues rather than allowing the issues to be settled rationally. They never completely commit themselves to ideas, arguments, individuals, or groups. They withhold information and use it to serve their own purposes when useful to them. They compromise superficially without really accepting other points of view privately. When they find orders objectionable they do not try to get the orders rescinded but are slow to execute them. They exude confidence even when they make decisions in the face of considerable uncertainty. They always are the "boss" to their subordinates.[454] All of this requires artful acting and a willingness to lead a Machiavellian (and possibly ulcer-ridden) existence which may be a heavy price to pay for success. This is so particularly when the same person might be even more successful if he could achieve a more rational solution, merging self-interests with organizational objectives in which he could be "open," frank, and free to "level" with others, as required.

The man-in-the-middle who succeeds in solving the dilemma receives the accolade from both his superiors and subordinates. Of supervisors judged immediately promotable by their bosses, 75 percent were seen as "pulling for the company and the men" by their subordinates. On the other hand, among those supervisors judged questionable or unsatisfactory by their superiors, only 40 percent were seen by their subordinates as pulling for both the company and the men.[412]

Conflicting Channels of Communication

The supervisor is a member of a formal organization based on the patterns of formal relations between job occupants above and below him. He is also in an informal organization based on relations between persons regardless of the jobs they occupy. The informal organization is likely to diverge from the formal, particularly when formal upward channels of communication are "noisy" or blocked.[525] The man-in-the-middle is a central relay station, and the development of conflicting informal patterns may depend to a considerable degree on his performance. He must learn to accommodate and use the informal organization if a strong one is present. What he receives from superiors, subordinates, peers, and others will depend on how much attention he pays to each source of communications.

Differential Attention

Thirty-two executives indicated how much they consulted with their boss, peers, subordinates, outsiders, rulebooks, or only themselves when faced with various kinds of problems such as whether to participate, how to plan something, or how to assign rewards. No matter what the problem, some executives attend strongly to the rule books; others do not. Consistent differences also existed among these executives in how much they consulted with their boss, peers, subordinates, and themselves, but not persons outside their organization. On the other hand, the nature of the problem led to no consistent response differences.

In a laboratory simulation of the pressure confronting the man-in-the-middle, this differential attention was a function of the general orientation of subjects. When the boss threatens and subordinates are dissatisfied, self-oriented and interaction-oriented supervisors increase their communications to the boss. Task-oriented supervisors increase their communications to their presumed subordinates.[48]

Attention Depends on Evaluation. A supervisor's behavior and attention depends on what bases he is evaluated and who evaluates him. If foremen spend two weeks in a training program emphasizing the need for supervisors to be considerate of the welfare of their subordinates,

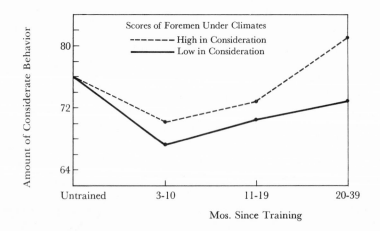

Figure 5.6: Comparison of Considerate Behavior by Foremen Who Return After Training to a Climate High or Low in Consideration. (After Fleishman, 1953, p. 216)

they will agree at the end of the two weeks that they ought to be more considerate. But three years later, back on the job, they only will behave this way if they believe their boss expects it of them.[211] Foremen returning to a climate (a boss) high in consideration are compared in Figure 5.6 with those returning to an inconsiderate boss.

Various other studies present similar conclusions. Foremen who changed more as a consequence of training in leadership received more encouragement from their superiors, felt more secure in their relations with their superiors, and perceived greater opportunity to try out new ideas on the job.[438] Supervisors in an insurance firm tended to model their own proneness to be coercive or permissive on whether their bosses were coercive or permissive.[357] Still another study corroborated the finding that supervisors conform to what they thought their boss expected of them.[330]

Who Evaluates?   But "if you try to please everybody, you may not please anybody." For there appears to be no correlation between the evaluations foremen receive from their subordinates and their superiors[65] although two superiors' evaluations tend to agree, and to a lesser extent the evaluations of two peers of supervisors show some agreement with each other and with superiors' evaluations.[629]

Above and beyond these considerations is the almost complete lack of agreement between what the supervisor thinks he does and what his subordinates say he does. Table 5.4 shows the glaring discrepancy by

TABLE 5.4   COMPARISON OF SUPERVISORS' DESCRIPTION OF THEIR BEHAVIOR WITH EMPLOYES' DESCRIPTION OF THEIR EXPERIENCE*

Asked of Supervisors: "How do you give recognition for good work done by employes in your work group?"		*Asked of Employes:* "How does your supervisor give recognition for good work done by the employes in your work group?"
Percentage of supervisors who say "very often":		*Percentage of employes who say "very often":*
Gives privileges	52	14
Gives more responsibility	48	10
Gives a pat on the back	82	13
Gives sincere and thorough praise	80	14
Trains for better jobs	65	9
Gives more interesting work	51	5

*After Likert, 1961, p. 91

comparing supervisors' descriptions of their own behavior with the experience reported by workers in the same utility company. For example, while 52 percent of the supervisors say that they give privileges very often, only 14 percent of the workers say they received such privileges.[410]

Importance of Immediacy. Most complicating of all is the probability that the evaluations to which a supervisor gears his own actions direct how he spends his time; and how he concentrates his efforts will depend on relatively immediate evaluations. Yet "ten years after an executive is discharged from his job, his associates may reflect that he was the best executive they ever had on that job."[599]

Situational Influences

While some kinds of behavior are reported or expected of leaders in all situations, many types are required only under specific circumstances.[622] According to one survey, in situations where the group has a high degree of control over its members, the leader is expected to dominate and actually does so; while in groups where members participate to a high degree, these expectations and reports of domination do not occur.[294] A study of transferred executives indicated that some behaviors of the transferee in the new situations such as his tendency to delegate authority, to spend time in public relations, to evaluate, read and answer mail, to read technical publications, and to spend time with outsiders, are characteristic of himself rather than the position. Other behaviors such as his amount of personal contact time, time spent with superiors, time spent in supervision, coordination, and writing reports are characteristic of the situation.[646]

The initiation and consideration of executives, their planning, controlling, and deciding, may be restrained or influenced by government agencies, labor union leaders or arbitrators, trade association rules, clients with contracts, sellers and buyers of the firm's products, customs, traditions, and sanctions of society.[666] Any or all of these may become matters of company policy. For some supervisors formal statements in rule books about what is expected of them become paramount in their resolution of conflicting interests.[48] These same men are likely to be uncomfortable in the absence of guiding rules. This intolerance for uncertainty or the need to take responsibility for decisions when conflicts arise among self, boss, subordinates, peers, and outsiders may be a manifestation of an authoritarian personality.

Example. Illustrative of such situational influences was the case of two medium-sized companies which differed in policies. Authoritarian policies predominated in one company. It was interested only in profits; all else was secondary. Subordinates had to understand what was expected of them. Personal qualities of leadership were emphasized. There was no joint participation in decisions, and all company information was restricted to management except where it clearly applied to an employe's job. The second company had a democratic focus and was concerned about employe and public welfare as well as profits. Permissive leadership was stressed as a matter of policy. There was joint participation and a maximum effort to inform employes about company matters. Table 5.5 shows how the supervisors of the two companies differed in their attitudes toward consideration and toward initiation. Note the complete reversal of emphasis which was statistically significant. Supervisors under democratic policies favor consideration; supervisors under authoritarian policies favor initiation. Of course, we do not know whether policies influenced a supervisor to be one way or another after he was selected, of if policies influenced the selection of only those who would behave in a manner consistent with policy. But, in either case, how the supervisor views his job and what he does is strongly associated with company policy.[637]

Position and Problems. Whether a supervisor is at the first, second, or higher level in the firm, and whether he is in a line or staff position makes considerable difference in the problems with which he is most concerned. When 211 such supervisors were asked to post and select problems for discussion in 26 discussion groups, 58.8 percent of first-line supervision, 35.3 percent of middle management, and only 5.9

TABLE 5.5 RELATION BETWEEN COMPANY POLICY
AND SUPERVISORY ATTITUDES*

	Company Has Authoritarian Policies N = 58	Company Has Democratic Policies N = 28
Attitude of Supervisors Toward—		
Initiating structure	56.4	50.1
Consideration	52.6	54.5

*After Stanton, 1960

percent of those in staff positions wanted to talk about the motivation of
subordinates to follow instructions, to meet deadlines, or to maintain
quality and quantity of production. On the other hand, 40.9 percent of
staff supervisors were concerned about dealing with resistance to
change, a concern of 36.4 percent of middle managers and only 22.7
percent of first-line supervisors. While half of the middle managers
wanted to discuss deficiences in their superiors, only a quarter of the
first-line and staff supervisors were willing to focus on this issue. Most
salient for the first-line supervisor were disciplinary problems and problems of promoting, rating, and classifying employes, while middle managers felt most ready to talk about problems of selecting, orienting, and
training employes. For the staff, issues of identifying problems, communicating solutions, and maintaining perspectives were most important.[628] It is interesting to note that regardless of position, most of the
problems seen as worthy of discussion by these supervisors and managers involved dealing effectively with other persons in the organization.
This concern for people conforms to what we know about which abilities
are required for effective supervision.

THE ABILITY TO SUPERVISE

A review of over 100 studies of leadership concluded:

> The average person who occupies a position of leadership exceeds the
> average member of his group in the following respects: (1) intelligence, alertness,
> verbal facility, originality, and judgment; (2) scholarship; . . . (4) knowing how
> to get things done; . . . (6) alertness to, and insight into, situations.[644]

The supervisor needs to know what to expect from each member of
his group and realize his own abilities and limitations. However, it
should be pointed out that leaders should not be too much higher than
the led in these various abilities,[341] for communications between the
leader and the led might be subject to confusion; the supervisor might
not appreciate lack of understanding of his subordinates; the subordinates might develop defensive reactions to repress feelings of inferiority
in the face of the leader which disturbed the interpersonal relationships,
and so forth.

In the post-Sputnik era, many big business recruiters of management trainees overreacted from their previous policies of hiring "all-
around" graduates with "gentlemanly C averages" to concentrating now
on the top scholars of the class. Both concentrations seem unwarranted
as there are needs for both brilliant as well as less-than-brilliant execu-

tives in the large firm. In the same way, the ability must be relevant to the task. Highly specialized engineers are not the best office supervisors; accountants, limited only to a traditional business education, are not likely to succeed as production managers.

Knowledge from Position

Knowledge and ability will lead to successful leadership behavior regardless of whether the knowledge is an attribute of a person or is due solely to his position. For example, one communications experiment found that the person most influential in a communication system was the one placed in a position most central to the system, providing him with the easiest access to receiving and sending information.[359] Anyone who is a company president obtains much of his ability to influence others in the firm from the special information he receives as a consequence of his position.

Social Ability

The successful leader demonstrates certain social skills. He can coordinate the different jobs of his group; he explains why he does things while he makes rules and regulations clear. He treats every member alike yet takes account of each as an individual. When he makes decisions it is for the group, not for the individual. An extremely important aspect of leadership is the ability to delegate authority wisely.[294]

Ability and Persuasiveness

The effort to shift supervisors from authoritarian, coercive, domineering behavior to democratic, permissive, considerate action has distracted attention from the efficacy of persuasion. Willingness to attempt to influence others is still important. For example, if two members of a group both have ideas that will produce superior solutions to the problem faced by a group, it is the more talkative one who will be more influential in getting the idea accepted.[557] A supervisor with ability to help solve the problems faced by his group can guide them to the correct solutions. If his subordinates agree that he has the best ideas on the subject, they may both publicly and privately accept his opinions. But the supervisor must be alert to whether his ideas are accepted only publicly yet not privately and only because of his power over the subordinates rather than because of the quality of the ideas. He also must recognize that if his promotion of his own point of view reduces opportunities for subordinates to be heard, then he is likely to be seen as initiating too much. Perhaps, the supervisor needs to become a member of his group, no more, but no less. That is, in the desire to be permissive some supervisors needlessly inhibit their own contributions to their group, believing that any persuasive efforts on their part will be seen as an attempt to dominate the group. But up to some point, persuasive efforts by the supervisor may be accepted for what they are worth, with the supervisor gaining, not losing, esteem in the eyes of his subordinates. Thus air crews were more satisfied with decisions to mock problems when the crew leader stated his opinion after the group had discussed the issue than when he never revealed his own opinion but only guided the discussion.[763] Moreover, somewhat better decisions emerge when the discussion leader breaks a problem into parts and sees that these are discussed separately than when he poses the problem and remains permissive thereafter.[431]

Persuasion has always been regarded as the most legitimate form of influence in our society, the favored method for bringing about everything from legal change to economic exchange. It still has an important place in the relations between supervisors and subordinates.

A Comparative Experiment. To test this point, 12 business students simulated supervisors who primarily use persuasion. They each dealt with three assigned subordinates by stating their decisions and why they were thought to be the correct one. Twelve other students simulated supervisors who use coercive methods, stating "this is how the decisions ought to be since this is the way I want them"; and 12 others were permissive, collaborating with their subordinates in reaching the decisions. Each of the 36 subordinates met with all three supervisors, but the order of the meeting was counterbalanced so that some met one kind of supervisor first, another kind second, and so on, while other subordinates met types of supervisors in a reverse order.

Table 5.6 shows how the subordinates felt about the three supervisors with whom they met. Clearly they disliked being coerced, but except for the fact that they felt slightly less responsibility for the decisions reached by supervisory persuasion (and therefore might be less willing to execute the decisions) they felt equally satisfied with their persuasive and permissive supervisors and the quality of the decisions reached.

That persuasiveness may be as adequate as permissiveness was

TABLE 5.6   COMPARISON OF REACTIONS OF 36 "SUBORDINATES"
TO COERCIVE, PERSUASIVE, AND PERMISSIVE LEADERSHIP

	Reactions to:		
	Coercive Leadership	Persuasive Leadership	Permissive Leadership
How satisfied were you with the decisions your team reached?	4.8	7.6	7.9*
How much responsibility did you feel for the decision?	3.7	6.4	6.9
How much would you prefer to be with your partner again, if you had to repeat the same task?	4.3	6.7	7.2
How much did you influence the decision?	3.7	6.4	7.0

*9 = Completely satisfied; 1 = Completely dissatisfied.

demonstrated also when the leader of adult women's discussion groups deliberately was persuasive or permissive. When persuasive, the leader talked 53 percent of the total time, gave much opinion, interpretation, and related information about a film on mental hygiene. Afterwards, the leader was described by the discussants as persuasive as well as interesting, frank, satisfying, purposeful, enlightening, and industrious. When deliberately permissive, the leader talked 17 percent of the time, expressed agreements, reflected and rephrased statements, and asked questions. Seen as permissive, the leader now was described as open-minded, reserved, cautious, reasonable, practical, and modest. Both persuasive and permissive leadership were accepted, but with different evaluations.[507]

Ability and Esteem

Whether a supervisor can persuade his subordinates may depend more on whether they perceive that he is able to help solve the problems facing them. Thus, military field studies concluded that the leader who is seen by his men as able to satisfy the needs of his men by successfully handling their day-to-day common problems develops a group which works harder and better for him.[257]

This value which is attributed to a supervisor is his *esteem*, his worth as a person regardless of his position in the organization. The supervisor who actually has more ability is likely to be more esteemed, but he may be esteemed for other reasons. Another employe may esteem him because he is judged similar to the employe. Since the typical worker tends to esteem himself positively, if he judges a supervisor as similar to himself in attitudes, interests, and abilities, he will tend to esteem the supervisor. The supervisor may be esteemed as a consequence of stimulus generalization—the tendency to react in the same way to new but similar stimuli as to old ones. He may be seen as looking or acting like another supervisor who was truly an able and esteemed figure.[41]

When the superior lacks esteem, he in turn is likely to be more influenced and conforming, particularly in ambiguous circumstances.[291]

Esteem and Influence. How much one is esteemed by his organizational associates correlates as high as .50 with how much influence he can exert among them. Such results have been reported for 168 administrator trainees, 84 shipyard foremen, 123 foreign-service personnel, and 202 civil-service administrators.[36]

There is a practical application of the relation between esteem and influence for a good predictor of the subsequent success of a man promoted to supervisor or executive is what his peers or buddies think of him before he is promoted.

Self-Esteem and Influence. Whether one will even attempt to persuade others will depend on his own estimate of whether he has something to contribute as well as whether he actually does have the required competence. Laboratory experiments indicate that subjects are more likely to attempt to lead others if they have exclusive possession of expert knowledge relevant to the solution of the tasks on which they are working with others. They are also more likely to attempt leadership if they feel esteemed or personally accepted by the others, they are concerned about doing well on the task, and they expect that the task solution will be achieved if their suggestions are followed.[295]

POWER TO COERCE

Status and Influence

A supervisor has options as to how he will influence his subordinates. Instead of trying to persuade them, he may depend on his *status*—the importance of the position he occupies in the firm—to influence his subordinates. Evidence of the degree to which his status makes it possible for a supervisor to influence his subordinates was found by placing 131 management personnel from different echelons in an oil refinery in one-hour initially leaderless discussions. The correlation was .88 between rank and tendency to be rated influential by impartial observers.[50] The correlation was higher if the discussion concerned company matters and somewhat lower if the discussion was not about the company.[49]

Figure 5.7 shows unpublished data from a management training laboratory further demonstrating the impact of status on influence. During the first week of training, 36 managers and supervisors met in nine two-hour sessions away from the plant and rated each other's influence over each session. There was no appointed chairman, and no man was in a discussion group with his own immediate boss, yet status in the company determined one's influence. The four echelons of management represented were influential in direct proportion to their status back at the plant. After the fifth session, the 36 participants were informed about how status had determined influence to stress their overattention to status. It was pointed out that the lower status foremen were needlessly inhibiting their own potential contributions. The ideas of the high status department heads were being accepted uncritically not nec-

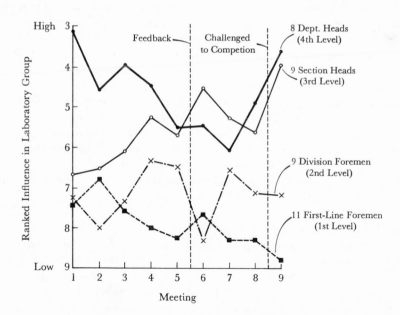

Figure 5.7: How Management Level in a Company Affects Influence in a Laboratory Away from the Company. (See Also Figure 9.1.)

essarily because of the worth of the ideas, but because of the source. At the same time, the department heads were made aware of how influential they were even when they, themselves, were not even trying to persuade their colleagues of lower status. As Figure 5.6 shows, this feedback succeeded in temporarily reducing status effects somewhat although men from the upper two echelons were still seen as more influential than those from the lower echelons. And later in the week when a specific challenge of group competition was initiated by the staff, the discussants responded by restoring the status hierarchy with which they had begun.

Status, Power and Influence

Status results in influence because of the *power* a higher status person has over a lower one. The superior can reward the subordinate for compliance with his proposals—or he can punish the underling for failure to comply with the proposals. The supervisor can grant or deny important rewards to his subordinates through his responsibility for recommending them to higher-ups for pay raises and promotion. Indeed, if such recommendations carry no weight "upstairs," the supervisor loses much of his real power to reward or punish. Subordinates may only "pay lip-service" to such a powerless superior stripped of all but his legitimacy and his symbols of his office. Thus, supervisors in an electric utility company who attempted leadership failed to obtain changes in their subordinates if they, the supervisors, had no influence "upstairs," while supervisors with such power were much more likely to succeed in influencing their subordinates.[518]

If a worker accepts the suggestion of his supervisor to avoid punishment or in hope of a reward rather than because of the intrinsic merit of the suggestion, he is publicly accepting an idea which he privately rejects. He is being coerced. Such coerciveness has both functional and dysfunctional aspects.

Functional Aspects of Status as a Source of Influence. If rapid decisions must be made, as in emergency situations, or if groups are frequently changing or unstable, strongly authoritative direction may be preferred by subordinates.[294] Survival experiences of 200 groups under conditions of isolation and stress showed that the power exercised by the formal leader, the man with highest rank, was one of the most important forces in holding the group together. When this power was not exercised, panic, disorganization, loss of life, and other unfavorable conditions resulted. When the official leader failed to exercise his power and to organize the group to react to the stress, there was an overly long period of shock and too much lag in compensation and adaption of the group to the new situation.[683]

Relying on status to influence is functional when the status differences are legitimate. For example, if a person of higher status is seen to have more knowledge and ability as a consequence of his office, his influence is accepted without resistance. His communications downward are regarded as authoritative and authentic. Men of very unequal abilities and importance can work together willingly for long periods.[31] Orders and commands from above are tolerated in the formal organization where they would be rejected elsewhere.[177]

Coercion shades into persuasion. A subordinate reacts to legitimate orders by acknowledging, "I publicly agree and while privately I have my reservations about the authoritative order, I will accept it privately since (a) it is expected of me; (b) the higher authority must know what it is doing; (c) I relieve myself of any responsibility for the decision by carrying out orders from above; (d) I must cooperate if I and my superior are to continue to work effectively together; (e) I achieve security by following orders; or (f) the orders provide me with a way of coping with a situation which I do not have the time or ability to handle by myself."

A Demonstration of the Legitimate Use of Authority.   On a holiday weekend between sessions of a management training laboratory, 18 wives of the management personnel each met for 10 minutes with one of the managers (not with their respective husbands) to reach decisions about the basic operating efficiency of households. Then they each met with a different manager to reach comparable decisions about the basic operating efficiency of companies. The managers who acted as their supervisors to reach decisions either were deliberately coercive or permissive; that is, they dominated the decision-making process, or they shared equal responsibility for the decision with the wives. Approximately one-fourth of the wives were paired first with coercive supervisors, then with permissive ones for the 10-minute interactions. Another one-fourth received the reverse treatment. These all first discussed household matters, then company matters. The remaining half of the wives' group were paired to discuss company matters first and to reach decisions about household matters during the second 10-minute pairing, again with either coercive supervisors first and permissive ones second, or the reverse. Table 5.7 shows the feelings of the wives after working with coercive and permissive supervisors to reach decisions about household or company efficiency. Note that the wives did not react negatively when

TABLE 5.7   REACTIONS OF 18 WIVES TO PERMISSIVE AND COERCIVE
SUPERVISION BY MANAGEMENT PERSONNEL PLAYING ROLES AS
SUPERVISORS IN DECISION-MAKING ABOUT HOUSEHOLD
EFFICIENCY AND ABOUT COMPANY EFFICIENCY
(9 = HIGH; 1 = LOW)

| | Decisions Made About | | | |
| | Household | | Company | |
Wives' Reactions	*Coercive Supervisor*	*Permissive Supervisor*	*Coercive Supervisor*	*Permissive Supervisor*
Satisfaction with experience	4.7	7.7	6.7	8.7
Hostility toward supervisor	3.3	0.3	1.0	0.7
Felt responsibility for activity	6.3	6.5	4.7	6.7

supervisors dominated the decision-making process when the problem concerned company issues. However they were quite put out when men attempted to dominate the discussion about household operating efficiency. In the first instance, when discussing the company, the superior position of the supervisor in the pair was legitimate; in the second, when discussing households, it was not. Coerciveness reduced satisfaction with the experience much more for the wives treated coercively than permissively when discussing household affairs than when reaching decisions about company efficiency. Much more hostility was generated towards the supervisor who was coercive when the talk was about household matters than when considering company issues. When the matters concerned household affairs the wives felt equally responsible for the activity whether the supervisor was coercive or permissive. In other words, they refused to accord the supervisor a legitimate role when the discussion was about household affairs, consequently when such a supervisor attempted coercion to reach decisions, they were far more hostile towards him.

When legitimacy of supervision is brought about by placing in office those elected to it, again, workers are more likely to accept behavior prescribed for them by the elected supervisor. Here they both publicly and privately accept the suggestions of such a supervisor.[545] We infer that when legitimacy comes about through election, the supervisor now has esteem—value as a person regardless of his office—to persuade his subordinates.

Dysfunctional Aspects of Status as a Source of Influence: The Inadequacies of Using the Power to Punish.   To examine the effects of the supervisor who obtains compliance by using his power to punish, paid subjects worked at a simple task of sorting IBM cards according to the total number of holes they contained, purportedly a real assignment, as part of a research project. The supervisor was presented as someone associated with the research project who needed the cards counted. Subjects were fined for failure to maintain speed and accuracy of performance up to standard. In comparison to subjects rewarded extra when they reached and maintained the standard, subjects punished by fines for failure to do so were more likely to show signs of resistance to maintaining production. After four working periods had occurred, punishment for failure became deleterious to speed and accuracy. It was felt to be a less attractive situation in which to work. There was a greater desire of subjects to leave the experiment. They also were more likely to want to do something else and to make suggestions for changing the work situation. They also showed greater feelings of aggression, liked their supervisor less, and were less likely to accept the supervisor as competent to evaluate their work when they were fined for failure to maintain standards rather than rewarded for maintaining standards.[221]

Other comparable experiments demonstrated similar results finding that punitive supervision resulted in increased worker tension and lower productivity.[160]

Overconformity.   In a similar experiment, levying fines when subjects failed to conform against their will to demands of supervisors led subjects to overconform to the suggestions of their supervisors. Such overconformity in minute detail and beyond orders by some of the subjects "recalled the behavior of the IWW workers who were reputed to systematically disrupt operations of factories" by similar techniques.[545, p.96]

Hostility or Withdrawal.   Using one's authority to levy penalties or to threaten workers in an effort to cajole them into productivity may produce various other side effects despite the outward conformity or overconformity to supervisory demands. Workers may react hostilely by making deliberate mistakes, overdoing orders, sabotaging, or striking as a consequence of the punitive supervision of the "hardboiled autocrat." Or they may withdraw from work by arriving late, being absent, quitting, or by showing apathy and indifference to the job itself. Thus, in seven British factories, departments with punitive foremen were more likely to be low in productivity and high in absenteeism and labor turnover.[12]

Spread of Negative Affect.   Punitive supervision produces a spread of negative affect. Twenty-four groups, each containing four subjects, had to follow elaborate blueprints to assemble models of molecules of pegs, springs, and various colored balls. In this complex task, they were subjected to either punitive or nonpunitive supervision as well as to close or general supervision. Punitive and close supervision, in contrast to nonpunitive and general supervision, tended to increase subjects' feelings of aggression towards their co-workers, as well as toward their supervisor, significantly lowering productivity.[155]

Even more insidious effects of punishment follow. Not only does the worker show more aggression toward his fellow workers as well as his supervisor when subjected to a punitive supervisor, he also tends to build up mistrust towards outsiders. When laboratory subjects were made fearful through electric shock, they even tended to see more maliciousness in photographed faces presented to them.[202]

A chain of events is set off. A man who is treated punitively by his supervisor will respond by being punitive to those below him in the hierarchy. Thus students who were subjected to insult and failure were more responsive to the suggestion that they now be punitive towards others.[725]

Recognition of Dysfunctionality of Punishment. Even when disciplinary rules call for punishment, a majority of foremen appear to avoid using it, cognizant of its inadequacies as means of controlling workers. When 172 groups of foremen played roles in the case of a worker who had violated a no-smoking rule and the rule called for a three-day layoff of the worker, only 35 percent of the foremen applied the three-day penalty. Fifty-two percent of the foremen were more lenient, either giving only one or two days' layoff, or forgiving the worker with a warning, reprimand, or entry into his personnel record, or consulting with other workers as arbitrators. Punitive solutions were less satisfying to all participants — those acting as foremen or workers — in the situation. Foremen who played the part of workers said they would have been more likely to reduce their future production as a consequence of their punishment. They also felt they would have been more inclined to file a grievance.[428]

Conditions Affecting Reactions to Supervisory Punitiveness. How workers will respond to coercion also will depend on other factors. A superior who arbitrarily violates the expectations of his subordinates would be downgraded particularly if his arbitrary behavior were countermanded by higher authority. On the other hand, if he corrected his own arbitrary violation and reformed as a consequence of the requests of his subordinates, he might be likely to increase in favor with his subordinates.[315]

The negative consequences of arbitrary behavior by the superior depends upon a number of other factors. Subject only to the veto power of a superior, 108 experimental subjects used models to design a city. Work was interrupted twice by the arbitrary, powerful superior. Some of the subjects were permitted to meet privately without the supervisor to discuss the situation. Others were not. Subjects who met privately were more aggressive, hostile, and independent of the supervisor than those who did not meet. The latter tended to be somewhat more positive in their evaluation of the power figure and more likely to cooperate overtly with him. Thus, when we gain the opportunity to deal as a group with coercive supervisors, and we can develop some sense of countervailing power, we can respond more hostilely to such supervision. Presumably workers without such opportunity to gain group support for their feelings either bottle them up or dissipate them in some other way.[650] Thus while all students frustrated by the "illegitimate" refusal of their teacher to repeat his instructions showed a loss of span of attention, a decrement in learning, and a rigidity in solving a test problem, those most severely affected by the arbitrary coerciveness of the teacher were students without any peer support who were led to believe that all fellow students fully accepted the teacher's behavior.[247]

A Summary Description.   The supervisor who uses his power primarily to punish in order to influence his subordinates reveals a pattern of attitudes and behavior in himself and his subordinates as follows:

> [He believes he] must constantly check up on everyone to keep up production. He gives the orders and the employes carry them out. He believes that the only way to get conscientious performance is to expect and secure discipline and immediate acceptance of all orders. He is careful not to spoil the employe with too much praise, believing that because the employe is paid to work he needs nothing else. It is the employe's place to carry out directions, not to question or always understand them. This supervisor is usually very conscious of his position and authority and believes that employes cannot be trusted very long on their own initiative.
>
> There is some submission to the supervisor's authority, but resentment and incipient revolt underneath (of which the supervisor probably is not aware); no one assumes more responsibility than he is forced to take; and buck-passing is a common pattern of behavior. Employes display irritability and unwillingness to cooperate with each other, and there is considerable backbiting and disparagement of the work of others. Only a fair level of production is maintained, and the work slips markedly whenever the supervisor is not present.[79]

Dysfunctional Aspects of Status as a Source of Influence: The Inadequacies of Using the Power to Reward.   We have seen that subjects given rewards for meeting production standards are most satisfied and more productive than those punished for failure to meet standards set by their supervisor. However supervisors who rely primarily on their power to grant or deny rewards to influence and control their workers produce work groups which are less effective than supervisors who use their power to foster participation and shared decisions.

A supervisor who depends mainly on his power to reward has been described as "a benevolent autocrat" who would be startled to be told that he was autocratic:

> . . . [for] he is interested in his employes, wants to see them happy, praises them as much as he criticizes them, is seldom harsh or severe, and likes to think that he is developing a happy-family group. He urges employes to bring their problems to him and is interested in all the details of their work. Actually, he trades benevolence for loyalty. The crux of his autocracy lies in the technique by which he secures dependence upon himself. He says, with a pat on the back, "That's the way I like it . . . I am glad you did it that way . . . That's the way I want it done;" or "That isn't the way I told you to do it . . . you are not doing it the way I want it." In this way he dominates employes by making himself the source of all standards of production. Any failure to live up to these standards he receives with hurt surprise and intense anger as personal disloyalty to him.
>
> His employes are fairly happy in their work, and most of them like the supervisor. Those who see through him however, dislike him intensely.
> . . . No one shows initiative without first ascertaining the reactions of the supervisor, and there is a definite reluctance to accept further responsibility. . . . The group is characterized by submissiveness and lack of individual development. . . . Because of their desire to meet the supervisor's expectation, productivity is fairly high as long as he is on hand to give directions.[79]

PERMISSIVE LEADERSHIP

A supervisor can use his ability and knowledge to persuade his subordinates; he can use his power to coerce them. However he may employ his authority to permit his subordinates to share in the decisions with him. Interested in avoiding the conflicts produced by coercion, the permissive supervisor uses his power to set the boundaries within which his group will work towards some outcome or decision. He learns when to use his power and when to avoid using it.

As long as the group continues to progress within the general boundaries the supervisor has set, he may contribute his own knowledge to the solution of the problems facing the group primarily as a resource person or as merely another member of the group whose ideas are to be weighted about the same as any other members' opinions. He permits the alternatives to the solution to a problem facing his group to be explored, imposing only those restrictions which keep his group from straying too far afield. He may use his power to solicit increased contributions from some members and reduction in the total input by others.

Permissiveness Promotes Acceptance

By sharing with his subordinates the power to make decisions affecting all concerned, the permissive supervisor increases greatly the acceptance of those decisions by those who must execute them. By promoting participation in the decision-making process, setting conditions for exploration, selecting and evaluating alternatives, and working toward a consensual approach to problem solving, the permissive superior is able to achieve from his subordinates a commitment to the solutions for the problem and a willingness to carry out the decisions involved. Thus foremen who call their men in to discuss decisions have subordinates who report themselves to be more satisfied with their foremen. Moreover, workers will tend to enter or withdraw psychologically from groups as a function of their ability to make decisions in the respective groups.[355] Workers who are involved in decision making by their foremen but not their shop stewards tend to share management values and goals; workers who are involved in decisions by their stewards but not their foremen tend to share union goals and standards.[330] Again, the merit-rating behavior of one group of foremen was significantly improved by permitting them to discuss and make decisions about more realistic ways of evaluating others. A control group of foremen were lectured on the subject in an attempt to persuade them to modify their behavior, but only the discussion group actually modified rating procedures significantly more in desired directions.[403]

Permissiveness Provides Opportunity
to Participate and to Decide

The permissive supervisor fosters both participation and opportunity to make decisions by considering matters with all of his subordinates as a group. But this creates conditions allowing each subordinate to observe how everyone else in the group feels about a matter under consideration. Such conditions reduce the individual's resistance to suggestions and change of opinion. Students were found much more likely to volunteer to serve as experimental subjects if they perceived that almost all other members of their class volunteered. In this mass audience situation, the observation of near-consensus and the opportunity to make public decisions increased volunteering more than did opportunity for discussion.[62] In a more tightly controlled experiment, ten groups of five subjects each were permitted to discuss the appropriate rank ordering of the size of cities after first making private judgments.

Ten groups were not permitted discussion after their first private judgments. Half the groups permitted discussions (or five groups) were asked to make group decisions; the other half were not. In the groups not permitted discussion, secret ballots about the appropriate ranks were collected from each individual, and in half of the groups the results of the balloting were announced while in half the groups, the results remained secret. Then, regardless of treatment, all subjects made a second set of private judgments. The increased correlation among members' judgments on the second set compared to the correlation of judgments on the first set provided a measure of the group's *coalescence*. Table 5.8 shows the average coalescence achieved under each of the conditions for the 100 subjects working together on ten problems. Maximum increase in agreement occurred when both decision and discussion were permitted. Decision alone and discussion alone both contributed to coalescence. In the absence of either, there was no change at all.[520]

In a field study to contrast the effects of decision and participation, employes had an opportunity to set the goals and standards of production or merely to talk about them. Over five or six weeks, five order checkers discussed their work while five mail openers set group goals. In the same way, six swatchers discussed their piece rates while six other swatchers set group goals. As seen in Table 5.9, again, as in an earlier

TABLE 5.8   MEAN COALESCENCE AS A FUNCTION OF
DISCUSSION AND/OR DECISION*

	Discussion Permitted	No Discussion Permitted
Decision permitted	.38	.23
No decision permitted	.30	−.01

*After Pennington, Harvey, & Bass, 1958

TABLE 5.9   TABULATION OF GOALS SET AND ATTAINED*

Week	5 Mail Openers Group B		6 Swatchers Group D	
	Set	Attained	Set	Attained
1	55	57.3	250	286.2
2	55	56.6	290	246.6
3	60	58.3	290	260.4
4	60	55.1	275	254.3
5	60	53.2	260	242.9

*From Lawrence & Smith, 1955

study at the Harwood Manufacturing Company, workers set goals higher than they could attain. Goal setting both by the office workers who opened mail and goal setting by the swatchers raised productivity during all five or six weeks in comparison to their performance before the experiment was begun. On the other hand, discussion alone had mixed effects.

Figure 5.8 displays the changes in production during the five or six experimental groups for discussion groups and for groups who set goals in comparison to their productivity prior to the introduction of the experimental conditions. Goal setting had more marked and consistent effects than did discussion.

There was no difference in the attitudes of the workers towards both experimental treatments. Seventy-three percent felt the meeting time was well spent, 69 percent felt they learned something new, and 64 percent wanted to continue to meet in the same manner, whether continuing discussions or continuing goal setting.[385]

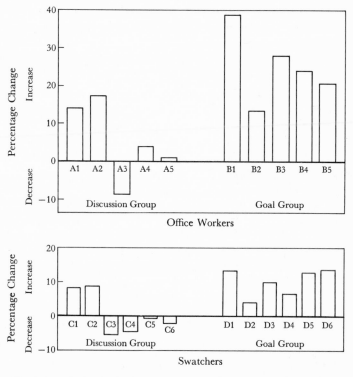

Figure 5.8: Individual Percentage Increase or Decrease in Productivity During Experimental Period Compared to Control
Period. (After Lawrence & Smith, 1955, p. 335)

Permissiveness Provides a Feeling of Freedom to Participate and Decide.
The feeling that a subordinate has the opportunity to participate and
to influence decisions affecting him seems more important than the
amount he actually participates in the decisions. When groups of 300 or
400 graduate students discussed how grade credits would be distributed,
their satisfaction with the decisions reached were unrelated to the number of points they personally received nor to the degree to which they
personally participated in the decisions. On the other hand, their satisfaction was strongly associated with how much opportunity they felt they
had to participate and to influence the decisions.[307]

Figure 5.9 suggests that in some companies at least, the supervisor
who is permissive enough to hold frequent group meetings with his
subordinates is judged more promotable by his superiors than supervisors who hold group meetings with their subordinates less frequently,
permitting less participation.[412]

But participation without much felt opportunity to influence decisions may have only minor utility at best, perhaps serving only to
ventilate feelings. Figure 5.10 shows that whether workers feel their
supervisor is good in dealing with them depends much more on whether

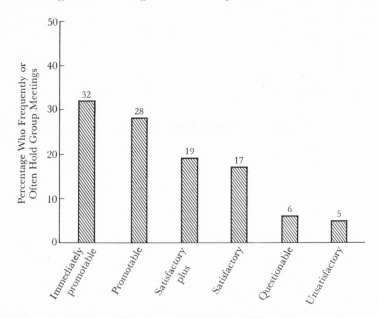

Management's Evaluation of Supervisor

*Figure 5.9: Relationship Between Management's Evaluation of
Supervisor and Frequency With Which He Holds Group Meetings.
(After Likert, 1961, p. 27)*

Of the workers in work groups where the men feel that the supervisor likes to get their ideas and tries to do something about the ideas, the percentage who feel the supervisor is good in dealing with people is:

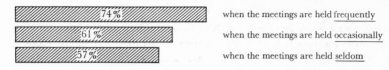

74%	when the meetings are held <u>frequently</u>
61%	when the meetings are held <u>occasionally</u>
57%	when the meetings are held <u>seldom</u>

But of the workers in work groups where the men feel that the supervisor is <u>not</u> interested in their ideas, that it is just talk, and that they don't really get a hearing for their ideas, the percentage who feel the supervisor is good in dealing with people is:

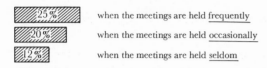

25%	when the meetings are held <u>frequently</u>
20%	when the meetings are held <u>occasionally</u>
12%	when the meetings are held <u>seldom</u>

Of the workers in work groups where <u>no meetings</u> are held:

39%	feel their supervisor is good in dealing with people

Figure 5.10: The Proportion of Workers Who Feel That Their Supervisor Is Good at Dealing With People as Affected by the Frequency of the Supervisor's Use of Work-Group Meetings and His Use of Ideas Which Emerge in the Meetings. (From Likert, 1961, p. 28)

they believe him interested in their ideas than on the frequency with which he meets them, although the frequency is of some importance. At the extremes, 74 percent of those who meet with their supervisors frequently and who feel their ideas carry weight believe their supervisor is good in dealing with people, while only 12 percent who meet seldom and feel their own ideas do not count believe their supervisor is good in his dealings with them.[412]

Simply because an executive assembles his subordinates frequently for meetings does not mean he is demonstrating permissive leadership; executives often use conferences to "sell" their own solutions as well as to aid in problem solving, assuring colleagues' acceptance of their solutions, and explaining their own preferences.[263] Often executives call meetings with subordinates to hold a one-way conversation with them. The executives do all the talking; the subordinates are supposed to be listening. These executives see meetings as a way to transmit information and to make announcements rather than as an opportunity for sharing information and opinions or for reaching decisions.

Permissiveness Implies Willingness to Accept Subordinates' Proposals. The feeling of freedom to influence the course of events is enhanced by a supervisor who is willing to comply with the requests of his group when such requests are appropriate. When one leader deliberately complied with the requests of his subordinates and another did not, it was found that subordinates increased their evaluation of the competence of the supervisor who complied with their requests and also felt more secure with him. Most important, their productivity was significantly increased as a consequence of working under a leader who complied with their requests. The reverse was true under the leader who failed to comply. He was downgraded for his failure.[159]

Permissiveness Implies General Rather Than Close Supervision

By avoiding supervising too closely, the permissive leader maintains feelings of freedom among his subordinates. And in turn this affects how he feels towards his subordinates.

Close Supervision and Mistrust. In a laboratory experiment, two "subordinates" were monitored by a subject who served as the laboratory "supervisor." High output was required on a dull task. One of the subordinates was monitored closely; the other was checked very little. Both subordinates performed equally well, but the attitude of the supervisor towards the two subordinates was quite different as a consequence of how he had to supervise them. The supervisor following orders to monitor a subordinate closely felt the subordinate was less to be trusted, was less dependable, and was complying with the supervisor's request because he was being watched. On the other hand, the supervisor felt that the subordinate he had been asked to check very little was complying because "he is a nice guy" or he "wants to."

Mistrust feeds on itself. If a supervisor feels compelled to supervise a subordinate closely, he increases his belief in the need for close supervision of that same subordinate. At the same time, if conditions are permissive and the subordinate does his work equally well, then the supervisor increases his belief in the trustworthiness of the subordinate, and presumably he is able to become even more permissive in his dealings with the subordinate.[652]

Close Supervision and Productivity. According to a similar laboratory experiment, tension is lower in workers and productivity higher under general rather than close supervision.[16]

A real premium from general rather than close supervision is the extent to which *partial reinforcement* effects can keep workers at their task in the absence of the supervisor. Experiments suggest that the learner who is checked as correct or incorrect after each trial in the learning process will extinguish or forget more quickly what he has learned, if the correction suddenly ceases, than the learner who has been corrected intermittently. Some schedule of partial reinforcement is most efficacious. This fits with the observation that the permissive, general, supervisor can be absent from his work group with less deleterious effects on the productivity of the group than the close supervisor. When the close supervisor leaves, one is likely to see an increase in fooling around, wandering off the job, and horseplay among the workers.[79]

Permissiveness Promotes Productivity

In addition to fostering acceptance, agreement, change, satisfaction, and trust, permissive supervision in many circumstances seems to contribute to the quality and quantity of output by subordinates. Work groups were more productive among those first-line supervisors in an insurance company who encouraged their workers to participate in decisions, were more permissive in their dealings with them, and supervised them less closely.[661] Again, 975 delivery men at 27 parcel delivery stations throughout the United States rated the extent their opinions were asked for by their boss and the ease they felt in getting their ideas across to the boss. The ease and freedom they felt in communicating with their superiors at a station correlated between .39 and .48 with the average deliveries the men completed daily relative to the standard time allotted for completion. Employes also felt more influential and more likely to be supported by their boss at the more productive stations.[324] And as already noted, workers permitted to set goals, whether in office or factory operations, significantly raised their productivity although mere opportunity to discuss work had less effect on performance.[386]

Permission Not License

Critics confuse permissiveness with lax, uncontrolled, unrestrained supervision. In this case, the supervisor avoids attempting to influence his subordinates and shirks his supervisor duties and

. . . has no confidence in his ability to supervise and consequently buries himself in paper work or stays away from employes. He may also be the one who believes that to be a "good fellow" means licence. He leaves too much responsibility with the employes; sets no clear goals toward which they may work; is incapable of making decisions or helping the group arrive at decisions; and tends to let things drift . . .[79]

Such laissez-faire leadership should not be confused with the permissive supervisor who

. . . whenever possible, . . . shares with his group the decision-making about work planning, assignment, and scheduling. Where a decision must be made by him, he helps the group to understand clearly the basis for his decision. He is careful to develop as much participation, opinion-giving . . . and a feeling of responsibility for the success of the work on the part of everyone. He is concerned that each employe clearly understand his work and have opportunities for success in it . . . He encourages worthwhile suggestions and the development of new procedures . . ."[79]

Permission Does Not Necessarily Lower Decision Quality

Critics also argue that if a supervisor permits his subordinates to participate in the decision-making process, the group product will be inferior. The supervisor, with his special knowledge and training, is in the best position to evaluate the situation and can make the best decision. The compromises resulting from group discussions are regarded by critics as likely to reduce the quality of solutions. But the evidence runs counter to the criticism. Experiments generally show that group decisions are superior to decisions reached by the average member of that group, although it is also true that the group decision may not be as good as that of the best member in the group. But how often is the supervisor the best? If this could be guaranteed, then decision quality might be better when decisions were made by the supervisor alone.[41] When 66 air force officers wrote decisions prior to discussion and then met as an *ad hoc* staff to write the decisions, the decisions written by the staff were superior to the average quality of decisions written by individuals without discussion. At the same time, the quality was the same after discussion whether the decision was written by the staff or by the commander who had listened to the staff discussion. Group discussions contributed to better decision-making, whether or not the final decision was written by the group or by the person leading the group.[419]

More will be said about this matter in Chapter 6.

Some Negative Consequences of Permissiveness

While the usual concerns are unfounded that permissiveness will promote licentiousness, lowered standards, anarchy, and less control, there are some potential negative consequences. The person who shares in the decision-making process not only derives greater self-satisfaction from his job, he also develops greater frustration with it, according to a nationwide American mental health survey.[268] Having

a personal stake in the outcomes of decisions taken . . . can be a satisfying, even an exhilarating experience, but it can also lead to sleepless nights.

This mixed blessing which power sometimes represents is illustrated by the experiment in a large clerical organization . . . in which about 200 clerks were given greater responsibility to make decisions about some of the things that affected their work groups. In general, morale increased in these divisions as a result of the change in control. Clerks felt more satisfied with the company, with supervision, with their work in general. They were, in large measure, favorable toward the increased control which they were able to exercise. However, despite the general increase in satisfaction, the clerks felt less of a sense of accomplishment at the end of the work day. They were also less satisfied with their present level in the organization. . . . In acquiring an increased feeling of responsibility for the work through the added control which they were able to exercise, the clerks no doubt developed standards of achievement which are harder to satisfy.[665, p10.]

When Permissiveness is Contraindicated

Permissive, and to some extent, persuasive supervision appear, in general, most effective in promoting satisfaction and productivity among employes. Nonetheless, numerous circumstances require more authoritative action by the supervisor, more direct application of his power to reward or punish, and more decisions by him without consulting his subordinates.

When Interaction is Restricted. When contact between superior and subordinate is restricted because of the size of the group, infrequent meetings between superior and subordinate, or poor communications, the supervisor must be ready to direct and to structure the situation — to give orders and see that they are obeyed. In small, intimate groups, where interaction between supervisor and all members is quick and easy, the supervisor can remain permissive. In the small, intimate, communicative group many more attempted leadership acts can occur in a given amount of time than in the large, distant group. Conversely it is more important that each attempted leadership act be successful and effective in the large, distant group, if it is to reach the same degree of effectiveness as the small, intimate, communicative one in the same amount of time with the same expenditure of energy. Each leadership attempt must "count more" in the large group since relatively fewer are possible.[41] As groups become larger than 30, the demands from subordinates for strong, central leadership become stronger. There is more reliance placed on whoever is appointed leader, regardless of who he is personally. There is more tolerance of leader-centered direction in larger groups.[293]

Figure 5.11 shows how the productivity of scientists in a medical research laboratory is greatest when they have daily contact with their group chief, but only if they are treated permissively and allowed to share in decision-making or given the freedom to make most of their own decisions. Permissiveness is best when meetings are frequent. But when contact between chief and subordinates is only a few times a week or less, productivity falls off with this same permissiveness by the chief. Permissiveness is thus contraindicated when interaction is low between leader and led.[519]

The Nature of the Task. The task may mitigate against permissive approaches because it restricts interaction. A person who is at the center of a network of communications from four peripheral locations will promote the fastest, clearest, most accurate communication system if he accepts the responsibility for making the decisions for the network (See Chapter 8, Figures 8.1 and 8.2). Those in the periphery are unsatisfied with this arrangement, but the system works most effectively if the central person is authoritative. On the other hand, if all locations are interconnected, more equalitarian decision-making becomes possible.[395]

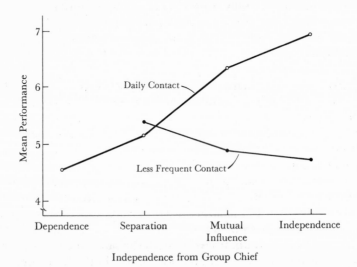

Figure 5.11: The Relationship of Scientific Performance to Independence from Group Chief and Contact with Chief. (After Pelz, 1957)

Whether the task is simple or complex may make a difference. If the task is easy and uncomplicated for the worker, close supervision of what he is doing is likely to be detrimental since he already knows what to do and how to do it.[442] On the other hand, if the task is complex or the worker has little understanding of how to tackle the task with which he must cope, permissiveness may be contraindicated. The worker may prefer a great deal of guidance and attention from his supervisor until he has mastered the job, particularly if it does not involve much creativity from the worker but only attention to routine details which he must learn.[63]

Higher Authority.   If rules and regulations set by higher authority restrict subordinates' decisions, then as seems obvious, supervisors dominate the group, make the decisions, and structure the situation. They are also less likely to be informal and to mix with their men, according to a survey of 100 groups.[296] Higher authority indirectly can prevent participation in decisions by subordinates by demanding immediate answers from supervisors with no opportunity allowed for workers to be consulted.[667]

Both in a progressive petrochemical refinery and in a national food processing firm, the extent a supervisor felt he should be considerate was positively correlated with how highly he was merit rated by his superiors.[38, 40] Yet in other companies no such correlation has been found,[543] and one can easily imagine settings where considerate, permissive superiors would be severely downgraded by their bosses. A real conflict is likely if top management insists on sacrificing all else in the interests of maximizing productivity and has the power to coerce workers into the effort.

Maximum Productivity Demanded.   Since workers and managers tend to seek *satisfactory* not maximum levels of goal attainment, permissive techniques may serve to reduce tensions, hostility, and frustration at the expense of failing to yield maximum output, particularly when such output is to some extent irrelevant to the income or other satisfactions of the work group.[14] If a maximum effort is demanded, promises of reward or punishment may be more effective in the short run than discussions about the matter.

Expectations of Subordinates.   If custom restricts what the worker is permitted to decide, the supervisor will define and structure the work.[296] Thus, whether Norwegian factory employes would participate in decisions depended on whether they deemed that it was legitimate activity for them.[223] Similarly, Israeli sailors who had expectations that their commander would be authoritarian were as satisfied with him as with a permissive commander.[216]

Studies in other more traditional cultures like Japan and Great Britain generally support the utility of permissive techniques, but more analyses repeating American experiments need to be done abroad.[708]

Military field studies indicate that more important to the effectiveness of the team is whether the leader conforms to the role expected of him by his subordinates, not whether he is permissive or coercive.[257]

Personality and Ability of Subordinates.   Supervisors will have difficulty in promoting participation among their subordinates in decisions if the subordinates lack the capacity to express themselves or the interest and ability to become involved or appreciate what they could contribute. Subordinates may personally dislike making decisions. They may dislike living without immediate decisions from supervisors and remaining under ambiguous, unstructured circumstances. Such intolerance for ambiguity is one of the characteristics associated with authoritarian attitudes.[3] Individuals with *authoritarian* rather than *equalitarian* attitudes are likely to reject permissive leadership. A survey of Philadelphia residents disclosed that highly authoritarian personalities wanted powerful, prestigeful leaders who would strongly direct them. They emphasized material support, wanting the leader to serve their special interests. On the other hand, equalitarian persons preferred leaders who could help them solve the problems with which they had to cope. They wanted warmth and consideration in their leaders.[578] In the same way, authoritarian infantrymen and airmen worked better under authoritarian leaders while equalitarian men did better led by equalitarians.[257] In a study of 108 supervisors in a retail parcel delivery service, productivity was found correlated with felt influence on decisions much more among equalitarians than among authoritarians.[705]

Personality and Expectations of the Would-Be Permissive Leaders.   An authoritarian manager who cannot tolerate uncertainty, who has strong power needs, and finds himself unable to accept equalitarian attitudes toward his fellow men may be more effective if he does not try to disguise his true feelings by a superficial display of permissive practices. If he maintains a consistent authoritative position, his subordinates, at least, may be able to develop a consistent, reasonably tolerable way of getting along with him. They know what to expect and, although they may react to coercion in the ways described earlier in the chapter, they will react possibly even more strongly to the executive who forcefully declares, "We'll be democratic around here, or else. . . . " What we are saying is that it pays to be permissive, but some managers may simply be unable to bring themselves around to a way of thinking and behaving that is required for a true sharing of leadership between supervisor and subordinate. In such cases, they may be better off maintaining practices with which they, at least, will be more comfortable. Otherwise, their own conflicts in what they prefer to do and what they actually do may generate even more difficulties with subordinates. For example, the professor who lectures for the full 50 minutes to his classes and refuses to allow time for discussion because he simply cannot tolerate or deal with questioning or skeptical students may be more effective in refusing to open discussions with students that he would be if he allowed time for interaction likely to arouse hostility, anxiety, and conflict in himself and, in turn, his students. He might effectively solve his dilemma by informal discussions with individual students outside of class. Naturally, it might even be better for all concerned if he were not teaching at all or if his personality were different or could be changed; but given his current state, his inability to deal with uncertainty or rejection suggests he is wise to avoid the possibility.

The disparity between equalitarian belief and permissive managerial practices takes on worldwide proportions for these practices have been exported from the United States, particularly since World War II. These practices conform readily to the fundamental American value of equalitarianism (Chapter 1), but such a value, per se, is by no means universally shared. Essentially, we may have been exporting the practice without the value underlying it. In Japan, for example, equalitarianism has been pushed by the dictates of the military government of an occupying power. An extremely subservient people simply accepted this like any other authoritative demand. Japanese executives subscribe to such practices as participative management even more than U.S. executives in a comparable sample![279] But, the question remains as to whether the practices can be made to work without true acceptance of the value of the individual that underlies the practices.

A cross-cultural survey of approximately 2,800 managers at training centers in 14 different countries noted a surprising degree of uniformity in how much these managers say they accept such permissive practices as participative management, sharing objectives, self-control by subordinates through commitment and understanding rather than control by coercion. Yet, except for the U.S. sample, there was little comparable acceptance in any of the other countries of the underlying beliefs on which permissive leadership is based; for example, that individuals — employes as well as supervisors — all have the potential to exhibit initiative, share leadership, and contribute to the problem-solving process in organizations. Fostering permissive management practices in such countries as Spain, France, Italy, Belgium, Denmark, Norway, Germany, and

Sweden (the lowest in mean acceptance of individual employe leadership potential) may be "a little like building the techniques and practices of a Jeffersonian democracy on a basic belief in the divine right of kings."[279, p.98] However these societies are all changing, partly influencing the extent management practices can become more progressive and partly being influenced by more progressive practices in government and industrial administration.

Emergencies. Subordinates want to be told what to do, and in a hurry, when danger threatens. Time does not permit a democratic discussion of alternatives. Rapid, decisive leadership is demanded.[294] From half to two-thirds of 181 airmen, asked their opinions about missile teams, rescue teams, scientific teams or other small crews facing emergencies, strongly agreed that they should respond to the orders of the commander with less question than they usually do. The commander in an emergency was expected to "check more closely to see that everyone is carrying out his responsibility." Half to three-fourths felt that "the commander should not be 'just one of the boys.'"[684]

Analyses of the survival experiences of 200 crews requiring them to fight hunger, cold, fatigue, and the enemy suggests that the effective leader in such stressful circumstances differs from the ineffective leader in the extent he exercises power, maintains communications in the group, rapidly restructures the situation, and maintains the group's goal orientation so that panic will be avoided. Panic occurs when members suddenly seek individual goals—everyone for himself.[488] Although the best decisions occur when the leader accepts information, ideas, and opinions of members for evaluation, still, he must express his own opinions, assume responsibility for making decisions, and when required, make decisions without consulting the group.[686]

*   *   *   *   *

The impact of the supervisor on his work force is such that we often can describe his behavior just by observing his subordinates, their productivity, grievances, absenteeism, and lateness, and by noting how apathetic or energetic they are about departmental matters.

Supervisors vary from each other in many ways. Most significant in effects on their organization are the extent they initiate structure, show consideration for their subordinates, and balance their objectives and loyalties. They differ in use of their abilities to persuade subordinates, yet often this is an effective style of leadership. They can use their power to coerce subordinates with promises and threats, but this has open and hidden costs. With power and ability they can treat subordinates permissively, setting the constraints liberally within which their subordinates can pursue objectives, sharing in decisions with subordinates, and discussing with them matters which affect all concerned. However such permissiveness is less efficacious when groups are large, when time is limited, and in a variety of other circumstances limiting interaction possibilities between superior and subordinates. Yet, in the aggregate, where it is feasible, permissiveness pays off, particularly in the small, face-to-face working situation. But to understand it, requires a more comprehensive examination of how groups develop and the processes they employ when permitted by their supervisors to search for group decisions. This examination now follows.

In Brief

MUCH OF THE BEHAVIOR OF THE INDIVIDUAL EMPLOYE CAN ONLY BE UNDER-stood in the context of the small group in which he works. Commitment to production goals, acceptance of leadership, satisfaction with work, effectiveness of performance all tend to depend on the relations of a man with his immediate face-to-face co-workers.

A group reaches maturity when members have learned to accept and trust each other, when they can communicate openly and share in decisions about the group, when they can identify their individual goals with the group's objectives, and when the governance of their behavior is based on mutual support and restraint.

Groups can be too large or too small depending on their task. In the same way, the task determines whether it will be efficacious to assemble employes into groups according to their similarities or differences in ability and attitude.

Decisions are reached in groups in many ways, but it is profitable to strive for real consensus rather than settle for majority vote or decision by a single person. A group will also be more effective to the extent that expectations of the members' roles are clear, the members are cooperative rather than competitive, are tolerant of each other, and provide mutual feedback as a self-corrective mechanism for learning.

Chapter 6

WORKING IN

GROUPS

THE MECHANIZATION OF ENGLISH COAL MINES DESTROYED THE TRADI-
tional face-to-face teams of two to four miners. As a supposed move
toward greater efficiency, the new "longwall" method broke the operation in a series of steps—cutting, ripping, and filling—to be completed
during three shifts by about 40 men. But the expected increases in productivity failed to materialize. Instead there were increases in absenteeism, turnover, sickness, and the incidence of psychosomatic disorders.
Remedial action was taken. Small, stable, responsible teams were reestab-
lished with some opportunity to set their own pace. Following this social
modification there was as much as a 30 percent increase in output.[748]
This case illustrates how the primary work group often determines what
its members will do. Management may set quotas, but the primary work
group of peers may decide whether or not its members will meet those
or some other standards established by the group, with or without management's blessing. The extent the group can set and maintain standards
for its members, we have seen in Chapter 2, depends on its cohesiveness.
The cohesion of members in a work group strongly influences how hard
they will work and their satisfaction with work.

Group Character and Member Performance

The character, composition, and history of a work group will
strongly affect the performance and attitudes of its members. Consistently observed differences in the character of 300 groups in 30 plants
made it possible to distinguish four types: apathetic, erratic, strategic,

and conservative. In each type, the members revealed distinct patterns of behavior differing from the behavior of members in other type groups. *Apathetic* groups had few grievances. Low in prestige, they took little concerted action against management. Neither were they a bother to the union. *Erratic* groups, high in prestige, ranged from near apathy to explosive activity. They started "wildcat" strikes over minor issues. Also high in prestige were *strategic* groups, holding important assignments with the firm. These groups exerted strong and continuous pressure on management, helped by their own cohesion. *Conservative* groups were composed of highly skilled workers who obtained what they wanted without pressure.[582] Subsequent analyses suggest that strategic and conservative groups are more likely to win grievance disputes than apathetic or erratic ones.[565]

Horizontal and Diagonal Relations

In the last chapter we focused on the superior-subordinate relationship. In this we study what is becoming possibly more important in industry, the relation among peers, among men at the same level and with the same status who must join together to plan, to innovate, to produce, and to evaluate.

While a foreman may order Joe, a carpenter, and Bill, a brick mason, to build a retaining wall, the quality of the work, the speed with which it is done, and the satisfaction that Joe and Bill get from the work may depend as much or more on how Joe and Bill relate to each other than how each respond to their foreman. And to some extent Bill and Joe can be more or less productive and satisfied as a consequence of whether they have learned how to work as a two-man group.

While more attention has been paid to vertical relations in industry, the quality and quantity of output and worker satisfaction may depend as much or more on horizontal relations along the system of work flow. As the parts are processed and assembled, moving in a batch or flow, the relations between each operator and the one before and after him may critically determine his performance and attitude. He is likely to become dissatisfied if his work piles up as a consequence of the slowness of the man next down the line or if he has to correct mistakes of the man who handles the material before it reaches him.[555] In the same way numerous diagonal relations are frequent and important, particularly in assembly line operations.[340] A foreman on the line may find himself soliciting the aid of workers from the maintenance department, for example.

Grouping as a Function of Technology

Some industrial tasks are conducive to group effort, but not all.[72] Steel production requires that work be carried out by highly integrated teams of men working closely together. Steel workers are likely to comment: "I like working with men I know and working like a team. . . . We carry on a lot of conversation and joke and time passes very quick. . . . Every man works as a member of a team and tries to turn out as much steel as possible."[710, p.61] On the other hand, such integrated team work is impossible on the automobile assembly line where only loose ties between men on the line can occur during work. Although assembly workers can talk with the men nearest them on the line, no set of workers will maintain the same contacts to form a stable, informal group.[713]

Importance of Group Effort in Industry

"A camel is a horse designed by a committee." So quip critics of group effort in business. But work in groups, by both management and workers, is commonplace in industry. Why? A first reason is that modern technology usually makes it difficult for one man to assemble, organize, and digest the facts necessary to make an appropriate decision or complete an operation. An individual very often finds himself, as in the case of steel fabrication, forced to depend on his peers, and they to depend on him in order to complete their mutual tasks successfully. An operator of a new catalytic cracking unit in an oil refinery may be puzzled about the unusual behavior of an instrument metering the input of feedstock. He may need to consult with an instrument maintenance man, a chemical engineer from the design department, the operator on the night shift, his own foreman, the shift foreman, and possibly also his old buddy who works on the unit next to his. A meeting of design, maintenance, and operating people may be called to discuss the problem. No one man has the knowledge or capability to deal with the problem alone. Thus it is not a question of whether groups are better than individuals in problem solving and in quality of performance than individuals working alone, but rather that there are numerous working situations in which it is impossible or most inefficient for an individual to handle alone: repairing heavy equipment, piloting a large boat, monitoring the output of a utility plant, manufacturing shoes, or designing merchandising displays. Management, at all levels, is a group effort. It is for this reason that 81.5 percent of a cross-sectional sample of executives

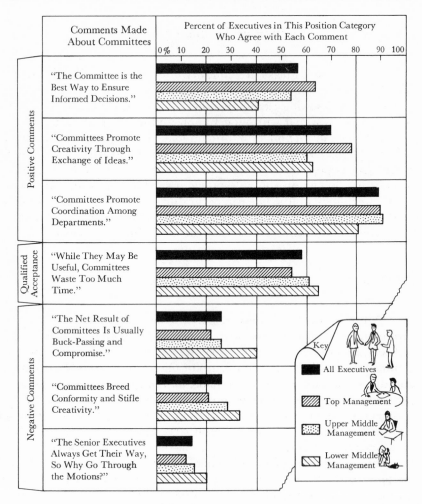

Figure 6.1: Committees—How Do Top Executives Appraise Them? (After Tillman, 1960, p. 163)

reported that their organizations maintained regular or standing committees; only 8 percent would abolish these if given the chance. Figure 6.1 shows what the sample thought about various aspects of committee work. As can be seen, a sizeable majority agreed that committees promote coordination, creativity, and informed decisions, although many also felt that committees tended to be inefficient.

The average executive spent three and one-half hours per week in formal conference and nine and one-half hours in informal meetings with others. As can be seen in Figure 6.2, larger firms make more use of committees as does top management compared to lower echelons. Top management committees are most likely to deal with policy and planning, marketing committees with reviews, and production and finance committees with planning and operating decisions.[680]

Working Together or Alone.   Actually research, accumulating since the turn of the century on whether the group or its individual member turns out the superior product, indicates that the group does a better job than its *average* member. (Otherwise, teachers might not need to proctor examinations.) Yet group products or solutions to problems are often not as good as the output of the *best* member of the group when he works alone.[418] There are some circumstances where even the average member proportionately does better alone than the group as a whole. For example, the sum and overall quality of ideas generated in response to a problem by individuals, each working alone and then added together, is considerably greater than where the same individuals who have not worked much together before meet as a group to try to "brainstorm" the same variety of ideas.[669] But, again, often we must work in groups. Rather than argue whether it would be better to work alone, we wish to explore in this chapter how to maximize the effectiveness and satisfaction of the group when work *must* be done by a group, as for example in industries with continuously flowing production. For instance, in the petrochemical industry, management decisions are usually made by committee because no one man normally has the variety of technical and business acumen to decide by himself.[751]

The Group as an Instrument of Permissive Leadership.   In the last chapter we noted that ordinarily permissive leadership pays. The supervisor who would be permissive sets up conditions permitting all of his subordinates to join him in deciding as a group how to operate. He uses the power of the group to bring about a more productive effort by all concerned. Yet whether or not the permissive supervisor can achieve his mission will depend upon the effectiveness of the group within which he must operate.

If the supervisor's boss does the same, then the supervisor will find himself a member of two groups in which he must work effectively; one composed of himself and his subordinates, the other composed of his boss and his peers. The supervisor serves as a pin linking the two groups. An entire organization of overlapping groups emerges if each superior would be permissive with his own subordinates and the effectiveness of group action becomes paramount within the organization.[412]

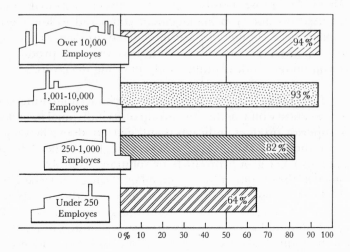

Size of Company   Percent of Companies Having Committees

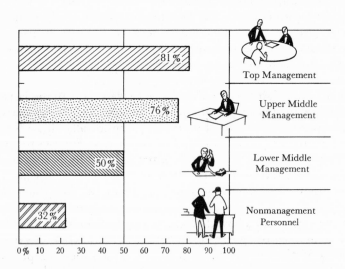

Percent of Executives Serving on Committees   Position Category

Figure 6.2: Committees — How Many Companies Have Them; How Many Executives Serve on Them? (After Tillman, 1960, p. 11)

GROUP DEVELOPMENT

Like individuals, groups learn. The eventual performance of a group depends on both individual learning of its members and how well the members learn to work with each other, how well they make use of each other, and how well they coordinate their efforts. Performance of a group will be impaired if members are too hasty and superficial in their agreement, substituting their initial unanimity for a rational analysis of the problem they face. Performance will also be impaired if decisions are compromises to resolve conflicts to save "face," rather than if the decisions are based on a careful deliberation of the problem and a thorough exploration and evaluation of all other alternatives. Taking a quick vote before any really serious discussion has been completed often "short-circuits" the formulation of a high-quality solution to a problem by a group which it has the resources to make.[33] Groups can and must learn how to use the resources their members bring to the group. Four stages have been described in the learning process for committees, discussion groups, and many kinds of work groups.

Stages in Group Development

A four-stage learning process describes the development and maintenance of typical management committees or conference groups responsible for innovation, planning, operating decisions, sharing information, or evaluating. First, members must learn to accept each other and develop mutual confidence and trust. Only after this has occurred can they proceed to communicate openly and freely and to act and react with their full resources to set and achieve desired goals at a high rate of productivity. Finally, when such productivity has been demonstrated, the immature, formal controls based on power can be modified so the group operates with more spontaneous informality. The members move from concern about trusting each other to concern about how to communicate effectively. From there they proceed to concern about what goals to set and finally to concern about how controls shall be maintained.[237]

First Stage: Developing Mutual Acceptance and Membership. Members initially are hampered by their mistrust of each other (which they are often quick to deny). They respect the motives of others, but they fear their own inadequacies as well as those of other members. Protection is sought in cliques and mutual admiration pairings. They resist initiation of new ways of operating through legalism and quibbling. Remaining defensive, they restrict the range of permitted behavior through conformity and ritual.

When members learn to accept each other and themselves, they can easily express their feelings and conflicting attitudes. Norms are established about how they will proceed, but individual differences are tolerated. Legitimate influence is accepted, and members develop a liking for each other.

Second Stage: Communication and Decision-Making.   During this phase, what were first ambiguous expressions are clarified in meaning. Strategy, gimmicks, and tricks are replaced by problem-solving behavior. Caution, pretense, and protective phraseology give way to open communications and reactions. Sufficient time is spent in reaching decisions.

Third Stage: Motivation and Productivity.   The group has reached maturity in resolving problems of its members' motivation when creativity is observed in sustained work, when members are involved in the work, when extrinsic or irrelevant rewards are not needed to maintain as high a level of productivity, and when members cooperate instead of competing.

Fourth Stage: Control and Organization.   A group has succeeded in organizing effectively when work is allocated according to abilities and by agreements among those involved. Members are interdependent, but the organization remains flexible and ready to change in the face of new challenges. Informality and spontaneity are stressed with actually little concern about the form of the organization.[237]

The Mature Group

Eventually, the mature, effective group that emerges has the characteristics enumerated by 250 respondents who were each asked to use a checklist to describe an efficient and an inefficient work group to which they had belonged. They described clerical, sales, manufacturing, business, maintenance, and military work groups. The five clusters of statements which best discriminated the effective from the ineffective work groups were (in order of importance):

  1. The members function as a unit. The group works as a team. The members do not disturb each other . . .

2. The members participate fully in group effort. They work hard when there is something to do. Members do not loaf if they get the opportunity. . .

3. The members are oriented toward a single goal. They work for common purposes. . .

4. The members have the equipment, tools, and skills necessary to attain the group's goals. The group members are taught various parts of their jobs by experts. The group is not shorthanded. . .

5. Members ask and receive suggestions, opinions, and information from each other. If a member is uncertain about something, he stops working and finds out. The members talk to each other frequently. . . . [35]

Thus the effective work group is one in which the individual members are highly interdependent, coordinated, and cooperative in their efforts. They are capable and highly motivated as individuals, and information flows freely among them.

We shall now look at conditions conducive to the creation and maintenance of an effective work group. Two basic questions confront us: how large should a group be, and who should group with whom.

FORMING THE EFFECTIVE GROUP

How Large Should a Group Be?

When one man does not have the resources to cope with a particular task, say, shackling loads and moving them by a hoist, the resources of several men must be combined to complete the task. The job obviously will depend upon the quality and quantity of resources each man contributes. The group will be more effective if its individual members are capable, skillful, and knowledgeable about what needs to be done. But not so obvious is the fact that the success of the group effort also will depend on how much and how well they interact with each other. A disaster will ensue if the crane follower or hoistman helper fail to signal the hoist operator or, in turn, if he misreads one of their signals. The team's speed and accuracy will be high when signals are on time, are clear and complete, and are accepted or trusted as reliable.

Of course some or all the interactions between workers may be irrelevant to the performance of their jobs. Much talk may mean less work. Thus shoe factory teams that did the most talking did not turn out the most work.[314] Music on the job appears to enhance productivity, partly because it reduces the amount of irrelevant talk between workers. But completion of a mutual task often requires effective interaction.

The quality and quantity of interaction among men working together will depend upon a number of factors. For example, as the group
enlarges to increase its total resources, the quality and quantity of interaction between any two members decreases. In the large group there is
much more competition possible in who will send and who will receive.
Contrast a ten-man with a two-man group. If only one man can "send"
signals in a ten-man group at any one time, then the chance to send at
that moment is denied to nine-tenths of the group. In a two-man group,
only half of the group must wait. In the same way, if all ten can signal
at once, then there is almost one hundred times the interference among
signals in the ten-man group as among the two men.

An Example.   Figure 6.3 illustrates the severe mechanical effects of size
in thwarting the potential interaction of members. Forty-eight groups
varying in size up to 96 were presented with a public relations problem.
They spent the first 30 minutes listing suggested solutions and the next
30 minutes evaluating them. As can be seen in Figure 6.3, the percentage
of students who reported that they had ideas they did not express and
the percentage who never talked directly increased as the groups en-

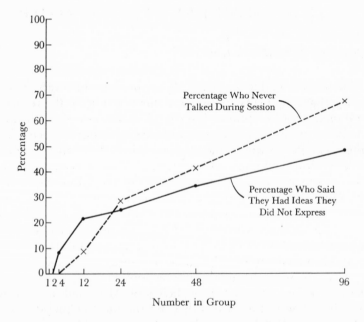

*Figure 6.3: Percentages of Members Who Are Unable to Express
Their Ideas Because of the Size of the Group. (Data from Gibb,
undated)*

larged. In addition to the obvious mechanical limitations imposed by the larger groups, students who failed to interact felt more threatened in the larger groups stating that more often they did not express themselves for fear that, "I might be misinterpreted by the group"; "someone else said it before I had thought of it clearly enough to express it in words before the group"; "it is easier to let someone else express my ideas"; or, "I thought my idea might sound silly."[235]

Interaction Potential and Size. So we are faced with a dilemma. We need to enlarge a group to increase its resources to handle a complex task. At the same time, such an increase reduces relatively the *potential* of its members to *interact* to cope with the problem facing the group.

Thus for a given problem there is an optimum size. If the group is too small it will not have the resources to do the job adequately or at all. If the group is too large members will interfere with each other's attempts to interact — unless special organizational strategies are adapted. Optimum size depends on the task. The manufacture of steel requires a large corporate organization of men and equipment. Steel cannot be produced efficiently without massive resources. On the other hand, small, individually owned tool and die shops operate at substantially lower costs than large, captive shops. Although skilled labor is paid more in the small independent shops, small scale operations here are more efficient.[514]

A summary of 250 small group studies concluded that smaller groups generally perform better in operational settings and on laboratory tasks than larger ones assigned to the same tasks, although members feel they are going to be less competent as a group compared to larger groups. Yet despite the fact that these smaller groups do not have large resources at their command, they do actually perform better because members have fewer difficulties interacting with each other. More ideas per member are expressed, and more mutual influence occurs in smaller groups. Also smaller groups see less need for guidance from higher authority, and their leader does not have to spend as much time in coordinating their efforts or clarifying rules and standards.[464]

Size of Working Group and Output. The relative output of 239 work groups in two British automobile factories was generally greater in the smaller groups. The groups varied in size from 10 to 50 men each. Foremen and workers favored the smaller combinations because better relations could be obtained among members of the smaller groups. They could see each other and what each was contributing to the group effort.[447]

Sears, Roebuck surveys concluded likewise that small units had higher morale and were more productive.[753] Again, it was in the smaller among 228 work groups varying in size from 5 to 50 that men were likely to be more attached to the group and committed to its goals.[592]

Norms for Size.   What size groups companies establish cannot tell us much about what is optimum, but they can provide clues as to what at least is satisfactory as far as their managements are concerned. The average size of work groups seems to vary with the industry. According to a census of 618 British groups, in chemicals it was 16.8; in engineering, 20.6; in food processing, 25.9; in clothing, 28.4; and in textiles, 33.3.[286] A survey of 940 American work groups suggested that the group can be larger if the foreman has an assistant. But it is likely to be smaller than average when workers operated as a gang, or if they are highly skilled.[266]

Why Are Oversized Groups Maintained?   If smaller units are more efficient, what prompts management to establish and maintain groups considerably larger? First, it is probable that management pays more attention to what appears to be the engineering and technical aspects of designing an organization. It considers what resources must be brought to bear and the minimum amount of administrative superstructure required.

Two groups of fifteen men would require two foremen, while one group of thirty requires only one supervisor. Or the fifteen-man groups might each have a lead man reporting to a foreman, requiring three supervisory personnel instead of one. However we can speculate that the total organizational operation would be far more efficient and satisfying if work groups generally were made much smaller than now is current practice. The technological imperatives, which led to the seemingly efficient assembly line of say thirty workers responsible for a particular section along one of the lines, caused management to ignore the psychological imperatives; that is, the same worker will be far more effective as a member of a five-man than a thirty-man work group. Serious consideration needs to be given to the relative economics of allowing technological rather than sociopsychological factors to dictate group size. Smaller groups are likely to learn tasks faster[105] and to perform them faster.[408] The problem is how to organize the same number of personnel now in a few large groups into many more smaller groups without increasing the number and layers of supervision. In the next chapter we will consider some possible organizational plans that attempt to do this.

Size and Effectiveness of Discussion Groups.   Interaction becomes paramount when the main purpose for meeting is to share information or reach joint decisions. The range of tolerable sizes for work groups becomes much smaller than the range possible for groups where the workers can operate alone for considerable portions of the day, interacting only for social reasons, for monitoring work completed, for correcting errors, and so on. We can even be quite specific about optimum numbers, for several experiments all seem to point to the same optimum — five or six members. Five is the size preferred by experienced executives, according to a survey, although committees on which these men serve are likely to contain about eight members on the average.[680] (Practice deviates from preference.) A problem-solving group, a management committee, or an evaluation panel examining complex problems seem to be most effective when they contain about five or six members. Below this they may not have the varied resources to fully deal with the issues confronting them; above this they begin to have difficulties interacting. Full participation in a discussion by 50 people is impossible; among 15, quite difficult.

Despite the custom and legal status of the twelve-man jury, twelve men operate more ineffectively and with less satisfaction than men in groups of five.[288] Larger conference groups are more disruptive than smaller ones; members feel more frustration and less sense of belonging to the larger discussion groups.[483]

Factor analysis of the interacting profiles drawn fron seven research studies revealed several specific effects of enlarging groups. As a group enlarges, the average member becomes less likely to ask for information, confirmation, and help, and he becomes less likely to reveal his tensions. He becomes less willing to give or seek opinions, evaluations, and analysis and to express his feelings.[283] This failure to show feelings and tensions in larger groups, no doubt, contributes to a polite but superficial level of activity, not conducive to real progress.

The optimum size shrinks to two when only simple, solitary judgments are required, where adding members mainly adds redundant information to the group. For single, uncomplicated judgments a two-man panel seems to do the best job, since interaction interferences are minimized. Two-man groups have been found more accurate and satisfying than those of three or four in size in a variety of such simple judging operations.[225]

Odd Versus Even. Even-sized groups, such as those composed of six men, reach more accurate decisions than those containing an odd number of members, say five or seven. Odd-sized groups, when faced with close decisions, resolve the issues quickly by taking a vote. A majority can be obtained often after only cursory examination of the problem. Such hasty decisions cannot always be obtained in even-sized groups on close and difficult problems. Here tie votes are common. The even-sized groups must continue to discuss the issues further and are thus prevented often from making hasty and superficial decisions.[225] It is interesting to note that executives prefer odd- to even-sized committees.[680] Here preference deviates from what would produce effectiveness—an example of why a science of management cannot depend on executive opinion and surveys of current practice to establish verifiable propositions about effective organization without resort to experimentally controlled tests.

How Groups Should Be Composed: The Case for Homogeneity

Suppose we have decided to form six-man teams from an available pool of 72 men. If we assemble in teams those men who are most alike in interests, abilities, and personality, we will promote interaction within each team. Members can communicate more easily with each other. There will be less conflict, fewer differences in opinions, standards, and ways of doing things.

Homogeneity and Influence. Members who are alike can influence each other more easily. There is less resistance to influence where members are similar rather than different. This was illustrated by an experiment where it was found that the experimenter could more successfully condition his subject verbally if the experimenter and his subject agreed on what are proper ways to interact. That is, the experimenter could more successfully make the subject respond each time in the same way upon hearing a particular verbal cue in order to obtain a reward or avoid a punishment. In addition, when experimenter and subject were compatible, conditioned responses took longer to extinguish when they no longer were reinforced by the experimenter.[579]

Homogeneity and Mutual Acceptance. We tend to like those similar to us and to reject those whom we think are unlike us. Members, who are alike or who think they are alike, will be more satisfied with the group, as well as with each other, than members who see differences between themselves and others in the group.[41] This was demonstrated by the following experiment:

Eleven trios of supervisors in a training laboratory were made up of men who beforehand agreed that a particular one of five alternatives should be employed to handle ethical problems in education and politics. Thirteen other trios deliberately were composed so that each man in a trio favored a different alternative. As seen in Table 6.1, interaction difficulties and dissatisfaction were greater in trios where men had differences in opinion than in trios where they initially agreed on the correct alternative.

Productivity If Task Is Simple.   If the task facing a team is a simple one, say, folding and packing equipment into containers where a variety of resources are not needed to complete the task, but merely six pairs of hands instead of one pair, then a *homogeneous* team is likely to be highly productive also. For example, 64 pairs of subjects completed nine jigsaw puzzles, alone and in pairs. The speed of the pair was greater, the greater the speed of each partner working alone and the less the difference in speed between the partners when they worked alone.[745]

Productivity If Task Demands Cooperation.   If productivity depends on easy, smooth, cooperative, conflict-free, coordinated efforts among the members, all of whom have been highly trained to interact routinely and automatically, then again a homogeneous membership, a membership where men are alike, should prove more productive. Thus teams were

TABLE 6.1   EFFECTS OF WHETHER TRIOS CONTAIN MEMBERS SAME
AND DIFFERENT IN OPINIONS BEFORE BEGINNING A PROBLEM-
SOLVING DISCUSSION

(9 = Completely satisfied; 1 = Completely dissatisfied)

	Trio Members Share Same Opinions	Trio Members Differ in Opinions
Difficulties in trying to get own ideas across	1.4	4.8
Difficulty in understanding what was presented by everyone else in trio	1.4	2.7
Freedom felt to participate	8.9	8.4
Discomfort during discussion	1.1	2.1
Satisfaction with final decision by trio	8.9	7.5
Would choose same partners again	8.0	7.6

clustered to work on assembly problems on the basis of whether or not they were compatible; that is, subjects were grouped according to whether they agreed on how much power, status, and affection should be used to maintain satisfactory interpersonal relations. Compatible teams were more productive than incompatible crews on an assembly task which required a high degree of cooperation under some pressure.[589] But compatibility was less important if the tasks did not require as much cooperation among the members of a team. Compatible and incompatible teams were compared on three tasks: an intercept problem requiring agreement and coordination among members for each decision, a plotting problem requiring some division of labor and cooperation, and a coding problem requiring little interaction among members. Compatible teams were particularly better than incompatible groups on the intercept problem requiring coordination, but compatibility made no difference in adequacy of coding where little coordination was needed.[590]

These results were corroborated in an industrial study of how the optimum mix of men in a group depends on how much cooperation is required. The 567 shop workers were in 62 groups, ranging in size from 4 to 13, at a maintenance base of an airline. The groups were rated as requiring a low, medium, or high degree of cooperation among members of the same group. For each group an index was calculated of how homogeneous the members were in response to psychological testing. This index of homogeneity correlated .53 with group productivity in those groups requiring a high degree of cooperation, but it correlated .01 and .05 in groups needing only a medium or low degree of cooperation within them.[415]

Productivity if Task Is a Chain.   Where a chain of reactions is required of a group, the total chain may depend upon the adequacy of each and every link. Again homogeneity is favored, for the group is no better than its poorest member. One link failure will destroy the entire chain. On some tasks the group can proceed no faster than its slowest member. In some groups one member can veto the decisions of the entire group or be so deviant in opinion as to block a group which cannot convert him, compromise with him, or expel him from the group. Under such conditions, such as when subjects had to coordinate completely an interlocking system of levers to turn on lights of a group maze, the typical group did worse than its average member working alone.[461] Presumably the more varied in abilities the members in such circumstances, the more likely the group to contain an extremely poor member who would drag the performance of the group down to his level.

How Groups Should Be Composed:
The Case For Heterogeneity

Where speedy, smooth interactions are less important than a crea-tive solution of a complex problem, a *heterogeneous* group—a group where members differ in abilities or opinions—may be more desirable than a group in which members are alike.

If Task Is Complex.   The main reason for grouping often is because no single individual has the varied resources to deal with complex prob-lems. If we wish to ensure that each of the 12 teams drawn from a pool of 72 men will have the varied resources for handling a complex problem, say, designing various components for a missile system, then heterogeneous assemblies of men may prove more productive.

If Speed Is Deleterious.   The very speed with which a homogeneous group can reach decisions may prove a handicap. When members have already reached the same opinion even before they have discussed an issue, they are less likely to make a good decision as a group as when they are in disagreement when they begin deliberations.[453] Like odd groups compared to even, groups homogeneous in opinion may close debate too quickly with a decisive vote.

A fictional illustration of this is the movie *Twelve Angry Men.* Eleven jurors are ready to convict an innocent boy on superficial evidence with-out any discussion. They are saved from a quick and erroneous decision by the skillful interposition of one juror who has some doubts and in-sists on a delay in the final vote to permit discussion of the evidence. As the discussion proceeds, one by one the jurors draw forth from their own memories information that was obscured during the trial but which when put together points to the innocence rather than the guilt of the defendant.

If Creativity Is Required.   While men who are alike may do a better job facing assignments requiring routine, coordinated, or linked efforts, men who are different are likely to be more creative as a group although they may experience more difficulties interacting. Mentioned earlier were the 24 trios of men in a management training laboratory composed of those with the same or different opinions about ways to handle ethical and educational problems. The most creative trios which could generate additional alternatives were those whose members differed initially in opinion but subsequently could reach a team decision. At least two-thirds of these trios came up with one or more additional solutions, while only half of those with members alike in opinion did so. Least creative were those trios whose members disagreed initially and could never reach a team decision. Only about a third of these could think up other alternatives when pressed to do so.

The importance of varied resources to creativity is illustrated by the data shown in Table 6.2, comparing open groups where members change from time to time with closed ones where members remain the same.

Sixty-four groups of two, three, or four had to compose captions for a *Saturday Evening Post* cartoon. The captions were evaluated for fluency and originality. Where a group added, removed, or replaced members during its efforts, fluency and originality were higher than when it remained the same in membership.[766]

More conflict and difference of opinion will be observed in heterogeneous groups; but assuming these groups learn how to tolerate and use conflict, they can make better decisions although they are likely to have more difficulties interacting and take longer to reach decisions.

In a related experiment, groups were formed on the basis of Guilford–Zimmerman Temperament Survey scores of individual members. (The Survey permits the respondent to indicate how much he sees himself as energetic, moody, ascendant, sociable, emotionally stable, objective, friendly, thoughtful, cooperative, and masculine.) Groups with members who were similar in personality profiles had less difficulty in regulating their internal relations but more difficulty in creative problem-solving than groups of heterogeneous membership. Where members differed in personality, they more often rejected an easy choice of two superficial alternatives to a problem offered to them and developed on their own, a third, more creative, integrated solution.[306, 429]

TABLE 6.2   THE CREATIVITY OF OPEN AND CLOSED GROUPS*

	Open Groups: Member Added, Removed, or Replaced	Closed Groups: Membership Remains Unchanged
Ideational fluency	9.6	7.3
Originality	25.9	18.7

*After Ziller, Behringer, & Goodchilds, 1962.

Optimum Mix. As there is an optimum size for groups depending on the task, there is also an optimum mix of men for a given group task. If men are too different, they have so much trouble interacting that they cannot begin to bring to bear on the complex problem they face the varied resources they have. If men are too similar, they reach agreement too easily and too often on the same wrong answers. They are more likely to fail to consider various alternatives and to explore the problem as widely. For simple, routine assignments, the optimum mix is of fairly similar types of men. For complex tasks with creative demands, the optimum becomes a more diversified assemblage. For assignments requiring easy, cooperative interaction, the optimum again is of similar men. But, when, such cooperation is less important, the men can differ more.

How Else to Compose Groups to Promote Interaction?

In addition to considering the number and homogeneity of men to assign to a group, we may foster interaction and the ease with which men can work together by grouping together members who are already familiar with each other, who already are attracted to each other, who esteem each other, who are geographically and socially close to each other, and who can communicate fluently, accurately, and rapidly with each other.

Familiarity Breeds Interaction. If we are intimate, familar, or experienced with other persons, we feel more comfortable about initiating and maintaining interaction with them. Our familiarity makes it possible to predict with less risk of error, their likely reactions to us. We feel more secure about interacting with them. In turn, continued interaction breeds familiarity, so we are more likely to interact with those we have interacted with before. At a gathering we usually approach friends before strangers.[41]

Since they interact more readily, friends can work together faster than strangers. Thus an experiment found that pairs of close friends could solve codes, puzzles, and arithmetic problems more quickly than pairs of strangers.[322]

Mutual Esteem, Attractiveness, Interaction, and Productivity. We have detailed earlier that cohesive groups (groups in which members are attracted to each other, groups in which members choose each other as work partners, groups in which members value each other's potential contributions) may be highly productive or highly unproductive, de-

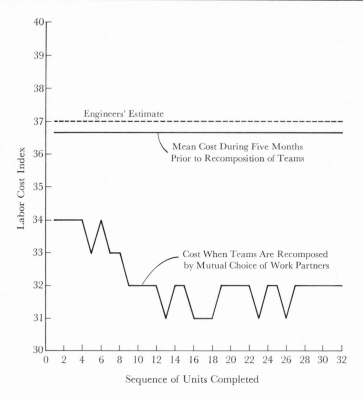

Figure 6.4: Labor Costs of Sociometric Group as Compared With Mean Pre-experimental Group and Engineers' Estimate of Labor Costs. (After Van Zelst, 1952, p. 182)

pending on whether the members share management's goals for high productivity. They could just as readily set goals of low productivity as a means of maintaining job security or as a hostile reaction to management. Members of cohesive groups will conform more closely to whatever standards—high or low—are set by their group. But normally, unless high productivity is seen by workers as a threat to their own job security, one expects that the average American worker, still imbued to a considerable degree with the Protestant ethic that work is good, will opt for setting high production goals—goals so high, in fact, that they may need to be lowered somewhat in order to be attained (see Table 5.9). He is sufficiently competitive to feel that a satisfactory level of output provides a sense of accomplishment. Moreover, satisfactory output contributes to the health of the company which in turn means, hopefully, more job security and benefits. The typical American worker has a dual allegiance for he does not normally see as incompatible the in-

terests of management and labor, even where they are.[540] For these reasons, generally, we expect that composing groups so that they will be
cohesive is likely to promote their productivity. This was demonstrated in a field experiment where costs of labor and materials to construct rows of housing units were reduced significantly when carpenters
and bricklayers were allowed to choose their work partners.

The workers were union men on fixed wages with at least seven
years experience who had been working on a current housing development for an average of five months. During this period they had considerable opportunity to learn much about each other on different job
assignments and at lunch. Workers were asked to nominate the first,
second, and third persons with whom they they would most like to
work. All but eight were paired or grouped with their first, second, or
third choices who, in turn, had chosen them as well. As can be seen in
Figures 6.4 and 6.5, right from the start the sociometrically assembled
crews were more efficient than the average crews previously. They took
less time to complete a unit, reducing labor costs. They wasted less
material, reducing material costs. Efficiency continued to improve until
about the completion of the twelfth unit of houses when it leveled off

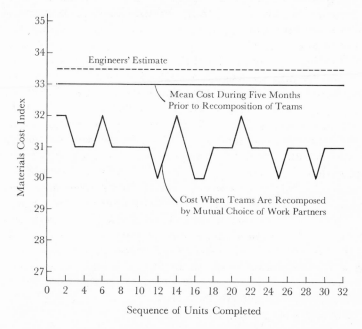

Figure 6.5: Materials Costs of Sociometric Group as Compared
with Mean Pre-experimental Group and Engineers' Estimate
of Materials Costs. (After Van Zelst, 1952, p. 183)

and fluctuated on a plateau. At no time did the mutually chosen crews ever slip back to operating at the previous costs. There was about a 5 percent overall savings in total production costs, and the turnover index dropped from 3.11 per production period to .27 per period.[698]

Worker satisfaction with the new attangements was attested by the following comment: "Seems as though everything flows a lot smoother. It makes you feel more comfortable working—and I don't waste any time bickering about who's going to do what and how. We just seem to go ahead and do it. The work is a lot more interesting when you've got your buddy working with you. You certainly like it a lot better anyway."[698, p.183]

Distance.   Relatively little attention has been paid to impact of geographical distance of members of their ability to work together. Yet data from 69 jury deliberations show that the mutual esteem between any two jurors, hence the amount of their interaction, their mutual influence, and the likely effectiveness of communications between them, increases the closer together they are seated at the juror's table.[654]

The importance of geography to group effectiveness is seen in the problems of the forest service where rangers are isolated from each other for long periods of time. Diaries must be kept, and many written reports are required as a means of maintaining the needed flow of information in the service.[71]

In the same way any national distributor of goods is likely to have only a few sales and servicemen in each of many widely dispersed territories. Face-to-face contact between salesmen and supervision is limited to a few visits a year and to occasional sales meeting held at a central location. Travel time and costs are great. Communications are one way. The salesmen send in routinized daily reports (usually regarded as a deadly chore to them), which are monitored at a distance by supervision. Corrections in performance need to be judged from these reports. Only after considerable delay can remedial action be undertaken by supervisors on the basis of filtered, erroneous information. Increasing the speed and amount of communications by more generous use of the telephone is one obvious, but expensive, way to help overcome some of the negative effects of distance on interaction and group effectiveness. Frequent teleconferencing by telephone, teletype, and television is likely to become common in the future as a way of facilitating the group effectiveness of sales and service personnel, all working at different geographic locations.

Communications.   The effectiveness of a group is markedly affected by the speed and accuracy of its communication processes. One approach is to code information before sending it. Coding into special language promotes accuracy and speed. Each message is made more easily discriminable from the next by substituting for similar sounding B, C, D, the distinct codes Baker, Charlie, Dog. We jam a great deal of unambiguous meaning into code (for those who know the code) speeding accurate communications in a message such as: "Debug the Fortran routine with the canned 101 and then remove the garbage." More will be said in the next two chapters about communications as they affect efficiency.

EFFECTIVE UTILIZATION OF THE RESOURCES AVAILABLE TO THE GROUP

Some groups of the same size and composition as others are likely to be more effective, to utilize their resources more fully. The way a decision is made by a group will strongly influence how satisfactory the decision is to its members, how much their collective judgment is fully mobilized to deal with the issue in question, the quality of the decision, and the speed and accuracy with which the decision is implemented or carried out. The cooperativeness of the members, their tolerance, their ability and willingness to carry out functions, as needed, and to provide feedback for each other will also influence their group's effectiveness.

Who Shall Decide?

Let us suppose that an executive wants to be a permissive leader. He wants to become a member in good standing in a group composed of himself and his subordinates and share with them responsibility for decisions which together they have the resources and authority to make. How should decisions be reached—by his canvassing the group for its opinions and then deciding by a show of hands, or what? What are the consequences of reaching decisions one way or another? What obstacles do groups face in reaching agreements?

Proposals That Fail Even to Be Considered. Sometimes decisions to shelve plans, policies, or operations are made without considering them at all. Many potentially good proposals may be offered by members of a group that never are discussed. Numerous factors increase the incidence of rejecting proposals without discussing them.

Proposals that fail to be discussed by anyone else after they are presented — proposals that are never brought to a stage where they could be acted upon — are a common occurrence in new groups, groups which have not established goals, groups whose members are unfamiliar with each other but who are reasonably free to try to contribute to the group's progress. We are likely to see such unpopular proposals offered by members whose self-esteem is higher than the esteem accorded them by their fellow members. This is a common event if the members have just assembled for the first time, since no one really knows much about anyone else. Here, members with past success in such groups may make efforts to make decisions for the group; but if they neither have the legitimate authority of the chairman nor personal esteem in the eyes of other members of the group, their initial efforts to decide matters for the group are likely to end in failure. Similarly, in new groups, members with a great deal of personal initiative, energy, and a strong desire to get the job done are likely to try to get the group to agree quickly on specific activities. If such members happen to be of low status; that is, if their position in life or at work is not particularly important to the rest of the group, their efforts to "start the ball rolling" are likely to end in failure.[41]

Failure is likely also when the initiator of the attempted decision trys to push his own favorite idea without giving others the opportunity to discuss the question. Likewise, he will fail if he has difficulty in communicating his ideas to the rest of the group. Perhaps he lacks verbal ability, or perhaps his intelligence and knowledge are so far beyond that of the remainder of the group that he leaves them behind when he attempts to propose new courses of action for the group. A would-be leader may be too dull, or too bright, to succeed in his group.[41]

Suggestions are likely to be rejected without consideration if they are originated by a new member who attempts to start running things upon his entrance into the group. The new member first must be accepted by the others in the group. He, in turn, must accept some of the norms, standards, and previously agreed-upon ways of behaving developed by the group. Only after this will the new member's ideas be seriously entertained by the others in the group.[473]

In groups facing difficult problems, suggestions are more likely to remain unconsidered. The same is likely to be true in highly motivated groups and among highly motivated members. Again when members all differ in their goals, some wanting to go one way and other members wanting to go another, there will be a high rate of rejection of new ideas.

Often a group is not ready for a new idea. Yet the same idea presented again at a later time may be accepted when the group has
matured sufficiently to understand the proposed idea. Groups can progress under these conditions if members are persistent in the face of
failure. The member who is overly concerned with being accepted by
others, with being regarded favorably by others, no doubt will hesitate
to reintroduce an idea that has failed to be discussed earlier. On the
other hand, the member strongly concerned about getting the job
done, the task-oriented member, is probably more likely to try again.[42]

The occurrence of these aborted attempts is not necessarily a sign of
wholly ineffective operations. If members were overly concerned about
failures, if they felt like the traditional Japanese that making a proposal
that was rejected would mean a loss of "face," it would seriously slow
the group's progress. Something must be ventured, if something is to
be gained. If a group of executives at a meeting share the belief that he
who makes no mistakes is likely to advance in the organization and a
second belief that it takes only a single mistake to ruin a man's career,
the number of proposals that fail will be few for few will be introduced.
Positive contributions to the group's progress are likely to be severely
limited. Members will reduce offering proposals to the group if failure
is punished; on the other hand, members will contribute suggestions to
a group to the extent they see themselves being rewarded and accepted
for doing so.[41]

"Brainstorming" procedures attempt to avoid the punishing aspects
of failing to have an idea considered.[505] Here members present new
ideas to the group for consideration without the ideas being evaluated
until a later time, without receiving any censure from the group for
presenting unusual, bizarre, or "outlandish" ideas. "Brainstorming"
yields a flood of proposals most of which are unacceptable eventually.
But this large number can be obtained in the same time that only one or
two ideas might have been offered if the typical reaction of a group to
the presentation of a new idea would have been to let it drop without
discussion. The search for new ideas is much broader and more fruitful
when proposals can be accepted temporarily without approval or
disapproval.

Self-Authorization as a Means of Deciding.   Self-authorized decisions in
groups are commonplace. Although he may regard himself as democratic and say he wants to share in making decisions with his group, the
typical company executive often calls a committee meeting not for the
committee to make decisions concerning questions facing the group but
rather to gain acceptance for the decisions already reached by the executive. What appears to be a meeting to reach a decision may, in fact, be a

meeting called by the executive to assure discussion of his proposal, to secure the motivation of his subordinates, and to impart information about his decision.[263] This authority-obedience pattern is a hard one to break. It is easy for the executive to present a plan of action to his committee not realizing that the nodding of heads and the agreement shown to his proposals have relatively little to do with the adequacy of the proposals or their evaluations by his subordinates. Rather, the subordinates are responding to his power over them. Saying "yes" is much easier for the subordinates than "bucking" authority. This self-authorized decision-making, made possible by the power of the chairman or the department chief, is self-perpetuating. For example, early in his career with his subordinates the chief may show hurt surprise, may express his feelings of being challenged, and may in many other ways block a healthy discussion of reasonable alternatives to what he is proposing and pushing. The silence of headnodding with which he is greeted on subsequent occasions is interpreted by him as agreement with his ideas rather than a hopeless resignation that his ideas must be accepted even if they are not really liked or valued.

In committee meetings and work groups among peers or where a permissive chairman provides complete freedom to share in the decision-making process, self-authorization still is a common occurrence. Here a member with a great deal of self-confidence, self-esteem, and a strong amount of initiative may present a plan of action. Before the group has an adequate opportunity to consider it, the originator of the idea may proceed to move into the next phase to discuss the details of his proposal. Only much later does the self-starter wake up to the fact that his original proposal has not been accepted. At such times he may find himself "out on a limb" without the rest of the group being there with him. If the self-starting member with initiative is highly esteemed by others in the group, he may succeed in gaining immediate acceptance for his self-authorized proposals. However, he cannot continue this for long without losing the regard that others have for him. He will be courting a real loss of prestige if he continues this way of pushing his ideas.

Self-authorization may succeed particularly when the members are unclear as to what they are doing and why they are doing it. They may see in some self-authorized activity an easy way out of the dilemma they face: "I don't know what's going on; but if Joe thinks he does, well I'm happy to see him trying."

Self-authorized actions are also likely to be accepted and effective during emergencies. There may be no time for discussion. The group wants a decision, any decision. They may see in the use of authority, decision-making by one man, a way to get fast action. More often than

not, however, this appeal to authority and self-authorization is an inefficient way that groups seek when they are experiencing strong feelings
of anxiety or when they are unclear as to where they are going and what
they are doing, yet no particular emergency exists. In the long run, such
self-authorized solutions are likely to slow down rather than speed up
the group's total progress toward its goals.

Minority Decision-Making.   One member proposes to cut prices in
order to bolster sales; a second member "hand-clasps" the first with,
"That is a great idea, Joe; why not tell us how we go about it?" And
the two launch into an hour discussion about the details of a campaign in which no one else may be interested. Actually the rest of the
group may want to pursue a product improvement program rather than
a price-cutting campaign. Often two or three in a group may make
such important decisions for a group in which they are only a small
minority. Figure 6.6 is a hypothetical chart showing how the number in
a group who make a decision determines the public and private acceptance of the decision. A minority of two or three in a group of ten can
carry along several more who believe the minority actually represents

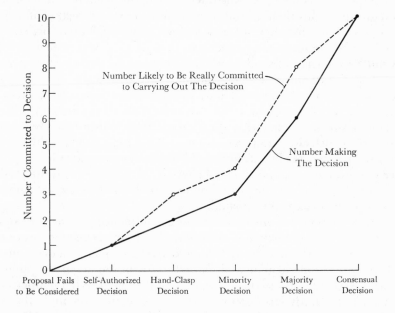

*Figure 6.6: Hypothetical Group of 10 Men Showing How Their Com-
mitment to a Decision Is Likely to Depend Upon How Many Participate
in Making it.*

a majority viewpoint since the remainder of the group has been silent. For, only the minority has had an opportunity to express itself before committing the group to a time-consuming examination of a sales campaign. The minority itself is deluded about where the rest of the group stands for people tend to overestimate the number of others who agree with them. "Even minorities comprised of only about ten percent of the group in one experiment tended to estimate that more than half of the group shared their opinions."[649]

Majority Decision-Making. Our cultural heritage and our legislative practices make it most popular for a group chairman to call for a vote to allow the majority to decide for all. Once a vote is taken it strengthens the convictions of the majority winners, converts some of the minority, and may leave a few remaining members embittered, unconvinced, and ready to work against what the majority has decided.

If the vote was made in haste without complete consideration of the issues, it may lock the group into an inflexible position from which it will have difficulty extricating itself since the majority has now been reinforced in the conviction that it is right and the minority is wrong.

Experiments have demonstrated clearly the tendency of members of a group to shift their attitudes and behavior in the direction of majority opinion or what they see as a majority opinion. Linguistic, ethical, and musical judgments have been found to shift this way. The judgment of time is similarly affected.[489] While 60 percent of subjects shifted their social, political, and economic opinions further toward majority positions when they were revealed, only 4 percent moved away from them.[735] Even when majority opinion defies the senses such as when a group of "planted stooges" states that the shorter of two lines is longer, some subjects in such circumstances who hear the stooges will actually believe they see the shorter line as longer. Others will go along with the group decision even though they do not believe it. Even after the group has disbanded the effects of majority opinion on changes in the behavior of others in the group will remain.[17]

Most demonstrations that persons are influenced by majority opinion have been about situations where the decisions to be made were not clear. The affected persons held little conviction about the decisions or felt reasonably inadequate and tended to see in the majority opinion a more correct solution to the problem than they held. What happens if a person holds fairly strong convictions on a matter, yet finds that the majority of his group feels otherwise according to a formal vote? Does he readily shift and accept what the majority thinks? He may publicly shift, but privately he still may feel that the group decision was unsatisfactory. Such a minority member who does not shift in private feeling and attitude towards the majority opinion is likely to feel coerced. He may go along with the group because these are the rules of the game—the parliamentary rules of voting. He may go along with the group to avoid further disputation, but he will not be as ready to accept or work hard for the goals selected by the majority. He may feel hurt and rejected as a consequence of the way the vote turned out. His confidence in himself may be impaired as well as his confidence in a majority of the group. This potentially disgruntled minority, resulting from majority victory and minority defeat in voting, contrasts with what happens when true consensus has been reached.[405]

Consensus: False, Forced, and True.   Full participation of all concerned, with a matter to obtain complete agreement on a decision is the ideal toward which an effective group strives.

False consensus may be mistaken for true agreement. For example, silence does not mean consent. When relatively few members speak out on issues, it is just as reasonable to assume that they are against a proposition as they are for it. Each member must express his view (if he has any) if the group is to achieve true consensus, or he must indicate when he does not care which way a matter is decided. At the same time, it is the responsibility of the group or its chairman to see that everyone has an opportunity to speak before a decision is made.

Consensus cannot be *forced.* If members are silent, it is unwise for a chairman or a self-appointed leader to point his finger at each member in turn to ask them how they stand on a matter. It is equally unsound for the group to agree to, "Let's go around the table to see what each person thinks we ought to do." A member may have to render an opinion when he does not really have one, or he may have to offer an evaluation before he has an opportunity to hear what some more knowledgeable co-workers have to say. His best potential contributions may be inspired after his turn to speak has passed, and he may now hesitate to interrupt "going around the table" since he feels he has been given his chance—although he has not used it fully.

True consensus only comes when members feel free to express their opinions and are willing to keep working together to develop a decision which meets the desires of the group as a whole. True consensus occurs when members may use fully whatever resources they can bring to bear on the group's problems. Mechanical procedures such as voting or taking turns to force contributions are avoided, but everyone who has something to contribute has a chance to do so and a chance to see his contribution considered and if possible worked into the final decision. Thus true consensus was likely among aircrews if they could express disagreements openly when working together on simulated survival problems. These same crews were found later to be more effective in combat.[685] Analyses of over 100 conference groups in business and government noted that true consensus was likely to be achieved in a group focused on one issue at a time, in a group which followed orderly, understandable, problem-solving procedures, not formal parliamentary methods. True consensus was more likely if members recognized a need for unified action, not when they felt a sense of urgency to reach a decision quickly. A friendly atmosphere also helped.[263]

Groups that strive for true consensus must be ready to settle for less than complete agreement on all matters. Thus if the conflicts in the conference groups were emotional, only simple issues could be resolved while complex questions had to be postponed. In fact, a majority of conflicts did not end in complete agreement.[263] Yet a group is more likely to operate effectively if it knows on what its members stand in disagreement than if it obscures the situation with majority decisions or forced or false consensus.

When agreement is impossible, then members at least feel the matter has been fully examined; and they may be more willing to commit themselves to an alternative solution to a problem not of their own choosing. Or when consensus cannot be obtained, at least everyone is aware of the fact and is not seduced into believing that complete commitment has been obtained, as might be the case if a decision were based on a majority vote.

While consensus may not produce the best possible solution to a problem, neither will a majority vote. Yet a consensual decision is likely to be a satisfactory one and one which is more likely to be executed efficiently than a decision based on a majority vote. Where opportunities to work for consensus are provided, members show more agreement with each other and more satisfaction with activities than members who do not have the opportunity to interact as much or to move in the direction of consensus. Consensus-directed discussions by school administrators at first produced much defensive behavior. But with continued meetings the consensual discussions yielded increased warmth, friendly attitudes of members toward each other, and better overall performance. Similar results were obtained with aircrews and research engineers.[41]

The chairman of a committee or the supervisor heading a department can serve an important function by using his power to move his group to a state of maturity where all members will share in the group's leadership, where all will share in stating issues, in summarizing, in testing for consensus, in making proposals, in giving support and encouragement to others, and in influencing the course of group action.

The chairman or executive, the man with more power than any other person in the group, can help the group to achieve decision-making consensus in many ways. He can prevent self-authorized agendas from developing. He can block members who seem to be monopolizing the group's activities or trying to dominate the group. By using suitable questions he can take on a member who continually argues and opposes without logical consistency. He may bring into the discussion members who seem to be uninterested by asking them for their advice and opinion. The powerful figure may do nothing more than show his willingness to share his power to provide the arena in which the group, including himself, can explore together the basis for obtaining group agreements. He may provide the kinds of information to the group not formerly available to it which will serve to set the boundaries of the group's responsibilities and authority.[41]

Further Impediments to Effective Utilization of Group Resources

In addition to inadequate decision-making processes and interaction difficulties mentioned earlier, such as those caused by enlarging a group, a variety of other causes of group ineffectiveness have been demonstrated. Removing these impediments should result in improving a group's performance.

Unclear Role Expectations. Trouble arises when members are unclear about what others expect of them. Moreover they become defensive if unable to forecast what other members are likely to do. Thus when "stooges" of an experimenter remained silent, the groups in which they were supposedly members remained less productive, more dissatisfied, and defensive. When these silent plants clarified the reasons for their silence and their rules became predictable and understandable, their groups improved in effectiveness and satisfaction.[618]

Competitiveness. If members see each other as competing for the boss' favor, competing for promotion, recognition, or pay raises, self-interest will conflict with the need to cooperate with other members to work toward group goals. When such self-oriented needs become dominant, consensus becomes most difficult to obtain.[262] Competitors see each other as less similar in personality than those who can achieve mutual rewards through cooperation.[571] Therefore, competition among members increases perceived differences in a group and consequently reduces the potential to interact and the likely effectiveness of the members as a group.

In comparison to groups in which members must cooperate with each other to achieve personal rewards, members who must compete for rewards are less coordinated and vary more in what they contribute.

Their activities are less likely to be subdivided, and they are less attentive to each other. There are more misunderstood and differently evaluated communications. They are more disorderly, less productive in quantity and quality, less friendly and less favorable to the group, its products, and its functioning.[164]

Unstable, Ambiguous Environment. A group is likely to standardize the behavior of its members to a degree, making it inflexible in the face of new demands on it, particularly if the new demands are ambiguous. Groups ritualize ways of handling problems which were once successful and which are now outmoded. In an experimental comparison, groups were more likely to maintain obsolete, irrelevant procedures rather than create new methods when new conditions they had to learn were unclear. On the other hand, when the new signals were distinct in meaning, there was more innovation and less ritualism in the group.[284]

Intolerance. When one member in a group takes an unpopular position, different and opposed to that maintained by all the others, the dominant majority first tries to convert the deviant; then, if he will not convert, they psychologically eject him from the group, acting as if he did not exist, paying little or no attention to him thereafter. The rejection is even more severe if the group (except for the deviant) is highly cohesive.[583] Yet the deviant may be the one member in his group with the right idea, the pioneering attitude, the most original outlook on the problem, who if listened to might shake the group out of its comfortable but pedestrian approach to work to attain a more creative solution to the problem faced by the group. As mentioned earlier, hasty decisions are pushed in groups in which most members are alike. Such groups are most intolerant of deviants. On the other hand, recent unpublished research suggests that where members are highly task-oriented, deviant opinion is more likely to be tolerated.

Absence of Specialized Resources or Activities. Ordinarily, effective groups may suffer lowered productivity and dissatisfaction owing to the failure of any of the members to accept a particular responsibility or to take a particular role when needed by the group. The problem-solving process will be disrupted, for example, if no one offers the group an evaluation of alternatives.[236] In the same way, a weak or missing link in the chain severely reduces group effectiveness. For instance, inadequate secretarial service was a strong factor in retarding effectiveness of 72 observed conferences.[259]

Absence of Positive Feedback. Groups are less likely to solve problems effectively, and members are likely to be more dissatisfied with their work, if feedback is not provided indicating the success with which the group is carrying out its assignments.[537] But merely learning about the group's success only contributes slightly to team performance.[759] On the other hand, performance of individual members working as a group improves the most when they receive constructive information about their individual efforts as well as the group's success as a whole, particularly if the problems are difficult.[759] Equally useful is personal feedback of one member to another in improving problem-solving efficiency of all.[619] Yet only emphasizing what is wrong with an individual member's performance serves to increase his defensiveness in the group, particularly if remarks are personal.[236]

*   *   *   *   *

Often the key to effective and satisfied employes lies in forming and maintaining attractive and effective work groups. At the same time, if one enters an organization in which the groups are already committed to processes which are inadequate or to goals which are in conflict with the aims of the organization as a whole, one may be able to bring about desired changes in the individual employe only after his group has first examined and accepted the possibilities of changing procedures and directions.

Understanding group life becomes essential in the promoting of the effective organization, for much of the work of modern organization must take place in groups as individuals lack the resources to handle alone so many of the problems of the large productive organization. And group products are likely to be better than what could be produced by the average group member, although they might not be as good as what could be turned out by the best member.

Groups develop in characteristic stages. Maturity is reached when members have learned to accept and trust each other, to process information effectively, to set mutually acceptable goals within self-imposed constraints. For a given task, there is an optimum group size, an optimum mix of talents, and an optimum amount of contact between members. Maximum utilization of the resources within the group are most likely when consensual decisions are sought, when members build upon each other's contributions, when role expectations are clear, when deviation is tolerated, and when members can give and receive feedback about their participation in the group effort.

Paramount to increasing the utilization of resources of the members of a group, particularly as the group enlarges to meet greater and more complex challenges, is how members are formally organized. This is the subject of what now follows.

In Brief

THE CONSISTENT PATTERNS OF RELATIONS AMONG LARGE GROUPS OF MEN may be formal or informal. The patterns are studied by case analysis, sociometry, and many other procedures, including mathematical and laboratory simulations. Classical organization theorists provided what appeared to be a logical set of rules for formally promoting and maintaining task patterns. However, because the relations to be regulated are among people as well as among people and positions, the rules need to be qualified in the light of modern behavioral science. Broadened objectives giving more weight to human factors suggest a variety of new ways of designing large organizations.

One important issue is an organization's growth and how it changes as a consequence of its own expansion. To understand an organization's development and behavior one needs to inquire into its objectives, how they are set and changed, and how the organization progresses towards its goals. One also needs to examine what obstacles or constraints inhibit the achieving of its objectives. Although intended to foster coordination of effort, the organization's rules often constrain behavior, as does the formally imposed pattern of relations. The task and technology of the organization are likewise important in affecting how the organization operates.

Chapter 7

INDUSTRIAL

ORGANIZATION

CERTAIN JOBHOLDERS WORK IN CONSISTENT, PREDICTABLE WAYS WITH other jobholders in the company regardless of who they are personally. Whoever holds the job of maintenance supervisor will order whoever is a maintenance mechanic to inspect a faulty machine upon the request of whoever is the foreman of whoever is the machine's operator. This predictable pattern, combined with all such possible patterns, is the *formal organization* of the company. The patterns may be prescribed in written rulebooks; they may be unwritten and maintained by custom, historical precedent, or specific arrangements made in the past by specific jobholders and handed down to their successors.

On the other hand, the *informal* organization is the pattern of consistent relations among jobholders, regardless of the jobs they occupy. Interaction between jobholders may occur because they went to school together, they are brothers-in-law, one admires the other, they happen to work next to each other, they are in the same car pool, or they live next door to each other. The operator with the faulty machine may be the next-door neighbor of the assistant foreman. The two may discuss the problem at home or at the plant because they are neighbors and friends.

As will be seen, any analysis of an industrial organization must deal with both its formal and informal aspects.

SPECIAL METHODS FOR THE STUDY OF ORGANIZATIONS

In addition to employing survey, field, and laboratory experiments, organizational research relies heavily on techniques specially applicable to studying the formal and informal relations between job occupants.

These methods include: case analysis, sociometry, position analysis, discretionary analysis, analyses of communications, comparative analyses, laboratory exercises, business games, and mathematical simulation.

Case Analysis

The case history is a detailed essay describing a business firm over a period of time. The writer attempts to account for current events in terms of the dynamics he observes and the history of the firm. Studies of cases are a favorite management training technique in which one is supposed to learn how a specific firm's behavior involves a complex interaction of many principles. Unfortunately, case-by-case examination does not contribute to the verification of any particular principle, for it is a matter of opinion as to which and how much of each principle is in effect in a given case. If the many available published cases were in a standard form, it might be possible for independent judges to abstract principles from them. For example, if each manufacturing firm could be clearly identified on a dimension revealing whether it produced units to customer orders, produced batches, mass produced items, or continuously produced a product (as in oil refining), and if each of these same cases also gave an objective or subjective estimate of the ratio of lateral to vertical communications in the manufacturing firm, we might be able to uncover the relation between production technology and the direction of communications in a plant.

Sociometry

By asking each member of a group to choose or to rate all the others, we obtain a picture of the informal social structure of the group, its cliques, its isolates, and the centers of decision within the group. This method, *sociometry*, has some special uses in organizational research.

For example, each employe is asked to indicate the persons he contacted most frequently in the past month. From the contacts named by all employes we can draw the perceived communication pattern of the organization and show the extent to which it does or does not conform to the formal organization. (See Figure 7.1. The dotted lines show the pattern of contacts. The solid lines show the prescribed formal organization.)

A more complete analysis is provided if we ask each employe to indicate which relations he *prefers* and which he *rejects*. The reports of those he said he had contacted give an estimate of his *actual* contacts. The *prescribed* relations are obtained by determining whom the employe

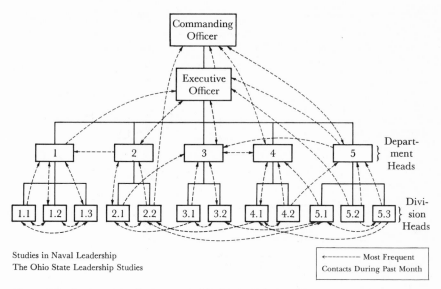

Figure 7.1: Sociometric Pattern of Working Relationships in a Small, Formal Organization Based on Each Person Identifying Other Most Frequently Contacted During the Past Month. (After Stogdill, 1949, p. 282)

was supposed to contact. The employe's understanding and satisfaction with the formal and informal organization can be obtained by examining the differences among his preferences, perceived contacts, actual contacts, and the relations prescribed for him.[456]

Position Analysis

Suppose we rate each job in an organization on how much knowledge, intelligence, versatility, and skill in handling people are required to successfully perform the job to obtain an index of a job's demands. Then suppose we rate on the same dimensions each person who happens to occupy the job to provide an index of employe capability. The ratio of these two indexes indicates how close an employe's capability matches the demands of his job. If the index is 125, for instance, the employe is judged better than his job; if the index is 82, the job is too big for the job occupant. Figure 7.2 displays such ratios found in a particular company. The manager with a ratio of 82 has more than he can handle: the traffic manager with 125 can do more than is now demanded of him. By moving personnel and changing the demands of given jobs through reorganization, it is possible to match more closely job demand and the capacity of job occupants as is seen in Figure 7.3.[226]

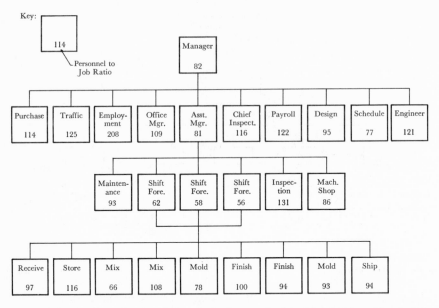

Key:

114

Personnel to
Job Ratio

Manager
82

Purchase	Traffic	Employ-ment	Office Mgr.	Asst. Mgr.	Chief Inspect.	Payroll	Design	Schedule	Engineer
114	125	208	109	81	116	122	95	77	121

Mainten-ance	Shift Fore.	Shift Fore.	Shift Fore.	Inspec-tion	Mach. Shop
93	62	58	56	131	86

Receive	Store	Mix	Mix	Mold	Finish	Finish	Mold	Ship
97	116	66	108	78	100	94	93	94

Figure 7.2: An Organization Before It Is Reorganized to Match More Closely Job Demand and Personnel Capacity. (After Gaiennie, 1950, p. 45)

Discretionary Analysis

Another analysis of potential use in understanding an organization is based on the freedom of the jobholder. In the typical line enterprise the manual or clerical worker has at most one-half to one full day of work assigned him to complete using his own discretion, judgment, and initiative without review by his superior. A skilled craftsman may go one week to a few months without review; a foreman, six months to a year; a production manager, from months to years; and a member of top management may be free of review for many years. The amount of time without review correlates highly with pay expectations. In instances where one or the other is out of line, changes may be in order in pay or in amount of discretion permitted.[336]

Analysis of Communications

Logging the pattern of communications and contacts made by each job occupant shows the whole pattern of communications in an organization. But it is also informative to follow a single communication through an organization to see at what relay points it is delayed, distorted, elaborated upon, or completely blocked. Such a tracing is done by asking each member of an organization, "By no later than noon today did you know about _____ or any part of it?" Respondents can indicate how much, if any, of the information they had and what time they learned it. For each individual and for each department, it is possible to calculate the percentage of information received relative to the total information they could have received. How much a particular communication spreads out in the organization can be determined. Also, we can see the extent to which individuals and departments initiate communications relative to their opportunities to do so. The speed of the informal "grapevine" can also be compared with the speed of the formal chain.[148]

Communications can be content analyzed. That is, they can be coded according to a theoretical scheme to increase understanding of what is going on. For example, in order to find out whether an organiza-

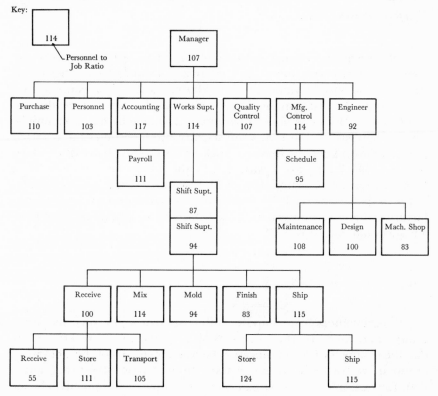

Figure 7.3: An Organization After It Is Reorganized to Match More Closely Job Demand and Personnel Capacity. (After Gaiennie, 1950, p. 49)

tion is operating effectively, it may be useful to classify its communications as goal-oriented, means-oriented, or irrelevant to the company's goals.[272] Presumably, operational efficiency would be high when the proportion of irrelevant communications was low.

Comparative Analyses

Organizations and organization units can be compared in a variety of objective ways. For example, factor analyses of checklist descriptions of 188 New Orleans manufacturing firms made it possible to scale them on such independent dimensions as how much they provided retirement benefits, attractive jobs, sickness benefits, insurance benefits, and discount sales to employes.[509]

Cross-Cultural Analyses

Often what we regard as the only way turns out merely to be the American way. Inspection of how organizations operate in other countries provide insight into our own idiosyncracies. For example, the research administrator in the Soviet Union has the status of an administrative clerk. Decisions about operations are made by the nonadministrative scientists. In the U.S. a top scientist often becomes the research administrator. Then he devotes much of his energy to activities which in the Soviet Union are performed by the administrative clerk.[351] In West Germany the technical head of a manufacturing firm is equal in status to the commercial. He therefore has more authority over manufacturing than his counterpart in the U.S., who would merely serve in an advisory-staff R & D role.[208]

Laboratory Exercises

Experimenters can impose different structures on laboratory groups and measure the effects. Basically, structures are created so that the channels of communication between members of the laboratory group are restricted in systematic ways. In the "circle" structure (Figure 7.4), for example, members can only communicate to immediately adjacent ones; in the "wheel" all members can only communicate to one at the hub of the wheel. As will be discussed in detail in Chapter 8, anal-

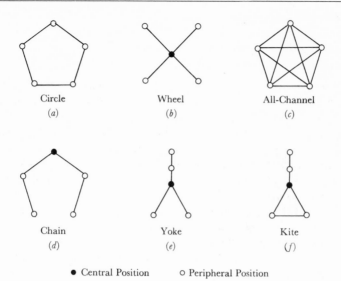

Figure 7.4: *Different Kinds of Communication Structures Studied in the Laboratory by Opening or Closing Communication Passages Between Members of a Small Group.*

yses can be made of the effects of the different structures on the number of errors, correct solutions, speed of solution, number of messages per problem, distribution of influence by position, agreement about distribution, satisfaction of members with their position and with their group's performance, and consistent patterns of interaction emerging within the various structures.[243]

Organization can be studied in the laboratory in other ways. In the Common Target Exercise, three players, although back-to-back, must learn to cooperate without communicating. Each must contribute a number so that all three numbers sum to the target number (of 31 or less). Study is concentrated on how the three men organize to solve the problem.[393]

How men organize for productive activity can be studied by manufacturing exercises. Quartets literally purchase tinker-toy materials at fixed prices, assemble the toys, and sell them in a fixed market.[522] The Case Institute exercise is similar; a Purchaser obtains letters of the alphabet, a Manufacturer forms words, a Salesman sells them.[117] In the Bass–Leavitt word-sentence production game, trios coin words from the letters of a master word, then "sell" sentences based on the words. Unused words are excess inventory. Bad words and sentences are scrapped. Actual production must proceed without communication, thus placing emphasis on pre-production planning.[47]

Business Games

The prototype business game, Top Management Decision Simulation, and most of its 200 successors present a rich display to players of markets and costs of plant, equipment, labor, and production. The game requires a variety of rational decisions by the individual or team of players: selling prices, advertising expenditures, research budgets, capital investments, and so on. Play over successive periods can be against other players or against random or biased mathematical scorekeepers. The complex calculations often are made by a high-speed computer. In addition to general management games, there have been created simulations of materials management, manufacturing, sales management, inventory control, maintenance scheduling, systems improvement personnel allocation, warehousing, production scheduling, service station operating, wholesaling, financing, stock market portfolio management, research management, and bank managements. Many of these can be used for studying decision-making processes in selected property-rich environments. One can also study here individual differences in the ability to abstract, to organize data, to forecast and plan, and to use information in a complex and diffuse environment of risk and uncertainty.[47]

The Carnegie Tech game, in which players operate one of three companies competing in a fairly accurate simulation of the real detergent industry, is sufficiently complex to combine the economic decision-making processes with real concern for internal management. So many decisions must be made by so many persons to meet the demands of the game, so much data must be processed by the players, that the game affords opportunities for studying in detail the effects of the organization of the players on their performance.[125]

In the Production Organization Exercise, companies of about 15 men each — practicing industrial managers in a training school — are created and literally compete with each other in efficient production and sale of products made from IBM cards by cutting, assembling, and stapling. Special restrictions imposed on players, preventing more than one-third of a company from meeting face-to-face, generate many of the social psychological phenomena of the large manufacturing enterprise, including perversion of management goals from maximum gain to minimum loss, collective bargaining with labor about the wrong issues, promoting of labor agitators, wildcatting, communication filtering by middle management, "overorganizing," and stealing of trade secrets.[44a]

These games and exercises offer management the opportunity to test new organizational strategies in advance. They enable the researcher to see the effects of a particular mixture of structures, objectives, and constraints. The research can also test radically new organizational designs, hardly possible with an operating company.

Mathematical Simulation

If the processes of an organization can be described mathematically and the dynamics matched by appropriate mathematical functions, it is possible to simulate a real system in its complex entirety. This was done, for example, for the distributive organization of H. J. Heinz. Given factory and product characteristics, data were generated mathematically about distribution costs as a function of customers, salesmen, carriers, warehouse locations, even forecasting the effects of changing consumer habits.[608] In the same way United Airlines found answers to crucial questions about routing and maintaining their aircraft by means of a simulation of a maintenance factory.[470] How well the mathematics match the processes observed in the real organization and accurately forecast what happens in the company indicates how well we understand and can abstract the important dynamics of the real organization.

CLASSICAL ORGANIZATION THEORY

The Need for Organization

For large numbers of men to coordinate their efforts on complex problems of work, each must be able to predict and account for the behavior of his associated workers. Coordination of effort would be impossible without such predictability and accountability. Predictability and accountability can be obtained informally, particularly in smaller groups where members can develop more familiarity with each other. But for larger groups, classical rules of organization provide a way of predicting and accounting for what each worker will do. Many of these rules were originated by the Romans or earlier civilizations and transmitted to our industrial society by church, government, and particularly military tradition and practice.

These traditional rules have been refined and perfected by management theorists such as Frederick W. Taylor, L. Urwick, and E. W. Reilley.[549] While they appear reasonably logical, they are unfortunately predicated on mythical assumptions about human behavior. They assume that workers must be persuaded, rewarded, punished, controlled, and directed if the coordination of effort is to be achieved. In fact, no work at all will get done unless there is active intervention by management. This is because the average man is naturally lazy and will work as little as possible. He lacks ambition, dislikes accepting responsibility, and prefers to be led. He is only concerned with his own needs and not with the goals of his organization. He resists change. He is not a good decision-maker. As much as possible, all decisions within the organization should be routinized so that under all circumstances the individual will require a minimum of thought without alternatives. Indeed, he must be told in detail what to do or he will not be able to do his job. He must be prodded with external incentives and close surveillance.[278, 466] The assumptions seem to fit the Roman military master and his captured barbarian slaves better than the typical American manager and his subordinates.

It is interesting to note that the traditionalists are likely to accuse others in the organization of fitting the above description, but naturally they always exclude themselves.[278]

The reader's own experiences and what has been said in the preceding six chapters cannot help but make the reader aware that these assumptions are erroneous.

Workers who fit the description can be developed, and the classical rules of organization generally contribute to such development. The rules do not follow from the assumptions; rather, the rules make the assumptions seem less in error. For by creating indolent, irresponsible, disinterested work forces, they perpetuate the assumptions that workers inherently are this way.[466]

Close adherence to these rules is likely to create organizational conditions increasing the likelihood of such negativistic behavior by the work group. As stressed in the preceding chapters, conditions at the work place, the nature of supervision, the previous history and experiences of the worker and the organization, and the society within which the working situation is located will determine whether a worker withdraws or is attracted to work, whether he is self-concerned rather than committed to the organization's goals, whether he resists or welcomes change, and whether he is interested, willing, and able to make decisions.

Traditional Rules of Formal Organization

Let us consider some of the classical rules to see whether each measures up to what we know of human behavior in the light of modern findings in the behavioral sciences.

1. *Someone should be responsible for supervising all essential activities.*

While this rule may be most efficacious in an emergency, research of the past 20 years points to the utility of shared leadership. Under a permissive supervisor each member of a group has the training and willingness to accept leadership responsibilities when he sees the need to do so. For example, every member will feel free to participate in suggesting new ways of approaching a problem facing the group. Sharing of leadership increases the likelihood that at a given point in an organization's or a group's life, those members with most ability to solve the group's problems are most likely to step forward to accept the leadership roles required of them. Where there is strict adherence to the rule that a particular activity is to be led by a particular individual, the group or organization is forced into a mechanical mold in which the led often know more about the solutions to the problems facing the group than does the formally appointed leader.

2. *Responsibility for specific acts should not be duplicated or overlapping.*

Logically, duplication may mean wasted effort. Yet there are numerous instances where duplication and overlapping are not only desirable but even mandatory. The reliability of a response system is increased by building into it one or more back-up systems, so that if the first fails to detect or respond to some particular event, the back-up system will do so. Overlapping responsibilities make possible shared efforts. This encourages the positive dynamics of groups described in the preceding chapter. Cross-training occurs as a consequence of such duplication so that one worker can move readily into another employe's position if the latter is absent or transferred. Specification to eliminate duplication may increase difficulties of coordination with a consequent loss in an organization's flexibility. If one worker makes the wheels and a second makes the gears for a wheel-gear assembly put together by the second employe, then anytime a wheel component is sent to the second worker unready for assembly, he must return it to the first worker rather than fix it himself. If the wheelmaker falls behind, then the gearmaker can only stockpile gears or stop work.

Again, completely independent duplication of effort may increase waste, but at the same time such freedom to duplicate lies at the heart of the competitive system. We may ask three designers in a single department each to submit plans independently for the same project, hoping thereby to generate a single best proposal from three potential sources instead of one. This may or may not be more productive than asking the three to collaborate in the first place; but it is certainly likely that however we do it, the three designers will provide us with a variety of choices.

3. *No one position should have too numerous or complex duties. Duties should be meaningfully clustered so that position holders do not have responsibility for a wide assortment of unrelated acts.*

While at times this rule may be economically sound and a stimulus to efficiency, it is completely contrary to what we know about the need for job challenge, job opportunity, job interest, and job involvement, particularly for skilled employes and those at higher levels. A wide assortment of tasks may be preferable to a job restricted to performing only one. Often jobs need to be enlarged. Even at the lowest levels on the assembly line, the girl who is given the opportunity periodically during the day to rotate from packing to inspecting, to a rest station and then back to packing is likely to experience less boredom on the job and more satisfaction with it.

4. *Responsibilities should be written, clear, and understood by job occupants.*

This rule may be needed if there is no other way of providing understanding about one's job, but it opens up the possibilities of jurisdictional disputes, concerns about responsibilities rather than objectives, competition between adjacent job occupants, disputes about words instead of work, and the likely tendency to perform at a level lower than actually possible. Work can be avoided, actions sidestepped, even when badly needed, by simply stating, "I am not supposed to do that; that is not my responsibility." Experience with team learning, particularly where coordination and project outcomes are complex, suggests that it is difficult, if not impossible, to specify in detail the boundaries of a job. Job incumbents who must collaborate, if given the freedom to explore with each other to learn the best possible ways of relating to each other, develop an organic organization which is far more efficient than might have been specified in advance by organizational planners.[111] An organization handicaps itself unnecessarily if it restricts unduly the scope of an assignment to an individual, impressing him with his assignment responsibilities rather than the objectives of his job. When objectives are paramount, he discovers higher levels of performance which could not have been expected of him in advance of his own discoveries.

Regardless of this traditional rule and even where job descriptions are clearly written, what executives do who are transferred from one job to another depends considerably on themselves rather than the job to which they are currently assigned.[645] Each executive seems to develop a pattern of behavior with which he is able to operate reasonably efficiently. Forced changes in the ways the executive operates may make for a neater organization but may do little to improve the executive's effectiveness.

Obviously some job structuring is needed. The suggestion is that we do not overstructure the situation by wordy job definitions emphasizing responsibilities instead of objectives.

5. *Authority to make decisions should be commensurate with responsibility for those decisions.*

Such a statement ignores the fact that much authority resides in the person owing to his value as a person or the esteem his associates have for him rather than the position he occupies. In fact, it is commonplace in organizations for subordinates, by presenting certain kinds of information to their superiors, actually to make the decisions which according to this rule should be made by their superiors. The rule fosters irresponsibility for organizational objectives, for individual members can plead, "I did what I could" or "I did what I was supposed to do, for it was no business of mine to pay attention to the matter which led to a disastrous outcome for the organization."

The rule places the staff advisor in a peculiar position in an organization, for if he has no authority over decisions but can only advise, then he can feel completely irresponsible for any decisions that are based on his advice.[278]

6. *Authority should be delegated so that decisions take place as close as possible to the point of action.*

If this rule could be applied or if it were consistent with the preceding rules, it would conform to the suggestions of behavioral science. But the hierarchical organization which must be created as a consequence of the preceding rules places decision-making in an organization at least one echelon higher than the point of action. Each superior is supposed to tell each subordinate at one echelon below him what to do. Paradoxically, more consistent with this rule but conflicting with most of the preceding ones is the recent proposal to organize overlapping groups (Figure 7.5) in which each supervisor would see himself as a pin linking the group composed of his peers and boss with a second group composed of his subordinates and himself. This proposal would actually move the decision-making process to the level at which the decisions will be executed.[412] The current pattern, following traditional rules, is for decisions affecting one's own activities to be made by one's immediate superiors.

7. *Executives should have no more than five to seven subordinates reporting to them; first-line supervisors, no more than 20.* (Many classical theorists argue for limits of only three subordinates at the highest levels in the organization.)

To follow this rule about "span of control" means that a steep, vertical hierarchy is required as an organization enlarges into the thousands. Sometimes such a hierarchy is necessary, but numerous negative effects result from such a many-layered organization. Messages initiated at the bottom of the hierarchy are unlikely to reach the top. If they do, they are likely to have been filtered, modified, and distorted. The goals of those at upper echelons become completely divorced from those at the lowest ones. Job tenure becomes more important than organizational objectives. As environmental problems change, the organization finds

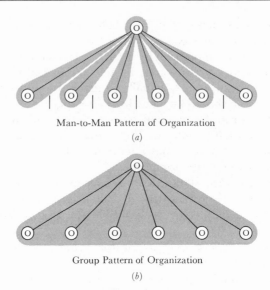

Man-to-Man Pattern of Organization

(a)

Group Pattern of Organization

(b)

Figure 7.5: Man-to-Man Versus Group Pattern of Organization. (After Likert, 1961, p. 105)

it difficult to react rapidly to such external demands. While persons promoted to higher echelons are more satisfied, those at lower levels, who form the vast majority of the pyramidal organization, remain relatively dissatisfied because of the invidious comparison. The pyramidal organization contributes to a few satisfied chiefs and a multitude of dissatisfied Indians.

As Sears, Roebuck has shown, even the largest organizations can be flattened drastically. One vice president can have 200 subordinate store managers if both he and his store managers have access to objective, reliable, and accurate measures of store performance and employe morale within the stores. Maximum freedom for subordinates is prized. If effective communication procedures are developed and maintained, extreme decentralization of this sort becomes feasible. Actually, a survey of the satisfaction of 1,900 managers in "tall" organizations with many echelons or "flat" ones with few echelons suggested that flat organizations provide more opportunity for self-development and self-actualization. However, it failed to reveal many consistent effects leading to the conclusion that this "span of control" rule often may be irrelevant compared to other factors such as sheer company size in determining how satisfied executives are with their organization.[535]

8. *Every occupant of each position should know to whom to report and who reports to him. The chain of command should be recognized and followed.*

Perception of the actual communications occurring in any large organization shows that such a chain often is ignored, for it makes much of the important, needed communications extremely difficult. It forces much reporting, evaluating, and examining to go up through one chain and down another to achieve some horizontal contact. The head of Division 3.1 (Figure 7.1) needs to give a report to the head of Division 2.1 in order for the organization to reach certain objectives; Division Head 3.1 must send his communication through Department Head 3 and the executive officer, who in turn transmits it down the line through Department Head 2 to Division Head 2.1. Some organizations do enforce this kind of awkward communication process. Some department heads enforce or try to enforce this type of organizational functioning. Indeed, imbued with the sanctity of this chain of command rule, Department Head 5 may develop strong feelings of insecurity and chagrin at learning that Division Head 5.2 has bypassed him and communicated directly with the executive officer.

Chain of command looks good on paper, but it is impractical. It is supposed to tell who takes orders from whom. The commanding officer is supposed to make decisions for the executive officer. The executive officer is authorized to make decisions for the department heads. The department heads are supposed to make decisions for the division heads. More often, it is the subordinates who are in better positions to make decisions affecting their own behavior than their superiors, and, in practice, the subservience plan of organization is unlikely to work well if followed. More often, it is not followed.[67]

In actual practice the chain of command may be a neat fiction. For as Figure 7.1 shows, the actual pattern of communications, transmission of reports, ideas, suggestions, proposals, advice, orders, and decisions flows in complex paths not shown by the traditional organizational chart. Figure 7.1 indicates which persons each member of the organization said he had contacted the most during the preceding month. Note, for instance, that Division Head 5.1 appeared to have contacted more frequently Department Head 4 rather than Department Head 5.

Modern Alternatives to the Classical Organization Theory

Classical organization theory is actually a collection of hortatory rules based on nineteenth-century military formulas modified for the purposes of industry. One organization, the pyramid, is generated by these formulas. Organizational search for new approaches to the changing environment is impossible. Phenomena associated with interactions between individuals are ignored, and individuals are treated as units.[392a]

What does modern behavioral science offer as a substitute to provide the needed predictability for coordinated effort? It suggests:

> More effective organizations are made about interested and able people; in
> small, freely communicating, face-to-face groups; under articulate and dedi-
> cated leadership; deeply committed to a clear and challenging objective and
> thoroughly involved in solving the problems which stand in the way of achieving
> the objective.[344, p.550]

Along lines discussed in preceding chapters, subordinates participate in setting objectives in collaboration with their supervisors. All feel
free to contribute and assume responsibility for achievement. While
individuals remain responsible for decisions, particularly those affecting
their own performance, the group develops a sense of responsibility for
supporting its individual constituents. Information is freely shared
rather than restricted to chains of command, and the best resources are
brought to bear on given solutions.[344]

The modern emphasis is on wide participation in decision-making,
face-to-face group action rather than the individual as the basic unit of
organization. The supervisor is the agent for maintaining intragroup
and intergroup communications rather than the agent of higher authority. The supervisor has the objective of helping his subordinates
to increase their effectiveness rather than externally controlling them
in the performance of their tasks.[604]

There are two ways of producing these suggested changes in relations among organization members. We can continue to employ the
formal hierarchy of the kind shown in Figure 7.1, but modified by permissive policies and by emphasis on management by objectives. Or, as
we shall see later, we can develop new organizational structures, specifically designed in the light of current thinking in modern psychology.

A Synthesis of the Modern and the
Classical Approaches is Needed

It is likely that different organizational arrangements are called for,
depending upon the nature of the work to be done, the abilities and attitudes of those who will man the organization, and the environment in
which the organization must operate. But some advocates of the behavioral approach have taken an extreme position, preferring to abandon completely everything from the classical school of thought. As one
critic quipped, classical organization theory concerns itself with "organizations without people," but the modern behaviorists tend to think about
"people without organizations." Yet there are numerous organizational

imperatives which still must be considered with due regard for what we know about human motivation, learning, and perception. Material and economic success are still critical (Chapter 3), permissiveness is often contraindicated (Chapter 5), individuals differ in their motivation (Chapter 4), and organizational goals are multidimensional (Chapter 1), as are those of the individual at work (Chapter 2). The classical rules were deduced from faulty assumptions about human motivation, learning, and perception. But behavioral scientists may be formulating principles deduced from erroneous assumptions about economics, technology, and production.

What is needed is a systems approach which seeks to blend concern for authority, responsibility and control, on the one hand, with concern for motivation, perception, learning, and interaction, on the other. We need to incorporate knowledge about information transmission, strategies, choices, probabilities, and sequences in order to optimize a system of strategies for cooperation within organizations and competition between them. The traditional school's emphasis on efficiency at work and the behavioral school's concern with the effective collaboration of men can be merged in the search for an optimum system to meet customer demands with production and institutional programs which balance growth, innovation, and stability.[233]

ORGANIZATIONAL GROWTH

Instead of rules for forming organizations, it is more important to understand what factors are involved in an organization's growth. If we develop understanding, then we can predict what will happen; and finally we may be able to control what will happen to an organization.

Stimulants to Organizational Growth

What makes firms grow? What stimulates some into almost continuous expansion? What motivates managers and planners to strive for bigger and larger systems to operate even when they have their hands full just keeping up with past developments? There are the nonmaterial values described at the end of Chapter 1 that may dictate decisions for expansion by management. Managers may thrive on adventure and risk and may seek prestige, power, and security in bigness. But, in addition, there are many completely rational reasons for the growth of business firms and agencies.

First there are external stimulants. We live in a growing economy

and a growing population. If one firm or agency does not plan to continue expanding its service, a competitor will fill the vacuum. Within
the growing economy the bigger a firm becomes, the more it faces a
reasonably stable market. That is, if a firm's share of the market annually
is about 40 percent, it is much less likely to fluctuate widely in relative
terms than if it has only 4 percent of the market. A drop of 1 percent in
market favor will be drastic for the small firm, but mean little to the large
one. The large firm has more control over its market to the extent that
it can bring to bear its advertising and pricing powers. The larger firm
can meet a customer's demands for complete service. It can introduce
new products faster. Its very survival in a highly competitive market
may depend upon its potential to grow at the expense of competitors.

Then there are technical reasons for organizational growth. A firm
attempts to "master its own technology." It will grow as it attempts to
integrate its activities from the processing of the raw materials to the
distribution of its wares to the customer. A meatpacker will eventually
try to own its own stockyard facilities, fatten its own pigs at one end of
its business, and sell finished products directly to chain stores at the
other end. In the same way if a firm is in the meatpacking business, it
attempts to make and sell everything but the pig's squeal and obviously
expands its production and distribution as its research and development
discovers new by-products of the original business activity.

Then there are economic reasons. Up to some point, costs per unit
of production are lowered as more units are produced. Bigger and more
efficient equipment can be employed. Revenue and profits are likely to
increase up to some point as the organization grows.

Finally there are rational needs of the membership that can be satisfied by continued growth. Growth provides more room for men in the
organization to move upward. Managers can be promoted faster when
new departments are formed. Workers can move into better and more
responsible jobs as production is expanded. And as the organization
grows so do the salaries of those who run it. (Executive income depends
more on the size of the unit administered than on its profitability.)[638]

Limitations on Organizational Growth

With all these forces toward expansion, what besides competition
with each other keeps firms from exploding? Some of the most important restrictions are the limitations imposed by the specific objectives
and products of the firm which rule out a wide range of possibilities for
expansion.

If one makes turbines, there are just so many that will be needed by the economy annually. The number produced cannot exceed the normal increasing demand for electric energy, power station construction, and so on. It may be economically wasteful to produce anything but turbines. The plant, equipment, and work force are of no use in manufacturing anything else. Expansion into foreign markets seems feasible, except that foreign competition may be as great as domestic, if not greater.

Government works against monopolistic growth as a matter of national policy. It also influences the growth and expansion of firms through direct regulation; for example, it controls how much oil may be pumped out of the ground, what business may and may not be engaged in by railroads and what minimum wages must be paid to workers.

As firms enlarge, the need for coordination places increasing burdens on the communication network within the firm. Internal complexities create more and more difficulties as firms continue to increase in size. Moreover, many of the other negative sociopsychological problems described in the preceding chapter accompany increasing size. There is also likely to be much resistance to the changes which accompany expansion. Finally the available management manpower may put the brakes on continuing expansion. A company may hesitate to create an additional division if it is unsure about whether it can locate or train the brainpower to run the division.[638]

And again, nonmaterial managerial values may inhibit growth. Cautious, conservative managers may prefer to avoid the risks of expansion more than they wish to seek potential gains from growth.

Upward Versus Downward Growth

Characteristic changes occur in organizations as they grow. For example, firms that grow by mergers tend to develop upward-growing control superstructures to direct and control the merging units. When company A buys companies B and C, their presidents are replaced by general managers, and the combination is headed by a chief at a new higher level. Those that grow primarily through their own differentiation tend to develop downward-growing control hierarchies.[298] If company A is split into divisions 1, 2, and 3, new division heads are created at one level below that of the president of company A. The merging units headed by general managers with a superstructure tend to experience more difficulties in centralizing their efforts; the downward-growing differentiating units led by division heads tend to have more difficulty in decentralizing. Open conflict is probably more frequent as a consequence of upward growth since each unit head, like the general manager, previously used to running an independent entity with a unique history and pattern of operating norms, now must subordinate himself to higher authority. He must coordinate efforts with other formerly independent units with different ways of operating. On the other hand, downward differentiation is accompanied more often by relative upward mobility of the individuals with seniority in the proliferating hierarchy. The new division heads have been reared in an older, undifferentiated firm and share common ways of behaving, so are less likely to conflict in opinions and actions.

Administrative Growth Versus Total Growth

The popular misconception known as Parkinson's Law[510] is that as organizations enlarge, the number of administrative employes increases faster than the rate at which the total organization increases. This supposedly occurs because an executive wants to multiply subordinates, not rivals. Also, officials are supposed to make work for each other, so that each bureaucrat added means ultimately the need to employ several more. It is a case of a statement being more interesting than true, for a survey of 211 manufacturing firms in Ohio showed no relation between their size and the proportion of administrative officials in them. Again, study of the growth of a major banking system failed to support the hypothesis that the administrative component of an organization increases in size at a proportionally greater rate than the organization as a whole.[671] Indeed, other studies of American manufacturing establishments and German concerns showed an inverse rather than a direct relation between size and the percentage of individuals within the organization devoted to administration.[24] Some consistent changes in structure and types of employes do seem to occur with organizational growth. But the extent to which the numbers of clerical, service, and administrative personnel increase faster or more slowly than the total growth of an organization appears to depend on the kind of technological activities involved in the organization's output. For example, in the construction industry a professional labor force, needing little direction, provides its own rational administration without the need of a power-based, bureaucratic superstructure. Workers are mobile, have special competence, and are rewarded directly as a function of their contribution to the organization's output. Contracts define their individual responsibilities. On the other hand, in mass production industry a hierarchy of administrative authority is involved in planning, supervising, and controlling the assembly line operations. Administrative staffs maintain lines of communications and the continuity of operations.[642]

This difference in administrative overload between the craft-contractual and the mass production approach to coordinating efforts was seen in an analysis of anthropologists' descriptions of 150 nonindustrial societies. In the simplest systems, contracts were enough to maintain arrangements among productive workers. Somewhat more complex were societies which rewarded workers according to what they did. Still more complex organizations were found in which, in addition to contracts and specialized rewards, superiors determined the rewards and used administrative staffs and hierarchical authority to achieve coordination.[691, 692] Only in these most complex arrangements was administration likely to increase with increasing organization size.

An analytical review of many studies of the ratio of administrative (A) to productive employes (P) concluded that once a firm reaches approximately 100 employes this A/P ratio becomes independent of further increases in the size of the firm. Technological effects, just enumerated, are regarded as more important in affecting the A/P ratio. The ratio increases with time, but it is argued that this is probably the result of increasing technological complexity, new requirements, and additional activities undertaken by the firm.[638]

Changes in Composition and Structure Accompanying Growth

Systematic changes have been noted with growth. Generally as the base of the pyramid of the typical business firm expands, so its height in echelons increases.

If we know the average span of control (S) that is, the average number of subordinates under each superior, then the total number of men (M) comprising an organization will depend upon the number of levels (L) in the organization:

$$M = \frac{S^L - 1}{S - 1}$$

When $L = 2$ and $S = 5$, for instance, $M = 6$. If $L = 3$, then $M = 31$.

If the number of subordinates increases per supervisor, then again the number of men will increase.

When $L = 2$ and $S = 9$, $M = 10$. If $L = 3$, then $M = 91$.

Conversely, if M increases, either the number of levels of an organization or the average span of control must be increased. Since several surveys involving hundreds of large firms find that they tend to conform to classical theory in that spans of control at management levels, S, increase on the average from only about five to nine at most, no matter how big the firms become, it follows that the number of levels, L, is most likely to increase with continued company growth. The pyramid gets taller as its base expands. A firm with 20,000 management personnel would need seven levels of management to maintain an average span of control of five.

Other structural changes accompany growth and aging. Departmentalization increases. The first formal subunit to appear in an expanding firm is likely to be a production department, then a sales department, then one for purchasing, followed by a quality control unit. The pattern in which other specialized subunits will appear is less predictable.[638]

Still other changes accompany the increasing height and complexity of the pyramid as companies grow and age. Thus a study of the growth of 30 business firms in Southern California between 1947 and 1955

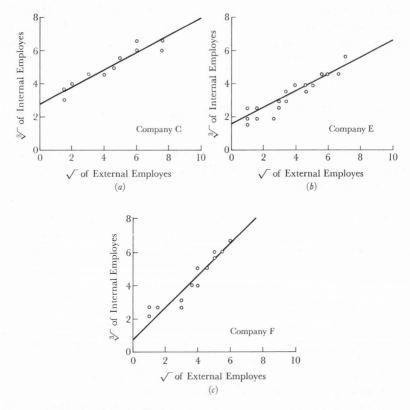

Figure 7.6: Comparison of the Square Root of External Employes and the Cube Root of Internal Employes in Three Companies at Various Times in Their Histories. (After Haire, 1959, p. 287)

found that the growing companies tended to shift from functional and geographic departmentalization to product departmental organizations. That is, instead of servicing all the needs of a region with a single department, they began to create separate departments for different products.[467]

Surface Versus Internal Growth. "Outside" employes work primarily with things outside the firm. They include purchasing and shipping workers, receptionists, and labor negotiators. Production employes, line supervisors, and the like are "inside" employes. The square cube law, which describes the growth of physical bodies, also seems to apply to organizational growth. The *surface* of a sphere increases by its *square* as the *volume* of the sphere increases by its *cube*. As the cube of the volume doubles, the square of the surface doubles. A straight line describes the increase of the cube root of the volume plotted against the increase in the square root of the surface of the sphere. Such straight lines seem equally applicable to describing the relative increase in the numbers of external and internal employes as companies enlarge. Data for three companies are shown in Figures 7.6a, 7.6b, and 7.6c for the years from their founding to the date at which data were collected in the late 1950's. For these three companies and a fourth not shown, the correlations are .99, .96, .95, and .97, respectively, between the square root of external growth and the cube root of internal growth of the companies at various stages in each company's development.[276]

ORGANIZATIONAL GOALS AND ORGANIZATIONAL BEHAVIOR

As we stressed in Chapter 1, an organization has many goals. The goals affect each other and the behavior of the organization. For example, if stabilized employment is regarded as an important goal, sales, production stabilization, better inventory control, sales forecasting, and dynamic programming all may be required, as may employes who are willing and able to transfer from one assignment to another.

Naive observers believed all goal attainment could be reduced to profit attainment. But accountants can disclose or hide profits with complete honesty, depending on their bookkeeping procedures.[278] Current profits may be transitory, misleading, or fictitious. One company, on the brink of disaster, may show a picture of high profits as a consequence of a tax loss carryover; another may show a loss because of a rapid depreciation schedule, yet be building a future value. It is interesting that institutional investors and banks indicate a company's worth in terms of how well it is meeting other objectives such as growth, management development, share of the market, and prospects for new products. And as mentioned in Chapter 1, chief executives of firms in confidential interviews stress as their goals satisfaction to management and employes and service to the community, as well as interest in growth and product quality.

We will now look at the relations among organizational goals, their importance, who sets them, and how and why goals change.

Independence Among Organizational Goals

Attainment of one goal does not imply the achievement of other objectives. Happy workers are not necessarily productive workers. Productive organizations are not necessarily profitable ones. Profitable organizations are not necessarily healthy ones for the community.

Table 7.1 shows the extent to which five different goals were achieved by 72 wholesale warehouse divisions of a nationwide pharmaceutical firm. It can be seen that quality and quantity of production and satisfaction (as measured by lack of turnover) are unrelated to each other. Dollar earnings are reflected only in quantity of output. Among these criteria of attainment, only quantity and profit are affected (neg-

TABLE 7.1   CORRELATIONS AMONG FIVE MEASURES OF GOAL
ATTAINMENT BY 72 WAREHOUSE DIVISIONS*

	Quantity	Errors	Profit	Product	Turnover
Number of products processed in filling orders per man-hour		.01	.36	.59	−.01
Number of errors in filling orders per man-hour			.00	.00	.15
Net profit (gross margins, wage rates and occupancy costs)				.56	.03
Product value (sales per man-hour production)					−.01
Turnover					

*After Katzell, Barrett, Parkway, 1961

atively) by such factors as the size of the unit, the size of the city in which the unit is located, wage rates, unionization, and the percentage of males employed rather than females.[357] As first stated in Chapter 1, maximization of any of these outputs is likely to be achieved only at the expense of each other or excessive demands on one or more inputs of men, money, or materials. Choices must be made and an optimum system is to be sought of maximum output in the aggregate at the cost of minimum overall input.

Importance of Organization Goals. A premium is placed on concern for organizational goals as we shift away from conventional views that higher authority is responsible for organizing men, money, and materials solely for economic ends and that higher authority must direct, motivate, control, and modify subordinate members to fit the needs of the organization. Subordinates, in the conventional view, would be passive or resist organizational needs without the intervention of this higher authority.

In preceding chapters we have seen that conventional ideas about what makes work attractive need considerable modification. Where subordinates can share the goals of the organization, where they can attain their own goals by directing their efforts toward organizational efforts, the role of higher authority can be drastically altered. Orders and instructions are replaced by information and advice. All participants in the organization, regardless of their level, develop a sense of responsibility for various aspects of the organization's objectives. But for this to occur, the organization's goals must be clear, acceptable, and understandable. Equally clear must be the individual's subgoals, whose attainment contributes to the organization's achievement of the broader goals. Feedback of progress in subgoal and goal attainment is also critical.[466]

Who Sets Goals for the Firm?

Management's goals are supposedly set by its board of directors, who in turn are elected to represent the interests of the owners and sponsors of the firm—the stockholders. Yet such boards seem to limit their interests. Furthermore, often management dominates the board rather than vice versa. A survey of 32 corporate boards revealed that future business prospects, competition, and output were the most frequent subject of meetings. Less frequently discussed were distribution matters, labor relations, taxes, pricing, stock inventory, product quality, and stockholder relations. And to an even lesser extent the boards dealt with such questions as income distribution, public relations, company morale, government relations, and new capital. A board responsible to stockholders and catering primarily to their interests may be more fiction than fact.

Relations Between Board and Management. While it is usually thought that the board sets the goals and policies to be followed by another body, the company's managers, actually the top management may be the board. For example, a number of the 32 boards surveyed contained only members of the firm's management. The board and top management were essentially the same. More than half the 32 boards had one or more members of management on them. This matches other findings showing that by 1935, in 75 percent of 200 of the largest American corporations, 43 percent of the directors were salaried executives. In almost half of the companies they formed an absolute majority of the board![250] Management thus may be relatively free of any higher level authority. Freewheeling management presents dangers that the stockholder's needs may not be met. For this reason, investors may have to form independent watchdog committees.[143] It also means that management is freed for long-range planning and growth and can afford to be less concerned only about immediate profits. Satisfied stockholders may be less important to a freewheeling management than maintaining the integrity of the organization, growth, good products, employe satisfaction, and management self-esteem. While it is freed to award itself both earned and unearned material rewards in bonuses and stock options, management is likewise freed to make a variety of other satisfying decisions. Management does not have to justify in terms of present or future profits additional costs of a new office building which is architecturally pleasing rather than a drab eyesore. The building is satisfying to the organization. That is enough justification. It would be difficult to explain away the architectural costs solely as an expense to promote the corporate image. Thus, often we must look at management, particularly key men in management, to locate where and how a firm's goals and subgoals are set.

Changing Goals

Influence of the Economy. Organizational goals change with changes in the economic environment. In the U.S. 1940–48 was a production-oriented period. Big and little business subscribed to a superordinate goal of national survival. Goals were to produce as much as possible and to produce new, completely different products as dictated by military needs. Profit depended on how much was produced. From 1949 to 1957, a sales-oriented period, goals were to sell as much as possible of the products produced. Sales growth and diversification were most important. Profits were maintained by raising prices as costs increased. Beginning in 1958 marketing became most important. Sales goals were recast into surviving and growing in the face of competition by finding out what could be sold in the market and producing it. External market conditions now determined the purpose and nature of the organization. [310] While profits on a new product are important, the manufacturer must share his increasing return due to his efficiency with the consumer in order to expand the market for the new product. "The organization which furnishes society with the highest level of service may reap the highest profits."[414]

Special Events. Transient conditions raise some goals in saliency at different times owing to specific events, personnel changes, or sudden changes in the consumer. Management may suddenly become safety conscious after a dramatic accident.[139]

Cultural Influences. Different environments produce industrial organizations with completely different goals. For example, interviews in 53 Japanese factories reveal organizations whose goals are quite divergent from comparable American plants. Employment is a personal commitment between employer and employe. There is little separation of work and private life. The employe is rarely laid off, nor does he quit. There is a surplus of cheap labor in the factory. Technological innovation is avoided, and adjustment to external demands is difficult.[1] In the Soviet Union equipment is difficult to replace, so that a premium is placed on maintaining machinery in contrast to the U.S., where both tax laws and mass marketing foster rapid replacement schedules and relatively less attention to maintenance.[253]

Labor Versus Machinery. Dynamic interactions of labor and equipment modify organizational goals over time. The cost of manual handling of materials in Great Britain from 1938 to 1950 increased faster than the costs of fork-lift trucks, resulting in a steady shift toward the employment of the trucks. But this meant that each worker was now more productive and valuable, capable of forming a stronger union, resulting in moving labor costs even higher. This in turn pushed management toward the goal of further mechanization.[472]

Goal Setters. Goals set at the top by a firm often are modified by those below who are supposedly working toward the established goals of those at the top. Within each firm, it is necessary to look at key individuals and how they modify organizational objectives in terms of their own experience. To appreciate directions that will be taken by different subsystems within the total organization, the goals and biases of these individuals must be assessed.[232] When 23 executives were asked to study some standard case materials in terms of company-wide considerations, each actually concentrated on those aspects of the case relating specifically to goals of his own particular department.[157] When a team of sales managers plays a top management business game against a team of accountants, the sales team may sell more goods than it has the plants to produce, while the accountants suffer from overcautiousness and emphasize competing by cutting prices. It is for this reason that business executives often make poor government administrators — and vice versa, for they change jobs but fail to change job objectives.[209]

CONSTRAINTS WITHIN THE LARGE ORGANIZATION

Rules and Regulations

The behavior of members within an organization is affected strongly by the constraints under which they operate as well as the goals towards which they work collectively. Within the organization, management control is exerted through prescribed rules of organization and prescribed rules for individual behavior. One may view these rules as demands for reliability, predictability, and accountability. They tell the employe what he is supposed to do, when he is supposed to do it, and how he is supposed to do it. If he fails to behave according to the rules, he must be prepared to defend himself against sanctions by higher authority. The potential threat of punishment for failure to abide by the rules then should increase the reliability and predictability of every member's behavior within the organization. But there are costs. Fear of violating rules can lead to rigidity of behavior. Employes must react to each other impersonally according to prescribed ways of interacting rather than spontaneously. Personal, informal socialization may provoke sanctions. Achieving the goals of the organization become less important than maintaining the organization's reliability. Decisions are made by categorizing situations and referring to the appropriate rules for dealing with the situations according to the category selected. New circumstances are forced into old categories.[475]

Rules, Status, and Power. Rules make status differences visible by informing everyone in the organization of who can reward or punish whom and who can make what decisions for whom. Differences in the status of employes are legitimatized. Again unwanted side effects result. Status differences may increase interpersonal tension, the desire for equalizing power, feelings of coercion, and demands for close supervision by higher authority.[251]

Rules and Specialization. Responsibilities and duties are specified by rule for occupants of different positions within the organization. As a consequence, different employes assigned to different jobs develop different specialized competence. As they develop these specialized skills, more authority is delegated to them in their specialities.

The predictability, reliability, and fixity of relations between specialized positions makes for considerable efficiency. It promotes objective methods of selection and development of employes as well as objective standards for discipline. Despite external changes in the environment of the organization, the internal affairs can be held more stable. In contrast to an informal organization, a highly bureaucratized one clarifies for its members to a great degree their standing in the organization and how well they are doing.[175] The formal rules make it possible to train, control, coordinate, and integrate the work of all despite the fact that the various employes within the organization are quite diverse in their interests, potential, and training.[175]

The importance of predictability, of being able to know the decision rules, is illustrated by an experiment with 20 four-man teams working on a manufacturing assembly problem. The teams were composed of a vice president, a department head, and two workers. They literally purchased supplies for the construction of toys, then constructed and sold the toys to a buyer. Unknown to the department head and workers, the vice president deliberately reneged on his prior commitments to the department head that he would sanction in advance any prospective transaction between the department head and the supplier. For half of the teams, the vice president gave no advance notice of his intentions to approve or disapprove. In fact, he made decisions about accepting or rejecting deals made by the department head without any basis known to the department head or to the workers. With an unpredictable vice president, net profits were significantly lower than where advance notice was served about what the vice president would do.[521] But programmed specialization has its costs. It may result in increased costs of changing personnel, departmentalization of interests, conflicts between employes, conflicts between department and organizational goals, and

greater emphasis on success as an individual employe or on departmental effectiveness rather than emphasis on organizational goals.[597]

Rules and Goals: Flexible Programming.   Rules can focus on goal attainment rather than on the means to the goals. Some of the most successful
organizational arrangements permit considerable flexibility of relations
and a high degree of decentralization of authority but maintain predictability and accountability by focusing attention on objective measures of
performance of individuals and departments. The relative effectiveness
of the various agencies and individuals within the organization become
matters of public knowledge.[174] It may be that such emphasis on the
attainment of objectives rather than on obedience to prescribed procedures makes visible and discernible the differences in esteem of individuals (their value as persons regardless of the positions they occupy)
so that influence within the organization can be exerted by those who
are most able and esteemed, instead of only by those whose status
and power are prescribed by rule.[41] Indeed, such attention to objectives makes it possible for the formal organization not to stand in
the way of effective cooperation between individuals, regardless of the
positions they occupy. Thus, while lines of authority may be set up,
sufficient flexibility is maintained in the horizontal flow of necessary
information.[388] DuPont's organization features a top management
policy committee divorced from immediate administrative responsibilities which sets broad organizational objectives. Twelve decentralized
autonomous units aided by more highly centralized service units in
finance, engineering, and so on, translate these broader objectives into
divisional operating goals.[154]

The importance of prescribing objectives rather than prescribing
methods, of establishing goals rather than controls, is illustrated by
the following paradox:

IBM's many computers have increased greatly management's
opportunity to control and constrain the behavior of its employes. Yet
one of the top executives of IBM noted that IBM itself "probably would
have lost a great discovery which became the heart of IBM's random
access computer, the memory unit, if its controls had been more effective. It was developed in one of our laboratories as a bootleg project."
A courageous handful of men risked their jobs with the company to
disregard a management order to stop developing the device in which
they believed. "Could they have done this if my company's control
system were more precise?" asked the executive.[718]

In sum, higher authority prescribes rules to increase the ability to
predict what the employe will do. Rules allocate jurisdictions over
subparts of the total operation and make legitimate the differences in

the status and power of different members within the organization. But men are not machines. Creating a division of labor and making status differences legitimate and visible lead to a variety of side effects such as increased rigidity of behavior, status struggles, separation of individual and organizational goals, and increases in conflict between individuals and departments within the organization.[442] In formulating the rules for an organization we need to pay more attention to the humans for whom the rules are intended, to allow them flexibility so that their decision rules are self-corrective, modifying the job to make better progress toward relevant goals. Job occupants need to be programmed to be problem-solvers who change their own rules of work to adjust to their own learning and to changes in the goals and constraints on their jobs. But if such flexibility is permitted, faster and more accurate communications about change need to be developed to maintain predictability. Similarly, job occupants will require more information about how changes will affect them as well as others.

Formal Structure as a Constraint

While employes can and do bypass the prescribed channels of communication, the formal organization chart does impose constraints on behavior. Different formal structures give rise to different behaviors. Thus two Norwegian firms showed distinct differences in how much independent action employes would take. Decisions to act independently depended on the organization structure and how much access men had to information about the organization.[168]

Geographic Dispersion Versus Functional Specialization. Rational simplification may lead management to revise departments which, say, perform three functions, *A*, *B*, and *C* as shown in Figure 7.7*a*, into three overspecialized departments, each performing only one function as in Figure 7.7*b*. Although the functional specialization would seem more efficient, it moves decision-making, particularly needed for interdepartmental coordination, to a higher level in the organization. More decisions affecting the department are made outside of it. Only concerned with one component of production, the specialized activity is less satisfying. Opportunities for job enlargement are less. Often despite the seeming economic good sense of specialization, overall productivity is less with specialization because of its effects on morale, the need for more coordination, attention to quality control, tighter scheduling, less flexibility of operations and opportunities for diversification within departments. Supervision must be closer. Interdepartmental conflict

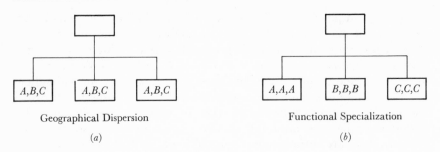

Figure 7.7: Functional Specialization of Departments.

is likely to be greater. Demands for interdepartmental coordination and scheduling increase staff work and details of procedures rather than concentration on objectives.[753] Functional organizations stress specialized training. It is more difficult to transfer personnel from one specialized department to another without a retraining program.

Again we are faced with a dilemma. If we focus only on what rationally seems most efficient from an engineering point of view, we may increase human costs and losses to a point where the whole system is actually less rather than more effective.

The typical highly *centralized* organization emphasizes functional specialization. Each unit is devoted to a different operation, as are groupings of the units. The units are serviced by staffs from head-quarters. Decision-making about unit goals occurs at headquarters. The typical highly *decentralized* organization emphasizes geographic dispersion. Each unit is fairly self-contained and self-supporting. In fact, units often buy and sell to each other in competition with the out-side market. Authority is delegated away from headquarters to the unit heads who in turn may or may not decentralize within their own units. But often they do not.[278] Although decentralization would seem to involve opportunities for independent action and hence job satis-faction, organizational decentralization may stop at the level of the unit head who actually vests all power in his own hands instead of further delegating authority downward within his own unit. This may be the reason a survey of 38 companies in the Philadelphia and Balti-more areas failed to reveal any differences in turnover, absenteeism, accidents, or grievances as a consequence of how centralized or decen-tralized they were as organizations.[723]

One penalty paid for centralization is that executives become specialists and cannot move readily from one department to another. With decentralization, the same executives may obtain general ex-perience in sales, accounting, personnel, and production and can move readily to another unit with similarly broad problems.

Technology and Organization

Technology exerts constraint on the organization as a whole and the relations within it that often is unrecognized. The classical rules of organization and the traditional hierarchy were supposedly applicable to any form of corporate enterprise. Yet it can be argued that the many-layered organization made up of units in which one boss communicates with many workers, as shown in Figure 7.8a, does not describe the current relationship in much of modern technologically advanced industry. Figure 7.8a was applicable where each worker did a simple job and the boss know the jobs of all the workers. Today, particularly in continuous flow operations like chemical production, the connections are more like those shown in Figure 7.8b. One operator has many advisor-consultants. Here there is almost an inversion in connections from what was prescribed by the classical rules of organization.

Technology determines what the pattern will be. Interviews in the spinning department of a synthetic textile mill suggest that the pattern of communications between superior and subordinate depends

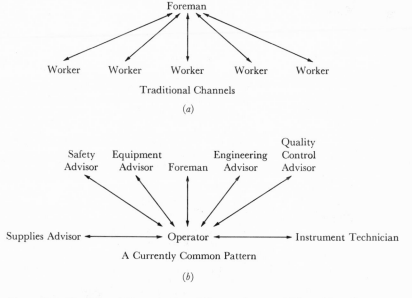

Figure 7.8: Traditional Organizational Connections and Those Now Common in Some Industries such as Industries Requiring Continuous Flow Processes.

directly on the amount of mechanization of the job. There is much instruction of the subordinate by his superior when mechanization is low. The subordinate in turn must feed back progress up the line. When mechanization increases, more of the subordinate's work is paced by machine. There now is less close communication between superior and subordinate. However, where mechanization is extremely great, such as in fully automatic operations, a great many communications will occur between superior and subordinate as a consequence of breakdowns.[612]

Interviews were conducted in 100 firms in South Essex, England, ranging in size from under 100 to 8,000 or more employes. The classical rules about span of control could not account for the wide divergencies found among these 100 companies. Thirty-five percent were straightline organizations while the remainder had more specialized line and staffs. The span of control of the chief executive ranged from 2 to 19,

Production Systems in South Essex Industry

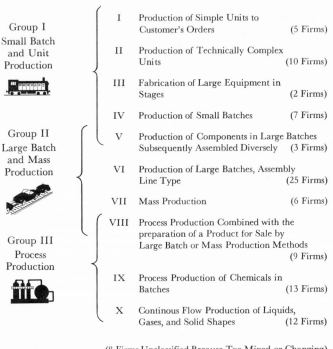

Group I Small Batch and Unit Production	I	Production of Simple Units to Customer's Orders	(5 Firms)
	II	Production of Technically Complex Units	(10 Firms)
	III	Fabrication of Large Equipment in Stages	(2 Firms)
Group II Large Batch and Mass Production	IV	Production of Small Batches	(7 Firms)
	V	Production of Components in Large Batches Subsequently Assembled Diversely	(3 Firms)
	VI	Production of Large Batches, Assembly Line Type	(25 Firms)
	VII	Mass Production	(6 Firms)
Group III Process Production	VIII	Process Production Combined with the preparation of a Product for Sale by Large Batch or Mass Production Methods	(9 Firms)
	IX	Process Production of Chemicals in Batches	(13 Firms)
	X	Continous Flow Production of Liquids, Gases, and Solid Shapes	(12 Firms)

(8 Firms Unclassified Because Too Mixed or Changing)

Figure 7.9: A Classification of 100 Firms in South Essex, England, According to Their Production Systems. (After Woodward, 1958, p. 11)

and the companies had from 2 to 12 echelons. At the first-line supervisors' level, the span of control was from 7 to 90. The companies also
varied greatly in the ratio of administrative and clerical employes
compared to those in hourly paid brackets. The range of ratios was
from 3 to 1 up to 1 to 14.

What appeared most important in determining the organization's
structure was the nature of its technology. It was possible to classify
92 of the firms according to their production systems as shown in Figure
7.9. At one end of the scale were five firms engaged in the production
of single complete units to customers' orders, such as custom-tailored
men's clothing or turbines for hydroelectric dams. At the other end
of the scale were industries, such as the petrochemicals, engaged in
the continuous flow production. Batch and mass production were in
between. This ten-fold classification scaled the extent to which "control can be exercised over the physical limitations of production." Firms
in the same industry were not necessarily in the same classification on
the scale. For example, two tailoring companies were found, only one
of which custom-designed its clothing. The other mass produced its
output.[751]

Technology and Hierarchy. Figure 7.10 shows how the number of levels
of authority in the management hierarchy of the 92 surveyed organi-

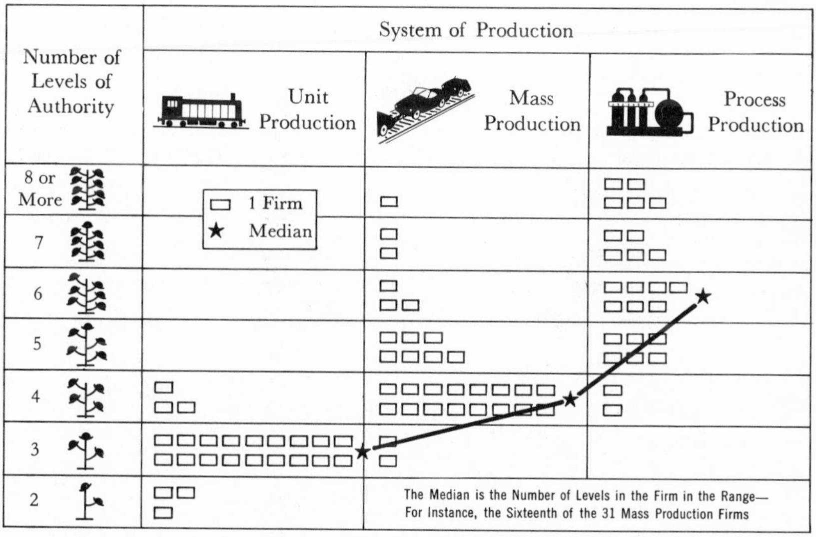

*Figure 7.10: How the Number of Levels of Authority in a Production System
Is Related to the Mode of Production. (After Woodward, 1958, p. 12)*

zations appeared to depend on their system of production. Companies engaged in unit production tended to have mainly three echelons in their organization. They were flat organizations. Mass production industries tended to have four or more echelons while the firms with process production were tall, averaging six echelons in the typical organization engaged in continuous flow output.

These differences in hierarchy were not a matter of overall size differences between the three types of companies. Table 7.2 shows how little the ratio of supervisors to workers (the number of workers in the company per single supervisor) varied as a consequence of the sheer size of the different organizations. However, as seen in Table 7.2, these ratios varied greatly as a consequence of the type of production system used. Note that regardless of size, the ratio remained almost constant for the process industries at seven or eight workers per supervisor. Regardless of size, the ratio was much higher in mass production. Table 7.2 and Figure 7.10 show then that for the firms surveyed, regardless of their size, those engaged in unit production had the flattest organizations containing the fewest echelons with relatively few supervisors for many employes, while at the other end of the scale of technical complexity, continuous flow organizations tended to be taller with many more echelons and fewer subordinates per supervisor.

Technology and Structure. A number of other systematic differences between the 92 firms appeared as a consequence of the technical complexity of their production processes. As technical complexity increased, so did the number of administrative and clerical employes per production worker as well as the proportion of professional and technical employes engaged directly in production. (In unit production and in mass production these same professionals were more likely to work in research and development.) Mass production firms were most likely to clearly define and specify duties and responsibilities, to emphasize

TABLE 7.2   THE NUMBER OF WORKERS PER MANAGER AS A FUNCTION
OF THE SIZE AND TECHNOLOGICAL COMPLEXITY OF 92 FIRMS*

	Size		
Technological complexity of production	*400–500*	*850–1000*	*3000–4600*
Unit	22	37	25
Mass	14	15	18
Process	8	7	7

*Modified from Woodward, 1958

written rather than oral communications, and to specialize their managements.

The favorite organization of unit production industries was a straight-line organization where each manager of production was supposed to have the technical skill based on experience to supervise all his subordinates. There were few specialists available. On the other hand, mass production industries favored a line and staff organization. Planning, scheduling, and quality control were staff functions separated from the work of the line supervisor. In still different fashion, process industries tended to develop functional organizations where each production executive had to be a kind of scientific advisor to those working under him.

Optimum Structure.   There seemed to be optimum arrangements for each type of production system. Thus, the most successful firms of each type were those close to the mode or median in their organizational structure for their kind of operation. For example, the unit producers with three levels of authority in their management hierarchy were more successful than those with two or four, and as seen in Figure 7.10, three echelons was the median number found in all the unit producers. Successful operations were most likely to occur where the organization's structure was closer to the average for all of the firms with the same type of production system.

Decision Process.   Characteristic differences in how management decisions occurred were also apparent as a consequence of the technical complexity of production systems. Decisions in the simplest producers, those engaged in unit production, were likely to have short-term effects and little further impact on policy or general problems. At the other end of the scale, in the process industries, decisions were likely to commit the company for a longer period of time and although occurring less frequently were likely to involve policy. Shorter term problem-solving decisions of an emergency nature might occur as a consequence of a crisis, but these were not the frequent, independent type of decisions seen in unit production and to a lesser extent in the mass production industries. In contrast to decision-making in the unit producers, the most technologically advanced industries involved in continuous flow were less likely to use hunches and intuition and more likely to make rational and accurate decisions. They face fewer unknowns, for once the product and process have been developed, then limited production can be undertaken which expands or contracts as a consequence of market forecasts and market demand. The unit producer must obtain a marketing order and then develop his product as specified, while the mass producer often must produce large batches of items and then sell them.

Authority and Technology.   The rationality and professional training of management in the technically advanced industries make it possible for managers to delegate authority easily. In the mass production and the unit production operations, management superiority depends on experience, and there is less certainty about the relative abilities of subordinates. Decisions made at lower levels are more likely to be reversed higher up in the organization in mass production and unit production systems. In contrast, in the continuous flow producers there is more management by committee, and senior executives make fewer decisions by themselves. They spend more time in formal social duties, in coordination, and in concern with personnel at higher levels in the organization. Reflecting to some extent what is shown in Figure 7.8*b*, the technological approach to production determines the nature of the supervisory-subordinate relationship. "In process firms the relationship between superior and subordinate was much like that between a travel agent and his clients than that between a foreman and operators in mass production."[754, p.30] While the foreman in mass production has to watch that the worker does not leave early before quitting time, the foreman is almost irrelevant in process-flow operations, for the worker arrives early to allow the man he is replacing to leave early. As long as the two workers overlap, it makes no difference when one leaves and the other arrives. Their foreman is of no consequence.[751]

Individual Jobs and Organization.   Workers and working conditions appear to affect organizational arrangements. For example, a survey of 98 American firms showed that the first-line foreman's formal span of control was greater if his subordinates were less skilled, had more varied assignments, occupied floor space, and were on group or individual incentive plans.[266]

Technological Change.   Changes in technology often have direct effects both on the formal and the informal organization. For example, in the old hand-rolling steel mill, ten men worked together rolling sheet steel. These men depended only on the preceding and following shifts of equivalent small groups. Now, in the continuous hot-rolling mill, operations are spread over several hundred yards involving subgroups of men of different occupational specialties in contact with a variety of management subgroups and staff services like steel research, quality control, and personnel.[592]

The Assembly Line

Assembly lines, characteristic of mass production industries, often fail to yield the production results expected of them. Each job is simplified as much as possible, making for dull, highly repetitive work.[690] The individual worker has lost control over his own fate. His work is paced by a conveyer belt with which he must keep up. He even must conform to schedules for personal and bodily physical relief. The machine dominates the worker. This machine pacing is the single most disliked aspect of the situation. His tools and techniques are determined, and changes in them are made by engineers, not the worker. The worker deals with only a fraction of the product and has difficulty attaining any sense of accomplishment from his work. Little learning is involved in the task, and there is little chance for upgrading. Only financial benefits can be increased as a consequence of continued work on the assembly line. The noise or the layout of the work inhibits social interaction or the formation of informal work groups. Most workers in this circumstance are bored and dissatisfied; only about 10 percent of 1068 interviewed at home liked or were indifferent to their work on an assembly line. Most of these workers preferred more variety than typical on the line.[713]

In the 100 English firms discussed earlier, human relations problems were found most often in those engaged in mass production. It is not surprising to find that absenteeism and turnover are much greater for workers on the assembly line in the same mass production industries than for workers off the assembly line, and that the propensity to strike in the United States between 1942 – 1948 found automobile manufacturing among industries with the highest incidence.[363] The foreman's relation to the worker on the assembly line is quite different from either his relation in unit production or in continuous flow. The assembly line may reverse the flow of requests. The worker asks the foreman for help. The foreman does not direct the worker, rather the machine does. The foreman's job is to adjust the assignments of workers as a consequence of absenteeism or to check on maintenance problems.[71]

Technology and Crowding. One characteristic of mass production has been the crowding of large masses of workers into a relatively small working area. Historically, the straight line of production in the large factory was dictated by the use of shafts powered by the water wheel, then by the steam engine. In both instances it was necessary to crowd as much equipment in a straight line as close together as possible, for the steam itself would dissipate as a function of the distance to be covered. The massing of workers, generally in straight lines, continues, yet the technology no longer demands this, for with electric power running the machinery it often makes better sense to disperse the workers in smaller plant units at a distance from each other. In fact, it may be easier to transport the materials to these smaller units located apart from each other which are more easily accessible to the workers than to crowd all the workers together in one location where it is more difficult for all to live and transport themselves to the single location. However, unfortunately for the worker and for urban development, the costs of production include the transportation of material, but not the time spent by the worker transporting himself to the workplace.[56]

Transportation developments have permitted certain kinds of firms to decentralize into smaller plants scattered over the countryside. It is not uncommon now to see pleasant suburban locations for small, light industries or for industrial research parks. Technology is even forcing dispersion. The aerospace industry must locate its propellant production facilities over a vast acreage for safety reasons, for example.

The Impact of Automation on Industrial Organization

Automation represents an acceleration in the rate at which machines replace men in the productive process. Computers and other types of automatic equipment are becoming substitutes for human skills, even at management levels. Like earlier technological innovations, automation is creating higher-level jobs yielding greater satisfaction, benefit, and return to the individual worker. At the same time it is also routinizing other kinds of jobs with a consequent reduction in satisfaction and opportunity. Like earlier technological innovation, automation increases the productivity per hour per employe greatly. It increases the quality, quantity, and standardization of goods produced and the quantity and accuracy of information involved in the production process. It creates a smaller number of new jobs requiring greater skills but dramatically reduces the number of production jobs. In comparison to a decade earlier, in 1954 a million fewer workers were engaged in mining and manufacturing in the U.S., yet productivity was at the same level in these industries as when the million greater number had been engaged in the work! In the 1950's the number of workers engaged in oil refining dropped from 147,000 to 137,000, yet output increased 22 percent![332]

Effects of automation depend upon the type of production involved.

A study of 125 workers transferred to an automated automobile plant suggests that automation increased the social isolation of workers and their dependence on each other as well as their need for teamwork. Yet automation increased the interdependence of workers in an accounting office.[197,441] Automation in the automobile business increased the closeness of supervision, the number of contacts between worker and foreman, and the number of foremen needed for each worker. But as a consequence of automation in another location, electric power plant production, workers' jobs were enlarged, as was their scope of responsibility and the training required. This was in contrast to the accounting occupation, where automation led to both upgrading of some jobs and downgrading of work requirements on others.[439] It led to less specialization of effort in the office than occurred as a consequence of automation in the automobile factory. Still a different outcome occurred as a consequence of introducing the first continuous seamless pipe mill in the U.S. Here close teamwork had to be developed, yet it was more difficult because of the loss of face-to-face contact with fellow crew members. Smaller work crews made for more close contact with supervision, however. The new jobs were physically easier but mentally more demanding and stressful.[711] There were some common effects of automation on all the situations, automobile production, steel pipe fabrication, electric power production, and accounting office work. In all locations automation increased the costliness of mistakes and a need to concentrate on avoiding error.[711,712]

The Changeover.   Introducing automation introduces a set of problems of transition. Some workers must continue to work under the old system, feeling neglect and indifference, while the new automated equipment is being introduced. There is an increased tendency towards nightshift work brought about by the need to utilize fully on a 24-hour basis the expensive automated equipment. During transition several systems must be operated simultaneously, the old, the new, and the conversion system. There are ambiguities, uncertainties, and insecurities about whether all the older employes can operate in the newer world of work. Each employe is concerned about his own adequacy for the new complex demands to be imposed upon him. Employes whose work is being phased out may face layoff, job transfer, and reassignment, less familiar or comfortable arrangements. Their future career with the company is in the hands of higher level planners. Apprehension, confusion, and resistance to change are commonplace under these circumstances.[439] A premium is placed on the supervisor's ability to cope with the interpersonal problems of the transition. After the changeover has been completed, however, those employes who have moved to bigger and better jobs, as occurred for most when transferred from a conventional to an automated power plant, are likely to be more satisfied with their enlarged job and greater responsibilities. However, they also are likely to report greater tension in their new circumstances.[439] On the other hand, if automation results in reduced benefits to the employes who are shifted, as occurred in the continuous seamless pipe mill, where employes lost 25 percent in take home pay as a consequence of automation, they were quick to demand and then enforce the introduction of an incentive plan by means of a slowdown until the company accepted the incentive plan. Following this, production jumped 50 percent.[711]

Impact of the Automation of Information Processing on Industrial Organization. An organization involves the flow of energy and matter on the one hand and information on the other. In the last decade it has been the automation of information processing that has had the most spectacular effects on organizational behavior and is likely to bring about even more change, particularly at management levels, in the years to come. For electronic data processing (EDP) will continue to grow as the basis for transmitting information within organizations. Hence obsolete equipment used previously for the same purpose, like bookkeeping machines, can be replaced at a cost the same as EDP equipment. Computers can be housed and maintained more cheaply than the number of employes who would be needed to complete the same amount of work. Companies can borrow on machines but not on employes. Equipment can be depreciated to provide major tax savings; employes cannot be depreciated. Finally EDP is part of the larger technological advance continuing in industrial societies in response to the continued pressures by labor for increased wages and shorter hours.[311] In addition to reducing costs for processing information, computers increase the speed, reliability, and precision with which data can be handled in comparison to manual methods. Indeed, in the next decade there is likely to be continued reduction in the costs of EDP coupled with greater speed. Computers are superior to man particularly in their long-term storage of immense amounts of information and their ability to search by iteration; that is, repeated cycling through the same search technique, at very high speeds, to solve problems or find answers which would be impossible for hand workers to complete. There are no human relations problems to face with the computer. On the other hand, man is still superior to the computer in dealing with ambiguity, vagueness, uncertainty, the absence of complete information, efficient cross-indexing of similar but not the same items, and the recognition of patterns after they have been transposed, rotated, or translated. (It is difficult to program a computer to recognize a triangle different from some standard triangle, once it has been distorted in size, shape, or direction.) Men can spot their own mistakes and correct them. Normally the computer stops work when a mistake occurs or goes on making the same mistake, although it is less likely to make mistakes than men doing the same job.[191] Apparently the computer is a stupid giant able to make large quantities of simple decisions extremely rapidly and repeatedly. However it is possible to program computers with an "artificial intelligence" so that they can learn from their own mistakes and develop a network of their own instructions to begin to cope with ambiguity and uncertainty. We are in the early stages of such program development, but presumably in the coming years we will begin to see computers dealing with higher level problems that are now reserved for man. This simulation of higher order thinking by the computer, coupled with its speed and developments in statistics, mathematics, and operations research, suggests that planning will be moved from middle management to higher level specialists, staffs of direct aid to top management. Decisions currently made by middle management will be programmed and routinized. There will be a greater separation of middle and top management. Research and development, innovation and creativity will continue to increase in importance. Top management will become increasingly research-oriented.[397] Middle management, freed from routine decisions, may actually be released for attention in less structured areas requiring more imagination and insight than before, dealing with decisions with many unknown elements and unquantifiable variables. More attention will be paid to the nature of the problem rather than its solution. It may be that middle managers will take on some of the roles currently played by top managers, while top management is freed to look at the system as a whole, to spend more time on personnel problems, to spend more time in the community outside and with other organizations.[11]

Automation commits the company to relatively rigid production systems in a market that might be quite fluid. Decisions are more expensive, more irreversible, and made for longer periods of time. Therefore a premium is placed on planning.[321] Except for more routine jobs that are created, like those of keypunch operator, most jobs in the new system are completed with a smaller yet more capable and intelligent work force, many of whom are hired from the outside, like programmers.[135] The new technical elite of data processors is introduced into the organization. These people are more likely to have a higher educational and social status than others comparable to them in the organization. They are less likely to be conforming and more likely to be self-directing. They will tend to initiate their own projects and their own changes. They are likely to cut across many departmental lines of the traditional hierarchy, since they are involved directly on questions of processing the flow of information itself, of central significance to the whole organization. Many former management functions, like scheduling and some phases of planning and control, are taken over by the elite that operates the electronic data processing. Centralization of such functions as bookkeeping, order filling, and related operations occur as a consequence of EDP.[311] There is a considerable increase in formalization of relationships and a concentration on rules rather than informal decisions. In fact, EDP itself makes many decisions formerly made by older employes or employes of high status in the organization. EDP sets the pace, not the employes. EDP deadlines must be met rather than deadlines set by individual employes. For example, all data of a given kind must be available at a particular point in time before processing by computer can be completed efficiently. Therefore all employes involved in gathering the appropriate data must meet this particular deadline. Any one employe's failure in this circumstance will cause the entire system to stop. A premium is placed also on coordination.[441]

NEW ORGANIZATIONAL DESIGNS

Need for Flexible, Not Fixed, Arrangements

The business world today requires rapid response to changes in the marketplace. It is important to determine what can be sold in the market, then to produce it.[310] This places a premium on the upward flow of communications, particularly from the sales force in the field. Rapid information processing and ability to analyze the causes of variance in the market are critical. The organization needs to be flexible enough to change with the changing demands placed upon it.

The Challenge of an Organization's Past

A second problem facing an organizational designer is that the typical organization in which he must work often grew and reached a high level of complexity not in any logical sequence but to accommodate to relatively transient and historical needs. The current organization may reflect the kinds of products that are currently produced as well as those that were produced in the past; geographical considerations, both past and current; particular personnel strengths and interests of person-

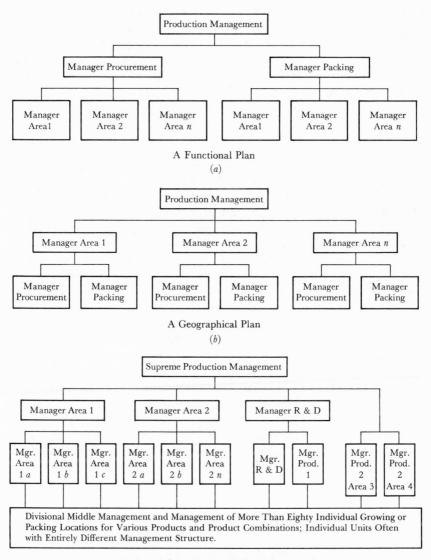

A Functional Plan
(a)

A Geographical Plan
(b)

An Actual Organization (Calpak) Organized
As a Consequence of History and Transient
or Specialized Needs of the Firm
(c)

Figure 7.11: Comparison of Organizational Plans Based on Function, Geography,
and History. (After Falk, 1961, p. 24)

nel which may or may not be currently still on the scene. While we might have expected that a canning organization, Calpak, would organize according to function as in Figure 7.11a or to geography as shown in Figure 7.11b, it actually is complexly and not logically organized as shown in Figure 7.11c, combining functional, geographical, and product arrangements.[196] Effective reorganization may have to contend with organization history.

The Need to Permit Organizational Learning

The survey of 30 Southern California firms mentioned earlier found that those companies which planned for expansion were no more effective than those which did not plan but grew organically to meet demands as they occurred.[467] Developments often take place as needed without planning, or even in spite of it. Operators within an organization often learn how to relate with each other much more efficiently than originally expected if they are given the freedom to learn how to improve these relationships. Any considerations about organization design should take into account the need to permit the organization to modify itself as a consequence of its learning and changing environmental demands. The importance of learning how to operate an organization was illustrated when groups of 40 men each were assigned to operate a simulated air defense system. The organic organization that finally developed handled several times the load with which the system was originally engineered to deal.[112] Operators first try to organize their relations with others in terms of their own previous experiences. Following a period of trial and error, organizational inventions occur, not foreseen by the organization designers, improving the relationships.[721]

The Line-Staff is Obsolete

Most current organizations are built around the concept of a line directly responsible for operations and a staff supposedly only able to advise line officials. In Figure 7.12 the production managers are the line managers of the manufacturing department, while personnel, quality control, production planning, and administration are staff. The line managers supposedly decide on the company's manufacturing operations while personnel offers advice on whom to hire, train, and promote. Quality control and planning advise the line on performance

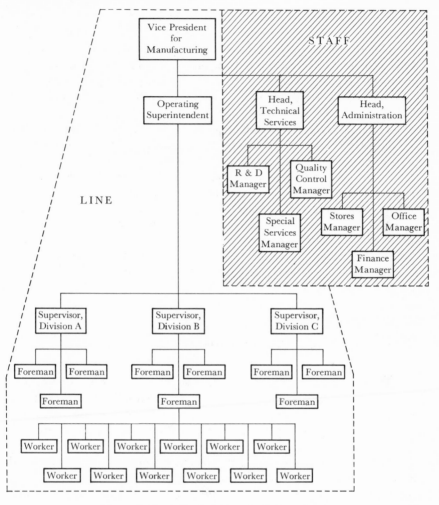

Figure 7.12: A Typical Line-Staff Organization.

and optimum schedules while administration buys, sells, and pays wages and salaries to assist the line. In practice, personnel may actually shape the nature of the work force, quality control may set its standards, and planning and administration may really be in charge of what and how much is produced. Yet the line-staff calls for the separation of the planners from the doers; and even where the rules are followed, this seems to be less effective than where the planning and doing are combined in the same employes. Thus, in a series of three experiments, trios of management trainees were given twenty minutes to plan how they would organize themselves to "manufacture" words from a key word like *architect* when the key word was given to them and how they would assemble the words into sentences. During manufacturing and assembly, they were not to be permitted to talk with each other but merely to produce. Trios that executed their own plans, rather than those developed by other trios, tended to be more efficient in sentence production, and they manufactured fewer meaningless sentences.[47]

The military line and staff arrangement was introduced into American industry in the early 1900's by Frederick W. Taylor. Quality control, personnel, and planning were made staff functions and removed from the line foreman's assignment. The staff concept was carried by executives who transferred from manufacturing to other kinds of industrial activity. The staff remained advisory as long as simple product lines were the rule, as in the early 1900's. Now, however, product lines are complex, and main concerns often are what to produce, not how to produce it. The staff, supposedly advisory and supportive, often is actually decisive. For example, it would be unreasonable to regard those in finance as merely advisory, when their decisions on how to treat costs may basically alter total operations.

Examples of Some New Organizational Designs

As a consequence of dissatisfaction with the traditional organization, some innovations in design now are being attempted which provide for more learning, flexibility, and greater recognition of the realities of group effects. They also may dispense with line and staff distinctions.

Overlapping Group Form.   The typical organization of today builds around a man-to-man pattern as shown in Fig. 7.5a. Yet, as we have noted, particularly in Chapters 5 and 6, groups are likely to exert more influence on each member than one man on another. Groups provide opportunity for participation, contribution to planning, open communication, and commitments that produce binding decisions. The overlapping group proposal is to convert the man-to-man relationship (Figure 7.5a) between a superior and each of his subordinates into a group containing a superior and all his subordinates (Figure 7.5b). Then each man in the organization above the first echelon except the chief officer becomes a member of two groups, one composed of his peers and their common boss, and one composed of his subordinates and himself (Figure 7.13). Each group at one echelon overlaps with all those at an echelon below. While relatively little seems changed in the shift to overlapping groups, a number of important consequences are likely, assum-

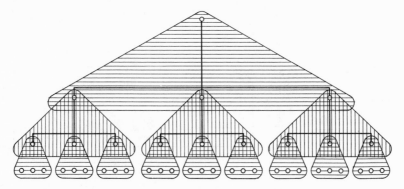

Figure 7.13: The Overlapping-Group Form of Organization. (After Likert, 1961, p. 107)

ing that the groups will operate under relatively permissive supervision. First decision-making is moved down one echelon so that planning and deciding are conducted by those who will execute the plans and decisions. Instead of a foreman planning the overtime schedule for his men, the group as a whole develops the schedule. Instead of the superintendent handing a production schedule to each of the foremen, all the foremen and the superintendent work out the production schedule together. With such shared decision-making, the organization benefits by using more of its human resources. Many more ideas may be generated in considering a plan.

People can be motivated to communicate more to each other both vertically and horizontally within the confines of the small group. Group responsibility for outcomes increases the flexibility with which its members will apply themselves. As members learn about each other's problems, often one can help out another who is temporarily overloaded. Sometimes such group functioning may result in reducing the total number of men required to handle the work formerly done by all as individuals.[412]

Some elements of this group approach will be found in a number of the other proposals for redesigning organizations even more radically.

A Functional Plan. This plan replaces the traditional line-staff arrangement with a functional teamwork design. Figure 7.14*a* shows how a company might be organized under the functional teamwork concept. Figure 7.14*b* shows how the process functions might be organized under the director of process functions and his assistant directors. All necessary tasks are covered by functional groups. Each is given appropriate weight and authority. The functions are grouped logically, not arbitrarily. The

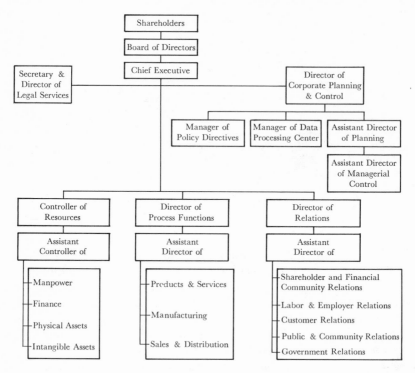

*Figure 7.14a: How a Company Might Be Organized Under the Functional-
Teamwork Concept. (After Fisch, 1961, p. 76)*

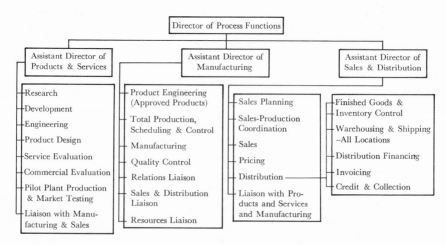

Figure 7.14b: How Process Functions Might Be Organized. (After Fisch, 1961, p. 76)

functional groups cooperate from day to day with minimum need for formal committees. Coordination is achieved at the lowest possible level, and only major conflicts between groups need to be resolved by top management. Inspection of Figure 7.14 shows that the groupings are in a time sequence under the director of process functions and his assistant directors. For example, under the assistant director of products and services are teams beginning with research, then development, then engineering, then product design, and so on. Teams dealing with the various necessary resources, manpower, finance, physical assets, and intangible assets, are grouped under a controller of resources. Finally teams concerned with communications and relationships within and outside the company all are grouped under the director of relations, as shown in Figure 7.14a.[208]

A Systems Design. A more flexible scheme, particularly applicable to engineering management and research and development, emphasizes a systems approach. Instead of different teams taking over at different times in the research and development of a product, different individuals are placed on the engineering team during different phases of a product's development. As shown in Figure 7.15, initially an elite group high in technical competence and intelligence and creativity conducts the basic research and creative work on the problem and its solution. Some of the elite are replaced as the project moves into the second phase involving detailed specification and design. Some of the original planners remain to oversee the activity until it moves into the third phase of manufacturing, when some of the design personnel are phased out and some of the production experts take over. As seen in Figure 7.15, the organization moves and changes during the three phases.[109] Like the military task force, theoreticians and specialists are on the development team in its early phase; later operations-oriented executives take over and the theorists are now free to move on to a new project. Finally some line operating management are introduced to the team as others are phased out of it.

When new products, new ideas, and new technologies are of major importance to an industry, the task force approach may dominate the management organization ultimately.[744] More generally, it has been proposed that executives be moved back and forth between operations and planning in cyclical rotation at the same level based on product changes and cycles, changes in methods and processes, and various other periods of significance to the company in order to increase the likelihood that men who execute various operations have something to do in the planning for them.

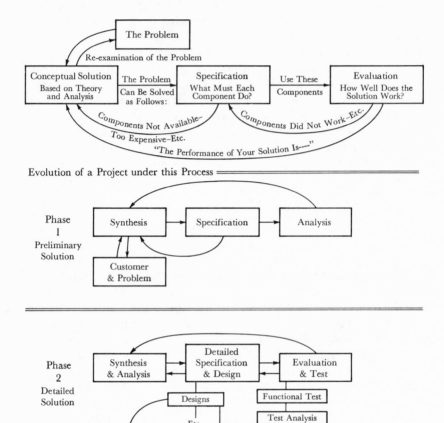

Evolution of a Project under this Process

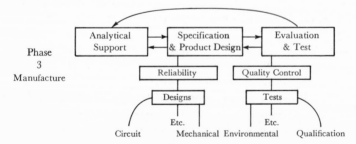

Figure 7.15: The Cyclic Process of Systems Engineering. (After Chamberlain, 1961, p. 93)

Combining Systems Flexibility and Line Reliability. Figure 7.16 shows how planning flexibility can be combined with more stable service units, such as may be required in the aerospace industries manufacturing extremely complex, but almost custom-tailored, rocket engines in limited amounts. The programs are run on a task-force basis, as described above, and are formally linked in the program and services council, where overall long-range needs of both programs and service divisions can be discussed. Questions concerning the sharing of the resources of the whole organization are dealt with here. The heads of the service divisions, manufacturing, testing, adminstration, and research development, serve on the program council as consultants to the program personnel. But the consultants have two objectives: to service the program and to maintain an efficient, healthy service organization. Completion of a given program should not be at the price of exorbitant costs in

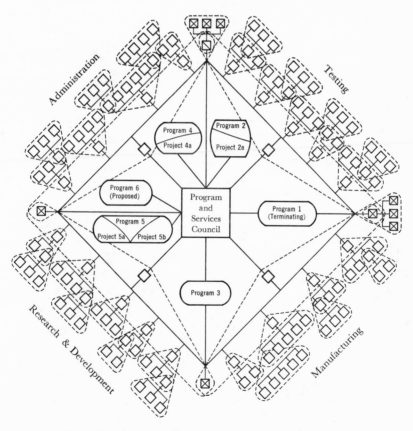

Figure 7.16: An Organizational Design for the Space Age.

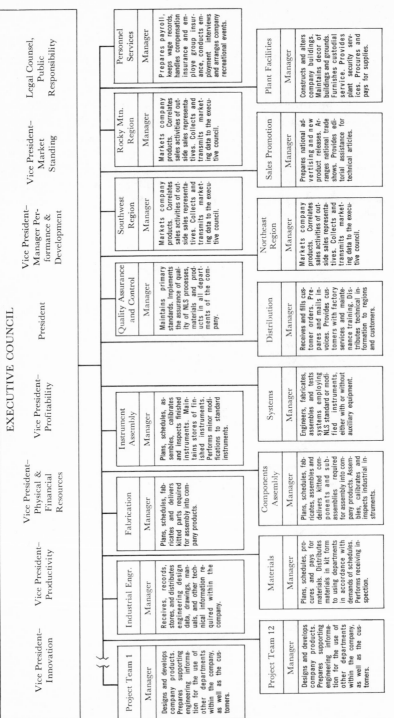

Figure 7.17: The Horizontal Organization, Non-Linear Systems, Inc.

money, materials, or men.[44] Lateral communications, of the greatest importance in service units of the type shown here, are fostered by a number of organizational devices. Overlapping groups making each supervisor a linking pin between his subordinates and his superior are introduced. Liaison men with joint appointments in two service organizations are also included to promote lateral connections between the organizations. For example, one executive is in both administration and in and R & D unit. He can be a center of information about new problems in a service unit as well as new research findings from the firm's laboratories. He may help to speed the translation and application of new developments by the organization's service and program units; he may also serve to keep the laboratory alert to new demands facing the service and program units.[272]

Effects of Introducing New Designs

In a rare experiment on an in-plant organization, an *autonomy* program was introduced into two divisions of a large, big business organization, promoting increased participation by rank and file employes. It had some elements of the overlapping group proposal discussed earlier. At the same time a *hierarchical* program increasing the amount of decision-making by upper management was introduced in two parallel divisions. The autonomy program to increase participation by employes resulted in increased productivity and satisfaction with the company, with the immediate supervisor, and with feelings of self-actualization. As expected, the hierarchical program reduced employe satisfaction but increased employe productivity also. Production costs decreased significantly under both treatments but more so under the hierarchical treatment, partly as a consequence of uncontrolled factors. Evidently attention to organization had positive effects on production regardless of what was involved, but the autonomy program raised satisfaction while the hierarchical plan lowered it.[491]

A more radical demonstration of the effects of an organizational design built on modern behavioral scientific concepts involved the complete reorganization of a company of 350 employes, Non-Linear Systems, devoted to the manufacture of analog digital converters, a high-quality precision product for transforming metered information into digital displays.

The new design included an emphasis on small-group decision-making, self-planning, a flat organization, and a number of other elements previously mentioned. The new arrangement is shown in Figure 7.17.

After eight years of reasonably successful operations as a traditional line and staff organization, the assembly line production organization was converted into small teams of six or seven workers, working together in 20- by 12-foot cubicles. Similar groupings were made in other parts of the organization. Currently the company is an extremely flat organization consisting of 12 project teams, seven manufacturing teams, nine teams involved in sales, and a personnel and plant facilities team. Each team is headed by a manager who in turn reports to an executive council of eight managers in charge of innovation, productivity, physical and financial resources, and so on. The 25 team managers consult directly with the executive council, which meets for several hours every day. There is no planning department, since each team is responsible for its own planning within the boundaries set for it by the executive council or by meetings of several relevant team managers. Each group is expected to plan and execute its own work. For example, a fabrication group may assemble, inspect, sign, and pack the completed units for distribution. Control of employe behavior is replaced by trust and reliance on individual responsibility. For example, the materials manager both purchases and writes checks to pay for goods and inspects them. No independent accounting system from another office in the firm is involved, as would usually be the case in a traditional company which felt it mandatory to have the accounting department as a watchdog that would make payments only after it had checked whether the orders for goods had been made properly and honestly. All employes, whether production workers or salesmen, are on a flat weekly salary so that labor costs are fixed. Salaries are raised in large steps only for visibly outstanding performance, change to a more important job, or because of inequities at the time of hiring. Payroll adminstration costs the company $50 a month, since all that is required is for the company to give a check once a month to the Bank of America covering all the salaries of its current employes. Most communication within the company is oral. Salesmen in all regions of the United States are expected to communicate directly by telephone to appropriate department managers. The managers of various departments get together to minimize or maximize inventories as assigned by the executive council. Department heads meet regularly with the executive council, and in turn members of the executive council freely circulate within the departments. The degree of oral communication is illustrated by the fact that the company executives rely on only two secretaries.

There was an initial drop in production when the changeover took place, but after nine months production was back to normal. Within 20 months it was 31 percent higher in the assembly department, for example, and was continuing to rise after this. In this department there were continual reports of discoveries of new and better ways of assembling materials. Customer complaints dropped during the period following changeover, and quality of items produced increased following the first nine-month recovery period. Technically competent members of the team were responsible for training their fellow team members who were unable to make the complex assemblies initially. The assembly departments became "The Academy," the training ground for future supervisors throughout the company. Worker interest in training led to their request for teaching machines to be used during the lunch period and for formal arrangements for night classes. Guaranteed salaries and steady employment made possible the maintenance of a steady flow of goods which are stockpiled when sales are low and sold off when sales are higher than capacity for production. The company, with fixed labor costs, knows in advance its break-even point and can maintain a posture of increased flexibility in establishing and forecasting profits as a consequence of sales. The teams compete with their own past performance rather than with each other. Each team is versatile. For example, each production team can now construct many different kinds of items.

Worker morale is what might be expected. Despite the fact that salaries are paid regardless of attendance, during the first two years following the changeover, absenteeism averaged less than 1 percent and never rose above 2 percent. Yet in the same San Diego, California area, comparable companies are experiencing absenteeism rates of 6 to 8 percent. Avoidable turnover is almost nonexistent. In a heavily unionized community, there is no effort even to attempt unionization. Individual workers have developed as a high degree of skill in calibrating instruments as if they were advanced technicians.[378] The organization is of limited size and will only be able to expand by duplicating itself in some other geographical location with complete decentralization of effort. Moreover, the nature of the task, demanding high quality, places a premium on the utility of high employe involvement. Further, the items are small and storable at relatively little cost compared, say, to perishable or seasonable materials. Within these limitations, the type of organization shown in Figure 7.16 and described above makes possible the high level of achievement of financial and material as well as human goals within the productive organization.

Toward a Bottoms-Up Organization

To sum up, if we design an organization by starting with the environmental demands, the stockholders' interests, and primarily rational concerns true about interlocking machinery but not about interlocking employes, we are likely to generate a typical hierarchical organization with variations in flatness, administrative staff, and the like as a consequence, primarily, of technological considerations. On the other hand, if we start at the bottom with the typical operating employe as described by modern behavioral science, we may design a radically different organization where the hierarchy may be hard to find, if it exists at all, because the organization design would have to provide for predictability and reliability by means other than establishing status differences, inflexible programs for each job, and so on. It would include the following characteristics:

1. Each job or individual system would have multiple membership in two or more larger or group systems.

2. Each individual system would have areas of discretion as well as programmed positions. Decisions would be made at appropriate centers, regardless of power considerations. At different times and for different purposes, decision centers would move to different systems, individual or group.

3. Each system would have as complete access as possible to human and material resources and to the information needed to fulfill its tasks and to its discretion to judge when its own program of instructions requires modification.

4. Each system, individual and group, as well as the total or supersystem, would have restructuring mechanisms available to it. When such restructuring of a system occurred, it would become known immediately to all other systems which might be affected so that they could make appropriate adjustments.

5. As much as possible, basic material income would not depend upon system performance. This would be given for willingness to accept and hold responsibility for a system. Overcoming job challenges would be the main source of satisfaction. Problems are not a scarce commodity, so that creating a work force that would find its satisfaction in problem-solving would mean that there was no limit to the supply of rewarding experiences (characteristics formulated by P. Lawrence and M. Horwitz).[647]

* * * * *

The reader should be forewarned that what has been presented here does little to describe current management organizational practices. There is a cultural lag of at least one generation involved. Corporate managements responsible for the organization of their firms still think primarily in terms of classical organization theory, individual authority, jurisdictional prescriptions, job simplification and specialization, spans of control, and chains of command. The typical member of an organization is made aware daily of his need to live within a system ruled to a considerable extent by classical theory, tempered only to a modest degree by current knowledge about human motivation, inter-personal dynamics, and the like. Yet as behavioral research continues to reveal how organizations really develop and maintain themselves so that we come to understand better organizational life, it will lead eventually to managements beginning to consider new organizational designs. These new prescriptions for coordinating the efforts of large numbers of men and equipment will balance technical demands on the organization with economic, social, and psychological realities; organizations designed for people as they really are, not as classical theorists would have liked them to be.

Central to this new approach is the study of the communications among the members of any formal organization. This is the subject of what follows next.

In Brief

COMMUNICATIONS CAN BE STUDIED IN THE LABORATORY AND IN THE FIRM. Centralized networks and one-way communications promote speed but not creativity or satisfaction providing a dilemma for management. Reception of downward communications depends on how the communicator is perceived, the medium employed, the order, style, and content of the message as well as the ability and motivation of the receiver. For the upward transmission of suggestions, questions, and grievances, the relaying supervisor is a key figure. Blockage and filtering of messages result in the spread of rumors. Much more horizontal flow of information occurs in organizations than is usually realized.

Chapter 8

COMMUNICATIONS IN

INDUSTRIAL ORGANIZATIONS

Method of Studying Communications

The effect of the organization on the behavior of its members has been studied in detail in the laboratory by systematically restricting the channels of communication open to members of a team working on common problems. The common problem is of this sort: at the beginning of each trial each of five subjects is given a card on which are printed five of six symbols. One symbol is missing from each card. Each individual lacks a different symbol. The problem each time is to have the group discover and record the one symbol that everyone has in common. The subjects are seated around a circular table and are separated from each other by five vertical partitions. They pass messages to each other through open interconnecting slots. These are the only ways of communicating among subjects.[53, 390]

All channels can be opened as in Figure 7.4c, or as many as 20 other communication networks among five positions can be examined. For example, in the wheel all members must communicate through the same single individual, shown in Figure 7.4b as a black position. In other nets such as the chain, yoke, and kite, again some members are likely to be more centrally located than others and are again shown in black. There is no central position in the circle or all-channel networks. Studying subjects in these circumstances provides an opportunity to examine how information is exchanged, how solutions are formed, and how answers are circulated as a consequence of the particular organizational arrangement to which the subjects are restricted.[264]

While it may be impossible to translate these experimental findings

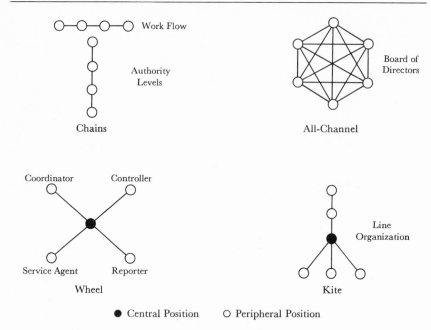

Figure 8.1: Linkages in a Company Analogous to Experimental Communication Networks. (After Dubin, 1962)

directly to large organizations, the results are suggestive and may help to clarify our later discussion about formal communications in industry, for these organizational networks are analogous to real companies. The chain is seen in the vertical and horizontal serial linkages in an organization such as shown in Figure 8.1. The horizontal flow of work is a chain. The vertical authority levels are also a chain. The board of directors is an all-channel network. The kite is a typical line organization. For many specific operations in an organization, persons will find themselves at the hub of a wheel.[178]

Particularly relevant for understanding communications in the large organization are research results with this technique on the effects of occupying a central position, of informal developments, of planning, of leadership, and of task demands.

Effect of Centrality

As might be expected, the more central a member is in the communication net, the less time it takes him to solve any problem requiring the giving and receiving of information. He is more likely to be satisfied with his position; he is more likely to communicate and receive communiations from others; and he is more likely to be identified as the leader of the group by others.[602] However, what seems to be most important about these central positions is the opportunity they afford the member who occupies them to be the decision-maker for the group rather than have decisions made for him by someone else.[687] In fact, this same increased satisfaction can be obtained by persons in peripheral positions by increasing the amount of information they have at the beginning of a communication problem. Centrality is satisfying because it permits one to know what is going on and makes one less dependent on others for decisions.[240]

Figure 8.2 shows how different is the task of any person who occupies a central position in a wheel network compared to the tasks carried out by those in peripheral positions. For example, as shown in Figure 8.2, only the person in the central position spends time, and a great deal of it, in compiling data, forming solutions, and transmitting answers. Those in peripheral positions spend a great deal of time pri-

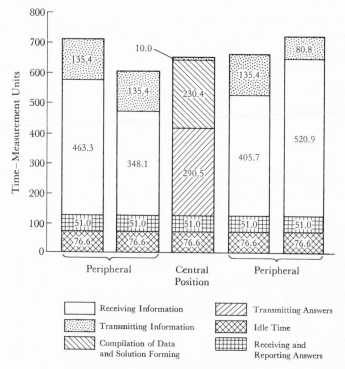

Figure 8.2: How Central Position Holders Differ from Peripheral Position Holders in What They Do in Solving the Problems of the Communication Network. (After Guetzkow & Simon, 1955, p. 238)

marily receiving information. Regardless of which person is placed in a central position of a network such as the wheel without any formal job specifications, his job and his attitude toward his job will be strongly determined by the communications imposed upon him by the system.

Informal Developments

Informal but consistent patterns of behavior among people can only evolve within the restrictions of the formal network. Little room is left for informality by the wheel net. The highly restricted wheel net cannot but rapidly develop a stable hierarchy conforming to the formal demands of the system in which the central person sends out information to all participants once he has received information from all. On the other hand, the all-channel groups can display much more variety in the informal organizations they build, particularly in distributing answers. Some evolve a system in which each person sends answers to every other member while others develop patterns identical to the wheel or to the chain shown in Figure 7.4. Those groups which are formally restricted to circle communication networks have the greatest difficulty in developing and maintaining any single informal pattern of communications. Over many trials they tend to fluctuate in the particular patterns of communications they use, especially in exchanging answers.[264] Generally speaking, any network which begins with a central position or which develops informally a centralizing procedure is able to complete the task faster with fewer errors.[493] However, centralization is likely to give rise to less satisfying peripheral jobs as well as less opportunity for members as a whole to modify their own organization, to learn about how the organization operates, to be flexible, and to be creative when new challenges are imposed upon the group.

Effects of Planning

Each individual is more likely to learn how to use his own position to the best advantage of the group where the groups are given opportunity for planning between trials and where they are connected with each other by open channels.[261]

Leadership and Communication Networks

Consistent with earlier discussions in Chapter 5, the type of communication network imposed upon the group determines which kind of leadership will be most effective. When the central member of the wheel or kite network and a designated member in the all-channel net are instructed to be coercive rather than persuasive, all three kinds of networks make fewer errors of information. However, the relative superiority of coercion over persuasion is particularly greatest in the wheel net, to a lesser extent in the kite network, and least apparent in the all-channel network. And under all three conditions members are less satisfied with coercion than with persuasion. In the all-channel and kite networks the same or similar amounts of decision errors occur with persuasive and coercive leadership. Only in the wheel are there fewer errors of decision under coercive rather than persuasive leadership.[41, 603]

The Task and Effective Communication Networks

While the highly centralized nets appear to produce the fastest solutions with the least errors and required messages in the simplest kind of problem-solving situation, such as finding the common symbol, the superiority of the centralized wheel or yoke disappears when the problem is made more complex by adding "noise" to the communications. Thus when subjects have to solve anagram problems where they may or may not need information from each other, noise in the communication system causes the disappearance of differences in the efficiency of the various nets. This and subsequent experiments lead to the conclusion that the efficiency of a communication structure depends on the characteristics of the task.[243, 292] No one network is universally superior. However, regardless of the network, central positions, positions with easiest access to all the necessary information, are more satisfying. The hierarchical structures like the wheel and the kite promote fastest communications and solutions to problems but offer less opportunity for creativity by the individual members.

COMMUNICATIONS DOWNWARD

Generally we will be concerned here with the mass message from one or a few managers to many employes below them. Even where these messages are given directly from the communicator to the employes by mail, in mass meetings, or on bulletin boards, we shall see that how much of the message is received and accepted will depend upon numerous aspects of who is sending and who is receiving as well as the contents of the message and the medium used to carry it. Downward communication in industry can be likened to messages from a central to all the peripheral positions. To begin with then, the previously discussed network studies suggest that we are dealing with senders who already have more access to information about the system than those who are to receive the message. The senders are more likely to be satisfied with their positions than the intended receivers and more likely to be involved in sending than receiving and in problem-solving. This in turn will dramatically affect the way in which the receiver screens out information from the message or recasts much of what was sent.

Methods of Downward Communication

Management uses a variety of media for communicating formally in mass to all its employes. A 1953 sampling revealed 76 percent of companies as routinely sending employes letters. Mass meetings with employes were used by 60 percent of these companies, while 72 percent published a magazine or newspaper periodically. Information racks and bulletin boards are commonplace, as are plant tours, motion pictures, and institutional advertising. During crises, management may pay for space on local radio or television stations or in local newspapers to communicate with its employes or to the public.[504] Finally management may insert messages in payroll envelopes, publish employe handbooks, safety manuals, and other special booklets as well as financial reports. It also may use public address systems. Despite all these formal media for downward communication, employes are likely to report, as did a sample of surveyed railway supervisors, that their principal sources of information were rumor and unofficial contacts.[316]

Centuries-old principles of rhetoric have guided management in the preparation of these materials. However, since the early 1950's these old ideas have been modified and new ones developed as a consequence of systematic research on mass communications.

Experimental Study of Mass Communications Downward

The method of study is relatively simple. An audience, usually a large class of college students, is asked to indicate beliefs, attitudes, opinions, or information about a particular issue, say labor-management relations. Following this, half of the audience experiences the impact of a particular mass communication, while the other half does not. Then the attitudes, beliefs, or information of the entire audience are resurveyed. How much change occurs in these as a consequence of the mass communication has been found to depend on the audience's perception of who is communicating to it, certain characteristics of the contents of the communication, the medium which is used, the order in which a communication appears in comparison to other competing messages, and various personal characteristics of the members of the audience.

Perception of the Communicator. If the communicator is labeled an extremist before he presents his point of view, he is less likely to bring about change in the attitudes of the audience than the communicator who is seen as moderate in position.[724] In the same way an impartial speaker who draws conclusions for his audience is likely to be most effective in changing audience attitudes; yet if he is suspect as an extremist, he will be even more ineffective if he is seen as a member of a class with a stake in the conclusions he draws. These effects occur despite the fact that both the speaker labeled as impartial and the speaker who is perceived as biased present identical communications.[318] Again, a well-liked, esteemed, trustworthy communicator can accomplish more change by advocating a greater change. On the other hand, an audience is likely to disagree more with a disliked communicator who presents identical messages.[587] However, this is complicated by the "sleeper effect." Messages are remembered longer than the sources of the messages. Therefore, over time, messages originally rejected because the communicator was disliked tend to increase in acceptability because the communicator has been forgotten. Thus an employe who has heard a message from an anti-union source may shift in attitude in the direction advocated by the source at a later date because he tends to forget the source of the communication faster than the communication itself.[319]

Taken as a whole, these studies suggest that to promote acceptance of its messages, management must build a reputation for itself among its employes as moderate in position on conflicting issues. Acceptance will also be greater if employes are generally satisfied with the management, like and trust it. But as we will see, such favorableness toward management does not necessarily lead to greater retention of the contents of messages from management.

The Medium. Media make a distinct difference. For example, in comparison to radio lectures, televised lectures are recalled better immediately and retained to a greater degree eight months later. However, printed lectures, as compared to radio and television lectures, are least likely to be recalled immediately or retained eight months later.

Most effective are combinations of media. Table 8.1 shows the mean accuracy on a test of recall completed by 528 employes in five different departments of Spiegel's, a mail-order house. The information sent down was about company benefit plans. Each of the five departments received the message in a different way. As can be seen in Table 8.1, employes in the department who received a letter mailed to their home and an oral presentation by their supervisor showed the greatest accuracy on the test of recall of the information transmitted to them. Next most effective was the supervisory presentation alone. Least effective in promoting accuracy of recall of the message was doing nothing but allowing the information to spill over from the four departments to a fifth by the informal grapevine.[142]

Regardless of the medium, however, many other variables can be tested which affect the degree to which a message will be accepted and remembered, although most of what follows is based on oral delivery or written delivery to assemblies.

Most of the research results to be described were obtained with college student assemblies, not employes. However, the results are suggestive of what to expect when management communicates formally with its employes in mass meetings, by mail, by bulletin board, by slips in pay envelopes, or even through oral presentations by supervisors in which little opportunity is provided subordinates to discuss the message with each other or with their supervisor.

Reception of Messages. There are certain characteristic ways in which messages are modified upon receipt. Audiences display an "indexing process" so that the headlines, captions, identifying backgrounds preceding or surrounding the message produce significant effects on judgment of the total message. Contrast effects can increase the change in attitudes produced by a message. For instance, a speaker on in-plant cost-reduction practices may begin with allusions to the size of the scrap pile.

TABLE 8.1   EFFECTS OF MEDIA OF COMMUNICATION ON ACCURACY OF
ANSWERS TO A TEST OF RECALL*

Medium	Number of Employes	Mean Accuracy on a Test of Recall
Combined letter to home and supervisory presentation	102	7.70
Supervisor presents only	94	6.17
Letter to home only	109	4.91
Bulletin board	115	3.72
Grapevine	108	3.56

*After Dahle, 1954

The salient features of a message are retained longer than the less striking parts, so that the message tends to be *sharpened* as well as *leveled*. Thus, for example, a mass communication describing all the details of the Taft–Hartley Labor Relations Act, including many points favoring unions and many more points favoring management, will be leveled by the audience, depending on their own previous attitudes, so that what is retained is a leveled overall attitude towards the Act as a whole with retention of only a few of the sharpest details, like the 80-day cooling-off period required by the Act. Thus no relation was found between how much each of 1,088 production employes knew about the Taft–Hartley Act and whether they were for or against it.[244]

Order Effects. The relative impact of a positive argument and a negative argument tends to depend upon the order in which they are presented. A *primacy* effect is created if there is a public announcement of the position of the employes before arguments against this position are presented. If competing or contradictory information is presented, that material which is heard first takes precedence in its impact compared to the material which is presented second. For greater change to occur in a positive direction, it is more effective to present the positive arguments first and then the negative arguments, rather than in reverse order. Again, more change occurs if the most desirable reasons are presented first and then the less desirable are offered.[587]

Style and Content of Message

While a debate between apologists, say management and union, each defending his own point of view, tends to move listeners in the direction of its pre-existing biases, an exposition which is frankly favorable to a particular point of view is more likely to shift the audience in the direction of the argument. At the same time an impartial presentation of both sides serves to moderate the attitudes of the audience as a whole.

For better educated employe groups, at least, messages containing sound evidence and fact tend to promote more acceptance and change than messages with generalities and assertations or messages emphasizing authoritative sources.[587]

Emotional Loading of the Language. Well-known is the ability to introduce strong opinion into what began as a neutral message by substituting an emotionally loaded term like "labor agitator" for a more neutral term like "labor organizer." Figure 8.3 illustrates such substitution in a series of news stories in the *Chicago Tribune*, a conservative newspaper, by comparing the words used in its stories with the similar, more neutral words employed by the *New York Times* to cover the same stories. The selected pairs of words, similar in meaning but differing in emotional content, were scaled by a sample of college students. Thus the average college subject rated "progressive" as having highly positive, unemotional value but its close substitute "radical" as quite "negative."[580]

Dealing with Opposing Viewpoints.

Further research with student audiences suggests that if management begins its messages with an explicit refutation of negative arguments it expects employes to advocate, it will promote a clearer understanding of the argument but actually will arouse antagonism among its employes and will inhibit the extent to which they will change their attitudes. Elaborating on the employes' counterarguments actually makes it possible for them to produce more ideas about why their position is the correct one. A message from management which contains no refutation of the opposing point of view changes more opinion than one which attempts to deal with counterarguments. However, an appeal will be weakened if it completely ignores well-known facts supporting the other side of the argument, although generally introducing unfamiliar facts supporting the other side will weaken one's appeal also.[674]

Employes are more likely to comprehend the intention of a message from management if conclusions are drawn for them by management. But only among less intelligent employes and among those who clearly comprehend management's intended conclusion will statements of the conclusion increase their change in attitude.[673, 674] But as mentioned earlier, if management is suspect, conclusions drawn are likely to be ineffective in comparison to letting the employes draw their own conclusions.[318]

The Effect of the Receivers

According to additional controlled experiments with college students, the impact of a message on employes is likely to be strongly dependent on their previous experiences, their existing attitudes and personalities. Information is more likely to be accepted if it is compatible with previously held attitudes.[516] Likewise it will be easier for employes

Terms Used in Reference to Same Event by:

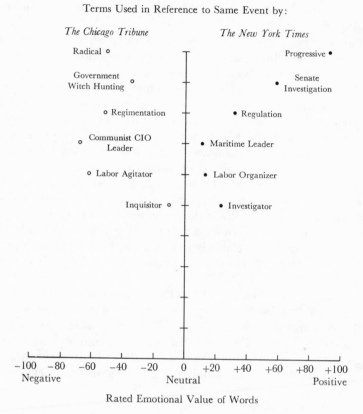

Figure 8.3: How The New York Times and The Chicago Tribune Differed in Emotional Loading of Words in Reporting the Same Events. (After Sargent, 1939)

to learn implausible arguments which fit with the attitudes they already hold than to learn plausible arguments which go against what they all believe.[343] In the same way, when the appeal for change is far from the employes' own current position, no change at all will occur, although an appeal which is closer to where they are now is likely to move them in the direction advocated. Employes are likely to see as unfair propaganda an extreme appeal, say, to reject seniority rights, while they will see a communication which is already close to their point of view as actually closer than it really is.[317]

Message Screening. Messages will be scanned and accepted or ignored and rejected to the extent that acceptance or rejection promotes cognitive consistency. For example, new car owners are attracted more to reading about the cars they have already purchased than about cars they considered buying.[192]

Some persons are easier to persuade than others, regardless of the message. Those who describe themselves as emotional or anxious with brief personality assessments are more likely to change their opinions as a consequence of efforts to persuade them.[207, 726] Similarly, they are more likely to accept propaganda if they are lower in self-esteem and self-confidence.[587] They are also likely to be influenced if the message advocates what fits with their own needs. For example, employes who are high in aggressive needs and need to punish others are prone to accept proposals for punitive handling of disciplinary cases.[587]

Messages from management lacking interest for employes will be screened out. A survey on what employes want to know concluded that they pay attention primarily to those communications concerning themselves and their jobs, about decisions and policies which affect them directly. Thus they are relatively uninterested in what happens to transferred management personnel in comparison to a proposed change in the cafeteria.[265]

A survey of the readers of the *Liner*, the company magazine of the Interstate Oil Pipeline Company, to which half of the employes and their families responded, indicated that almost all respondents gave the magazine a careful reading. Eight percent of the respondents noted that their spouses were readers; one-third said that their children read the magazine and over 10 percent noted that their friends and neighbors also read the magazine.

Stories concerning retirement, promotions, new construction, company operations, benefit plans, and service awards were most popular and also best remembered. The least popular items were those involving civic activities, the oil industry in general, regulations and legislation concerning the oil industry, company executives, and the parent company.[194]

Receiver Ability. The contents of a message may be too difficult to comprehend by most of the employes for whom it is intended. According to a check on the reading ease of 400 letters written at General Motors in conjunction with "My Job Contest" (see Chapter 2), the reading became more difficult, the higher the rank in the company of the writer. If such writing is for men at one level below the writer, the problem is not serious, but consider the implications if letters and other materials are being prepared from the topside for men at the bottom of the hierarchy.[424]

A 1951 analysis of 23 employe handbooks found at least ten to be pitched at a level of difficulty requiring one to read like a high-school graduate or higher in order to comprehend what was in the manuals.[101] Again, 65 percent of the material in an unselected sample of company papers was hard or very hard, such that most employes would lack the reading skill to understand the material unless they could read like high-school graduates.[544]

It is not uncommon to find that a manual prepared for the company foreman is written at, say, a level requiring the ability to read like a college student. Yet as a 1950 survey of 518 supervisors in seven plants showed, the mean reading ability of these men is equivalent to the tenth-grade level, lower still if the supervisor had less formal education than the average and if he was older.[127] Although the average foreman can read at the tenth grade, 10 percent may be reading only at the sixth-grade level. To ensure readability of the material by all the foremen, the company must scale it down to the lowest level of reading ability found among its foremen, but without losing the interest of its best educated men. To reach all the foremen the company will need to increase sharply the ease with which the material can be read by reducing the length of sentences, by increasing the number of personal pronouns, by increasing the human interest in the material, by using words with fewer syllables in them, and so on; for content analyses of reading materials have found that each of these affects the ease with which readers of a given grade-level can cope with the material.[215] When downward communication media such as weekly employment publications are increased in reading ease, human interest, and informativeness, survey results report considerable increases in the extent to which employes become favorable about the publication and take the magazine or newspaper home to their families, although the percentage of employes who read the publication may not change as much.[369] In the same way the speed of reading technical publications can be increased by increasing the personal references and human interest of the material, although immediate retention is not altered.[367]

Another approach to increasing message receptivity is to improve the speed and accuracy with which the messages can be received. This was done with 150 executives who met for 90 minutes once a week for ten weeks of training. They discussed topics like vocabulary building, skimming, and varying reading speed for different purposes. Films were used to provide pacing exercises. Speed and comprehension were checked periodically. The executives advanced from the 70th to the 82nd percentile on a standardized reading test for college seniors. Moreover, their average weekly reading speed went from 277 to 440 words per minutes during the ten weeks of training.[57]

Efficacy of Relevant Downward Communication

Adding downward communication systematically to feed back to employes information about the success of their performance has been shown to directly increase productivity. After life insurance agents attended a home office or regional training program of four days, the company kept in contact with approximately half of the agents by means of weekly production bulletins or personal letters distributed every two months commenting on the performance of each of the agents. A comparable control group of agents did not receive this attention from company management. Table 8.2 shows the average monthly production of the experimental and control groups of agents before they all attended the four-day training program and their average production during the six months that followed the program. Over half of the experimental group receiving the weekly bulletins and personal letters improved following the training, while only 37.7 percent of the control group without this continued follow-up increased in productivity. At the same time that the average production of the experimental group rose, the average for the controls fell.[730]

But there appears to be an optimum amount of communication downward. If there are too few of such formal communications, rumors will flourish in their absence, even on the executive level. On the other hand, the channels can get flooded with much irrelevant material so that the employe tends to "tune out" the whole system which is overloaded with messages. Even important messages may lose their saliency

TABLE 8.2 AVERAGE MONTHLY PRODUCTION OF LIFE INSURANCE
AGENTS RECEIVING PRODUCTION BULLETINS AND PERSONAL LETTERS
AFTER TRAINING AND THOSE NOT RECEIVING SUCH
INFORMATION AFTER TRAINING*

| | Average Monthly Production | | |
	Before Training	Six Months After Training	Percentage of Agents Improving
65 agents receiving training and information feedback	$18,542	$21,352	54.3%
68 agents receiving training but no periodic information feedback	$17,317	$15,496	37.7%

*From Weitz, Antoinetti, & Wallace, 1954

because they are imbedded in so much information of less consequence to the employe. Also there may be conditions under which a sense of frustration develops because the distribution of information results in everyone finding himself concerned with everyone else's problems, problems which he often cannot make any contribution to solving.[657] In the same way downward communications are ill-advised when they will serve no useful purpose but rather detract from organizational efficiency. For instance, there is no sense in punishing the department head with information noting that his costs are up 10 percent more than in other departments if he has no control over the costs. What is completely outside his sphere of influence becomes a personal defeat as a consequence of communications from above, stressing his increased costs. More useful would be budget information and cost standards over which the department head could exert some influence within his department.

Table 8.3 illustrates that for some people, at least, there can be too much as well as too little information received from above. Both supervisory and nonsupervisory employes were tested on their knowledge about the company. The knowledge had been disseminated by the company in the past. Employes also indicated their attitudes towards the company. Table 8.3 shows the correlations obtained between amount of information retained by employes and their attitudes towards their companies. As can be seen in Table 8.3, in the five firms surveyed, supervisors who retained more company information tended to be more *dissatisfied* with their companies, while generally office and opera-

TABLE 8.3   CORRELATIONS BETWEEN HOW MUCH INFORMATION COMMUNICATED BY A COMPANY IS RETAINED BY EMPLOYES AND HOW FAVORABLE ARE THEIR ATTITUDES TOWARD THE COMPANY*

Company	Supervisory Personnel		Nonsupervisors (Office and Operating Employes)	
	Number of Employes	Correlation Between Information and Attitude	Number of Employes	Correlation Between Information and Attitude
A	29	−.11	66	.04
B	15	−.43	44	.14
C	12	−.20	93	.12
D	11	−.25	79	.30
E	23	−.02	85	.12

*After Perry & Mahoney, 1955, p. 342

ting personnel receiving and retaining more information had more
favorable attitudes towards their companies.[523]

On the other hand, a 1957 survey of all employes in the headquarters offices of Standard Oil of New Jersey and affiliates found a
close relationship between the extent to which employes believed they
knew enough about internal company policies and their general morale.
Figure 8.4 shows how these employes responded to the question, "Do
you know enough about internal company policies?" as against their
index of general morale, measured by their overall satisfaction with
material benefits, the reputation of the company, supervisory practices,
and opportunities for self-realization on the job.

Those who felt relatively ill-informed tended to be younger, of
shorter service, lower paid, less educated, and less likely to be in supervisory positions. While 68 percent of those who felt relatively well-
informed about internal company policies agreed that "my supervisor
keeps me well-informed," only 26 percent of those who felt relatively
ill-informed regarded their supervisor as a satisfactory communicator.
Table 8.4 shows the preferences of the "informed" and the "uninformed" as to how they would like to be kept up to date. The informed
were generally more interested in the company newspaper as a medium
of information, but both groups tended to have the same preferences,
high in interest in meetings of the department with their supervisor
and low in regard for letters to their home.[658]

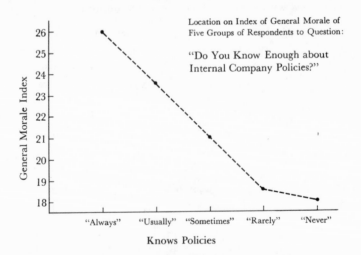

Figure 8.4: Relation Between Felt Adequacy of Communications
and General Morale of Standard Oil of New Jersey Headquarters
Office Personnel. (After Stuhr, 1962)

TABLE 8.4   RESPONSES OF STANDARD OIL HEADQUARTERS EMPLOYES
TO THE QUESTION: "HOW WOULD YOU LIKE TO
BE KEPT UP TO DATE?"*

	The Informed	The Uninformed
Company newspaper	57%	42%
Meeting with supervisor	54	58
Department meetings	56	56
Letters to home	13	17

*Adapted from Stuhr, 1962.

ONE-WAY VERSUS TWO-WAY COMMUNICATION

The effectiveness of downward communication is directly dependent on whether it is being complemented by effective upward communication. Like the manager who must send down a complicated set of instructions to his subordinates, a laboratory subject may be asked to send one of the patterns of rectangles shown in Figure 8.5 either by one-way or two-way communication with his audience. The subject describes how the rectangles form a particular pattern using words only, and his audience must try to draw the rectangle according to his verbal description.[390]

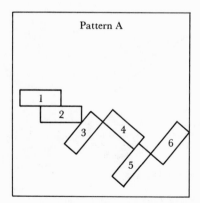 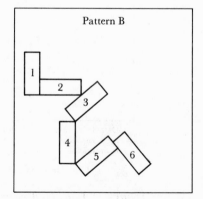

Figure 8.5: Patterns of Rectangles to be Communicated One Way or Two Ways. (After Leavitt, 1958, p. 121)

In a one-way, downward communication system the audience cannot interrupt the sender to ask any questions, while in the two-way situation they may interrupt the sender with questions at any time.

One-Way Communication Is Fast

As might be expected, one-way communication is considerably faster and more orderly. However, it is much less accurate than two-way communication. Thirty-three members of one audience under one-way conditions matched on the average only 1.1 rectangles of the six in a pattern, while the same audience was able to match 4.8 rectangles correctly when given the opportunity to communicate upward. However, they took three times as long to do the job when they could talk back to the sender.

One-Way Communication Is Frustrating for Receivers

Although faster, the one-way system is much more frustrating to the receivers. Figure 8.6 shows how 41 receivers felt about the two communication techniques; one-way was "quite" to "completely" frus-

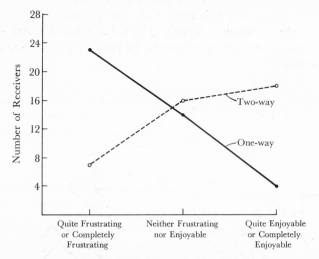

How Did You Like Working This Way?

Figure 8.6: How 41 Receivers Liked One-Way and Two-Way Communication Situations.

trating for a majority of them, while two-way tended to be rather en-
joyable. Unfortunately, the sender is likely to be more comfortable
under one-way conditions. In a two-way system he may find himself
attacked because his mistakes and oversights are disturbing the audience. They are likely to attribute misunderstandings to the sender's
inabilities to communicate rather than the receivers' abilities to listen.
The sender will have to accommodate himself to the slowest member
of the audience. He can block out all this negative feedback by operating
only a one-way, downward-flowing system, but it will be a very inaccurate procedure for the transfer of information.

In industry whether two-way communications will be permitted
is usually the prerogative of the sender, management. If management
wants to maintain orderliness, if management does not want its mistakes
to be recognized, if management does not want its communication inabilities to be aired publicly, if management wants to be able to blame
its employes for communication failures, then it will communicate
downward and maintain a one-way system. However, if its major concern is communication accuracy and satisfied employes, it will foster
a two-way system. If management maintains a closed door (Figure 8.7),
it shuts itself off from hearing many unpleasantries, yet at the same time
misses the opportunity to answer questions which might clarify its own
messages as well as information, ideas, and suggestions on how its
operations might be improved.

The Closed Door

Unless Management Makes a Special Effort
It Will Not Hear All It Should.

*Figure 8.7: The Closed Door. (From Ind. Rel. Dept., U.S.
Steel, 1953)*

Two-Way Chains

Since often we are dealing with a chain of communications in the typical industrial hierarchy, and messages must be relayed through many levels and positions, two-way communication is likely to promote completeness and accuracy of transmission as well as satisfaction of many senders and receivers involved in the flow of a single piece of information. The vulnerability of the many layered hierarchy to communication failure, as will occur with one-way transmission, is made apparent because it takes a blockage of two-way communication at only one link in the chain to produce an inaccurate or incomplete transmission through the remainder of the chain (Figure 8.8).[391] The superintendent will receive no feedback from the work force if he sends them a message through his foremen who transmit only one way.

Pressure to Talk Back

The typical industrial organization is geared primarily to downward communication. Yet there actually resides in those below in the system a strong tendency to want to communicate upwards. Two-way communication provides a tension-reducing activity for those of lower status. When experimental subjects are assigned to different levels in a hierarchy and permitted to communicate freely with each other, there is actually more pressure for those of lower status to communicate upward than vice versa. One of the frustrations of a lower-level position, no doubt, is the inability to communicate upward through many hier-

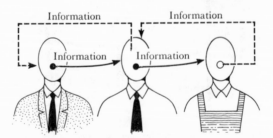

Two-Way Communication Is Through the Foreman.

Figure 8.8: A Chain of Two-Way Communications from Management Through Foreman to Worker. (From Ind. Rel. Dept., U.S. Steel, 1953)

archies despite one's needs to do so. Even where the experiment allows upward communication, subjects assigned to lower-status positions feel inhibited from doing so.[359]

Those of lower status are more likely to communicate irrelevant content, both upward and horizontally. It may be that such irrelevant communication is a form of catharsis or escape.

Various factors increase the pressure to communicate upward. More communication upward is likely to come from persons at lower echelons in the hierarchy who have the desire to be promoted but are unlikely to move upward.[359] Experimental subjects in low-status positions but likely to be promoted send more messages to other persons at their own level, while unpromotable subjects send more and longer messages upward.[123] Two factory studies suggest that workers with strong promotional desires tend to conceal from their boss job difficulties which might affect their chances for promotion, particularly if they mistrust their boss. As a consequence superiors are less likely to understand the job problems of their subordinates who have strong desires for promotion. The same upward communication failure seems to occur for those subordinates who actually are promoted rapidly.[548]

Perceived Versus Actual Two-Way Communications

Matters in industry are complicated by the fact that the superior often believes that he is maintaining a two-way communication system when his subordinates believe that it is primarily a one-way channel. For example, in one study, while 73 percent of foremen said that they always get their subordinates' ideas, only 16 percent of their subordinates agreed with them that the subordinates' ideas were obtained.[412]

An Example of a Formal Two-Way Mechanism

An active two-way communication system was created in a plant by establishing regular monthly work unit meetings. Foremen called their workers together for the final 45 minutes of the shift on the third Friday of each month. A foreman would spend the first five to ten minutes reporting company matters concerning his employes: vacation schedules, overtime during the next ten days or equipment replacement schedules. Then the foreman would ask employes if they had any questions, any ideas or suggestions for doing things differently. The employes were free to bring up different subjects, except politics,

religion, and the union contract. Outsiders like staff specialists or department heads might be asked to attend a subsequent meeting to review
in more detail a particular subject of interest or to answer more fully
certain questions raised by the employes.

An attitude survey was run by the National Industrial Conference
Board in this plant as well as in a comparable plant without this two-
way communication plan. The two plants were similar in unionization,
the nature of the employes' work, and their seniority.

The only difference was that one plant had the regular meetings,
the other did not. Employes in the plant with regular meetings felt
that their foreman was of greater help in keeping the employe up to
date on company matters, while in the comparable plant, employes
felt they were more likely to get the low-down on what is going on in
the company from fellow employes. In the plant with the regular meetings, employes were more likely to feel that they were told why they had
been asked to do something and that their foreman was more likely to
ask their advice before deciding things. They also felt they had a better idea on how they were getting along on the job. They also reported
more interest in the company's annual report. It was easier to talk
things over with their foreman or to get their ideas up to the top men
in the company, who they felt were more likely to be really interested
in the ideas. While 55 percent felt that the company with regular meetings did a good job of telling what is going on and what is being planned,
only 18 percent in the comparable plant without such meetings felt that
their plant did a very good job. Equally important, 62 percent of employes in the plant with regular meetings felt they really belonged in
the company rather than "just worked in the plant," while only 29
percent in the plant without meetings felt the same way. And finally,
45 percent of the employes with scheduled meetings felt their company was one of the very best to work for, while only 20 percent felt
the same way about the company without the regular meetings.[271]

FORMAL UPWARD COMMUNICATION

Supervisors can encourage employes to communicate freely with
them about work and personal problems. This information should be
evaluated and transmitted upward. Formal efforts can be made to
solicit such information, as for example, in the regular meetings of
supervisors and employes just mentioned. Or periodic counseling
sessions can be held, in which the main purpose is to discuss the progress
of the employe, how well he feels he is doing in attaining his goals,
and what the supervisor as well as the rest of the company can do to

support the employe in his efforts to do a better job. Supervisor and subordinate can collaborate in a mutual evaluation and goal-setting program.

Grievance Procedures

Ordinarily a union contract will include a formal grievance procedure. The employe who is dissatisfied in his upward communication with his own supervisor can make a formal complaint by means of his union steward who will then take the case to higher levels. In a way, the start of the grievance machinery means that upward communication has broken down.

Suggestion Systems

The formal suggestion system is a common way of promoting upward communications. As early as 1880 a suggestion plan was introduced in a Scottish shipbuilding company and at the Yale and Towne Manufacturing Company in Connecticut.[58] By 1941 half of 231 companies in a nationwide sample had installed formal suggestion systems.[591] Today suggestion systems are commonplace in large organizations.

A 1945 survey of organizations employing a total of two million eligible workers noted that about one out of five of these workers submitted a suggestion during the year. Over two million dollars was paid in awards to these employes.[5] In the Soviet Union in 1956 over 1.4 million suggestions from workers were put into practice.[253]

Role of Supervisor. The successful suggestion program depends heavily on the supervisor. For example, a 1957 survey at the Esso Research and Engineering Company found that the percent of employes of a particular department who participated in the program and the awards they were likely to earn increased as there was a corresponding increase in agreeing that "their supervisor is friendly when they discuss suggestions and other matters." Quantity and quality of suggestions increased directly with the extent to which divisional supervision supported the program, a program felt by over 93 percent of the respondents to be of value both to the company and the employe.[342]

One-third of the employes answering the survey by Esso Research and Engineering did not like the idea of submitting their suggestions to their supervisors before they were sent to the suggestions com-

mittee.[342] Many employes may hesitate about approaching their supervisor concerning the submission of a suggestion for fear they may be
placing themselves in competition with him. They may "show him up."
Or some may mistrust the supervisor, feeling that he may steal the idea
if he cannot participate in the suggestion program. Collaboration between subordinate and supervisor may be increased and competition
reduced by giving the supervisor a small percentage of the reward
earned by his subordinate for submitting an approved suggestion, as
is done in the Soviet Union. Both supervisor and subordinate are rewarded when the subordinate submits a meritorious proposal through
his supervisor.[253]

However, supervisors who push for sheer quantity of suggestions
from their subordinates may obtain a yield of suggestions which are
generally poor. Thus a group of office workers who submitted many
suggestions earned less than $12 per suggestion while those in another
department who submitted far fewer were paid over $33 for each sug-
gestion approved.[357]

Supervisory Participation.   Three out of four companies surveyed permit supervisors to participate in the suggestion program.[5] However,
often supervisors feel themselves to be ineligible for rewards, and professional and technical employes regard the program as one for nonprofessional employes. They tend to regard the creation of suggestions
as part of their routine assignment.[342]

Suggestions as a Symptom.   As with grievances, to some extent the number of suggestions may reflect a breakdown in upward communication.
The survey of office workers just mentioned found that departments
whose work productivity was low tended to submit more suggestions
than departments whose productivity was high, although the increased
quantity of suggestions was not matched by a corresponding quality.
It may be that employes in high producing departments are able to
suggest ideas informally to their supervisors without using the formal
system.[357]

Two-Way Arrangement Required.   Again the upward flow of suggestions
requires the maintenance of a two-way communication system. Rapid
and adequate downward feedback is essential. There must be an immediate notice that a suggestion had been received and is not lying
around in an unopened envelope or in a suggestion box. The suggestion should be evaluated within a reasonable amount of time, say
30 days. Reasons why the committee does not approve a suggestion
must accompany the rejection.[58]

Individual Differences. Employes differ in the extent to which they will submit suggestions. At Esso, although women made up 52 percent of the work force, only 14 percent submitted suggestions, while 84 percent of the men did so. College-trained and longer-service employes were also much more likely to submit suggestions than those with less than a year of service in the company or with high-school degrees only.[342] Effective downward communication from management on who can and should submit suggestions and how to do so may help to increase participation in groups where suggestions have been few in the past.

Rewards. Rewards must be commensurate with the value of the suggestion both in the amount of recognition given for it and in the size of the award for an approved suggestion. Most effective systems gear awards to the value of the suggestion to the company, to its products, to safety and working conditions.

It is important to avoid arousing feelings of inequity, as when an employe feels that the suggestion for which he received a $24 award saved the company several hundred thousand dollars annually. Objective schedules are set up to avoid this if possible so that an award will be made proportional to the estimated saving to the company if it puts the suggestion into effect.

Attitude Surveys and Employe Committees

Attitude surveys, described in Chapter 2, are another means of upward communication. Employe committees organized to promote, aid, or administer credit unions, recreational programs, job evaluation programs, merit rating systems, and public relations are also sources of upward communication.[58]

OTHER COMMUNICATION FLOW

Horizontal Communication

Formal organization charts usually make provision only for vertical communication. Yet a large amount of horizontal communication is expected between various staff services and line personnel as well as between, say, sales management, product planning, and line management. Even where it is unexpected, within the production line organization considerable horizontal communication of a formal nature takes place in order for work to get done.

Some Illustrative Data

In one plant 17 percent of the communications originated by a line production manager were horizontal, as were 22 percent of the communications he received. In another plant 41 percent of the messages originated by the line production manager were sent horizontally and 40 percent were received by him from peers in the same level in the organization.[381] Among supervisors in a textile mill interviews disclosed that most communications were horizontal. This was particularly true where the work process was highly mechanized. Machines instead of the foreman set the work pace of subordinates, reducing the need for much vertical communication or close supervision and increasing the percentage of horizontal flow of information.[612] In still another factory intensive self-recording of time spent with others showed that executives spent as much time with staff personnel as with their own subordinates. In fact, it was concluded that too much horizontal communication was taking place in this factory and too little between the different echelons for optimum operations. It may be that we find it most comfortable to talk at length with our peers, rather than with our superiors or our subordinates.[89] Organizational charts will become more realistic to the extent to which they show the horizontal lines of communication as well as the vertical.

Horizontal Communications in R & D. Research organizations are finding the need to formalize the horizontal flow of communications. Project directors must be able to communicate directly with those directing line services supporting the work of the projects.[44] Large government agencies such as NASA find it necessary to make provision for the flow of information from one station to another, between personnel at the same level in the hierarchy working on common problems, just as provision is made for the flow of information up and down within the same station.

One common horizontal transmission of particular importance occurs when one employe replaces another in a system. If the new man is equally experienced, according to a study of seven-man aircraft control and manning systems, then replacement of the old man has little effect on the system. But if the new man is inexperienced and must be "broken in" by the man who is being replaced, the entire system will suffer if the old job occupant passing the information to his replacement "has inadequate storage facilities." Maintaining the system when replacements occur will depend on how well horizontal communications can be sent and received between the man to be replaced and his replacement.[564]

Horizontal Communication and Organization Design

All the newer organizational designs presented in the preceding chapter tend to create structures promoting more horizontal flow. For example, the design based on overlapping groups (Figure 7.13) fosters such horizontal interaction by emphasizing the working together in groups of peers at the same level in the organization.

Horizontal Influence Is Persuasive. Influence downward may be coercive. The subordinate listens to the superior not because of the validity of the superior's ideas but perhaps because of the superior's status or power, his means to reward or punish the subordinate. Or, a superior can use his power to be permissive (Chapter 5). But horizontal influence must depend upon persuasion for the most part, where one employe persuades another of equal status and power because the influencer is esteemed as a person or his ideas are valued.

It may be that a flat organization entails more horizontal and less vertical influence. If so, we should also find more persuasion but less coercion or permissiveness in the aggregate than in the tall hierarchy. Again, where technology forces much horizontal communication, mutual persuasion is most likely to be involved in the influence process.

Rumor as a Substitute for Formal Communication

When formal communications in an organization are infrequent, slow to be transmitted, or given less than complete credibility, rumors are transmitted instead. Thus the grapevine is less likely to take root where management issues a reliable and trusted daily bulletin to all its employes. On the other hand, rumors will start and spread more often among subordinates in departments headed by executives who deliberately withhold information as a tactical device for maintaining control.[454]

Saliency.   The intensity of the rumors and their dispersion throughout the organization will depend on how important a message they contain. A rumor about mass layoffs will spread more widely and rapidly than one about a new medical clinic.

Meaning.   An ambiguous communication will spread more than a clear one, since the ambiguous message is more difficult to test against reality. Preceding events will make a difference, providing special meaning to a rumor. An item about economic recession or poor business prospects for the firm appearing in a local newspaper might speed greatly the transmission of a rumored layoff.

Diffusion.   Rumors will move faster among transmitters who are close in time and space. It will be spread more rapidly, say, in a department of employes who mingle with each other frequently than in one in which interaction is restricted. Rumors are less likely to reach isolated employes or isolated departments.

Where employes are free to interact in a department, the diffusion follows a logistics curve as shown in Figure 8.9.

If 20 employes of a department meet freely in random sequence with each other and each transmits a different message, say their birth dates, Figure 8.9 shows how many of the messages actually are known at each minute after the subjects began freely interacting. The diffusion of information first spreads slowly, then gains momentum, and finally slows down as everyone begins to become saturated with all the information. This diffusion can be almost perfectly predicted from deducing the probabilities that a knower of a particular bit of information will meet a non-knower at a given time.[171]

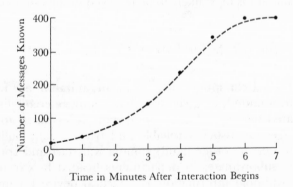

Figure 8.9: Logistic   Modeling   for   Diffusion.
(After Dodd, 1955, p. 399)

Motivation. The need for information directly increases word-of-mouth transmission in the absence of formal communications. The time begins to draw close when annual merit raises are to be made and one's superior is unable to indicate what will happen. The field is now fertile for the speedy transmission of a rumor that no raises will be granted this year.

Crises increase the need for information. Here it is almost impossible for formal methods to be quick enough to scotch rumors before they start spreading rapidly.[613] Particularly for those unable to tolerate ambiguity and uncertainty, any information, whether credible or not, serves to reduce anxieties. On the other hand, the more insightful persons with more prior knowledge of circumstances will be less prone to transmit rumors.[113]

Rumors Flow Horizontally. Although management usually pays more attention to vertical transmission, rumors spread most rapidly by means of horizontal chains. Such horizontal flow is heightened if liaison and staff personnel are distributed throughout the firm. Staff employes tend to be more active than line personnel in spreading information.[149]

Purposiveness. Rumors may be started deliberately as a consequence of competition. For political ends, a rival department or individual may be rumored to be incompetent, untrustworthy, or ignorant of outside affairs.[90] Or such rumors may be inspired unintentionally yet serve a competitive need to increase one's own ego by deflating another's among third parties. But most rumor developments and their distortion are not intentional, purposive, or functional to the organization, nor to the individual who relays the rumor. Yet the relayer's systematic distortions can be understood in terms of systematic perceptual errors and memory losses.

Systematic Distortions in Transmission

Condensation. The receiver of a message who in turn sends it on by word-of-mouth to the next person distorts the message in systematic ways. First what he sends will be shorter, simpler, and less detailed than what he received. He displays an indexing process so that only the salient features of the message are relayed, often in condensed coded form.[95] Contrast is enhanced within messages by sharpening up some details, reducing the visibility of others. What began in headquarters as the details of a reorganization proposal may gradually decay into rumors about personnel transfers.

As it is relayed, the middle of a message is more likely to be lost than the beginning or end; just as after learning a list of nonsense syllables, one retains the first and last syllable longer than those in the middle of the list.

Closure.   Where the input is ambiguous, as is often true about rumors, the relayer is likely to fill in, to bring closure to gaps in the message he hears. If he hears that an unknown visitor from headquarters is due to arrive on an inspection tour, he may transmit to the next employe the news that a staff inspector, probably George Smith, is coming. Further along the transmission line, the message may be that George Smith is definitely coming.

Symmetry will develop in messages as they are relayed. If ten persons are being transferred out of a department in the early phases of a rumor's development, later the message may contain the information also about ten persons to be transferred into the department.

Expectation.   Employes will err by relaying information in the direction of what they expected to hear in comparison to what they actually heard. Their expectations cause even more bias than their opinions about the message they are relaying, although needs, values, and opinions do play an important role also in distorting communications. For instance, one group of union officers in a gypsum plant were respectful of authority and submissive to management. They received many strong grievances from workers but registered only lukewarm complaints with management. The filtering process was only realized when a wildcat strike broke out and more aggressive union leadership took over.[251] Wishful distortion, distortion in the direction of one's own biases, occurred here as well as distortion to please the receiver or to avoid arousing his resentment.

Memory Bias.   Memory as well as transmission is biased. We remember those parts of messages likely to please those to whom we must communicate.[587] We tell the boss what we think he wants to hear rather than what he should hear. Sometimes we do distort in the direction of our own commitments. We have claimed that a program would be a success. When ambiguous reports are received, we interpret them to fit our prior commitment.

Adaptation.   Adaptation levels play a part. If we have been transmitting generally bad news, one bit of good news will be inflated when we send it on, out of proportion to its actual goodness. Or if we have become accustomed to hearing and sending bad news, we might find the good news incredible and hesitate to send it at all or convert it into bad news.

Association.   Associated cues may cause error. If most accidents in the past have been in the maintenance shop, a message that an accident occurred *near* the shop may be translated into a message that an accident took place *in* the shop.

Individual Differences.   Regardless of what they hear, some relayers will respond differently than others. Thus when a completely ambiguous, nonsensical situation is created by asking examinees to guess whether a question the examiner has in mind will have a "yes" or a "no" answer, ostensibly as a test of their extrasensory perception, reliable individual differences emerge. Some examinees consistently guess "yes," "true," "agree," "support," "favor," and so on, while others just as consistently guess "no," "false," "disagree," "reject," "dislike," and so on.[40] (See Chapter 4.) Some personalities are acquiescing, agreeable, and accepting while others are just as consistently skeptical, negative, and rejecting. Such personality differences become increasingly important in determining what will be relayed as the rumor becomes more ambiguous.

In the same way group effects are likely to foster distortion. If an employe hears similar false reports from several other co-workers, he is more likely to transmit the erroneous information than if no such group conformity effects are apparent.[95]

*   *   *   *   *

Analysis of communications requires studying the sender, the message, and the receiver as well as the formal channels along which the message can be transmitted. Emotional and rational issues are involved. The sender can thwart transmission by permitting only one-way communications, either because of legitimate concern for speed or because he feels unable to handle potential feedback. The sender will screen out messages, hearing only what fits with his needs, or understanding only what his vocabulary level permits him to comprehend. The message may be couched in language too difficult for the receiver to grasp or emotionally loaded with words resulting in immediate rejection of the contents by the receiver. A network where all messages must go to and from a central position will coordinate information faster, yet at a sacrifice in the satisfaction of those in peripheral positions, while a completely open network will generate more overall satisfaction at a sacrifice in speed.

The emotional and rational problems of communications are amplified when the sender is from one group and the receiver identifies with another. Misunderstandings multiply when a manager talks to a worker, when a union representative talks to a company executive, when the sales supervisor questions the production chief, or when an engineer tries to communicate with a nontechnical executive. These are the problems to which we now turn.

In Brief

WHETHER IT TAKES PLACE IN A GIANT INDUSTRY OR A SMALL DEPARTMENT store, conflict in a formal organization manifests itself in certain consistent ways. Those at different levels in the hierarchy are likely to disagree about the goals of the organization and what constraints it must work within. Trouble arises if status differences are confused or unassociated with real differences in ability and esteem.

Conflict in formal organizations usually can be seen as a nonzero-sum game permitting competition and cooperation for which there are adaptive and maladaptive resolutions. Questions of mutual trust are paramount issues here. But often the conflict between departments, between union and management, between technical and nontechnical employes, or between line and staff, is a zero-sum game, unfortunately. If one side wins, the other loses. A common pattern of highly predictable outcomes dominates such controversy.

When union and management play a zero-sum game, each has certain well-known competitive strategies. When negotiations can produce some satisfaction to both sides, a variety of collaborative arrangements is possible. And this is the trend in union-management relations—away from competition and toward collaboration.

Chapter 9

CONFLICT IN INDUSTRIAL

ORGANIZATIONS

STATUS DIFFERENCES

Although a division of labor is necessary in the large organization, the differences it causes in the rank and importance of members is a continuing source of conflict between them. The conflict is even greater if there is confusion about whose job is really more important or if a man of low esteem is elevated to a job of great importance.

Position and Status

Some individuals are assigned to more important positions than others. The position of division head gives the occupant much more responsibility for men, money, and materials than the position of first-line foreman. It gives him more power over more men and more authority to make decisions about more money and materials. Whoever occupies the position of division head has more status than whoever is assigned to a job as first-line foreman, regardless of what each is like personally. The foreman may be more valued as a person, more esteemed, but he still would not have the prerogatives of the division head.

Utility of Status

These status differences make it easier to forecast what a job occupant will do, what he will decide and when. Responsibilities are allocated, and successive higher levels of control are provided by the system.

The rules regulating the behavior of job occupants also protect them and may even give them freedom to show initiative in areas in which no rules apply.[85] Rule books often make it possible for a job occupant to know when he has freedom to decide about a matter and when he does not. Again, when multiple prescriptions are present, rules allow a job occupant to choose which rule to apply. If both customer goodwill and minimizing losses are seen as equally important as company goals, the job-holder is free to decide which is most important in dealing with a specific customer complaint.

Status as a Source of Conflict

As we have observed in previous chapters, status differences have other consequences for the organization, many of which are dysfunctional. Formally the superior is to tell the subordinate what to do, yet the subordinate seems to feel greater need to talk to his superior about what is to be done than vice versa. Anxiety may be aroused about one's status, interfering with work rather than facilitating it. How much deference one is receiving, whether one's pay raise is equivalent to that of another, whether an outsider will be brought in, thus blocking one's promotion, are commonplace "status worries."[229] Those strongly concerned about their status and likelihood for promotion are prone to conceal job difficulties from their boss, reasoning that revelation might affect their chances for promotion.[548] They also have least understanding of company policies and goals if highly frustrated in their efforts for promotion.[614] The struggle for status may manifest itself in competition for symbols of status: carpets instead of bare floors, auto parking-lot assignment, desk-top size, and so on. And how much status an employe has, has direct bearing on his control over his environment.[229] More status means more opportunity to participate in decisions and to influence others. It is little wonder that we find such a consistent direct relationship between status and job satisfaction (Chapter 3). Even among those in higher echelons, according to a survey of 1,958 executives, greater status brings greater need satisfaction, particularly with opportunity for self-actualization, autonomy, and esteem in the eyes of others. However, top management does not feel any more secure or more satisfied with social opportunities than do those at lower levels.[532]

A variety of other conflicts exist between those of different status. The subordinate may see himself as putting forth more effort and reaping less reward than his superior. Distasteful, boring, dirty, physically hard work offers less return than creative, stimulating, mental effort because the labor of one man with a strong back is simply of relatively little importance to the firm's overall performance compared to an idea for a new production technique. Both tradition as well as supply and demand keep rewards low for unskilled labor and high for management personnel. Top management, moreover, is often in a position to determine its own compensation because of the control it may have over the Board of Directors.

The extent to which the blue-collar employe has benefited from his efforts and raised himself from the marginal subsistence level of wages to income levels making possible a decent standard of living is related to his success in unionization, strikes, and other forms of open conflict. He has been aided by a gradual change in the past two centuries in industrial societies. The focus of legislation has changed from concern for property to concern for people, from complete lack of interest in the worker's fate in a ruthlessly competitive world to active concern for his protection from the rigors of supply and demand. Technological advances also have made it possible to continue to increase the distribution of benefits to employes for their labor as each employe has become more productive.

The gap between the rewards distributed to management and employes is narrowing in many industrial areas, particularly between such skilled, organized employes as the steel workers and their management. For example, a steel worker can earn as much annually as a foreman might elsewhere. As each individual blue-collar employe produces more with more complex and expensive equipment and with special skill, each productive employe is likely to narrow the gap further. Currently it is argued that skilled workers should be classified and paid according to the knowledge they must have to do the job, their mastery of technical skills needed, their need to assume responsibility and to endure punishment and risk.[617] In a socialist state like Jugoslavia, it is argued and made a matter of legislation that no plant worker's income should be less than 40 percent than that of the plant manager.

Pervasiveness of the Effect of Status on Power to Influence

High-status jobholders are legitimately more influential than those below them about matters affecting how they work together towards organizational objectives. This differential influence is prescribed in the regulations. But as first mentioned in Chapter 5, even where the job occupants are removed several hundred miles from the plant site, placed in unstructured training groups to discuss all kinds of issues, many having no relevance to the company, where no member is with his own immediate boss, company status still strongly affects who influences whom.

As described in Chapter 5, when 36 supervisors met off-site in groups of 12 for two hours and at the end of each meeting, rated each other on how influential each had been during the meeting, status in the firm strongly determined the patterns of influence. Figure 9.1 is a summary of the data of Figure 5.7 and shows the mean rated influence of supervisors according to their status in the company. The higher their status, the more they were seen as influential.

Status effects in these circumstances are often quite subtle. For days higher-status men will sit on one side of the table and low-status persons on the other without actually being aware that where they chose to sit is strictly according to their status on the job. Low-status supervisors have great difficultly in "opening up" with those of higher status, even in these situations where no one is with his own boss and discussion is often about matters outside work. Typically the department heads feel they are not trying to be influential nor exerting as much influence as others attribute to them. It often comes as a surprise for them to learn how influential even a shrug of their shoulders may be in shaping the response of those lower in status. When informed about what is happening, a sense of the illegitimacy of their pervasive influence leads them to sharply reduce their participation and actual influence. To illustrate this, the 36 men were formed into 18 pairs where one member was of higher status than his partner. The pairs worked on a series of half-hour problems together, one per day for several days. Before attention was called

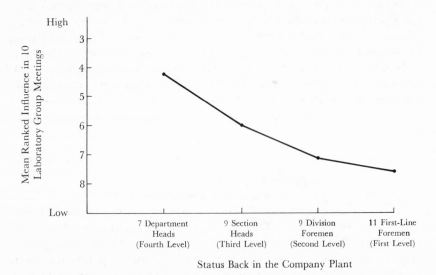

Figure 9.1: How Management Level in a Company Affects Influence in a Laboratory Away from the Company. (See Also Figure 5.7.)

to the importance of company status by showing data of Figure 9.1 to the men, two-thirds of the two-man teams were led in decision-making by the higher-status member of each pair. After Figure 9.1 was shown, two-thirds of the team decisions were influenced mainly by the lower status member of each team.

Status Confusion

The average apartment dweller, regardless of his own income and job, accords the apartment janitor less status than the janitor often accords himself. Further, many tenants will resent the janitor's income and new car.[245] There seems to be a general tendency to overvalue one's own job and to undervalue others. Thus 250 Boston residents tended to rate their job more highly than jobs very similar to their own.[98] First-line foremen are often caught in a conflict attributing more status to themselves than accorded them by their unionized subordinate employes, who collectively have more power over their foreman than vice versa.[754] Hostility is aroused particularly when a supervisor grants himself authority to make unpopular decisions when those below him do not feel he has such authority.[399] Again, the female restaurant waitress sees herself as having the authority to tell the male counterman what orders to fill. He resents taking such orders from a female whom he regards as of lower status than himself.[741]

Confusion is heightened because a person may have status in one situation but not another. The small-plant manager rotated to a staff headquarters position may find himself now a small frog in a big pond when he had been used to being the biggest frog in a small pond. A person may have high status within one branch of an organization but relatively little in another. The company chemist may have high status among his professional colleagues in other companies but relatively low status among his fellow salaried employes in his own company.

Status-Esteem Conflict

Ordinarily, more valued, more esteemed employes are promoted to higher status jobs. Yet the correlation is hardly perfect. It varies from one organization to another. When the correlation is low, status is not congruent with esteem, and the organization is likely to suffer from conflict and lack of effectiveness. Thus equipment maintenance was found poorest among those 40 radar crews that had lowest regard for their highest status member—their key noncommissioned officer.[508]

Informal contact patterns are likely to deviate more in organizations where status is not congruent with esteem. In a law enforcement agency the 16 members were more likely to contact those whom they esteemed, regardless of their positions. At the same time the less able and less esteemed men engaged in extensive and formal relations in their efforts to enhance their own attractiveness to their fellow workers.[70]

The administrator in research and development may have more company status than the scientists working for him. Yet he may be much less flexible, educated, and technically competent, causing dysfunctional conflict. "In scientific research, a hierarchy of power, which is not sustained by real differences in skill and contribution, recognized by all who work together, tends to produce interpersonal tensions and rivalries which inhibit creativity."[186] Often the administrator takes refuge in the ideology of the classical rules of how organization is supposed to operate. All must conform to the chain of command. He obtains further protection in his role by observing a rigid ritualism, which again is quite dysfunctional.[676]

A common source of conflict is the age-status inversion found in technologically advanced companies. Foremen are likely to be older, long-tenured men who came up through the ranks. Higher-echelon executives are likely to be much younger engineers or college graduates who entered the company much more recently. Similarly, staff personnel, supposedly in advisory positions only, yet actually often with the ability to make important decisions for the firm because of their specialized competence, are likely to be younger than the line executives to whom they are supposed to be of service.[145]

Where status confusions and imbalances are likely to produce conflict, one way to reduce it is by making contact between jobholders completely impersonal and objective. For example, the male counterman may resent less taking orders from an order slip placed on a spindle by the waitress than receiving orders directly from her.[741] Another way is to educate those in conflict about their own irrational feelings.

CONFLICTS IN GOALS AND ORGANIZATIONAL CONSTRAINTS

Unless they have unusual locations apart from everyone else in the firm, most employes, wage and salaried, have to resolve conflicts generated by many, many cross-pressures. The boss wants more production;

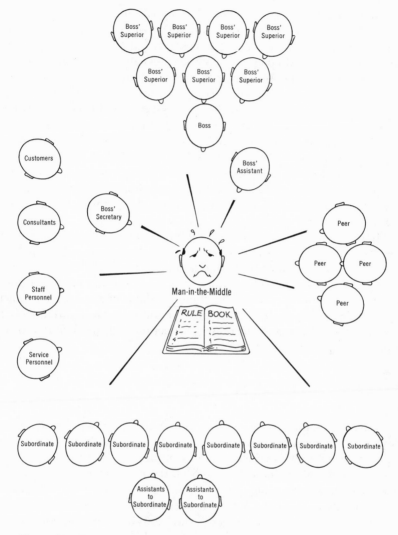

Figure 9.2: Sources of Cross-Pressure on a Member of a Formal Organization.

subordinates want more consideration. Customers demand faster deliveries; peers request schedule delays. Consultants suggest change; subordinates resist change. The rule book prescribes a formula; the staff says it will not work (Figure 9.2). It is not surprising that according to representative nationwide survey in 1961, only one out of six men in the labor force in the United States reports being free of tension on the job. Such job tension is higher among professional, technical, managerial, sales, and clerical employes than among blue-collar employes.[349a]

Many organizations have conflicting goals and constraints resulting in conflicting sets of rules. For the Spanish Colonial Empire murderous Indian slavery was economically necessary, but Indians were to be humanely liberated from paganism. Some rules called for colonial administrators to protect the Indians; other rules required administrators to condemn the Indians to fatal working conditions.[526]

Just as the Spaniards had the dual systems of church and civil authority, so does Soviet industry have dual systems of authority centered in a Party secretary and a plant director, each reporting to different superior organizations.[253] And many U.S. multiplant firms combine centralized staffs with decentralized lines to create the same dual authority in practice. A manager caught in the dual authority system may find his immediate line boss asking him to start a new project while a representative from central headquarters demands that he stop it.

It is easy to become confused about what is important, about the role one is supposed to play in the organization, about the upper and lower limits of one's authority, and about the obstacles to its exercise.[335]

Such conflict is likely to reduce overall organizational effectiveness. In laboratory studies simulating some of these organization conflicts, as might be expected, such cross-pressure was found to retard creativity, increase frustration, and decrease satisfaction with work and with the organization as a whole.[700]

Pseudosolutions to Conflict

Various escapes from conflict are commonly practiced. Some employes are hypocritical and insincere, practicing duplicity to avoid disapproval from above or below; for example, they tell their boss about how lazy their subordinates are and tell their subordinates what a slave driver the boss is.[682] Some develop blind spots in their environment so that they refuse to accept the existence of conflict.[147]

Delaying tactics are a protective device. When confronted with conflicting rules, the bureaucrat of the Spanish Empire would "obey but not execute."[526] An immediate demand was met by agreeing to do what was demanded, yet never actually doing it because it conflicted with a counterdemand. Hopefully the passage of time was expected to reduce the strength of one or the other demands.

Others deal with status conflicts by a form of withdrawal, wearing a "mask" seemingly neutral and objective.[525] One manager said that when his boss and subordinates disagreed, he would take his subordinate up to his boss' office and leave the two to solve the problem without him.

Some of the defense mechanisms described by Freud which are

false solutions to conflict faced by a person, yet protect his integrity, are seen frequently in industrial organization. For example, there is a common tendency to *displace* blame for conflict. We refuse to properly accept the source of conflict or its complexity. We avoid blaming ourselves or those whom it might not be safe for us to blame or to whom we are blindly loyal as partial causes at least for the difficulty. Thus managers account for a strike as the result of outside agitators who stirred up the workers to fight its management, instead of realistically examining the situational factors which led to the strike.

Or we take comfort in *rationalization,* socially acceptable excuses for real conflict, perhaps treating some "goldbricking" subordinates by saying: "I don't really care about whether you fellows take a break once in a while, but top management would start thinking about layoffs if they found someone loafing."

Six extreme examples of how employes cope with role conflict were drawn from a national survey to illustrate how coping attempts depend on the nature of the conflict as well as the personality of the man in conflict.

An assembly superintendent who has an obsessive-compulsive personality sees himself on a job with shifting demands that can never be fully met. So he develops guilt feelings about his own inadaquacies and copes with these feelings by overwork. "He doesn't *want* to keep busy; he *must* keep busy."

An executive has strong needs to be free of his superiors. He sees his superiors as retaliating against his struggle for autonomy because he projects upon them the threat he feels from his own subordinates. He actually acts towards his subordinates like he says his superiors act towards him.

A mathematician with poor administrative skill deprecates the need to be a good administrator.

A technically inadequate sales analyst copes with his job conflicts by becoming overly dependent upon his subordinates whom he also resents as a consequence.

A medical administrator deals with the conflicts between his professional and nonprofessional activities by withdrawing into a shell, avoiding any aggressive decisions and limiting sharply his efforts to exert influence.

A credit expediter reacts with guilt and anxiety because he really is more interested in a sales position where the aim is to increase the size of the customer's order rather than supervising the restriction of credit for the same customer resulting in a decrease in the size of the order.[349a]

To understand organizational conflict further requires examining the nature of trust and suspicion between members of any organization.

Trust, Suspicion, and Communication

A salesman of fork-lift trucks, overhead traveling cranes and monorail systems observed that whether or not his installation of labor-saving equipment aroused hostile employe reactions depended upon how the changes were introduced. As might be expected, no tension was created if the new equipment was first suggested by a worker or if it was for expanding operations so that it created no threat to job security. On the other hand, even where no jobs were threatened, suspicion and hostility were aroused by management if "everything was always treated as a big dark secret and the salesman was specifically warned by management personnel on frequent occasions not to divulge any information to employes." When trips had to be made into a plant for the purpose of taking field dimensions or checking a proposed layout, conversations were always held in guarded tones lest any secrets be disclosed. All this secret activity made workers feel that the installations would in some way affect their security, and they resented management's reluctance to inform them of proposed changes in operations.

And if job security was really being threatened, management secrecy often generated greater hostility than might have occurred if management had been more open about proposed plans, giving some workers who would have to be laid off more time for their own personal planning. For example, a bottling company had been handling all cases by hand in its operations. By changing the bodies of delivery trucks to accommodate pallets and by purchasing two fork-lift trucks, the company was able to reduce the needed number of workers in bottling operations from 115 to less than 50 men. The 115 went on strike and only after 110 days agreed to use fork-lift trucks, but tension was high for a long while thereafter.

Sabotage is a not uncommon reaction after suspicions and mistrust build up resentment to a fever pitch. One worker devised a method to jam the accelerator of a fork-lift truck to the floor, pointed the truck in the direction of the edge of a four- to six-foot high loading dock, then jumped from the truck before it ran off the edge. Again, two night employes linked the backs of two fork-lift trucks with a strong chain. Driving off in opposite directions, they burned out clutches, ruined transmissions, and shredded tires. It took several months for management to realize why the equipment was being worn out so fast.

Management Guilt-Feelings.   Management often adds to its own feelings of guilt by maintaining secrecy about the closing of a plant or a department in the interests of avoiding unpleasantries. The discharged employe will not be around after discharge to complain, so notice is withheld to the last possible moment. The desire to avoid open confrontation is illustrated by the great difficulties many executives have in discharging their own incompetent secretaries as compared to signing an order to lay off 100 line employes.

The Value of Openness

Evidence is accumulating in laboratory experiments that much of this arousal of hostility, fear, resentment, and guilt could be avoided by more open communications between the parties involved. If A and B are engaged in a game, as shown in Figure 9.3, so that both players will earn something ($+1$) if both choose "right," both players will lose (-1) if both choose "left"; but if one player, A, chooses "left" while the other, B, is trustingly choosing "right," A will win two points and B will lose two points. By choosing "left," either player can punish the other and perhaps himself, although this also offers the possibility of maximum gain ($+2$) to himself at the expense of the other. By choosing "right," either player offers to compromise if the other player will cooperate and choose "right" also so that both can earn something ($+1$, $+1$).[166]

Players will develop mutual trust and both choose "right," depending on each other to do likewise, if they can establish open communications with each other as to the relevant elements in the situation confronting them. Figures 9.4 and 9.5 show how opening communications affect potentially suspicious players of the "right or left" game.

Player B

		Left	Right
Player A	Left	$-1,-1$	$+2,-2$
	Right	$-2,+2$	$+1,+1$

Figure 9.3: A Two-Person Game of Competition and Cooperation. (The first value in each box indicates what A will earn, the second value indicates what B will earn, if the box is selected by the simultaneous choices of A and B. If A chooses left and B chooses right, what they earn, +2 for A and −2 for B, is shown in the upper right-hand box.)

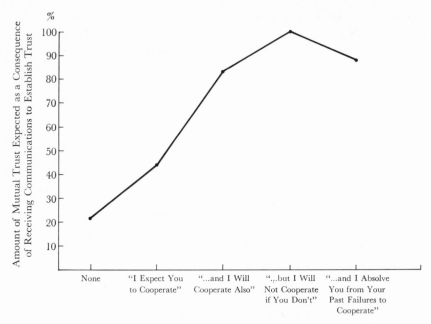

Notes Received by 18 Pairs of Players Under Each Condition

Figure 9.4: How the Amount and Nature of Communications Received Affects Expectations of Trust. (After Loomis, 1956)

Expectation (I expect you to cooperate), *intention* (I will cooperate also), *retaliation* (I won't cooperate if you don't), and *absolution* (I forgive you your past failures to cooperate) increase both trust and trustworthiness in those receiving the communications. Once mutual trust develops and is demonstrated to work, cooperative (right-right) behavior will be maintained. If communications are inadequate, if mutual trust fails to develop, uncooperative behavior (right-left) or (left-right) or (left-left) will continue.

Those initiating communications to establish trust are more likely to commit themselves to cooperation and are even more trustworthy than those who receive the information.[416] A two-way system of communications would seem needed to ensure maximum mutual trustworthiness.

Effects of Orientation and Concealment. Mutual trust is most likely when both players are positively oriented toward each other's welfare and when rules are clear about what will happen if trust is violated.[166]

But this is complicated by experiments that demonstrate that if *B* mistrusts *A*, *B* will conceal his attitude about an issue when he communicates to *A* while *A* will inaccurately perceive *B*'s real position.[471] In the same way when 36 management personnel in a training laboratory were repeatedly asked over several days in small group meetings, "How much that was in your mind did you tell the group today?" and "How much did others do so?" the trainees always felt that they personally were disclosing less than everyone else. They felt everyone else was being more open about matters than they admitted themselves to be.

Effect of Experience. Trust or suspicion grows from experience. If *B* is undependable, if the probabilities that he will choose "right" are low, *A* will be more suspicious than if *B* has exhibited consistently the tendency to choose "right."

Gradual escalation of mutual suspicion, resentment, and hostility is likely. *A* trusts *B*, but *B* violates the trust. *A* retaliates by choosing "left," increasing *B*'s suspicions of *A* and *B*'s own untrustworthiness. On the other hand, mutual trust can develop if *B* communicates his intentions and expectations and is consistent about living up to his commitments to *A*.[164a] For example, when each player was led to feel before beginning the game that the welfare of the other person as well as his own welfare is of concern to him and that the other person felt the same

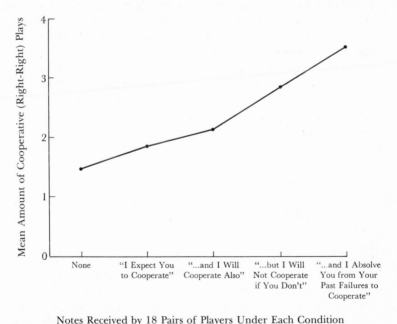

Notes Received by 18 Pairs of Players Under Each Condition

Figure 9.5: How the Amount and Nature of Communications Between Players Affects Their Actual Trustworthiness. (After Loomis, 1956)

way, he was likely to be trusting and cooperative during eight or more of ten plays. But if he was led to believe that his only interest was to do well himself or to do better than the other player, he was likely to co-operate less than four out of ten plays, particularly if he could not communicate with the other player before making decisions.

Effects of Dependency.   Other experiments have shown that suspicion is greater if one player is more dependent on the other than if both are equally dependent on each other. On the other hand, he will increase in trust of the other party if a third, disliked, party enters the picture. A player also will be more trusting if he sees the other making sacrifices beneficial to him. He will reciprocate with altruism on his own part.[164a]

To sum up, conflict is partly dependent on communications. It may be increased instead of reduced or held in abeyance if management remains secretive when it believes it is introducing goals and constraints into the organization likely to conflict with employe interests. While complete candor may not necessarily be the approach which will maximize cooperation and minimize mistrust, suspicions, and conflict, some degree of open communication seems preferable to complete secrecy in promoting cooperation and trust and reducing conflict.

But sometimes the game is not one in which cooperation is possible. One party will lose if the other wins. Such is often the situation when intergroup conflict and its side effects are observed. There are numerous win-lose occasions where compromise is impossible. For example, management may have to decide whether to expand one department's operation or another's. It can neither do both nor split the amount of resources it makes available. In the same way employes may have to vote for or against a union shop. If it is accepted, all employes must join the union within a specified number of days after they are hired. If there is no union shop, employes are free to decide whether or not to join the union.

INTERGROUP CONFLICT

Conflict between groups arises when one group can gain only at the expense of the other. The parties compete in a zero-sum game where one side must lose if the other is to win.[423a] If we ask two experimental groups each to create a product, say an essay on a particular subject, then ask both groups to judge which group did the best job, this win-lose structure is created.[69] The pattern of intergroup dynamics which results provides a general understanding or organizational conflict — conflict between union and management, conflict between two departments of the same firm, or conflict between groups of employes with different identifications such as younger staff engineers and older line foremen.

When Conflict Begins

Just as the announcement that war was declared used to bring on a gala celebration, so the announcement of a contest inspires and cheers the members within each experimental group. They become more attracted to their own groups. As the conflict between groups appears, each group becomes more cohesive. Loyalty grows for one's own group. Thus for 66 groups containing eight or nine members each, sharp increases were recorded in each member's evaluation of his group's goodness from before to after the beginning of a competition with other groups.[69]

Overevaluation of Own Group

Figure 9.6 shows how 36 management trainees evaluated their own and two opposing groups during such a competition. The sense of group goodness is maintained throughout the conflict and is only temporarily dampened by defeat. This favoring of one's own side against opposition extends so that if one's group must collaborate with an allied group against a common opponent, then the collaborating groups increase in our esteem, while the opposing groups are downgraded.[45]

Perceptual Errors

When each group has completed its product and is asked to study both products in order to judge whether the opposing group or itself has done a better job, certain consistent perceptual and cognitive errors occur. For instance, each of 20 groups was asked to study its own two-page essay and that created by a competing group. Then the members of every group were given a test of recall about both essays. Each of the 20 groups earned higher scores on the test of recall about its own creation than its competitor's essay. Each member tended to see items that actually appeared in both essays as appearing only in his own group's product. He perceived many more differences between the two group essays than actually existed.[69] This in turn seems to be due to certain learning

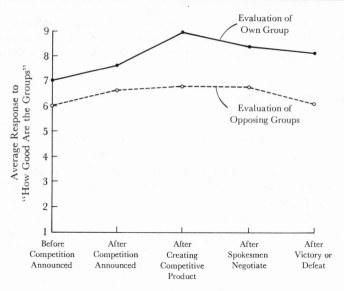

Phases in Intergroup Competition

Figure 9.6: How 36 Trainees in Three Competing Groups Evaluate Their Own and The Opposing Groups During the Intergroup Competition.

phenomena. For when the amount of learning about two objects is incomplete, differences between the objects become exaggerated.[94] Also we expect more differences from others, the more we see them as socially distant from us.[494] And the less favorably disposed we are toward the other group, the more likely we are to see differences between group positions. Thus employes actually underestimate the real degree of agreement between themselves and management. And they see more divergence of opinion, the more unfavorably they regard their management.[707]

So what began as a realistic win-lose competition turns into a more conflicting situation. Incompatible interests give rise to perceptual errors, biased memories, and distortions contributing to further conflict.

Conflict and Authority

Authoritarian leadership becomes more acceptable under the competitive threat from the outside. Members elect their strongest figures to central positions, those described by the group before the competition begins as most likely to assume leadership roles, to contribute to problem solutions, to pose problems for the group to discuss, to offer evaluations, to give suggstions about how to proceed, to eliminate group effort, and to push the group to stay on the central agenda.[69] Decisions can be made faster, commitments can be met more easily, and divisions within the threatened group can be prevented. The outside conflict increases the intolerance for differences within the group, brands deviation as disloyalty, and actually makes the groups more aggressive externally as well as towards dissenting members.

Conflict and Conformity

If a public vote is taken on the relative merits of each competing group's product, almost every member votes for his own group's effort. A few unsure members are slow to raise their hands, but once they view the overwhelming reactions of their co-workers, they quickly make the vote unanimous in favor of their own product. However, more than public pressure for loyalty is involved, for when a secret ballot is taken, the voting behavior is about the same. Regardless of the real quality of the two group products, most members remain strongly convinced that their own side did the best job, regardless of the arguments that follow and regardless of the fact that neutral judges can quickly decide that one product is clearly better than another.

This biased evaluation is not a consequence of an individual's need to maintain his own self-esteem, rather it seems based on the effects of group loyalty. This was demonstrated when one sample of students first competed as individuals to produce essays, then in groups. A second sample did the reverse. Students rated their own individual essay about half a point higher on a five-point scale than the essay of their individual competitor, but they rated their group product as two and one-half points better than that of their competing group.[224]

Resolving the Conflict by Negotiation

Spokesmen for competing groups are committed to their respective positions even more so than the rest of the membership of each group, for they usually have personally contributed more to the group's product. During negotiations with opponents they can agree on an agenda for discussing the competing products and on criteria for evaluating them, but almost never on the critical question as to which group did the best job. To capitulate would bring severe censure from the group one was representing. Only two such capitulations were recorded for 33

representatives in one analysis.[69] In another instance a spokesman capit-
ulated but in private discussion afterward admitted that he still felt his
group had done the best job. He had acknowledged defeat as an act
of revenge against two members of his group who had voted for the
opposition.

Whether the negotiations are public or private appears to make
little difference, although private negotiators may become somewhat
more moderate in their respective positions.

Mediation and Arbitration

In these win-lose situations, mediators who bring the conflicting
parties together and try to help them resolve the conflict do not have
much effect. If no compromise is possible, if one side must win and the
other lose, then higher authority must be brought in, in the form of an
impartial arbitrator. This seems to be the only way a decision can be
reached without resort to force.

How is the arbitrator viewed after he renders his decision? As might
be expected, it all depends on whether his decision is favorable to one's
side rather than the other. Winning groups see the arbitrator as more
practical, sincere, thoughtful, efficient, frank, capable, fair, open-
minded, astute, consistent, objective, progressive, resourceful, well-
informed, and impartial. Losers after defeat see these same arbitrators
as more slipshod, opinionated, impractical, biased, uninformed, unfair, partial, rigid, arbitrary, shallow, incompetent, stupid, superficial,
bungling, inexperienced, and irresponsible.

An executive in charge of two units may find himself called upon to
arbitrate such a win-lose conflict between the units. For example, each
unit may have made a budget request which it feels is essential to the
unit's survival. The executive must decide which request to grant since
he has only enough to satisfy one unit, not both. It can be seen that he
has to attend to some real "patching up of feelings" after he has made his
decisions.

Effects of Victory and Defeat

Characteristically the competing group awarded the prize tends to
rest on its laurels for some time afterwards. It is "fat and happy." Members tend to play or avoid working very hard. Such a reaction was reported by 32 of 33 winning groups and only 15 of 33 losing groups. On
the other hand, 28 of the losing groups and only seven of the winners
reported fighting, increased tension, or "flight" from the group.

The leadership is often overturned in the losing group, seldom in the winning one. Losing groups are much more likely to analyze the causes of their defeat. Winning groups go on to other matters. This is a common industrial pattern, for many companies who having been highly successful in competition tend to coast thereafter rather than to keep pushing for ever better records.[69] Management is often content with satisfactory levels of operations rather than optimum levels.[442]

Resolution of Differences (Where Compromise is Possible)

If the conflict can be described as a non-zero game so that both parties may gain somewhat by cooperation or agreement, then resolution of the conflict is much more likely. A resolution is more likely if both parties can see common goals whose attainment would be rewarding to both and whose attainment is only possible if both groups work cooperatively towards it.[604a] Bargaining may occur in which each side gives up something in exchange for obtaining something else. Or compromise may be achieved in which what is to be distributed is shared among the parties in dispute.

Whether groups will still fail to collaborate in a non-zero sum circumstance where compromise is possible will depend on a number of factors such as the following:

1. If each party has been successfully self-reliant, able to get along satisfactorily without an agreement, it will be less desirous of coming to terms in a dispute.[260] A company which has successfully remained nonunionized is unlikely to acquiesce quickly to a bargaining election.

2. Agreement will be less likely if the parties do not trust each other to keep the agreement or if there is no way to guarantee keeping the agreement. A company is less likely to agree to contract terms with a union which it believes the union is unable to keep.

3. Agreement will be less likely if it is seen as interfering with the independence of action by one party or the other. A nonunionized company is likely to balk at work rules it must accept if the union wins an election to represent the work force. The work rules reduce management's freedom of action.

Executive Assistance. There are a number of ways a person in higher authority can help disputants to settle their arguments. An executive facing two angry subordinates, each convinced that his own position is correct while the opposing position is wrong, can attempt to clarify the nature of the conflict and how a decision could be made. He can recognize and accept the feelings of the opponents, listening with understanding and avoiding evaluation. He can point out the creative alternatives available as a consequence of the differences, suggesting ways for the disputants to communicate to solve the problem together while he primarily works to maintain relations between the parties.

On the other hand, the executive can make matters worse by arguing that no differences exist, exploiting the differences to strengthen his own hand, or branding disagreement as disloyalty.[586]

Therapeutic Approach.   A therapeutic approach has been suggested.[68] Each side in a dispute discusses within its own group its perceptions and attitudes about itself and the other. Then representatives publicly present the descriptions each group has of the other. Now each group examines how the other group has described it. Finally the representatives attempt to help each group appreciate the nature of the differences, to correct invalid explanations of past incidents, and to separate real from unreal aspects of the conflict.

Rigid Versus Flexible Positions.   When both parties are relatively equal in power so that one cannot force a decision on the other, agreement is more likely if the parties can avoid a rigid position.[423a] Thus simulated union-management negotiators coming from groups who developed bargaining strategies were likely to deadlock in negotiations, but corresponding negotiators from other groups were able to resolve the bargaining issues easily when told merely to study the issues prior to negotiations to develop understanding of the divergent positions of union and management.[43] This was true particularly for negotiators who studied the issues by themselves rather than in groups.

Intergroup Conflict Within the Firm

The amount of conflict generated by competition between departments and individuals within the company is often greater than one might expect from units that are formally supposed to be cooperating in achieving the firm's objectives. A number of salient kinds of intergroup conflict can be noted within the firm.

Conflicting Interests.   Consider the likely conflicts of interest between the marketing and manufacturing divisions of a company. Stability is desired by the manufacturing department, flexibility by the marketing division. Marketing wants a special run for a customer to gain his goodwill; manufacturing is disturbed by the costs and bother of the special run. Marketing does not want to have to try to sell obsolete items; manufacturing wants to produce for large inventory to lower production costs. Marketing wants to produce to match varying market demand; manufacturing is interested in stabilizing production to maintain a secure labor force.[381]

When one branch of a firm improves its operations, increasing its profitability and returns to workers and management, it may bring on complaints from other branches without the same success.

Conflict as a Consequence of Differential Change in Performance. Girls on a bonus plan, spraying paint on partially completed toys passing on a conveyor belt, were given the opportunity to control the belt's speed after complaining of its rapidity and their inability to keep up the pace. As might be expected from earlier discussions about the impact of group decision-making, when the group members were given control, they increased rather than reduced the belt's speed, thereby earning bonuses 30 to 50 percent above the level expected for them. However, the extra production piled up in front of the girls' department and a vacuum was created behind in the production line. Other departments began complaining about wage inequities. Engineers lost prestige, and management felt it had lost some of its prerogatives — to set and coordinate the pace of output. Introducing group decision-making in one unit resulted in a conflicting imbalance in output and wages of the total organization. The conflict caused management to reverse its decision and to remove the self-pacesetting by the girls, six of whom then quit.[742]

Conflicting Professions. A sharp split often divides salaried employes, particularly in technically oriented companies, where at least half or more may be engineering graduates while the remainder either have degrees in business, science, or the humanities or none at all. While resentment of the bright, young, college graduate by the older first- and second-line supervisors is a common observance, the competitive feelings of the college graduate are not as well advertised. Yet a survey of the engineers and scientists of six companies found that most of them felt that operating management rather than the engineers and scientists received all the recognition in company and community. Eighty percent felt they were underpaid compared to other employes, while over 70 percent felt exploited by management, felt that their talents were misused by the company, and felt that management oversimplified their problems and lacked concern for long-range goals recognized by the engineers and scientists.

Technical Versus Nontechnical Employes. In technologically advanced firms such as in the aerospace or electronics industries there may be as many nonsupervisory engineers in operation as blue-collar union workers. Both are employe groups but with marked differences in skills, interest, background, and loyalty. Here are some of the intergroup conflicts observed by the management of a liquid rocket fuel plant employing about 5,000:

> Engineers pressure machinists to rush jobs; sometimes enthusiastic engineers do work which should be performed by bargaining unit personnel—a violation of the contract. Many engineers violate the contract knowingly and tell the union stewards so. But contract violation by engineers often is due to ignorance, since they seldom read or even comprehend the terms if they do read the contract.
> Engineers receive mainly negative information about unions. They tend to downgrade the individual union employe. Union employes identify all engineers with management, as arrogant and anti-union. They see line management as disrespectful of their capabilities.
> Outside social contact between engineering and union personnel is limited.
> Engineering delays result in idle operators whose job security is threatened as a consequence of the sporadic shopload.
> Union members fail to alert engineering group to difficulties that better design could correct. The engineering group fails to acquaint unionized employes with purposes, goals, and plans. Unnecessary complaints from both directions result. Engineers complain about lack of enthusiasm, slowness, and disrespect for company's commitments in general. The union members complain about design deficiencies and pressure for performance.

Staff Versus Line. Observations in three plants of 4,500 to 20,000 employes with 200 to 1,000 managers pointed to sharp conflict between those in line positions with formal operating authority and those in staff positions, formally supposed only to advise those in line assignments. The staff manager was likely to be younger but better educated than the executive on the line, who had more authority. The staff personnel actively sought transfer into line jobs but not vice versa. Their push for increased personal esteem, possibly because of their lack of status, increased tensions within staffs and conflict between line and staff.[145]

Interdivisional Pricing. Suppose the components for a console are made by Department *A*, and the console is assembled by Department *B*. Department *B* can also buy components from outside the company. The departments establish a price for the components. If the transfer price is above the prevailing market price, Department *B* is forced to operate at higher than necessary costs, while Department *A*'s gross income is raised. On the other hand, Department *A* may show a loss while *B* earns a profit, if the transfer price is set lower.[158] Conditions are set for a possible win-lose game, but resolution can be achieved if an arbitration committee from a central staff sets a price which appears just to both departments on the basis of current or past market prices for the same or similar products.[158]

Mergers. The cooperate-or-compete game shown in Figure 9.3 is played by many individuals and departments when a merger occurs. The merger brings on fear that what was a secure job will now be lost to a competitor from the merging unit. Worries abound that choice new spots may be picked first by the competing group and that status will be lost in the rearrangement. The merger may bring about physical movement to less desirable quarters. Unfamiliar superiors may be put in charge.

To smooth the transition and increase cooperation requires establishing and maintaining trustworthy, open two-way communications and the interchange of ideas and opinions in planning the integration.[193]

Functional Competitions

Competition can be useful to a unit, but it needs to be channeled so that each unit competes against itself rather than against other units that are supposedly collaborating to achieve overall organization objectives. For example, the 66 operating companies of Genesco and the departments within them each calculate monthly objective quantitative measures of performance, including productivity, results of morale surveys, accuracy of forecasts, and so on. Each company evaluates itself on the basis of its own gain over past periods in how well it uses the capital for which it is charged.[337]

Competition against outside agencies can be a functional spur, or it can produce dysfunctional blindness to one's own shortcomings and real needs and strengths. Care must be taken in examining with what groups we believe we are competing and why.

The single largest most important example of intergroup conflict found in business and industry is obviously that between the union organization and the company management.

UNION-MANAGEMENT CONFLICT

Reasons for Unions

There are many reasons why workers join unions. The reasons are social, psychological, economic, and sometimes even legal. Workers will join unions when their jobs fail to provide them with an adequate standard of living or necessary job security. Unions give workers a feeling of security, of status and integrity, of social equality, of satisfaction

in group effort, and a sense of belonging or having a meaningful place
in society. They also provide a release for frustration through aggression.[108, 246] Men may have to join the union to continue their employment if a union shop has been established in the union-management
contract.

Figure 9.7 shows the responses of 1,251 union members from 13
union groups representing about 14,000 union workers in a variety of
industries in the Mid-West and on the West Coast. It can be seen that
approximately three-fourths of the respondents gave favorable reasons
for joining the union, such as belief in unionism, the protection of
seniority, as means of obtaining better wages and benefits, and belief
in the value of collective bargaining. The minority mentioned such
adverse reasons as being forced to join the union in order to hold one's
job due to contract provisions or being forced to join because of social
pressure.[695]

Satisfaction with Unions. Other surveys support the generally favorable
attitudes towards unions by the local members. Of 392 men interviewed
in their homes, 93.4 percent said the union is needed in order to "buck"
management.[567] Table 9.1 details the favorableness of reply to a number
of specific questions about how a particular local handles union business.[150] Interviews and mail questionnaires of members of various local

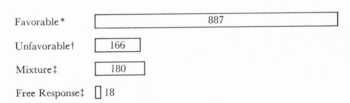

Favorable*   887

Unfavorable†   166

Mixture‡   180

Free Response‡ ☐ 18

    *Respondents could check any or all of these favorable reasons
for joining union:
1. Because I believe in unions.
2. Because the union provides job security through seniority
provisions.
3. To get better wages, vacations, paid holidays, etc.
4. Because workers as individuals have no bargaining power.
    †Respondents could check any or both of these unfavorable
reasons for joining union:
1. Because I had to join to hold my job.
2. Because union members made it unpleasant for those who did not
belong.
    ‡Mixture of the above.

*Figure 9.7: Comparison of Amount of Favorable and Un-
favorable Reasons Given for Joining Union. (After Uphoff &
Dunnette, 1956, p. 12)*

TABLE 9.1   UNION MEMBER OPINIONS OF SELECTED UNION
ADMINISTRATIVE PRACTICES AND PROBLEMS, ARRANGED IN
DESCENDING ORDER OF FAVORABLE RESPONSES BASED
ON 140 REPLIES*

Subject of Opinion	Total Favorable Responses	Total Unfavorable Responses
Worthwhileness of union meetings	90	9
Likelihood that present contract will be renewed without major changes	86	13
Administration of grievances	84	11
Desire to attend union meetings	83	16
Probability that members of the local personally support same political candidate	80	17
Local's comparative strength in bargaining	77	22
How well respondent personally understands labor contract	77	23
Extent to whoch local keeps its members informed on union matters	76	21
Extent to which union members in general are in the "right" when they call a strike	76	22
Opinion of present labor contract	73	27
Local's fairness in assigning jobs	70	26

*Adapted from Davis & St. Germain, 1952, Table 1, p. 287

unions of District 9 of the International Association of Machinists found
55 to 60 percent satisfied with what the union was doing in collective
bargaining, grievance handling, and political activity, while 67 percent
of the members were satisfied with the overall job the union was doing.
(Yet, in contrast, 85 percent of these same respondent were satisfied
with their company as a place to work.[569])

Political Reasons.   In comparison to European unions, which are often
primarily political action groups, American employes generally oppose
voluntary political contributions or much involvement in politics by the
union leadership.[567]

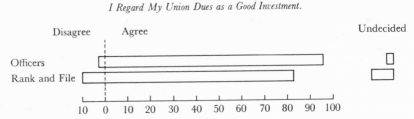

Figure 9.8: Extent Union Officers and Rank and File Regard Union Dues as a Good Investment. (After Uphoff & Dunnette, 1956, p. 32)

Attitudes of Leaders. As might be expected, active members and union leaders are more fully committed to the union movement and generally more favorable about their unions than inactive members.[594] Figure 9.8 illustrates the general tendency of union officers to be more favorable than the rank and file in attitudes towards the union. For example, of this sample of 1,251 members, 82 percent of the rank and file and 95 percent of the officers agreed that union dues were a good investment.[695]

Cultural Factors. More subtle, personal and cultural, factors may be involved. Thus it is more difficult to organize a union in a rural southern area without much previous history of unionism than to organize a new union in a large metropolitan center where most workers are unionized already.[29] In the same way white-collar workers regarding themselves as members of the middle class rather than the working class are more difficult to organize into unions.[373] Although one might expect individual differences to play an important role, relatively little has been found to discriminate the active unionist from the average workingman. While in the earlier years of the union movement the leadership had more of a middle-class origin, by 1945 a survey showed that approximately 60 percent were drawn from laboring families. Union leaders were more highly educated than typical of the general working population but were about the same in religion and political affiliation. The majority of these union leaders had worked as laborers in their industries, although by 1945 there was a trend towards career unionism in which the developing leader worked primarily as a professional white-collar worker for the union itself with only a short stint as a company employe active in the union movement.[485]

Rational-Economic Sources of Conflict

It is well documented that "bread-and-butter" issues dominate the open conflict in the U.S. between union and management. Thus

30 percent of all grievances at one large midwestern plant concerned wages; 28 percent, working conditions; and 10 percent, questions about seniority.[187] A factor analysis of 120 arbitration cases from 450 recent industrial disputes revealed five basic clusters of grievances. The central issues dealt with economic security, grievances about wages, hours, vacations, and insurance benefits. Next came questions of job assignment: promotion, seniority, layoff, and transfer. Union rights, activities, contracts, and security were another cluster, while supervision and working conditions were still another. Finally, different uses of coercion clustered together so that if a case involved disciplinary action, it might also invoke discharge, strikes, or lockouts.[173]

The material conflicts depend on the industry, its age, the current economic scene, and its past history of negotiations. Currently we are likely to see in service industries, at one extreme, disputes about recognition of the union as the bargaining agent. At the other extreme in rapidly automating manufacturing plants, where a generation of unionism has elapsed, we are likely to see primarily disputes about work and seniority rules, During the early 1960's pressures for wage increases lessened as the cost of living stabilized.

Psychological Sources of Conflict

As mentioned in Chapter 1, material conflicts are often the superficial dispute between union and management. The disgruntled worker will grieve about wages, or the union will organize a mass demand for a reduction in hours when the real issues are psychological, such as inconsiderate management, assembly line boredom, or worker hostility due to lack of job status. Wages are an objective issue, quantifiable and easy to discuss and dispute; feelings of frustration are not. Workers may vote to strike out of frustration with supervision, then justify the strike in the form of wage demands. And settling a wage dispute in favor of labor possibly may increase satisfaction with other less tangible, quantifiable, or easily seen aspects of the job, like job challenge or self-control over conditions. For experiments (as well as fraternity hazing) seem to indicate that we tend to reduce the dissonance in our perception of the value of our work and the value of how much we are rewarded for it.[204] It may be that given enough pay, we rationalize away the psychological displeasures of a job.

Perceptual and Cognitive Differences. The unrealistic differences in evaluation seen in the experiments with intergroup conflict are enlarged when union and company conflict. Real differences in interest produce unrealistic differences in what each side regards as important in the conflict, what are its chief causes, and in what ways the conflict should be resolved. Thus when 33 pairs of graduate students simulated union-management negotiations, although all were given the same background information, those serving as union representatives correlated only moderately (.61) with those serving as company men in ranking the importance of the nine issues about which they were instructed to bargain. They significantly disagreed on the relative importance of three of the nine issues. The company negotiators thought blocking the union's demand to have a representative on the Board of Directors was much more important than the union men considered it to be if they won the point. On the other hand, the union representatives attached more importance to their trying to win disputes about a checkoff system and a night shift differential in pay.[43]

In actuality, union and management enter conflicts with different information, so that some of their differences in evaluation of the situation are due to real differences in information. But much of the difference in how they analyze the causes and resolutions of disputes lies in their opposing commitments, identifications, past history, and motives. Consider how union and management in "Illini City" differed in reactions to the items shown in Table 9.2 dealing with the causes of labor disputes, methods of settling them, and whether open conflict is necessary and desirable.

As can be seen in Table 9.2, while the union member was more likely to regard a strike as due to unfair behavior by management, half of the executives blamed strikes on outside agitators. While one-fourth of management would outlaw all strikes, three-fourths of labor felt the strike was a basic right. More than half of the management sample felt unions interfered with the company's right to manage, while more than half of labor felt that they had to wring concessions from management by force.[326]

More specific differences about handling grievances were noted in comparing 396 management-oriented and labor-oriented officials drawn from labor, management, and government members of the Industrial Relations Research Association. Management men were significantly more opposed to outsiders entering negotiations and were more inclined to feel that success in negotiating depended on personality. They were more likely than labor-oriented officials to feel that "levels should be set beyond which some grievances cannot be taken." They also agreed more strongly that contracts should define the kinds of grievances that can be filed. On the other hand, labor-oriented respondents felt arbitration should be a binding last step in the procedure

TABLE 9.2   HOW UNION MEMBERS AND MANAGEMENT EXECUTIVES
IN "ILLINI CITY" DIFFER IN OPINIONS ABOUT
SELECTED UNION-MANAGEMENT ISSUES*

	Union Members	Management Executives
On Causes:		
Most strikes are caused by unfair tactics of employers	29%	7%
Most labor trouble is caused by outside union organizers rather than by discontent of workers with their wages and working conditions	14	54
On Methods of Settlement:		
All strikes should be outlawed	9	24
The right to strike is as justified as the right to own property	74	46
On Needs for Conflict:		
Most unions interfere with an employer's right to run his business as he pleases	21	59
Management usually has to be forced by unions to raise wages or to improve working conditions	58	34

*Adapted from Institute of Labor and Industrial Relations, 1953

and that complaints should not be considered grievances until formally filed by the union.

The management- and labor-oriented officials also disagreed about the purposes and values of various aspects of grievances. For example, compared to labor, more management men felt that the details of a grievance were relatively unimportant.

At the same time there were many areas of agreement. For example, both groups recognized the possible constructive elements in grievances, the need to make it possible for foremen to settle as many as possible, and the need for keeping a file of settlements.[388]

Perceptual Bias.   But at a deeper level, both sides are caught up in life-long perceptual distortions of each other. Seventy-six members of a

Central Labor Council and 108 executives, mainly in personnel and industrial relations, were shown photographs of two typical middle-aged men. One of the photos was shown to half the labor officials and half the executives with the man in the photo identified as the secretary-treasurer of his union. The man in the other photo was identified as the local manager of a small plant. The other half of the union and management personnel were shown the same photos but with the descriptions reversed so that the only differences in how the respondents as a whole described the personalities of the men they saw on an adjective checklist must have been due to the fictitious identifications of the two photos and the respondents' own perceptual biases. And differences they did see! The company executives checked whichever photo was said to be that of the manager as portraying a man who was conscientious, honest, trustworthy, and responsible as well as considerate, cooperative, fair, and impartial. The union officials did the same for whichever photo was identified as the secretary-treasurer of the union, although they were inclined to be a little less extreme in extolling the virtues of the secretary-treasurer.[274]

These union-management perceptual differences appear in childhood, depending on socioeconomic standing in the community, and are maintained into adulthood. Young children (age 12) express the union-management split in terms of personal characteristics of the antogonists; older ones (age 16) start thinking more about issues and their own allegiances. Those of lower socioeconomic background see the union as as economic force; those in higher brackets see it as a collection of people. While "lowers" see the boss as the man who tells people what to do, "uppers" see him in terms of power, money, and intelligence.[281]

Further Errors in Appraisal.   Conflict may arise out of the tendency of industrial managers to believe that labor leaders have more understanding and acceptance of good supervisory practices than they actually do, as revealed by tests of supervisory principles. Conversely, labor leaders underestimate management's tendency to understand and at least verbally accept the human relations approach to good supervision.[480]

Differences in Self-Appraisal.   As first noted in Chapter 5, Table 5.3, management and labor see themselves differently also. Table 9.3 shows the significantly different adjectives 463 management compared to 320 line workers checked in describing themselves. Management as a whole tends to emphasize its objectivity and intelligence; labor, its reliability and cooperativeness.[529]

TABLE 9.3 ITEMS DIFFERENTIATING MANAGEMENT
PERSONNEL AND LINE WORKERS*

Management Personnel	Line Workers
See themselves as:	See themselves as:
inventive	cooperative
loyal	dependable
resourceful	planful
clear-thinking	efficient
sincere	calm
fair-minded	thoughtful
responsible	reliable
dignified	civilized
imaginative	self-controlled
logical	adaptable
Do not see themselves as:	Do not see themselves as:
immature	quarrelsome
affected	moody
cold	stubborn
infantile	conceited
intolerant	nervous
foolish	careless
weak	selfish
rude	self-centered
rattle-brained	disorderly
submissive	fussy
self-pitying	hard-hearted
cynical	aggressive
dissatisfied	outspoken
sly	excitable
irresponsible	impatient

*From Porter, 1958, p. 106

Differences in Ideology. Management and labor are divided in opinion over many fundamental economic and social questions, such as corporate property rights or the contributions of unionism to the standard of living, which in turn may affect local disputes over concrete matters. Other idealistic and nonimmediate or even relative issues divide management and labor. Management continues to fret about its lost prerogatives; labor, about past injustices. Management puts lawyers in charge of its negotiations; unions use politicians.

Organizational Sources of Conflict

The union and the company are different forms of organization, and conflicts arise because of their differences. The authoritative appointed company executive expects the elected union official to have the same degree of control over responsibilities when in fact the union official is often in a relatively less reliable position. The union official is likely to have to consider internal organizational politics more than the appointed company executive. The humorous demagoguery of the cartoon in Figure 9.9 illustrates the point. Labor is likely to assume more extreme positions than management, often to dramatize an appeal to their own membership as well as to put management on the defensive.[717] The downward flow of communications in the union is more difficult, for union officials cannot as readily maintain contact with employes as can management. And the horizontal transfer of information across organizational boundaries has also been found to favor the company. Union stewards seem more willing to share information with their foremen counterparts than vice versa. In one plant of 3,400 men, for example, although top union and management officials espoused cooperation and mutual confidence, one-fourth of the union stewards did not share information with their respective foremen, while one-half of the foremen blocked the flow of information to their shop steward.[362]

One-Sided Approaches to Resolving
Union-Management Conflict

Both union and management often attempt to settle disputes by power plays, by marshalling strength and forcing their weakened opponent to acquiesce. Each side has its favored strategies which may work, provided the opposition is unable to being to bear equal counterforce, in which case a deadlock results. From then on there must be some compromising, some trading, some give-and-take for the stalemate to be broken.

Union Strategy. Collective rather than individual bargaining by employes adds obvious strength to their position in any economic test of strength with management. A management which must come to terms with its whole work force faces a potential work stoppage if negotiations fail. A management dealing with an individual employe bargaining for

GRIN 'N BEAR IT

**"I think we got management on the defensive, men!...
They're trying to counter our outrageous demands
by making ridiculous offers!"**

Figure 9.9: Union and Management Strategies in Bargaining.
(Pittsburgh Post-Gazette, May 31, 1963, p.2)

himself only has to consider the difficulty of replacing a single dissatisfied worker.

Seniority clauses in contracts give unionized employes special
protection against punitive action by management and at the same time
restrict management freedom. But abuses can result—such as feather-
bedding, in which companies must maintain employes on certain jobs
although no work by them is required.

Management's control and power to coerce employes arbitrarily
can be seriously weakened by union protective measures. For example,
in 170 cases in a variety of production and service industries where

management felt so strongly about a worker's incompetence, violation of shop rules, or alleged insubordination, that it discharged the employe, the subsequent conflict with the union led to arbitration which sustained management's right to fire only 58 of the workers.[528] However, it is not known what such a worker's future in the company is like after reinstatement. Is he shunted into less desirable jobs, harassed, or treated like any other employe? One wonders what the subsequent relations are between a reinstated worker and a foreman who brought about his attempted dismissal for insubordination, for example.

Formal grievance machinery makes it possible for workers to bypass their supervision with complaints. The grievances can become harassing weapons to test management's strength for forthcoming contract negotiations, to pressure specific supervisors and so on.

Finally there are economic pressures. Workers can slow down on the job or strike. Picketing may be tried to prevent company operations from continuing without the union men on strike. Further economic sanctions can be brought to bear against employers by boycott campaigns, sympathy strikes, mass demonstrations, and political action, although the latter is usually not popular with the rank-and-file.[632]

Management Strategy. Automation is the ultimate management refuge. Machines do not talk back or bargain collectively for higher wages. Another power play is to move the plant to a nonunion locale. But aside from the investment costs of moving or installing labor-saving equipment, seniority provisions sometimes make it difficult to do either without maintaining job protection for at least some of the employes who would have been displaced.

Management can also reduce potential union conflict by developing programs to maintain and increase employe satisfaction described in the preceding chapters, through better plans for rewarding employes and meeting their expectations, through better supervision, attention to group effort, communications, and organization.

If the firm can maintain a company union unallied with any national union movement, it usually can maintain much more control over its affairs. The company union has a small treasury and no outside advisors, and its union leadership is often more sympathetic to management.[632] However, a shrewd company union leader can use as an important weapon to win his demands the threat that his constituents will vote in the AFL-CIO, the Teamsters, or the United Mine Workers and will then be much more difficult to deal with.

A more subtle technique is to promote into management the more effective union leaders. Many foremen have moved into their positions as a consequence of their success as union leaders.

Although violence by either side has become less common in the past 25 years, there still remain militant managements who can engage in unfair, even extralegal, labor practices tantamount to breaking the unions without fear of legal sanctions because of the slowness of legal redress. Without a strong union treasury behind them, employes cannot wait years to settle a case in court about a job-security contract clause which they are likely to win because the employer was violating an agreement.

It has been suggested that the main reason for the success of the Wagner Labor Act of 1938 in promoting union recognition lay not so much in the legal penalties likely to be imposed on companies which failed to obey the law, but rather in the fact that managers who accepted unions were law-abiding. Although many could have blocked unionization (as some did and still do) extralegally, most did not use many of their most powerful weapons once they were declared illegal.

In the U.S., whether or not management had a more powerful strategy, depended much on political action as well as economic and social. Unions shifted from the weaker to the stronger positions in 1938 with the passage of the Wagner Labor Relations Act, setting up legal machinery that facilitated the right of workers to organize to bargain collectively. The Taft–Hartley Act following World War II probably balanced matters the other way again (although not to the extent to which government had supported the employer prior to 1938) by outlawing the closed shop (in which only union members can be hired), allowing employers to address employes on union-management matters, and providing against a quick strike by making a 80-day cooling-off period mandatory after employes had voted to strike.

Union-Management Resolution Through Collaboration

Resolution of conflict appears most difficult when labor and management are equally matched in a zero-sum, win-lose struggle. If unequal in power, one side can resolve the issue to its own satisfaction through its greater power. Ideally when the contest can be made into a nonzero-sum cooperative game, a resolution satisfactory to both sides can be achieved — sometimes at the expense of the public in the form of higher wages and prices. Even where one side is temporarily stronger, it may be to its own long-term advantage to cooperate rather than compete, to develop a history so that at a time of subsequent weakness, the other side will agree to cooperate although it in turn might gain a temporary advantage.[605]

Lockouts and hiring scabs by employers, and strikes, slowdowns, and sabotage by employes can force the basis for decision, although both sides may suffer in such a showdown. One-sided recourse to force and violence does still occur but is much less common than a generation ago.

In the U.S. as well as the rest of industrialized society in the Western world, the union movement is now in a "quiescent" state,[29] but management has also become less militant, resulting in a softening of the conflict. Negotiation of conflict is the rule now; resolution by force, the exception. "The battles [are] in the corridors instead of the streets, and memos . . . flow instead of blood".[367] Emotional, aggressive union leadership, which won the right to organize and bargain collectively, is replaced by those who can maintain the establishment cooperative, reasonable, and stable.[595] At the same time management has to live with the union and operate successfully with the established union as part of its environment. Hostility by management at this point would be self-defeating, increasing rather than reducing conflict without purpose.

The evidence is clear that the strike has been declining in frequency and duration throughout the industrialized Western world in the past 50 years, according to a statistical summary of days lost and numbers involved in strikes in 15 countries during this period.[572] Thus in recent years in Great Britain only 2 percent of total lost working time has been due to strikes, while 98 percent was due to absenteeism, illness, and layoffs.[37]

We have also moved from conflict resolution, which was only an armed truce, to truly collaborative solutions, from position X shown below to position Z, at least in many enterprises in the U.S. and even more so in other industrialized countries.[287, 632]

There are many reasons for the shift from militancy to industrial peace.

Dual Allegiance. An important reason for the shift from an armed truce toward collaborative conflict resolution is the tendency for workers to remain loyal to both company and union. Although management and union may see themselves in competition for the employe's loyalty, there is considerable evidence that most workers feel loyal to both. In a unionized plant with a long history of good labor relations, most workers were found to identify with both union and company, although those extremely management-oriented were likely to be hostile to the union. The employes as a whole minimized the perception of conflict between union and management and saw them both as pursuing the same objectives.[747] Dual loyalty was also found the rule among 800 meat packers and in Japanese steel mills and coal mines[542] as well as in other American firms.[156]

(X) *	(Y)	(Z)
Armed Truce	Working Harmony	Collaborative Effort
−	−	−
Competition for Worker Loyalty	Acceptance of Bargaining as Basis for Resolution	Joint Efforts Toward Mutually Rewarding Goals
−	−	−
Conflict over Scope of Bargaining Management Rights	Willingness to Compromise	Joint Problem-Solving
−	−	−
Relative Power of Disputants Decides Questions		Mutual Trust and Confidence

*Adapted from Stagner, 1956

In an interview study, dual allegiance was found in 73 percent of 385 packing house employes, 88 percent of the union stewards, and 57 percent of the foremen. As one interviewee put it, "The union don't hurt the company. The union protects the workers, that's all."[540,p.95]

In the same way those 202 employes in garment work, construction, trucking, grain processing, or metal products in "Illini City" who were favorable toward their company were also likely to have favorable attitudes about their union.[631]

Personality and response bias, as discussed in Chapter 4, may also play a part. Some employes are generally satisfied with anything and everything, while others are chronic gripers, so that finding that some men are favorable to both company and union may not indicate real dual loyalty as much as a generalized response to acquiesce.

Dual loyalty may be due to historical as well as psychological factors to some degree. The union battles the company to gain security rights for employes. Twenty years later the employes are favorable about the company because of the security of job tenure it offers.[540]

But whatever the reasons for dual allegiance, such shared favorableness towards both company and union must serve to mitigate the amount and degree of union-management conflict and to soften the ways it is resolved.

Mutual Tolerance and Sophistication.   Another contribution to the shift from militancy to peace is the increased sophistication of the disputants and their acceptance of each other.

Acceptance of collective bargaining by management and the decline of the strike and labor militancy have been paralleled by increasing acceptance of each other by the disputants and the substitution of negotiation for force. And understanding is replacing force as the basis of conflict resolution.

Interviews with 21 business agents representing a union of 40,000 members concluded that the agent sees contract negotiations as his main job, for which he needs skill in interpersonal relations, needs to match wits with management, and needs to remain valued by employes. Persistence, knowledge, experience, competency in problem-solving and communication skills are seen as paramount for success by these modern-day union leaders.[570]

Unions have followed management leads in making use of psychology in training and practice. "Not many years ago, labor intellectuals. . . were ambivalently worrying and sneering at management's use of group dynamics, role-playing, sensitivity training, leadership development. . . . Today, they have taken over the same techniques to resolve the problems of apathy, hostility, incompetence, and leadership succession that affect their own ranks."[403, p.257]

Support for labor-management collaborative effort is high among top and middle managers. Thus 81 percent of top and 71 percent of middle management in a large-scale survey of British industry supported the idea. Lower echelons of management do not appear so enthusiastic.[496] However, in the U.S., in contrast to other advanced industrial countries, a relatively large segment of employers, particularly those in small and medium-sized companies, have yet to accept the legitimacy of collective bargaining, preferring long court fights, state right-to-work laws forbidding union shops, and engagement in heavy anti-union propaganda about threats to move plants, shutdown, and the cost and corruption in unionism.[29]

Ritualization of Negotiations.   Another source of mellowing is to be found in the way union and management often carry on negotiations now. Continued experience with professional negotiators has resulted in the institutionalization and legalization of negotiation practices. To a considerable degree, negotiations have become ritualized.

"A large share of collective bargaining is not conflict but a process by which the main terms of the agreement, already understood by the negotiators, are made acceptable not to those in charge of the bargaining but to those who will have to live with its results!"[75, pp.64–65]

For example, union agents are aware that they can obtain only an 8-cent increase in hourly wages, but the union membership wants 20 cents. They fight hard with management for the 20 cents, while company representatives attack the 8-cent figure but grudgingly give in. Indeed, negotiators have been found quite accurate in forecasting what they will receive or have to give; and although they may be far apart publicly before negotiations begin, they usually are privately close to agreement but will engage in ritualistic debate whose final outcome both sides are fairly confident they already know.

Even seemingly overt conflict has become ritualized. Strikes are called for weekends or when inventories are high; management serves coffee to pickets. Plants are kept in working condition despite walkouts.

Real conflict, then, occurs only if mistakes happen or when one side fails to react when the other is ready to compromise. Real conflict is more likely to remain in truly democratic unions when workers can reject solutions achieved by their representatives. Industrial war may break out also if either side takes a strong, idealistic position and resolution is required over emotional issues.[75]

Informal Resolution. Mollification of the potential conflict also results from the tendency to abandon at lower levels the formal rules stipulated in the union-company contract for informal agreements in order to maintain effective operations. Indeed, the rank-and-file employe is likely to dislike a steward who is belligerent and does not compromise with management so concessions can be earned. They favor one who can settle grievances informally.[146] No doubt this informal tendency depends upon dual allegiance of employes and their own lack of strong union bias.

Social Change. Many of the social forces which terminated the growth of American unions in the 1950's also contributed to the shift from militancy to peaceful labor relations. Sweatshops had been legislated out of existence; work was made more pleasant; the worst jobs had been automated. The unions no longer needed to push for improved working conditions and benefits. Fringe benefits had become standard in company compensation programs. The very success of unions in achieving many of these improvements subsequently weakened their purpose for existing.

The decline in union militancy, membership, influence, prestige, and interest also can be traced in the post-World War II shift in the characteristics of the labor force. Employment in unionized areas such as mining, railroads, and textiles declined as much as 60 percent from 1940 to 1960. At the same time the numbers of white-collar, professional, and technical employes, traditionally less interested in collective action, increased greatly, as did the proportion in the work force of many other groups traditionally less interested in unionization: rural Southerners, Negroes, Mexicans, Puerto Ricans, and women workers.[29]

During these years, middle-class status striving may also have served to make employes less anti-management and less pro-union. Installment buying following World War II and the heavy indebtedness of the new work force made strikes of any duration harder to take.

Still another factor was the decentralization of large business, which made it more expensive to unionize multiplant operations.[87]

Although hindered in further development in states which passed right-to-work laws outlawing union shops, despite the overwhelming support of union shops by almost all of eligible employees in NLRB elections (1947–1951), unionism still thrives in unions strongly established by 1946 and in growing areas such as Los Angeles or Minneapolis where the industrial climate was already pro-union before the growth.[29]

Towards Constructive Labor Conflict Resolution

But the relaxation of union-management conflict may not be as important as moving it into constructive and peaceful channels. That is, peace enforced by the power of one side or the other may mean callous exploitation of labor at subsistence wages by an all-powerful management or an economy where an all-powerful labor limits enterprise to a point of stagnation.

Not all forms of conflict in industry can or should be eliminated. Conflict is an inevitable consequence of social change and to attempt to eliminate it in all circumstances for the sake of social harmony and integration can only have an inhibiting effect upon the introduction of new methods and procedures themselves designed to produce greater productive efficiency. There are, however, certain types of disintegrating conflict, especially those emanating from dominative authority, which can be avoided.[556, p.32]

When power is balanced, constructive negotiation is sought, in which each side is willing to settle for less than complete victory. A summary of National Planning Association Studies on the sources of industrial peace suggests that constructive negotiation between union and management is more likely when they accept each other's norms or standards of behavior. Management must accept the legitimacy of collective bargaining, avoid seeking to alienate workers from their union, and stay out of the union's internal affairs. At the same time the union must recognize that its welfare depends on private enterprise and the company's success.

Accord in bargaining will be reached where employe wage norms do not rise above those of the employer. (This congruence is maintained, for example, if the industry and firm are high-paying, but the plant is in a low-wage area.) Again, harmony is likely when there is mutual trust and negotiations are problem-centered rather than abstract or legalistic, and when there is joint consultation and wide sharing of information.

As mentioned before in discussing ritualization of negotiation, peace is more likely if each side can predict what the other will do and knows what to expect. Strikes occur when expectations are violated or are unrealistic.[632]

Mediation. In 1913 the U.S. Department of Labor began offering conciliation service to industrial disputants. Mediators were made available who had no power to force disputants to agree but who could persuade, convince, cajole, or sometimes force disputants to talk to each other constructively or otherwise. By 1952 about 75 percent of the states had mediation services, some requiring mediation if a strike or lockout impends.[566] Unfortunately, relatively little is known about the effectiveness of such neutral parties in trying to conciliate two disputants, nor how to increase the effectiveness in promoting resolution between the conflicting negotiators.

Some mediators have better reputations for success than others. Of 146 rated good, fair, or poor by their colleagues, those of middle age (40–54) were likely to be rated higher than younger or older mediators. Democrats were rated more favorably than Republicans or Independents, as were Protestants compared to Roman Catholics and Jews. Higher rated mediators earned high scores on the Wonderlic intelligence test and were more neutral in labor-management attitudes on a disguised attitude assessment.[734]

Interaction process analysis of the mediation of 12 disputes found that the success of negotiations was greater if negotiations were so directed that orienting responses decreased while suggestions and socioemotional reactions increased as negotiations continued. On the other hand, many hostile expressions early reduced the likelihood of a successful outcome.[380]

Some untested suggestions on how to play an effective role as mediator are:

1. The mediator must maintain his reputation for truthfulness, impartiality, and objectivity when speaking with one of the disputing parties alone about the other.

2. The mediator should try to direct disputants away from seeking to exploit some advantages due to problems which are inside the structure of the other organization.

3. The mediator can try to shift the blame for conflict on third parties outside the control of the disputants, such as business competitors.

4. The mediator can weaken the position of a disputant if he can get the latter to deviate hypothetically "just for the sake of discussion."

5. The mediator may help negotiations by reducing tensions when attacks become personal.

6. Each side should be encouraged to bare all its troubles. The ventilation may help feelings, direct frustration to outside factors, and possibly promote understanding.

7. The mediator may propose "hypothetical" packages of agreements with one side alone or with the other.[566]

Arbitration.   When disputants cannot reach agreement, one step short of force is arbitration — giving the power to a neutral umpire to decide the issue. We have already noted that a judge whose decision is unfavorable to a party is devaluated by the losing party. A continued experience of such unfavorable verdicts is likely to lead to a rejection of the arbitrating process and the resort to force. Another weakness of arbitration when it is compulsory is that disputes which would ordinarily be settled by negotiation are unresolved because the party with the somewhat weaker position feels he has little to lose and much to gain if for one reason or another the arbitrator should side with his less adequate point of view. Thus sometimes even minor cases cannot be settled without going to arbitration, if both parties previously have agreed to take unresolved disputes to arbitration.

An analysis of 197 arbitrated disciplinary cases found the arbitrator supporting management in only 38 percent. Arbitrators completely revoked management action in 31 percent or modified it. Arbitrators supported management's disciplinary action more often if the case involved a violation of shop rules or insubordination and less often if it concerned alleged incompetence or violation of the contract. Further analyses suggested that arbitrators often went beyond their authority to decide whether unfair discrimination was involved in case and modified the severity of management discipline, interpreting the severity as due to secondary motives such as the need for management to vindicate its status or demonstrate its power.[528]

Collaboration Between Union and Management

Collaboration, working toward common goals where each side supports the other, takes two forms: sharing information and consulting, and creating a common fate by sharing profits or costs.

Information Exchange. By 1949, 87 percent of 263 American firms, according to an American Management Association survey, had some form of formal cooperation with their union. Most commonly, the firms reported such formal cooperation in the areas of safety, waste elimination, the promotion of understanding of labor policies, attendance, insurance, quality control, job evaluation, and working conditions. Most frequent was information exchange. To a lesser extent, advice was exchanged. Still rare, however, was joint determination. In Great Britain a survey of 1,000 manufacturing plants found information exchange in 98 percent, mainly about hours, rests, and shifts. Half had joint consultation or exchange of advice which was judged particularly effective in matters of holidays, layoffs, dismissals, safety, and working conditions and least effective when about training, promotion, or turnover. [496]

However, the occurrence of joint consultation may be symptomatic of good union-management relations, rather than a contributor to it. In fact, it is argued that it may intensify conflict if no common basis of understanding exists before it.

But the mere introduction of democratic forms of consultative procedure will not be sufficient to eliminate conflict . . . unless attitudes and values are also changed. Research on joint consultation seems to suggest that where a sense of common purpose is felt, formal consultative procedures are largely unnecessary because informal consultation at all levels will be taking place in any case. Similarly, the introduction of formal procedures where there is no common value system will probably intensify conflicts between private goals and between the goals pursued by other groups and associations within the firm.[556, p.32]

Yet if the Human Relations Committee of the United Steel Workers and 11 major steel producers or comparable committees in longshoring and meatpacking are examples, there seems much promise in the continuing joint study of potentially conflicting issues long before formal negotiations about them must begin. In 1963 the Committee spent considerable time in formal joint study and discussion, after which contract negotiations were able to proceed smoothly and easily.

Sharing Profits or Cost Reduction. As mentioned in Chapter 3, the plan developed by Joseph Scanlon, a union official, is the prototype of plans in which the contract requires the union to cooperate fully in reducing waste and increasing productivity. All employes are required to join the union—a union shop is accepted. The savings in labor costs per unit as productivity increases are returned to the employes.[401] Management gains in more efficient use of investments, more production with the same overhead, and better quality of output as well as increased labor peace, job security, stability of profits, participation by employes in suggested improvements in operations and in training of each other.[632] A recent variant of the plan at Kaiser Steel provides for a sharing by management and workers in all cost reduction. In contrast to profit-sharing arrangements, labor participates in cost production and pro-ductive economies — matters over which it has much control. In profit sharing, despite labor's efforts, profits may not appear because of market conditions, investment problems, and so on.

The Future of Industrial Relations

Current trends in both unionism and in industrial technology sug-gest that substantial changes are likely in industrial relations during the coming generation. Fewer and more highly centralized union organ-izations will develop, as has occurred already in the Teamsters and Autoworkers unions. Planning and negotiating at national levels will be done with the aid of highly professional staffs. Local unions will be concerned with social and educational rather than economic activities. Local leaders primarily will be information transmitters.

Unions will be broadly based over a number of industries and oc-cupational groups. The typical multi-industrial union will cover clerical, professional, and technical employes as well as those in production. To cope with managerial programming of a flexible work flow utilizing different work groups, subcontractors, and a variety of material re-sources to optimize arrangements to reflect the current state of market, material costs, and so on, unions will attempt to cover the entire process with one integrated organization. This need to follow industrial process change will require highly specialized and centralized union staffs to coordinate union activities.

The prime purpose of bargaining will be the evaluation of management planning processes. Unions are certain to insist upon reviewing plans and pro-grams and upon the right to negotiate their revision in advance of being put into operation. Decisions on wages, work schedules, fringe benefits, and so forth will follow upon basic agreements on matters such as the nature and evaluation of jobs, installation of technological changes, procedures for hiring, layoff, transfer, and reassignment and the like, for a large portion of the worker's income over a considerable part of his future working career will be at stake. This kind of "job service" will become a major function of the union in replacing shop-level decision-making . . . unions will demand clarification of the criteria utilized in management's choice of possible programs and plans. . . . Almost every management policy will be subject to question, ranging from proposed capital investments to donations to charity or education. How these plans fit together with programs in the public sector will receive special attention. In sum, collective bargaining will no longer be the union's attempt to seek the Gompersian "more and more" but a vital balance wheel for settling major decisions about resource allocation and economic development for the whole society.[353, p.26]

One final trend likely in the coming years because of industry-wide and multiple bargaining demanded of management will be increased use of professional agents who are likely to identify more closely with their professional counterparts representing the unions, like career diplomats from different countries do.[353]

*   *   *   *   *

Traditionally the study of conflict in industry was regarded as almost synonymous with the study of labor-management relations. Yet we have seen that many of the intergroup phenomena characterizing labor management conflict also appear among people who officially are supposed to be striving for the same organizational goals. The production manager seems about as ready to compete with the head of sales for budget increases as he is ready to conflict with union bargainers. There may be differences in the intensity of feelings, but it is probable that as much heat will be aroused in sales and production managers as in union negotiators if a situation arises in which all the budget increase will go for advertising *or* all will go for new equipment, a zero-sum gaming situation. The particular kinds of groups the competitors come from may be less significant to understanding conflicts between them than the past history of the groups and whether compromise is possible.

As before, rational and nonrational elements are involved. And now we shall see that even where the executive would be completely objective and completely rational in his decisions, he is limited, often severely, in the extent to which he can be. His problem often becomes one of trying to make decisions with as complete objectivity as the uncertain and risky circumstances will allow. This involves developing understanding of the errors and distortions of his own perception and behavior when he faces ill-defined problems, ambiguous dilemmas, and vague guidelines so that he can correct for them as he makes his decisions.

In Brief

IN THIS CONCLUDING CHAPTER WE LOOK AT THE EFFORTS OF THE ORGANI-
zation members, particularly its executives, to reach decisions rationally
rather than on through the methods discussed in earlier chapters such
as bargaining, authority, persuasion, or group pressure. Sometimes
elegant mathematico-deductive procedures make possible optimum decisions. But usually complete rationality is impossible because the problems to be solved are too complex or ill-defined.

Problem-solving proceeds in three stages: perceiving the problem,
searching for or inventing solutions, and evaluating the solutions. Various characteristics of the problem and the problem-solver affect outcomes at each of the three stages. At each stage it is seen that despite
his intention to be rational, various attitudinal and motivational factors
limit the decision-maker, but much can be done at each stage to reduce
these restrictions on creativity, inventiveness, and accuracy of decision.

Chapter 10

PSYCHOLOGICAL ASPECTS OF

EXECUTIVE DECISION-MAKING

ACCORDING TO CLASSICAL PRINCIPLES OF ORGANIZATION, CONFLICT CAN be eliminated, or if it appears, can be resolved by programs of rules which can be applied to each problem as it arises to provide appropriate answers. Conflicts over returned goods can be resolved, for instance, if the firm has a routine, standard operating procedure for handling customer complaints. An applicable rule might be that refunds are automatic for all merchandise returned within a year costing less than $100. Other refunding is on a pro-rata basis reflecting cost and use. All problems about refunds can be categorized and decisions made according to rules for each category.

While such programming is possible, particularly for simpler problems, a variety of human judgments and discriminations are involved when the problem becomes more complex and is not subject to routine solution. For example, before appropriate rules can be applied to the problem of whether or not to discontinue a particular production process, it is necessary to classify the problem or to see if the problem can be classified according to acceptable categories for which rules are available. Even before this, someone may have to decide whether or not the firm has a problem—whether there is dissatisfaction with the current production procedure.

Nonrational Approaches to Making Unprogrammed Organizational Decisions

In Chapters 5 and 6 we discussed the ways that decisions are often due to socioemotional factors such as group pressure rather than any impelling rationale or logic. In Chapters 5, 6, and 8 we also looked at how discussion and persuasion may be the source of decisions. In Chapter 9 we examined the importance of negotiation and bargaining, even among executives supposedly working toward the same organizational objectives.

Decisions on how to handle problems may also be reached purely *accidentally*. Executives from two different divisions may happen to meet in a hallway and decide, as a consequence, on a subsequent production plan. If they had not been in the same hallway at the same time, they might never have decided on such a plan.

Decisions could be *random*. Management might be indifferent as to which of two departments will switch to a new plan first, so a coin might be tossed to decide the matter. Department *A* would start if the toss were a "heads"; *B* would start if the toss were a "tails." Sometimes random decisions are a rational or best possible solution to a problem. Suppose one wished to minimize the likelihood that a competitor could forecast in advance one's daily price change on a given day. A rational strategy would be to adjust prices daily on a random basis.

As mentioned earlier, power often decides matters. The most powerful person in the situation makes the decision regardless of the opinions and feelings of the less powerful. For instance, a vice-president for marketing strongly disagreed with the president of the firm about marketing strategy. He wanted to increase advertising expenditures. The president favored reducing the cost of advertising in order to offer the product at a lower price. Power settled the argument. Prices were cut, and the vice-president resigned.

But organizations are unlikely to survive if all their unprogrammed decisions are made accidentally, randomly, or as a consequence of power.

RATIONAL APPROACHES TO MAKING UNPROGRAMMED ORGANIZATIONAL DECISIONS

One rational approach would be to pursue a strategy of *minimax* loss in making decisions after we had calculated the anticipated gains and losses of the decisions. We will accept that decision which is likely to yield the least ill effect if the worst happens. For example, suppose we know (or think we know) what it would cost to locate stores in different sections of a city. We have estimates of the potential earnings of the stores at different locations. Determining what we hope to gain, we choose to locate the new store where we believe we will risk the least amount of loss for this given amount of gain.

We might pursue a strategy of *maximin* gain, working towards a minimum gain which is as large as possible. Thus we can fix the size of potential losses we are willing to accept. Then for this given loss level, we aim for the location where the greatest gains are possible. We might decide to build the store at a more competitive location, but where the traffic was heavier. We would risk facing more competition because of the greater potential gain from capturing our share of a larger market.

Finally, we might use a mixed strategy to avoid undue risk, yet achieve reasonable gains. We might, for instance, build two small stores where traffic and competition are light and one bigger store where both are heavier. Our choice of a rational approach, minimax, maximin, or mixed strategy, is not rational. The choice is a question of which aims we prefer, how much risk we can tolerate, and what we value most. (See Chapter 1.)

A variety of mathematical procedures makes it possible to order our estimates, calculate risks, and approach optimum decisions — saddle points — where gains are likely to be greatest or losses likely to be at a minimum assuming our estimates are accurate. *Operations research* is a discipline devoted to the determination of such optimums through the use of applied mathematics.

Operations research makes use of statistical decision theory, actuarial analyses, mathematical game theory, linear programming and other applied mathematico-deductive processes to derive optimum business decisions. Conclusions follow logically from assumptions and estimates. If the operating rules are correct and consistent and if our assumptions and estimates are correct, then the correct optimal solution will follow. Moreover, anyone familiar with the mathematics will reach the same exact solution if he starts with the same assumptions and estimates. Once these assumptions and estimates are given, the solution is determined.

Statistical Decision Theory.   Statistical decisions are the core of decisions about product quality and its control. By means of statistics, a manager can set up the risks of poor quality he is willing to tolerate; and with suitable sampling procedures, he can maintain the uniformity of his product within specified limits, knowing how often he may erroneously allow a defect to pass by. In continuous flow operations he can employ statistics to signal him when a correction is needed in the system. By relying on objective statistics, he can avoid overcorrecting the system every time a minor fluctuation occurs in it.

Statistical forecasting provides a completely rational procedure for an executive to reduce the riskiness of his decision in the face of an uncertain environment. With statistical analysis and an adequate sample of interviews, for example, he can obtain a better estimate of the probabilities that the public will prefer his DeLuxe to his Regular brand products than he might obtain from his own past experience or his intuition. But he still must decide whether he is going to follow the dictates of his statistical outcomes or his own hunches.

Actuarial and statistical analysis make it possible to formulate objective rules for decisions which minimize the possibilities of error and increase the likelihood that most of the information relevant to the decision will be considered. As an illustration of this, a credit house derived an objective scoring index for forecasting the likelihood of success or bankruptcy among several thousand small business firms. Success was found more likely among firms with over $10,000 capitalization, with more employes, if the owner was married and a young man rather than a woman or older man, and if no one in his family assisted him.[722] Observation of how oil and gas operators make drilling decisions by intuition, experience, and imagination suggested that much of the uncertainty in their decisions could be reduced by statistical decision theory. This would result in giving the operators greater freedom to consider the broader aspects of problems and the consequences of various decisions.[256]

Applying Game Theory. Sometimes the major elements in a business decision can be described and analyzed in a simple game matrix. Thus

. . . the Monsanto Chemical Company ran into a major problem regarding the timing of the release of its new product, the soil conditioner known as Krilium. . . . Monsanto worked for about ten years on a soil conditioner, the last two and a half of which consisted of field tests by independent technicians in various parts of the country. In 1951 the marketing problem came up. Monsanto feared leaks. For one thing, a number of technical papers by agronomists and other field workers had been completed and were being held up. A leak might mean that Monsanto would not get its trade name established first in the market. It decided to announce in December 1951 and did, with the desired effect. The product, Krilium, became famous overnight. The competition was taken by surprise. But there were difficulties. Monsanto had small production facilities and did not expect to get to market until 1953. It only wanted to say that the discovery was made and that its name would be Krilium, first in soil conditioners. Then the trouble began. Two other companies, American Cyanamid and American Polymer Corporation, looking at the chemical family to which Krilium belonged, were astonished and pleased to discover that they themselves were producing a product for oil-well drilling (a mud conditioner) which belonged to the same family. After a few field tests, this competition was soon on the market with an actual product. Monsanto managed to get to market in 1952, but after the others. . .[462, p2]

A matrix showing the estimated payoff of the choices confronting Monsanto about whether or not to announce the discovery regardless of whether or not Monsanto or its competitors were immediately prepared to market the soil conditioner might look as follows, assuming that getting the name before the public and getting to market first was equally useful to Monsanto and to its competitors:

Competitors
(Monsanto's Competitive Environment)

Monsanto is Unprepared to Market	Should Monsanto:	Prepared now to market	Unprepared now to market
	Announce now or	A +1	B +2
	Postpone announcement of new product	C 0	D +3

If Monsanto announced now (as it actually did) and its competitors were prepared to market (possibility *A*), this was seen as yielding a gain of +1 for Monsanto. Monsanto would have the lead in advertising, but the competition would begin profitable business as a consequence. If competitors were unprepared and Monsanto announced (possibility *B*), then Monsanto would have the advertising lead and would be ready about the same time or sooner to market products yielding a greater potential utility of, say, +2. On the other hand, if Monsanto withheld its discovery and its competitors were about ready to market the product (possibility *C*), Monsanto would fail to capitalize at all on its discovery while its competitors went ahead, yielding a payoff to Monsanto of 0. If Monsanto waited to announce until it was ready to market and caught its competitors unprepared (possibility *D*), it would stand to gain the most over its competition. Thus postponement was riskiest for Monsanto. It could gain the most (+3) or lose the most (+0). Making the announcement now would provide a gain to Monsanto of either +1 or +2. This was the alternative chosen, as it gave the greatest possible gain with the lowest possible loss.

Linear Programming. A typical problem which can be solved by linear programming is as follows:[120, pp.370-371]

A company has four plants *A, B, C,* and *D* with production capacities of 150, 150, 200, and 250 units per month respectively. It supplies three markets *X, Y* and *Z* having fixed requirements of 225, 200, and 175 units per month respectively. The company cannot fill any of market *Z*'s requirements from plant *C* because of a lack of transportation facilities from *C* to *Z*. Assuming that the objective is to minimize transportation costs, find the optimal transportation schedule. Unit transportation costs are as follows (dollars):

		Market	
Plant	X	Y	Z
A	5	2	8
B	4	3	5
C	2	4	—
D	6	3	4

That is, a linear function, in this case transportation cost, is minimized. Shipping totals are calculated from the four plants to the three markets so that shipping costs will be as small as possible, subject to various constraints such as the lack of transportation facilities between *C* and *Z*.

In the same way one could calculate the transportation program which would maximize profits, say, if profit depended on the time required for shipments to reach markets. Linear programming could also be applied to stochastic or randomly fluctuating processes. For example, it could find an optimal schedule if the three markets *X, Y,* and *Z* had mean requirements of 225, 200, and 175 units, each varying an average of 25 units from month to month.

Linear programming can aid in policy formulation and evaluation. Suppose a firm manufactures Regular and DeLuxe models. As a matter of policy it feels that at least 50 percent of its sales ought to be in DeLuxe models to maintain the company's image as a producer of high-quality items. Considering raw material costs, selling prices, and plant capacity, the firm can estimate its immediate profits producing 50 percent DeLuxe models. Then it can run another linear program maximizing its immediate profits. Comparing the two outcomes will indicate to the company the cost in immediate profits of its policy to maintain an image as a high-quality outfit. The results might produce a change in policy.

Linear programming can be applied to many types of organizational problems such as budgeting the firm's resources, reassigning manpower, or scheduling the flow of production. Linear programs covering a succession of time periods make it possible for management to predict and control required inventories, prices, labor forces, and so on. These dynamic programs help to dampen the oscillations in the system of the amount of supplies ordered, stocks in inventories, and finished goods assembled for inventory and for sale.

Complete Rationality Is Seldom Possible

Statistical analysis, linear programming, and other optimization procedures free the executive from depending on gross judgments about complex problems. Now for instance, all the executive must do is judge that his plants will produce as indicated and his markets will maintain demands as stipulated in the transportation problem. Even this risk can be reduced if markets are guaranteed by contracts which cannot be cancelled without penalty. Unfortunately, many if not most organizational problems cannot be defined so easily as the transportation problem. Many problems are so poorly defined that their ambiguity results in solutions depending considerably on the personality, aspirations, motivation, and past experience of the problem-solver.

Since this is a text in organizational psychology, we will concentrate here on the limitations to complete rationality, to completely rote mathematico-deductive approaches to decision-making such as linear programming, waiting-line theory, statistical decision theory, mathematical game theory, and other tools of operations research. Students of organization decision-making would be advised, however, to familiarize themselves with these elegant approaches whose applications to business and industry are rising rapidly.*

We will proceed in this chapter to look at the process of actual decision-making in organizations where rationality is intended, where considerable effort is made to cancel the effects of power, authority, and group pressure, yet where the decision is still of limited rationality

*A general theory of statistical decision functions is to be found in Wald.[709] Luce & Raiffa[422] cover and extend the original development of game theory by von Neumann and Morgenstern and provide the student with illustrative applications of game theory to business decisions. The classic text for introducing the operations research techniques of linear programming, waiting-line theory, and inventory replacement mathematics is that of Churchman, Ackoff, & Arnoff.[115] The less mathematically sophisticated student might wish to begin his studies in this general area with Clough.[120] A particularly lucid, non-mathematical examination of linear programming and its uses can be found in Bock.[78]

because the business executive is an imperfect sensing, learning, and calculating mechanism with built-in filtering and distortion components.

We will try to see how these imperfections systematically alter the way decisions are integrated. Understanding these systematic tendencies may help in suggesting means (distinct from mathematico-deductive approaches already mentioned) for improving the search and identification of better solutions to organizational problems where the decision appears to be aiming toward complete rationality.

Note that the usual decisions *in* an organization are not necessarily *about* organizational issues, as such. Thus we must deal with the general question of how one makes a decision when one intends to be rational but where one's own personal restrictions and the constraints imposed by the organization in which one works limits how rational the decision can be.

Organizational issues about which decisions must be made are like the following:

How should our capital expenditures be budgeted and allocated to the different units of the organization? How many echelons of supervision should we have? How can we remove the blocks to communications and coordination in the system? What should be the size of our various units? Should we diversify along product or functional lines? What transfer price should be set on a product made at one profit center in the firm and used by another? These kinds of problems have already been discussed in Chapters 6 through 9; now we are concerned with the general process by which one attacks and solves such problems, as well as the more common problems which face the executive or the administrator, such as how much service we can afford to supply with our new equipment, what type of compensation plan should be adopted, or whether we should use a fast or slow rate of depreciation in computing our taxes.

DECISIONS WITH
LIMITED RATIONALITY

When the problem deals with too many unknowns, too much complexity, or too many variables, quantification often becomes difficult or impossible eliminating the possibilities of applying mathematical analysis. Even the techniques of mathematical simulation fail when less predictable "people" variables become major causative factors in the system we are trying to simulate by means of a mathematical model. We can substitute probable errors for people in our equations, and the model may operate quite nicely. But although the model may work, it will still fail to match the processes of reality, our ultimate aim in constructing the model, if highly complex human behavior is involved in the real process. Transportation costs may be only one factor in our shipping decision discussed previously. In considering what to do we may need to judge the reliability of each transportation facility that will be used. We may need to be concerned with whether labor disputes may tie up shipments, with whether alternate facilities will be available, whether warehousing will be adequate and with some of the long-range implications of our schedule to plant development, maintenance, and depreciation. Here we may have to make shrewd guesses about future local and federal tax policies. Only limited rationality can be applied when the transportation problem is expanded.

Pure reason has its limits also, if we consider such diverse typical executive problems: Should the management committee be expanded? Should we accept the union proposal to form a joint-study group? How can we take more advantage of government and university research in improving our own products and processes?

Even trying to remain reasonable, as problems become more complex, ambiguous, or ill-defined, decision-makers are less able to remain completely rational in trying to solve the problems. Perceptual and cognitive distortions creep into their thinking as they attempt to discern the problem. Motives transform their understanding of the problem. Inadequate learning is applied in the search for solutions, and the range of search is usually highly restricted as a consequence of past learning. Expectations are unduly influenced by wishful thinking. A variety of judgmental errors are possible in testing the feasibility of alternative solutions to the problem. Even the post-mortem examination as to the wisdom of the choice may be swayed by the decision-maker's desire for wish-fulfillment.

Management may see a disorderliness in the storage of paper forms. They may quickly conclude that the filing system is inadequate—although it may be that they simply are generating too much useless information on paper. In selecting a new filing system they are likely to search their memories for a procedure that was used before. They are likely to adopt a customary method which has worked reasonably well in the past. Or they may look at what some other firms do and follow suit. These solutions have limited rationality in that they fail to take into account the special conditions of their firm, and they sacrifice the possibility of determining the best possible or *optimum* information collection and processing scheme yielding the most information with the least effort and expense. The filing plan based on limited rationality is satisfactory; it works fairly well, but it is not necessarily the best plan.

Psychology, Economics, and Limited Rationality

In its study of rational problem-solving, classical psychology dealt with the ability and motivation of the decision-maker. It was concerned with what in his experience resulted in modifying his discrimination of the problem facing him and what reinforced certain choices with consequential fixation on a particular alternative. The environment facing the decision-maker had some structure to it, which made it easier or more difficult for a decision to be reached and for learning to occur. It was a reasonable environment, which would react in consistent ways as controlled by the investigating psychologist. Where an alternative was no longer possible, the problem-solver was seen to generalize and to select a substitute alternative which was similar to what had proved rewarding in the past. Such a problem-solver had to have the capacity and learning to properly discriminate among his alternatives and their relevance to the problem at hand. Psychology has broadened its interests and now often examines the rational aspects of decisions where reinforcements are uncertain or are delivered intermittently or in various statistical patterns.

The science of psychology sees and tries to account for the limitations on a decision-maker's rationality in terms of his inadequate history, his inadequate repertoire of responses, his inability to discern and judge correctly differences in stimulus conditions and potential alternative responses. Although classical economics described a perfectly rational decision-maker in a world of certain and known characteristics, more recently microeconomists have come to prescribe what is rational in a world with uncertain or random elements which make outcomes a matter of probability rather than certainty. They also consider the *risks* of dealing with a world where even the probabilities of outcomes are unknown. Acts and objects have established values which guide the acts and objects chosen by the rational decision-maker. Economics has come to deal with rational aspects of decisions by showing that the decision-maker at a particular moment in time weighs the *utility* to himself of certain choices, the probability that he will receive the payoff, and what he must pay to obtain certain outcomes of use to him. His situation may be risky in that the outcome may be uncertain. He may reduce his risk by an increase in payment. What is now studied is how value is exchanged for payment under various conditions of risk and uncertainty.[611] Thus, psychology and economics have grown close in interests. They both aim to understand the behavior of an individual in an uncertain environment, an individual influenced in his choices by his personal motives and history.

Satisfactory Versus Best Solutions

Both modern behavior-oriented economics and modern economics-oriented psychology describe decision-makers in organizations as having only limited rationality, behaving like most people have been found to act in novel situations to which they cannot respond automatically and achieve the reward associated with overcoming the obstacles barring access to desired goals. And the world in which they must make choices is also imperfect. The consequences of certain options are uncertain; other options and their consequences fail to be discerned or are misperceived. Searching for new options and evaluating them is seen as a costly consideration which reduces the desire to search as widely as a purely rational being might search who was interested in a complete mathematical analysis of the situation confronting him. Therefore the typical business decision-maker searches for solutions only until he finds a satisfactory choice, but it may not be the best choice that could be made if complete information were available about the problem and alternative solutions to it. For example, an optimum output for a firm to yield the best possible returns to all its interests to provide for better growth, for more satisfaction to its stockholders, managers, and employes might call for the production of 50 percent A beams, 30 percent B beams, and 20 percent C beams. Yet, it is likely that the firm's president might decide to produce only A beams since marketing this product alone would yield a satisfactory profit and growth. In making this kind of decision he is acting as a *satisficer*, searching only until a satisfactory but not necessarily best alternative is found.*[442]

Heuristics Versus Algorithms

Behavior-oriented investigators see reasonable choices usually based on the past experience of the success and failure of various options rather than by pure logical analyses.[611] In the search for an all-sea passage to India for half a century Portuguese navigators followed a safe and satisfactory strategy of hugging the African Coast as they explored southward, each following after the other, but going a bit further south until Diaz reached the Cape of Good Hope before turning back. Yet

---

*Technically speaking, one can formulate "what will satisfy" as the objective function to be gained through an optimization procedure. However, as we observed in Chapter 1, what will satisfy depends on what is valued and whose values are involved. It may prove difficult to quantify what will satisfy all concerned with the operations of the system under study.

logical analysis of the prevailing winds led Vasco de Gama to strike out boldly toward the southern tip of Africa directly from the Cape Verde Islands, saving him sufficient time so he could round the Cape and continue on to India.

In following the coast Diaz employed *heuristic* reasoning based on the persuasiveness of the success of those who sailed before him. In taking advantage of the winds da Gama adopted an *algorithmic* approach to his goal, calculating how much time he would save by maximizing his use of the prevailing winds and currents and ignoring the actually less important need to always remain close to land.

While some mathematico-deductive investigators prefer to treat primarily what business decision-makers should take into account and how they might arrive at the best possible decision (like Vasco da Gama),[452] others are more interested in finding principles for predicting what business decision-makers actually will do under specified circumstances, even working out computer models to simulate or duplicate the behavior of actual businessmen like investment officers[118] or department store buyers.[140] The argument is that if we can program a computer to match the decisions of a businessman which he has based on his "rules of thumb," then we are beginning to understand how decisions are made. Once we develop such understanding then we can work on improving the decision-making process. If we only concern ourselves with the mathematically or logically elegant solutions to business problems, we will miss an important element in the process—namely, the decision-maker himself with the many restrictions and limitations on his actual rationality. Further, as said before, many business problems still remain outside the possibilities of mathematico-deductive analysis.

Routine decisions in organizations dealing with, say, the testing of new products or the distribution of the products to different warehouses can be handled by an elegant optimization calculus. Such routine problem-solving begins with the need to choose from specified alternatives. Each alternative has a known consequence. The organization chooses that alternative whose consequence is most useful or profitable to the firm. But long-range, nonroutine decision-making in organizations tends to follow a pattern better dealt with by the psychology of problem-solving. The problem itself may not be sensed. Or the problem may be obscure or inadequately defined. Worse, the real problem might be masked by false symptoms.

Alternative solutions need to be identified. But they may be obscure, and a costly search may be required to locate or screen among many potential choices.

The consequences of various choices are not given. They must be estimated. Or trial-and-error learning must be employed to test their effects. Again, estimates and judgments are subject to a wide variety of human errors which need to be considered to understand how decisions are made in organizations.[141]

Stages in Problem-Solving

Three broad stages complete the decision process. First the problem must be sensed and analyzed. Applicable elements must be discerned. Then solutions must be discovered, invented, or identified. To do this, known information is appraised and corrected for bias. Unknown factors are isolated. Third, the solutions must be evaluated to identify the one or more that best copes with the problem. For this to be done, we need to establish criteria for evaluation, weigh the pertinent alternatives and unknowns, project expectations of the impact on objectives, and synthesize our findings with a course of action.[2]

Figure 10.1 displays a flow chart of logical steps which might be involved in a complete or ideal problem-solving process. The problem-solvers, if they act like a computer, can proceed from one step to the next only if the test of whether they have completed the step permits them to pass on to the next.

The process usually begins with a sense of dissatisfaction with the current state of affairs. A memorandum may be written to the safety director viewing with alarm the increasing number of minor accidents to employes. If the safety director can assure the dissatisfied memo-writer that the rise in accidents is only a random departure from expectations and that the alarm is not warranted, the process may stop. If he agrees that the situation is unsatisfactory, he may call an *ad hoc* committee of his staff to define the problem. They may raise numerous questions. Is the unsatisfactory situation due to a change in reporting methods? Is it due to the opening of a medical first-aid center nearer to the workplace? Are only major accidents increasing? Are the definitions of minor and major accidents in terms of days work lost meaningful and do they help clarify the nature of the current problem? Are minor accidents on the increase in all or only selected departments and shifts? Has there been any recent change in worker morale? Has there been a slackening in the safety program? Are new employes more prone to accidents, or is the introduction of new, faster equipment with more risks for operators confusing the issue?

Following this examination, are we in a position to classify the problem? For example, can we say that the increase in minor accidents is due specifically to faster equipment. If it is, then we have a routine solution for the problem. We have available a special employe training program

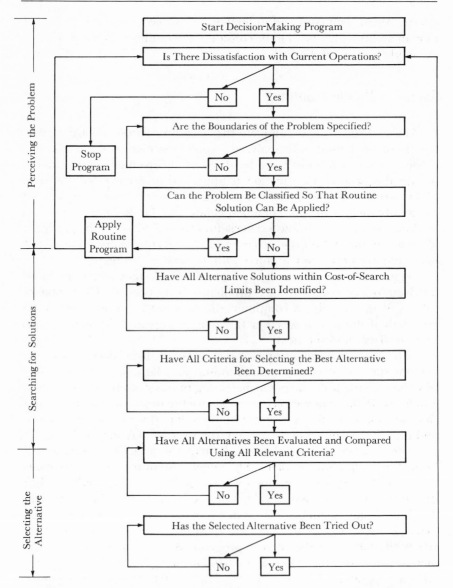

Figure 10.1: A Program of Tests of Logical Steps in the Decision Process.

to be used when new equipment causes difficulties for employes. Therefore we can follow standard operating procedure and end the decision
process at this time by contacting the training department about the
matter.

But suppose our analysis suggests that rather than being routine,
the problem is due to several causes. Moreover, it is judged to contain

considerable uncertainty[144] and therefore remains outside the bounds of routine classification and treatment. Therefore we now must search for alternatives until we can pass the test that all options have been identified or that continued exploration for solutions is not worthwhile. We may generate such alternatives as starting a special safety campaign, providing special programs for supervisors on attitudes toward supervisors, hiring a consulting psychologist to counsel individual employes who are accident-repeaters, hiring an engineer to redesign the equipment, and so on.

The criteria for evaluating the alternatives must be established. Efficacy, cost, and feasibility might be adopted as the three criteria to use in evaluating each option. As a consequence, the proposal to launch a supervisory training program might be judged as best in meeting the selected criteria. The supervisory program then will be tried out. A follow-up evaluation may eventually report favorably on the success of the new project, and the decision process will end with the conclusion that the accident problem no longer exists. Or if it reports that the project failed to reduce minor accidents, then there still is dissatisfaction with current operations and the problem-solving cycle is repeated as shown in Figure 10.1.

An Illustration. A staged process of problem-solving similar to the hypothetical one just described was seen in a detailed account of how a medium-sized corporation examined the feasibility of introducing electronic data-processing equipment into its accounting operations. First, for example, there was a considerable period in which a special assistant to the controller explored the problem by corresponding with experts, talking with salesmen and users, and reading journal articles before moving into the next stage.[141]

Problem-Solving by Computer

Step-by-step logical description of problem-solving makes it possible to simulate this heuristic process by computer programs. A General Problem-Solving Program has been written by a Carnegie Tech-Rand research group, which develops its own network of instructions to detect differences between the present situation and a goal, to retrieve from its memory or through search and analysis alternative ways of reducing the discrepancy, then to apply the alternative which will reduce the discrepancy between current state and objective. Similar programs have been designed which prove mathematical theorems and play checkers or chess.[611] The computer model indicates that relatively straightforward step-by-step procedures are sufficient. Left to their own devices, humans usually follow somewhat less orderly procedures. For example, analysis of four cases of business decision-making suggests, unfortunately, that the actual human decision process is not as rational or orderly as it might be. First, rough expectations apparently screen out obviously inappropriate alternatives. Thus one alternative to cutting costs might be to eliminate production of high-cost – low-profit items. But such elimination immediately brings on many new unwanted problems such as more seasonal unemployment and decreased use of full plant capacity. Second, the feasibility of implementing a particular decision is considered, as well as ways it can be evaluated. Most important is whether the solution is within budgetary constraints. There is some examination of the expected costs and returns of alternative solutions to the problem but little attempt to demonstrate that the expected net return on the chosen alternative will equal or exceed the expected return on alternative investments.[138]

But when forced into more orderliness, humans become more successful problem-solvers.

While computers *must* adopt such orderly processes, humans may find it efficacious to do so also for there is some evidence that a step-by-step orderly attack on problems increases the effectiveness of human problem-solvers. Orderly problem-solving proceeds in three stages: (1) delineating the problem, (2) creating and/or searching for alternative solutions, and (3) evaluating prospective solutions. Problem-solvers are most effective when they thoroughly consider one stage before moving to the next.

Efficacy of Staging.   After problems were assigned to four groups of ten persons each, the groups were forced to separate the discussion of alternative solutions from the evaluation of the solutions. Four control groups attacked the same problems freely. Groups forced to separate the stages saw themselves as becoming significantly more efficient than the control groups and were more satisfied by the experience. They felt no different from control subjects in apprehensiveness or inadequacy. At the end of the process they were significantly more committed to the decisions reached.[249] In similar fashion, staging was encouraged in 96 groups of four men each, while 50 groups served as free controls trying to solve a problem in work procedures. The "Change of Work Procedures" problem was as follows:

Time data were available to the foreman of a work crew. He knew that maximum efficiency could be obtained if each worker was placed on the job he did best. But the workers preferred to stay on their present jobs. The problem was to devise a plan which would increase the efficiency of the work group and be acceptable to the workers.

The 96 experimental problem-solving groups were asked to present the problem first to get everyone's views about it. Only after this sharing of views were they to explore and discuss all the important factors in the situation. Finally at the end of the search and discussion they were to use the list of factors to synthesize a solution to the problem. The control groups followed no particular order in solving the problem.

Table 10.1 shows how the experimental groups who discussed the problem in stages were more likely to emerge with integrated and therefore better solutions — solutions which satisfied the need to increase efficiency as well as avoid resistance from workers when adopted. About one-fifth of both the experimental and control groups emerged with the old solution to continue rotating men through all jobs, letting men help each other, and giving special training when needed. New solutions which moved each man to the job he could do best were reached by two-thirds of the control groups, while only 37.5 percent of the experimental groups decided to use this solution (which was likely to meet strong resistance from the workers). On the other hand, 41.7 percent of the experimental groups, using staging, created an integrated solution that was better than the old or new solutions. This integrated decision called for men to rotate only to jobs they could do well or to rotate but spend more time on jobs they could do best. Only 12 percent of the control groups invented such a clearly better solution which met the needs of production as well as the desires of the workers.[432]

Staging More Likely Among Better Administrators

Further evidence on the profitability of outlining the problem and screening alternatives before taking action is seen in the results of "in-basket" tests given to 232 administrators. These tests were a collection of

TABLE 10.1 EFFECTS ON QUALITY OF DECISIONS WHEN GROUPS ARE
INSTRUCTED TO VIEW SITUATION AS A PROBLEM TO BE SOLVED IN STAGES
RATHER THAN A DECISION TO BE MADE*

| | Solution Reached | | |
	Old	New	Integrative
96 Experimental groups (solve problem in stages)	20.8%	37.5%	41.7%
50 Control groups (no staging)	22.0	66.0	12.0

*After Maier & Solem (1963)

facsimiles of letters, memoranda, and other contents likely to be found in a typical administrator's in-basket. The administrator responded to the 32 problems posed by the contents of his in-basket by placing in his out-basket instructions for his secretary, memos, letters, reminders, and appointment calendars.

The contents of each out-basket could be scored on 68 aspects, such as number of unusual actions, number of superiors involved in action taken, or amount of information given to subordinates. Eight primary factors emerged in a factor analysis, showing the dimensions along which these administrators varied consistently. They varied in how much information they exchanged with others, how much they discussed matters before acting. how much they complied with the suggestions of others, how much they analyzed the situation before acting, how concerned they were with maintaining organizational relationships, how much care they took to specify in advance when work was to be done, how much they were responsive to outsiders, and how much they gave orders to their subordinates in writing.

Two higher-order factors accounted for the correlations found among the primary factors. Some executives did more work than others, making for higher or lower scores on the eight primaries. Most significant for our discussion of staging was the second higher-order factor, which suggested that these administrators vary on what stage of the decision process they concentrate. On the one extreme, some administrators concentrate on trying to clarify the problem. They spent somewhat less time on scheduling and organizing facts and even less on taking action. At the other extreme were administrators who were most likely to take action, paying less attention to alternatives and with even less concern about clarification of the problem or organization of facts about it. Further analyses disclosed that it was the administrators with more ability (as measured by aptitude tests) and administrative knowledge (as measured by a special achievement examination) who were most likely to concentrate on preparing for a decision rather than on taking immediate action.[218]

PERCEIVING THE PROBLEM IN ORGANIZATIONS

If staging is to be followed, the problem must be delineated during the early phases of the problem-solving process. Often this is the most important aspect of the decision process. Whether or not an emergency exists requiring an immediate decision, whether the problem is routine, or whether long-range policy-planning is involved depends on how we view the presenting conditions. It may be that no decision should be made, or no decision should be considered at this time.[656]

A number of principles drawn from general psychology can help describe what happens when organizations are faced with nonroutine problems requiring decisions, how they discriminate whether or not a problem exists, and if it does exist, how they establish its fundamental character, its significant elements, and its boundaries. These are formed into a meaningful pattern, sometimes quite unconsciously. The process of organizing the problem elements is rapid, but during it, the problem-solver forms hypotheses, tests them against present perceptions and against his memory, and revises his synthetization accordingly. The ultimate wrong decisions may result to a considerable extent from the problem-solver's failure at this first stage to attend to all significant elements of the problem instead of the few in which he is most concerned because of his past experience or his current motivation. But erroneous perception of the problem may be a consequence of its structure. For example, there may be too much time between cause and effect, so that the critical cause-effect relation is missed. There may be multiple causes obscuring the important underlying one. The cause may appear extremely different from the effect, so that the incongruity makes it difficult to associate the two.[400] (Consider the fission of the minuscule atomic nucleus and its cosmic effects.) What is perceived, what is in the pattern that is organized, will depend upon various attributes of the stimulating situation as well as various characteristics of the decision-maker.[733]

Some Effects of the Problem Itself as the Stimulus

Various stimulating properties of the problem itself affect the way it is perceived and defined. Arrangement of the problem (the set of stimulus conditions) into a meaningful pattern will depend on the proximity and similarity of its parts as well as on the tendency for observers to fill in missing parts and achieve cognitive balance in certain ways. As a consequence of their makeup, some parts of the problem will stand out and be enhanced in perception by contextual effects; other parts will fade into the background.[752] Some of these perceptual tendencies already have been briefly mentioned in Chapter 8 as they affect our receipt and transmission of rumors.

Proximity. Studies of how forms and shapes are perceived indicate that those parts of a pattern of stimuli which are close to each other will be seen to group together. Notice how the workers of Figure 10.2 are readily seen as four groups of six, not six groups of four. We will tend to identify employes in blocks depending on the department in which they happen to be working. If complaints in the grinding department are twice as high as anywhere else in the plant, we will tend to see all grinders as disgruntled. It may be that the high incidence is due to only one or two unhappy grinders.

Sameness.   We tend to group together things that are alike and to sepa-in our perceptions things that differ. Note how in Figure 10.3 it is easy to separately group managers and workers. Thus we are likely to see all Negro employes as a single homogeneous group. We easily perceive that we have a "Negro problem" if one or two altercations occur between white and Negro workers in the plant.

Common Fate.   Things that occur together, disappear together, or move together tend to be grouped. Some stocks whose prices tend to rise sharply and fall sharply together often are grouped together as "glamour stocks." Actually some may be sound growth investments while others are much more speculative.

Events that happen by chance or for other reasons tend to occur together may be seen to cause each other. Layoffs may occur as new machinery is brought into the plant. But the machinery may have been

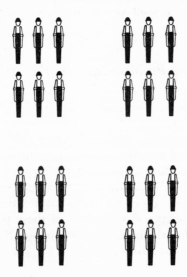

Figure 10.2: The Workers Are Seen in Groups of Six.

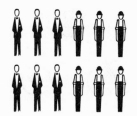

*Figure 10.3: The   Workers
and Managers Form Two
Groups.*

ordered two years earlier to expand some activities, while the layoffs
are actually due to a seasonal drop in sales.

Closure.   We tend to complete in the fullest fashion only partly sensed
figures. Thus in Figure 10.4 the coins form a six-pointed star. This is
most readily seen rather than 12 individual coins or small combinations
of coins. One readily sees a boy's face and a sailboat in the incompleted
figures rather than just a mass of irregular black spots.

Within the large company, the principle of closure may manifest
itself in two ways. First, there will be a desire to bring closure when it
cannot be seen. A marketing firm will push its salesmen to sell all sizes
rather than just the most salable models. In the same way order blanks
will be prepared requiring a considerable amount of relatively useless
information in order to complete the description of the order. Second,
closure will be seen when it does not exist. For instance, many matters
may be discussed at a meeting and people leave perceiving themselves
in agreement although they actually "talked around" the problem and
failed to examine whether they were in agreement at the end of the
meeting.

Saliency.   What stands out in a problem? What is *figure* and what is
ground in the picture that is seen? If we gaze up at night, the stars are
the figure and the void is the background. The stars draw our attention
with clear definition, form, and boundaries; the blue-black void is
formless and uniform. The stars are in front; empty space is behind.
The stars have more meaning; empty space has less meaning.

The figure in an organization problem is likely to be the current
griping about inadequate wages; the background, generalized dissatisfaction with company policies. Numbers are more salient than a climate
of opinion.

The figures in business problems are literally the numerical figures,
the quantitative stimuli. The qualitative data tend to be less salient.

*Figure 10.4: We See Forms and Figures as
Complete When Parts Are Missing.*

Thus when Wharton Business School students play business games,
they pay much more attention to quantitative than to qualitative data
when both are available. They concentrate first on the numbers, then
use qualitative data to confirm analyses and solutions of the problem
already reached from study of the quantitative data alone. They seem
to behave as required by the measuring system, disregarding other

forms of data. For example, like most business game players, they tend to ignore the importance of evaluating qualitatively their adversaries' strategies and probabilities of success, yet these may be among the most critical aspects of the problem with which they must cope.[421]

Contrast promotes saliency. The one ailing department among 30 successful departments gets all the executives' continuing attention. *Frequency* and *intensity* also draw attention.[373] When customer complaints suddenly rise dramatically, management is likely to be aroused quickly to the fact that a problem exists.

Context.   A grey piece of paper looks white if surrounded by a black piece. In the same way we judge a problem in the context in which it appears. In judging our own company's declining sales figures, if our *frame of reference* is an economy-wide contraction, we may view our decrease with less alarm than if our firm is declining while most firms are reporting increased business.

Our *adaptation level* determines the point at which we may become alarmed. If we have been accustomed to fluctuations up or down of 10 percent in annual sales, a 20 percent decline will have dramatic impact.

Cognitive Balance.   People tend to perceive various events and beliefs so that they will be congruent with each other. When a person becomes aware of an inconsistency in his system of beliefs, when he perceives that his beliefs or his perceptions of a situation contradict each other, he will attempt to reduce the dissonance, to reconcile the conflict.[204] For instance, we noted in Chapter 3 how, if we have to work harder than expected to reach a goal, we will tend to justify the harder work by increasing how much value we attach to the goal.

Often the reconciliation is maladaptive, resulting in inefficiencies or new problems. For example, a marketing firm was convinced that product acceptability strongly depends on advertising. They introduced a new tapioca pudding to the market with a lavish television advertising campaign resulting in instant sales success. Despite the continuing high rate of advertising, however, sales suddenly plummeted. To reduce dissonance, more money was plowed into advertising, for the strong belief in the power of advertising remained unshaken. If sales dropped, it was reasoned that advertising was inadequate. But alas, the pudding was not very tasty, and while advertising led shoppers to try the product once, there were few repeats. The advertising money could have been better spent on developing a better pudding. If the belief in the importance of good products had been stronger and the belief in the power of advertising less strong, presumably the sharp drop in sales would have been interpreted more realistically.

In business games, players usually reject data which run contrary to their own current beliefs.[421] A case in point is one foods executive who kept his team steadily reducing prices in a game, nearly to the point of bankruptcy. He did this because for 30 years he had been in an industry where share of market and profitability was maintained primarily by price-cutting. Yet he was now playing a game where it should have become evident by the second or third play that prices were only a minor determinant of customer demand. But he ignored all current data he was receiving and relied solely on his own beliefs when in fact one can only come to grips with the problems presented by business games (and presumably much of real business also) by adopting an experimental frame of mind, displaying willingness to shuck old beliefs when they fail to account for new facts, testing the system to check out new hypotheses, and avoiding falling into the trap of seeing in ambiguous results the confirmation of beliefs primarily because such confirmation is desired and not because such confirmation is valid.

Some Effects of Personal Factors

Of particular significance in organizational problem-solving is the obvious factor that persons are differentially sensitive to the same stimulating conditions and view the same conditions in different ways, using different concepts to organize their thinking. These differences may depend upon the *personality* of the job occupant coping with a problem or the *position* he holds.

Differences in Set. Some executives will be *set* to see a problem that does not exist; others will be insensitive to problems that do exist. A manager who is expecting trouble will react quickly and strongly to vague rumors of a wildcat strike. He may be overly sensitive to the possibilities of a class war. A colleague may dismiss the rumors as trivial.

Different Perspectives. Interpretation of the same events will depend upon the location of the problem-solver and his education. The same stimulating conditions may give rise to totally different understanding of the causes of the condition. Thus if too many defective parts are reported showing up on the assembly line, the engineering executive conceptualizes the problem as one of quality control requiring a reduction in defects from 4 to 1 percent. The personnel executive believes he has a problem of inadequate employe training. The production executive sees a breakdown in supervisory controls. All may be correctly viewing the same situation but with totally different perspectives.

This phenomenon was observed also in a marketing firm, 20 percent of whose sales force had been replaced the preceding year. The sales manager felt he was faced with a critical morale problem. The staff statistician saw the 20 percent quit rate in the firm's marketing force as a random fluctuation from a long-term average of 15 percent. The merchandising department saw itself shorthanded with a problem of completing work with an inadequate number of employes. The personnel manager remained unconcerned because turnover of 20 percent of the sales force annually was about average in his industry. Actually the staff psychologist found that most of the avoidable turnover was a consequence of discharge for incompetence. Salesmen leaving the firm did not quit because of dissatisfaction; they were usually fired because of incompetence. Men with ability were likely to survive and happily continue their service with the firm.

These same turnover data had different consequences for different executives and were interpreted accordingly.

Differential Personal Orientation.   Motivation obviously plays a strong role in directing the differential attention and interpretation of organizational members facing the same problem. A *self-oriented* executive may view a problem under discussion by his committee as an issue potentially harmful to his personal success in the company. An *interaction-oriented* executive may participate at the same meeting, more concerned about whether the problem is discussed in a relaxed, friendly way. The contents of the problem are a minor issue to him. The *task-oriented* executive focuses on the problem itself as a puzzle to be solved and remains dissatisfied if the meeting adjourns without having solved the problem.[42]

Differential Concern for Various Aspects of Organizational Problems.   Attention to who and what are involved in problems varies from one manager to another. What is salient in an industrial firm, what is figure and what is ground, varies from one member to another. According to a factor analysis of 109 factory management personnel, these differential foci of attention in an organization can be clustered into five areas. Some managers reflect more *concern for subordinates* than other managers when coordination is needed or decisions are required within one's department. Some managers reflect, more than others, greater *concern for authority,* for what the boss thinks about plans and innovations and what the rule book says about various matters. Still others focus on *concern for themselves*, primarily when the problem deals with distributing rewards in the organization and with what the boss thinks about their participation in organizational affairs. Some managers focus more than others specifically on *how rewards are distributed* and how superiors, peers, and subordinates feel about the distribution. And some emphasize, more than others, *general organizational concern*: concern for what peers think about coordination, concern for how the boss deals with conflict, and concern for what subordinates feel about planning and innovating.

These variations in concern about organization problems depend on one's position in the organization to a considerable degree. Department heads with less than two years in office are significantly more concerned about their subordinates or how rewards are distributed than those in office two to ten years. But those in office longer have greater overall organizational concerns. Time in the company has similar effects. Seniority brings less concern for oneself and how rewards are distributed, and more general organizational concern.

Concern for authority is highest among department heads whose employes are skilled rather than semiskilled or unskilled. But it is lowest when subordinates are semiprofessional.[699]

Effective Versus Ineffective Approaches to Perceiving the Problem

More and less effective ways of viewing a problem can be suggested from studies of successful and unsuccessful problem-solvers. Those likely to succeed almost immediately perceive through some familiar stimulus, word, or phrase, a point at which they begin their attack. They break up the problem into smaller parts, parts with which they are likely to have had some past experience. They eliminate redundancies while retaining the important points and tend to sharpen and bring the major elements of the problem into focus. They systematically reorganize the problem into a series of sub-problems, extracting key terms and ideas and simplifying their perceptions without losing the essentials. They handle each part of the problem methodically.

Unsuccessful problem-solvers fail to understand the statements of the problem they are given. They become confused about the requirements. They cannot fill in gaps in understanding with guesses at the possible meanings of elements that are unfamiliar to them. Worse still, unsuccessful problem-solvers are more likely to distort the problem and attack a newly perceived problem—one that is so dissimilar from the original that the solution has no relation to it. Often their failure to solve a problem lies mainly in this misinterpretation of the issue through unwillingness to devote the needed time to this first stage of problem-solving. These prospective failures often possess the knowledge necessary to solve a problem, but they cannot perceive it as being solvable with their knowledge. At the same time they believe that reasoning as such is of relatively little value in answering problems—either one has all the necessary information and therefore knows the answer, or he does not. Unlike the potentially successful problem-solvers, those likely to fail refuse to break up a problem into its parts.[73, 675]

SEARCHING FOR SOLUTIONS

In generating solutions those who ultimately fail to solve a problem satisfactorily have no plan of attack. They jump from one part of a problem to another and from one stage to another, neglecting the important details; they become sidetracked by external considerations; they wander off on tangents when some word suggests an irrelevant idea or an interesting incident. Before they have sufficiently engaged in considering alternatives, the failing problem-solver selects one on the basis of feeling that it "seems right." Often some trivial or irrelevant point is used to justify such a selection. Even if he begins with a systematic plan to generate solutions, such as one based on the criteria that the correct answer must fulfill, he fails to follow through with the plan and loses sight of it when difficulties occur during the reasoning process.[73]

For ultimate success in solving a problem, alternatives need to be identified, classified, discovered, and invented. Many of the perceptual tendencies which describe how problems are recognized also describe what happens in the search for solutions. Particularly important is the *set* one adopts.

Increasing Search for Alternatives by Using a Set to Avoid Criticism

Fundamental to improving the search process is promoting a set to increase the number of alternatives to be considered. As has already been discussed, decisions reached are better when stage-by-stage problem-solving forces problem-solvers to spend more time searching for alternatives before making a decision. If the cost in time for such searching is minor, then it will be profitable to *brainstorm*, to delay criticism, and to generate as many alternatives as possible before considering the quality of the proposals.

Brainstorming has been offered as a generally useful method for improving the quality of decisions by forcibly increasing the quantity of alternatives generated by the problem-solvers. Four rules are pre-scribed to create a brainstorming set. Evaluation and criticism of any presented idea is withheld during brainstorming. Idea generation as such is unrestricted in this search phase. "Wild" ideas are as acceptable as pedestrian solutions more easily seen as relevant to the problem. Quantity of output is stressed. Preceding ideas are reviewed only to generate new combining solutions; new ideas are synthesized from ear-lier ones presented to solve the problem. With this frame of mind it is possible, for example, to generate literally a hundred ways of, say, using a wire clothes hanger, many of which are both creative and original. Inhibitors to creative output are avoided, criticisms such as: "it's not part of our job, we've never done it that way, we haven't the time, we tried that before, our situation is different, it's too hard to administer, what will our customers think, or somebody would have used it before if it were any good."[116]

To demonstrate the efficacy of brainstorming, one sample of sub-jects were told to produce freely ideas for solving two problems. A con-trol group was told to produce only high-quality ideas. The control group also was to avoid poor ideas because it would bring penalties for them. Those free to brainstorm without fear of penalty for inadequate solutions actually produced more good ideas than those restricted by fear of penalties for poor proposals. Moreover, subjects who brain-stormed without previous exposure to the riskier situation where poor ideas were penalized, generated better solutions than subjects who freely brainstormed after first experiencing the need to avoid poor ideas. An earlier experience of restriction adversely affected idea production even after the restrictions were lifted.[469]

Group Versus Individual Brainstorming. It was thought that group par-ticipation would facilitate brainstorming, that members could build on each other's ideas and generate more good ideas collectively as a conse-quence of their interaction than they could alone.[505] However, 48 Yale students who brainstormed in real groups of four failed to match in number or quality the ideas of 48 students who worked alone but whose isolated contributions were assembled in nominal groups of four to eliminate duplications. Even after these duplications were subtracted, the nominal groups produced almost twice as many different ideas as the real groups.[669] Similar results were found for 48 research scientists and 48 advertising personnel of Minnesota Mining and Manufacturing, although the latter, at least, might have been expected to do better in groups.[184] Nor was personal orientation or group homogeneity impor-tant. Results continued to favor individual brainstorming when groups were formed according to the self-, interaction-, or task-orientation of members. Neither when members were all different in orientation, nor when they were all alike did the real groups produce little more than half the different ideas that the individuals in those groups could produce when working alone.[269] However, some unpublished work points to the possibility that real groups do become as effective or more so than isolated individuals if they continue to practice as groups and as members become more familiar with each other. Presumably members can learn to become more effective in groups, in building on each other's ideas. This would suggest that men who can work well together will be more productive in groups than working alone. Men who esteem each other highly, for instance, as noted in Chapter 6, should make more effective work groups and therefore should find group brainstorming more fruitful. Although some evidence has been found to demonstrate this point for two-man brainstorming pairs,[124] group advocates of brainstorming have yet to demonstrate that with enough training it is possible to form real groups which will generate more good ideas than the same trained individuals can do working alone.

Increasing Search by Adopting Other Special Sets

The search process is facilitated if the decision-maker adopts a *questioning set*. To help generate alternatives, he may ask in a systematic sequence: Why? Where? When? Who? What? How? What current resource could be adapted? Modified? Substituted? Transformed? Combined? Omitted? Reversed?[505] Along the same lines, merely adopting *a set to be original* increases the originality of ideas generated. That is, if we are given instructions to try to discover or invent unique solutions rather than just any solutions, we increase our production of such out-of-the-ordinary alternatives.[434] If we adopt a *constructive set* rather than a negative or critical set towards ideas, it helps to promote greater and more successful search for creative solutions.[323]

In the search for alternatives a number of tests can be made on how well the search has proceeded. Is the search broad enough and clear in its directions? Have some alternatives been ignored because they customarily are solutions to different problems? Has there been a failure to consider alternatives considerably different from the initially proposed solution? Have some alternatives been rejected without full consideration or because they are misunderstood? Are we holding onto one alternative because it has worked successfully before on a different problem or in a different situation?[702]

The frame of reference the organization sets for its problem-solvers is of particular importance. Venturesomeness and wide-ranging search for new and better ways of doing things are likely to be inhibited if emphasis in the organization is always on rules, clearances, and reviews, or if the payoff is to those who maintain stability and order rather than to those who innovate. Search will be inhibited if jurisdictional lines are stressed, so that one executive avoids making suggestions to another about the other's area of responsibility. On the other hand, creativity will be enhanced when the organization approves attempts to experiment, to innovate, and to challenge old ways of operating.[132]

Increasing Search by Special Effort

Upon finding that more good ideas appeared in the second half of a subject's brainstorming output, it was reasoned that extending the time devoted to search would increase the overall quality of ideas generated per unit time allotted for search. When the available time for brainstorming on a particular problem was extended from five to fifteen minutes, the last five minutes yielded significantly more good ideas than the first or second five-minute periods. There seems to be extra payoff in keeping subjects searching for new alternatives. An idea that emerges late in the search process is likely to be the best one.[511] In the same way when the same groups are asked to go back to tackle again the same problem for which they already had reached a decision a first time, they tend to discover or create new and better solutions. The previously-mentioned "Change of Work Procedures" problem was solved twice by 100 students. During the first trial only 16 discovered the integrative plan promoting both productivity and worker satisfaction; yet 52 created such a plan the second time they examined the same problem.[429]

Of course, there must be an optimum amount of time and effort one should spend in search. At some point it is no longer worthwhile to spend more time seeking additional alternatives. Problems can become stale. But since subjects reach plateaus in productivity, rather than cease further search altogether, often a temporary stop is helpful, for it may result in the appearance of further new ideas following the rest period. (During the rest period interfering irrelevancies may be forgotten, making it possible to evoke ideas which were inhibited by the interfering responses.) However, at some time a final halt must be called. For one can expend too much effort. Motivation may be too high. Extremely motivated subjects, for example, are likely to be more selectively vigilant in their search, depending on the nature of their motives. This will restrict the breadth and range of their search for original approaches. For example, hungry subjects will see more foods in ambiguous pictures they are trying to describe, restricting somewhat their seeing other possibilities in the pictures. The quality of ideas will be affected adversely also if motivation is too high. For instance, it is likely that housewives will buy too many food items they do not really need if they shop at a grocery supermarket just before lunch. In the same way incentives may be too large, stimulation too great, and pressure to perform too heavy. Thus scrappage and accident rates are likely to increase when machine-paced production is speeded up beyond an optimal point. Again, the average quality of suggestions may fall when management overdoes a campaign to increase the quantity of suggestions submitted by employes.

Increasing Search for Alternatives by Training

Relevant learning experiences increase the degree to which problem-solvers can discover, invent, or identify alternatives. For instance, in comparison to controls, subjects who first spent time examining lists of uncommon uses of objects they were subsequently to employ to solve a problem were better able to discover the unique way (not already mentioned) they would need to use the objects to solve the problem.[435] In the same way, in comparison to subjects without practice, subjects who practiced at generating original rather than ordinary responses to stimulus words, when later tested with new stimulus words, tended to generate more original responses to the new stimuli.[434] In general, further studies along the same lines supported the conclusion that originality of response is a form of learned behavior and follows the same principles of development as does learning in general.[436] More extensive training courses in how to brainstorm or how to generate more alternatives of high quality yield results which are consistent with this conclusion.[500, 512] For instance, a ten-week creativity program of one hour training sessions was given to 31 A.C. Spark Plug employes. In comparison to the rest of the plant without creativity training, the trained employes significantly increased afterwards the number of suggestions they submitted. Moreover, more of their suggestions were accepted; and in comparison to nontrained employes, they gained more in award money earned.[609] (It is uncertain as to how much these effects were due to change of *set* and how much to *training*, but nevertheless, training did increase the generation of good solutions and alternatives to current practices.)

Divergent Versus Convergent Search

So far we have concentrated primarily on the *divergent* search for alternatives. That is, we have been concerned with the production of as many diverse solutions to a problem as possible, assuming that many solutions may work although the best one is likely to be uncovered if the search is broad enough and continues long enough. In many situations the search becomes convergent, starting with many possibilities available and continually narrowing the range of alternatives or creating the best alternative out of some or all of the available possibilities.

Divergent search is usually involved when one is considering publishing a catalog of products for wheat farmers or formulating an advertising campaign for a client. Convergent search is usually involved when one is seeking to discover the proof of a mathematical theorem, what move to make next in a game, or at what point there has been a communication breakdown in one's organization.

> In . . . convergent thinking there is almost always one conclusion or answer that is regarded as unique, and thinking is to be channeled or controlled in the direction of that answer. . . . In divergent thinking, on the other hand, there is much searching about or going off in various directions. This is most easily seen when there is no unique solution . . . [265, pp.6–7]

Individual differences in success in convergence have been assessed by tests of picture or sentence arrangement, synthesizing objects from parts, identifying hidden figures embedded in more complex patterns, reasoning with forms, and completing numerical operations. Convergent thinking occurs when one tries to find the answers to multiple-choice questions. All alternatives are provided, but only one answer is correct. Individual differences in success in divergence have been assessed by symbol production tests, creating plot titles, planning air maneuvers, word listing, and inserting similes. Divergent thinking occurs on any completion test requiring the generation of as many correct answers as possible. The distinction is not always clear on some problem-solving tests. However, a number of factor analytic studies support the proposition that convergent and divergent search are logically and operationally distinct.[265]

Converging by Computer.   In trying to understand the step-by-step ways human beings deduce theorems, or detect and discover the answer to a problem through convergent thinking, it may be helpful to examine how computer programs must be written to obtain such a solution, for studies of convergent human problem-solving are often obscured because so much of the connected process is internalized. Even where the subject verbalizes what he thinks he is doing, one cannot be sure that his verbalizations are accurate portrayals of the process. Only indirect experiments can provide objective guides as to what is happening. For this reason, it may be that computerized models will provide a needed catharsis in the study of problem-solving. The models are sufficient. They may or may not do what human beings do, but they suggest that human beings might well look to the computer to see how much of what they are doing is unnecessary or inefficient.

A set of instructions was written for an all-purpose digital computer which converted them into a control system capable of inventing alternative solutions and testing their adequacy.[498] Such a system succeeded in proving 38 of the first 52 theorems of Whitehead and Russell's *Principia Mathematica*. The system was started with a *memory* of the axioms required to prove the theorems, certain *primitive information processes* which can operate on the memory, and *programs* of rules to follow in trying to prove each theorem. The required programs and processes describe how human problem-solving may work in the same way that difference equations describe how electrical circuits work.

Four rules of inference were sufficient to develop this Logical Theory Machine. A *substitution* rule made it possible to substitute a new element for an old element in an expression. However, the substitution had to be made throughout the expression. *Replacement* permitted the computer to replace a connective, such as "implies" in the expression A implies" B, with the definition of "implies" using other connectives. *Detachment* allowed that B was a true expression, if A implied B and A was a true expression. A syllogism rule made *chaining* possible. If a implies b and b implies c, then a implies c. Chaining could proceed ahead or backwards. An *executive* process coordinated which method would be tried; and if the trial was a failure, what method to employ next. It applied learning by sending into memory storage theorems that had been proved for possible use in the proof of subsequent theorems. The executive also used *matching* and *similarity* tests to check whether two subexpressions were identical.[498]

Computer-Human Analogs. The computer's step-by-step search for solutions was recorded, and provided a description of how problems can be solved (not necessarily how they always are by human beings). The descriptions seem to approximate what we have called in men—set, insight, and a hierarchy of responses. For example, if the computer had stored many proven theorems which it could now employ in a new proof, in obtaining the new proof it spent much more time in trial-and-error

testing the usefulness of these theorems than when it had only the axioms and the one essential theorem in its memory. In searching its memory it showed "insight" by working back from the new problem and examining only potentially useful theorems selected by similarity checks.
Only theorems were considered which were likely candidates for substitution attempts. The executive started with the goal of determining
the new proof (the problem) and by working backwards ruled out large
numbers of attempts without the need to consider them. It also ordered
the sequence in which sub-problems would be solved, working in the
simpler ones first.

New proofs did not come directly, but by detachment and chaining,
the computer generated alternative expressions to prove. The methods
employed to solve these and the sub-problems themselves formed a
growing network, a hierarchy of approaches to solving problems.

Active Instead of Passive. While most neurological descriptions see the
neurons of the brain as passive switchboards, acted on and modified by
stimuli, and behaving subsequently as modified, the computerized information-processing system suggests that for problems to be solved,
there must be developed and stored complex strategies which are
evoked by a problem stimulus. In the same way to be effective the human
problem-solver must take an active role in the formulation of hypotheses
and to realize that one does not need complete conviction that a particular hypothesis is the correct one before considering it.[73]

Such activity is necessary for a solution to be invented which is a
creative synthetization, a fresh approach to handling a problem, one
which often combines previously disassociated ideas. First a number of
potentially acceptable alternative ways of solving the problem need to
have been generated. The willingness to reserve judgment and continue
searching, discussed earlier, is a necessity. If only one ready-made solution stands out and is quickly seized as the only way, problem-solving will
be at an end. On the other hand, if none of the proposals uncovered
after continuing search carry much support, apathy may ensue. And if
they balance each other in support and are in conflict, they may produce
a stalemate. At this point for a creative solution to occur, the elements
in conflict among the acceptable solutions need to be identified. Then
the variations in these elements which are compatible can be searched
for so that a new solution can be formulated which encompasses what
has been acceptable among older, partial, answers to the problem.[306]

Computerized thinking is closer to these kinds of approaches to
understanding of problem-solving which emphasize organizing operations into strategies, step by step, where each subsequent step depends
on the outcome of the preceding one.[88] A problem is described as a

"schematic anticipation" for which means of solution must be found and applied. Priorities must be assigned to provide the order in which methods and evaluations will be tried. Long sequences of solution-methods are chained in a variety of ways. All of this convergent search can occur if the problem-solver has a memory, primitive information processes, and programs of rules for substitution, replacement, detachment, and chaining along with an executive controlling matching, testing, and priorities.

EVALUATING AND CHOOSING

Following the search process, particularly the divergent kind which has generated many solutions to the problem at hand, how does management evaluate the alternatives it has assembled? How does it decide on which alternative or alternatives to select to apply in solving the problem?

Evaluation is affected by how orderly and systematically it proceeds. Evaluation is affected by the error of the estimates of the cost of each alternative as well as the potential utility of each alternative. Evaluation depends on the *risk* and *uncertainty* of each prospective outcome. (We are involved in a 50 percent risk if we bet that a coin will land as a head instead of a tail; we are involved in 50 percent uncertainty when we have only half the information about what is affecting a particular outcome while the other half is unknown.)

Subjective rather than objective perceptions of risk, uncertainty, and confidence govern evaluations. Persons differ in their preferences for avoiding such risk and uncertainty, although most people share certain preferred risks. Groups will risk more than individuals, but the quality of the final decision will not depend on whether it is made by the group or the group chief after group deliberation.

An Orderly Approach to Evaluation

It appears profitable to adopt a systematic screening procedure. Failure to maintain an orderly approach leads to accepting answers to problems on vague feelings about their rightness rather than logical, rational, or objective considerations.[73] First, as noted in Figure 10.1, the *criteria* need to be examined upon which evaluation will be based. Weights may be attached to each of these criteria. A series of questions about risk preferences may guide our choices: Do we seek the anticipated outcome yielding the greatest probability of gain? Are we interested in the least risk of loss? Do we prefer the greatest gain regardless of risk or the least loss regardless of probabilities? What material, monetary, and human constraints limit what we may do? What are the consequences of implementing each alternative? What new problems will be generated by each particular solution?

Weighing Alternatives. After screening out obviously unfeasible or irrelevant alternatives, an orderly evaluator proceeds to examine and weigh the advantages and disadvantages of each alternative, using the selected criteria.[426] Often, a checklist of pros and cons is advisable. Each criterion in the checklist need not be given the same weight, but the checklist forces the decision-maker to be systematic in evaluating every alternative by means of each criterion. No one alternative is treated with favoritism. Wherever possible, supporting evidence and the confidence in evaluations is examined. A choice matrix may be worked out (as done for the Monsanto problem earlier in the chapter) and game mathematics applied in a search for an optimum choice.

Integrating Solutions. Often such systematic exploration makes it possible to see ways of combining and integrating solutions, particularly if one makes an effort to do so.[427] To promote such integration, it appears more profitable to look at each alternative solution with a positive constructive attitude rather than a negative set. When General Electric employes, for instance, reviewed ideas by asking, "What's good about these proposals?," they were more likely to incorporate the suggestions in the final solution. When they focused on what was wrong with the proposals, the ideas were likely to be rejected completely.[323]

Quality of Final Decision by Executive or Executive and Staff. One executive may believe that he should obtain the advice and consent of his subordinates about the problem at hand and possible solutions to it. Yet he still feels he alone must make the decision about which alternative to adopt. Another executive does not stop in his use of his group of subordinates after alternatives have been discussed. He collaborates with his group in making the final decision. Is one approach better than another?

If the executive is trying to capitalize on the values of group consensus (Chapter 6), if he reserves the last step, the final decision, for himself, he risks selecting an unfavored one through misunderstanding of how the problem and the solutions to it were seen by his group in his deliberations with them. On the other hand, if he maintains the group approach to the end of the process, hammering out a jointly constructed agreement, he risks obtaining a decision which he personally regards as less than the best. Actually if the executive and his subordinates are pursuing similar goals with knowledge of similar constraints, have achieved agreement on the problem, and have searched and evaluated the various alternative solutions to the problem, the final choice is likely to be very similar whether the executive alone makes it or it is made by the executive and his group. One experiment suggests that the quality of the decision will be about the same under both circumstances. Simulated *ad hoc* staffs of Air Force officers wrote decisions after discussion of a particular problem. The commanders of the groups also wrote a decision following a review of the opinions of the *ad hoc* staff. There were no significant differences in the quality of the commanders' decisions and those of their staffs. Of course, quality was better for both staffs and commanders who reviewed staff opinion than for commanders who did not have the benefit of staff consultation.[419]

Factors Affecting the Final Choice

Classical economics assumed that a decision-maker was completely informed about the choices available to him and their consequences. He was infinitely sensitive to this information and was completely rational. As such, he chose that alternative whose consequences would give him the greatest value or utility with the least cost. Where utilities for different alternatives were the same, the decision-maker became indifferent about his choice.[190] If these assumptions were correct, then there would be no need to study the behavior of the decision-maker, for we would only need to understand the decision-maker's environment and the choices available to him. Then we could determine mathematically what his choice would be.

Unfortunately most organizational decision-makers are not completely informed, are not infinitely sensitive, and exhibit only limited rationality. Therefore to understand how decisions are reached we must examine the decision-maker's expectations and his values. Although the decision-maker sees himself as orderly, systematic, and rational, he must estimate the likely consequences of each prospective choice, how much it will cost, whether it will work, and how much utility lies in making the given choice. In making these estimates he displays certain cognitive tendencies and judgmental errors. To understand fully what decision will be made we need to appreciate some of these propensities when human beings are faced with choices. The logical mathematics of the economics of expected utility do apply to understanding choice, but only in relatively simple situations.

Economics of Expected Utility. Logically the expected value of a choice is the amount to be gained from selecting an alternative, multipled by the probability that the solution will pay off. Thus a $3 certainty has an expected value of (1.0) ($3) or $3. The expected value, U_1, of a 40–60 risk involved in earning $10 is .4($10) + .6($0) or $4. If there were protection against complete loss so that instead of this 40–60 alternative yielding $10 or nothing, it provided $10 or $2, then its expected value, U_2, would be enhanced considerably, becoming .4($10) + .6($2) or $5.20, and would represent more potential gain than the $3 certainty. Despite the objectively more valuable but more risky proposal yielding a U of $5.20, many, if not a majority of persons, would prefer to choose the certain $3, particularly if the money represented a large amount. For example, some people may prefer an alternative which has a 40–60 probability of earning $10 than one which gives $3 for certain. But it is doubtful if many would prefer an alternative which has a 40–60 probability of earning 10 million dollars to one which will provide 3 million dollars for certain. Expected values based on utility and perceived probability of obtaining choices unfortunately do not forecast with too much accuracy how individuals of limited rationality will choose.[699] One reason is that decision-makers treat the risk of loss and the probability of gain quite differently.

Avoiding Large Losses. Studies of subjects given the opportunity to accept or reject different bets indicate that they dislike making logically equitable bets where there is even a low probability that they will lose large amounts. All things being equal, it is probable that except for professional gamblers, most people will reject a 1 to 10 bet where they stand to gain $1 and lose $10 although the objective probabilities are 9 out of 10 that they will gain the $1 and only 1 in 10 that they will lose $10. Yet a completely rational player would be indifferent, for the odds and values are mathematically equal.[190]

There is rationality in avoiding the risk of large losses to make small gains. A single large loss may terminate the game by using up all a player's capital. Or, at least, it threatens the player's sense of security. Any other kind of bet does not immediately hold such a risk.

Choosing Among Potential Losses and Gains. In line with this desire to avoid large losses, it may be that we tend to choose the lesser potential loss, if the choice must be made between two losses, regardless of the relative odds. But if the choice is between two possible gains, the surer gain is chosen regardless of its value. In other words, when choosing among two painful alternatives, expected (negative) utility of the choices determines our preference; when choosing among two beneficial alternatives, the expected probabilities of payoff determine our choice.[696]

It is only in relatively simple and transparent situations where the subject who intends to be rational can see and remember easily when he is being consistent, that he is able to maximize his utility if that is what he wants to do. Here he can select the choice which will cost him the least and gain him the most. "But as choices become a little more complicated . . . he becomes much less consistent."[610, p.258] This will happen, for instance, when the choices become less easy to discriminate. As this occurs, the subject will more often erroneously select the poorer of the two choices. Even where there are no real differences between, say, two pieces of ambiguous art or two completely random alternatives, subjects will err in seeing differences and will formulate hypotheses about those differences. And again, error will occur when a person is faced with real differences in likely outcomes which should be easy to discriminate, say, requiring him to choose between *plus* or *minus*, on a series of trials, when *plus* actually will be rewarded randomly on two-thirds of the trials and *minus* will be rewarded on only one-third of the trials. The subject would make the right choice in 6 out of 9 trials if he always chose *plus*. Yet the average subject *event matches*. He follows some nonrandom sequence of choices in which he chooses *plus* in approximately two-thirds of the trials and *minus* in one-third, and where as a consequence he makes the right choice in only 5 out of 9 trials. (He is correct on two-thirds of the trials when he chooses plus and is correct on only one-third of the trials when he chooses minus. That is, for the pluses, he is right $\frac{2}{3} \times \frac{2}{3}$ or $\frac{4}{9}$. For the minuses, he is also right $\frac{1}{3} \times \frac{1}{3}$ or $\frac{1}{9}$. And, $\frac{4}{9} + \frac{1}{9} = \frac{5}{9}$. If he *always* chose plus, he would be right $\frac{2}{3}$ or $\frac{6}{9}$ of the time since pluses are right $\frac{6}{9}$ of the time.[610])

Judgments about the probability of payoffs are complicated by one's past experience as well as by the value of the payoff, although the latter, at least, should have little to do with such judgment.

The utility of payoffs follow a logarithmic trend. To double the utility of $10 requires something worth $40, not $20. Like most psychophysical studies, which suggest that man tends to respond logarithmically to most stimuli, requiring, for instance, four times as much physical noise to hear a sound twice as loud, so it takes more nearly $40 to double $10 in its effects on human evaluators.* This has been demonstrated by seeing how long subjects would continue to react to a prospective payoff

*The actual relation between a physical stimulus (S) and the sensation or response (R) it evokes is described by a power curve, $R=aS^b$. In logarithmic form the equation becomes: $\log R = \log a + b \log S$, where a and b are constants obtained for the particular sense modality involved.

during extinction trials, that is, after payoff for effort was permanently suspended by the experimenter. Two hundred subjects pushed buttons on an electronic slot machine which paid off according to a prearranged schedule. Then payoff stopped altogether. The subjects pushed buttons in the absence of any further payoff to the logarithmic extent of the monetary value of the payoffs they had originally experienced, as shown in Figure 10.5. That is, when the machine ceased delivering coins, the average subject who had been accustomed to receiving a penny for each button pushed, pressed buttons only about 60 times more. When expecting a dime, they continued pressing about 65 times. For a quarter, they pressed about 70 times. When they had been accustomed to receiving 50 cents, they pressed the button without payoff only about 92 times on the average. The psychological impact of money, in this case at least, seemed to suffer a radically diminishing return. One cent generated 60 presses but an additional 49 cents could only yield an extra 32 presses altogether. Figure 10.5 displays these results.[407]

Groups Risk More Than Individuals.   Although the quality of the decision may not differ after the group has deliberated, the group's decision is

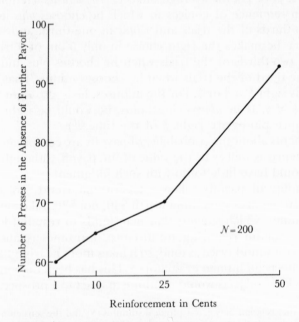

Figure 10.5: The Relationship Between the Amount of Money Reward and the Mean Number of Button Presses to Extinction. (After Lewis & Duncan, 1957, p. 117)

likely to take more risks than that made by a lone individual. In comparison to a control group of individuals making risky decisions in isolation, individuals who discussed decisions and reached consensus but remained personally responsible for the decisions increased risk-taking by about 5 percent. When their group as such became responsible, they collectively increased their willingness to risk by 12.5 percent. Thus discussion, consensus, and the diffusion of responsibility led to increased tolerance for risk.[715] We may infer that bank committees are likely to approve more risky loans than individual loan officers.

An Irrational Group Decision May Emerge from Rational Choices of Its Membership. A purely rational person is transitive in his choices. If Mr. Black prefers apples to bananas, and bananas to cherries, then he will also choose apples over cherries. (If $a > b$ and $b > c$, then $a > c$.) Consider that Mr. Black, Mr. Brown, and Mr. Green prefer the fruits in the following order:

	Members		
	Black	*Brown*	*Green*
First Choice	Apples	Bananas	Cherries
Second Choice	Bananas	Cherries	Apples
Third Choice	Cherries	Apples	Bananas

For Mr. Black, $a > b > c$; for Mr. Brown, $b > c > a$, and for Mr. Green, $c > a > b$. Suppose the trio votes on which fruit to choose. In each case a majority of two of three voters can decide the outcome. Apples are favored over bananas by Mr. Black and Mr. Green; so for the trio, if a vote is taken, $a > b$. Bananas are favored over cherries by Mr. Black and Mr. Brown; so for the trio, $b > c$. If the trio vote is completely rational it should be transitive. Since $a > b$ and $b > c$, then $a > c$; apples should be voted for over cherries. Yet in such a vote both Mr. Brown and Mr. Green favor cherries over apples ($c > a$) and so the trio majority would be irrational or intransitive despite the fact that each of its members, Black, Brown, and Green, are completely rational![568]

Systematic Distortion of Objective Probabilities. Understanding of choice is made more difficult by the increasing distortions which occur in individual's subjective estimates as the objective odds rise. A considerable percentage of the American public is addicted to illegal "numbers" lotteries in which the odds are 1,000 to 1, but the payoff for winning is only 600 to 1 (or 500 to 1 on certain popular numbers). There seems to be a general tendency to overestimate the size of low objective probabilities of success. In the same way we tend to underestimate probabilities of success of those choices with high probabilities. The speculator sees higher probability of success than 100 to 1 in his gambling on what is really a 100 to 1 shot. When the odds are 9 out of 10 that a plan will pay off, investors see less likelihood of success than 9 out of 10. At least, matters feel more risky than they actually are. And as observers of poker, dice, or horse players can readily note, it is usually these subjective probabilities that most determine bets rather than the objective realities of the situation. Slot machine players in particular are usually playing against impossibly unfavorable odds. Classical economics would suggest that no one would play a slot machine after he observed the pattern of payoff, for the player should act completely rational. He would maximize his holdings by not playing at all and keeping what money he had. But the 24-hour-a-day slot machine casinos of Nevada prove otherwise.

Confidence of Decision

Our willingness to risk is obviously directly related to our confidence that we know what outcomes are likely as a consequence of our choice. Studies of confidence provide clues as to how we move to reduce the uncertainty in situations before making final decisions.

As might be expected, we tend to be more confident that an alternative will work as a direct consequence of the previous experience of success or failure of that alternative. For example, when subjects must guess whether a light will signal and whether it will be a right or left light on a panel, they decide on the right light fastest when the right light responds 75 percent of the time, more slowly when the right light signals 50 percent of the time, and most slowly when it works 25 percent of the time.[420] As should be equally obvious, our confidence and how long we take to decide is directly affected by the real physical or social differences in the alternatives from which we must choose. Certainty and speed of decision of laboratory subjects is greatest when they must judge among physical differences which are likewise greatest.[203] Certainty and speed of decision also depend upon the intensity with which one emotionally favors one alternative over another. One is less likely to deliberate over choices about which he already has strong attitudes, for whatever the reason.[536]

We tend to be more confident when we receive more information about an alternative and if the information is more constant. We will attempt to increase our confidence before making a decision depending on the costs and gains from doing so. Thus subjects were given two packs of cards. Each card had a number on it. The subjects had to decide which pack came from a population of cards with a higher mean number. Subjects made more confident decisions about bigger packs and packs of cards on which the numbers did not vary greatly.[328] In this situation when prizes were given for correct decisions and costs attached to receiving more cards before deciding, subjects behaved quite rationally. When the prize was large, they requested and paid for more information before deciding. Conversely, when the cost per card was small, they were more likely to ask for more cards before deciding.[327]

Judgment is fraught with other errors. We have mentioned before the general tendency to accept or agree rather than to object or disagree. Such a tendency becomes more pronounced if we are confronted with more uncertainty and ambiguity. We also become more acquiescent if we are bored or indifferent.

Our judgment of one alternative will be affected by its contrast to other alternatives. It may look good simply because other solutions look bad. In the same way we may accept an alternative because it is embedded in a context of optimistic and hopeful statements, or because it is connected to other actually more promising solutions which are to be tried.

Following Up a Final Decision

The decision process is not complete even after we have made our final decision. For, as shown in Figure 10.1, we must follow up the decision to see whether the consequences were as expected. If the outcomes have occurred as predicted, then the problem is solved. Otherwise a reexamination of the problem may be needed, initiating again the cycle of steps in the decision process.

In the follow-up phase, a particular judgmental phenomenon which is likely to affect accuracy adversely is the tendency to seek justification and validation of one's decisions rather than an objective appraisal of the decision.

The Tendency to Confirm Rather than Disconfirm Decisions. Francis Bacon noted 350 years ago,

The human understanding when it has once adopted an opinion . . . draws all things else to support and agree with it. And though there be a greater number and weight of instances to be found on the other side, yet these it either neglects or despises, or else by some distinction sets aside and rejects; in order that by this great and pernicious predetermination the authority of its former conclusions may remain inviolate.

Once we have made a decision we tend to concentrate on corrobora-tion of its correctness rather than take equal note of subsequent con-tradictory evidence. We become blind to contrary evidence, particularly if the aftereffects of decisions are ambiguous or difficult to evaluate. Since cognitive balance is favored over cognitive dissonance, if the evalu-ation of the wisdom or efficacy of a decision which has been made depends on subjective judgment, it is likely that we will perceive the decision to have been beneficial rather than detrimental when actually it may have had no utility for us.[204] Errors of judgment in reaching the final decision, are thus reinforced, and our subsequent evaluations biased accordingly. For instance, most executives, when queried about the effects of some special training they have received, will respond favorably about the effects on them. And if they must decide on whether the program should be continued, they are more likely to vote to con-tinue than to suspend it regardless of its actual worth or lack of value to the firm.

*   *   *   *   *

Confucius said, "The superior man understands what is right; the inferior man understands what will sell." How can an executive increase his chances of being more like the superior man when faced with prob-lems that are not neatly packaged for him? How can he increase the likelihood that his organizational decisions will be based on reason rather than accident or power plays? These are the substantive questions of this concluding chapter.

Applied mathematics comes to the executive's aid in his efforts to use reason when he can quantify costs, risks, processes, and structures. But such complete rationality is seldom possible. To approach it in the face of the more usual uncertainties and vagaries with which the execu-tive must cope he must develop an understanding of how he actually solves ill-defined problems and the motivational and perceptual distor-tions to which he is subject when doing so. Furthermore, he must bring method into his own problem-solving behavior. He must learn to delay his search for solutions until he has sufficiently analyzed the problem he is attempting to solve; he must learn to delay his selection of solutions until he has thoroughly searched for alternatives.

Finally, in his evaluation of prospective solutions he needs to correct for his own judgmental errors, his confusion of objective risks with subjective preferences to avoid large losses, his greater confidence and irrationality in groups, and his tendency to seek confirmation and reject disconfirmation of the wisdom of his decisions.

REFERENCES

1. ABEGGLEN, J. C. *The Japanese factory.* Glencoe, Ill.: Free Press, 1958.
2. ABENDROTH, W. W. The research and decision-making process. In J. Shera, *et al.* (eds.), *Documentation in action.* New York: Reinhold, 1956.
3. ADAMS, J. S. Wage inequities, productivity and work quality. *Industr. Relat.,* 1963, **3,** 9–16.
4. ADORNO, T. W., *et al. The authoritarian personality.* New York: Harper, 1950.
5. ALGER, L. J. *Suggestion statistics.* New York: Amer. Mgmt. Assoc., 1946, Production series No. 165.
6. ALLPORT, G. W. The trend in motivational theory. *Amer. J. Orthopsychiat.,* 1953, **23,** 107–119.
7. ALLPORT, G. W., & POSTMAN, L. *The psychology of rumor.* New York: Holt, 1947.
8. AMERICAN MANAGEMENT ASSOCIATION. *Principles and patterns of executive compensation.* General Mgmt. Series No. 150. New York: Amer. Mgmt. Assoc., 1950.
9. ANDREWS, R. E., *Leadership and supervision: a survey of research findings.* Personnel Management Series No. 9. Washington: U.S. Civil Service Commission, 1955.
10. ANSBACHER, H. L. Attitudes of German prisoners of war: a study of the dynamics of national-socialistic followership. *Psychol. Monogr.,* 1948, **62,** 1–42.
11. ANSHEN, M. The manager and the black box. *Harvard Bus. Rev.,* 1960, **38**(6), 85–92.
12. ARGYLE, M., GARDER, G., & CIOFFI, F. Supervisory methods related to productivity, absenteeism, and labor turnover. *Hum. Relat.,* 1958, **11,** 23–40.
13. ARGYRIS, C. *Organization of a bank.* New Haven, Conn.: Yale Univ., 1954.
14. ARGYRIS, C. Research trends in executive behavior. *Adv. Mgmt.,* 1956, **21**(3), 6–9.
15. ARMSTRONG, T. O. Developing effective supervisor-employee communication. *Personnel,* 1950, **27,** 70–75.
16. ARONSON, E., & MILLS, J. The effect of severity of initiation on liking for a group. *J. abnorm. soc. Psychol.,* 1959, **59,** 177–181.
17. ASCH, S. E. *Social psychology.* Englewood Cliffs, N.J.: Prentice-Hall, 1952.
18. ASH, P. The SRA employee inventory—a statistical analysis. *Personnel Psychol.,* 1954, **7,** 337–364.

19. ASTIN, A. W. Dimensions of work satisfaction in the occupational choices of college freshmen. *J. appl. Psychol.*, 1958, **42**, 187 – 190.
20. BABCHUK, N., & GOODE, W. J. Work incentives in a self-determined group. *Amer. J. Sociol.*, 1951, **16**, 679 – 687.
21. BAEHR, M. E. A simplified procedure for the measurement of employee attitudes. *J. appl. Psychol.*, 1953, **37**, 163 – 167.
22. BAEHR, M. E. A factorial study of the SRA employee inventory. *Personnel Psychol.*, 1954, **1**, 319 – 336.
23. BAEHR, M. E., & RENCK, R. The definition and measurement of employee morale. *Admin. Sci. Quart.*, 1958, **3**, 157 – 184.
24. BAKER, A. W., & DAVIS, R. C. *Ratios of staff to line employees and stages of differentiation of staff functions.* Columbus: Bur. Bus. Res., Ohio State Univ., 1954.
25. BAKER, G. W. *Recruitment, assignment, and utilization of new research and development of Air Force officers: a study of needs as perceived by two status groups.* CRL-TM-54-1, Randolph Field, Texas, 1954.
26. BALMA, M. J., MALONEY, J. C., & LAWSHE, C. H. The role of the foreman in modern industry. II. Foreman identification with management, work group productivity, and employee attitude toward the foreman. *Personnel Psychol.*, 1958, **11**, 367 – 378.
27. BARBICHON, G., & MOSCOVICI, S. Analyse dimensionnelle de l'entreprise et du milieu de travail. *Bull. Cent. etud. rech. Psychotech.*, 1958, **4**, 291 – 398.
28. BARITZ, L. *The servants of power: a history of the use of social science in American industry.* Middletown, Conn.: Wesleyan Univ., 1960.
29. BARKIN, S. *The decline of the labor movement.* Santa Barbara, Calif.: Center for the Study of Democratic Institutions, 1961.
30. BARNARD, C. I. *The functions of the executive.* Cambridge, Mass.: Harvard Univ., 1938.
31. BARNARD, C. I. Functions of status systems in formal organizations. In R. Dubin (ed.), *Human relations in administration.* Englewood Cliffs, N.J.: Prentice-Hall, 1951.
32. BARNES, L. B. *Organizational systems and engineering groups.* Boston: Harvard Bus. Sch., 1960.
33. BARNLUND, D. C. A comparative study of individual, majority, and group judgment. *J. abnorm. soc. Psychol.*, 1959, **58**, 55 – 60.
34. BASS, B. M. Ultimate criteria of organizational worth. *Personnel Psychol.*, 1952, **5**, 157 – 173.
35. BASS, B. M. Feelings of pleasantness and work group efficiency. *Personnel Psychol.*, 1954, **7**, 81 – 91.
36. BASS, B. M. The leaderless group discussion. *Psychol. Bull.*, 1954, **51**, 465 – 492.
37. BASS, B. M. Development and evaluation of a scale of social acquiescence. *J. abnorm. soc. Psychol.*, 1956, **53**, 296 – 299.
38. BASS, B. M. Leadership opinions as forecasts of supervisory success. *J. appl. Psychol.*, 1956, **40**, 345 – 346.
39. BASS, B. M. Undiscriminated operant acquiescence. *Educ. psychol., Measmt.*, 1957, **17**, 83 – 85.
40. BASS, B. M. Leadership opinions as forecasts of supervisory success: a replication. *Personnel Psychol.*, 1958, **11**, 515 – 518.
41. BASS, B. M. *Leadership, psychology, and organizational behavior.* New York: Harper, 1960.

42. BASS, B. M. *The orientation inventory.* Palo Alto, Calif.: Consulting Psychologists, 1962. See also: Bass, B. M. and Dunteman, G. Behavior in groups as a function of self-, interaction, and task orientation. *J. abnorm. soc. Psychol.,* 1963, **66,** 419–428.

43. BASS, B. M. *Effects on negotiators of their prior experience in strategy or study groups.* Tech. Rept. 1, Contract Nonr 624(14). Pittsburgh: Univ. of Pittsburgh, 1963.

44. BASS, B. M. Industrial organization for the space age. *Pittsburgh Bus. Rev.,* 1964, **34**(1), 5–13.

44a. BASS, B. M. Business gaming for organizational research. *Mgmt. Sci.,* 1964, **10,** 545–556.

45. BASS, B. M., & DUNTEMAN, G. Biases in the evaluation of one's own group, its allies and opponents. *J. Conflict Resolution,* 1963, **7,** 16–20.

46. BASS, B. M., HURDER, W. P., & ELLIS, N. *Assessing human performance under stress.* Final Tech. Rept., Contract AF 33(616)134. Baton Rouge: Louisiana State Univ., 1954.

47. BASS, B. M., & LEAVITT, H. J. Experiments in planning and operating. *Mgmt. Sci.,* 1963, **9**(4), 574–585.

48. BASS, B. M., & VAUGHAN, J. A. Experimenting with the man-in-the-middle. Paper presented at the Ford Foundation Seminar on the Social Sciences in Business. Pittsburgh: Univ. of Pittsburgh, 1962.

49. BASS, B. M., & WURSTER, C. R. Effects of the nature of the problem on LGD performance. *J. appl. Psychol.,* 1953, **37,** 96–99.

50. BASS, B. M., & WURSTER, C. R. Effects of company rank on LGD performance of oil refinery supervisors. *J. appl. Psychol.,* 1953, **37,** 100–104.

51. BAUMGARTEL, H. Leadership, motivations, and attitudes in research laboratories. *J. soc. Issues,* 1956, **12**(2), 24–31.

52. BAUMGARTEL, H., & SOBEL, R. Background and organizational factors in absenteeism. *Personnel Psychol.,* 1959, **12,** 431–443.

53. BAVELAS, A. Communication patterns in task-oriented groups. *J. acoust. soc. Amer.,* 1950, **22,** 725–730.

54. BEHREND, H. Absence and labour turnover in a changing economic climate. *Occup. Psychol.,* 1953, **27,** 69–79.

55. BELCHER, D. W. Employee and executive compensation. In H. G. Heneman, *et al., Employment relations research.* New York: Harper, 1960.

56. BELL, D. A. *The end of ideology.* Glencoe, Ill.: Free Press, 1960.

57. BELLOWS, C. S., & RUSH, C. H. Reading abilities of business executives. *J. appl. Psychol.,* 1952, **36,** 1–4.

58. BELLOWS, R. M. *Psychology of personnel in business and industry.* Englewood Cliffs, N.J.: Prentice-Hall, 1949, 1954.

59. BELOUSOV, V. V. Experimental geology. *Sci. Amer.,* 1961, **204,** 96–107.

60. BENDIG, A. W., & STILLMAN, E. Dimensions of job incentives among college students. *J. appl. Psychol.,* 1958, **42,** 367–371.

61. BENGE, E. J., & COPELL, D. F. Employee morale survey. *Modern Mgmt.,* 1947, **7**(1), 19–22.

62. BENNETT, E. B. Discussion, decisions, commitment, and consensus in "group decision." *Hum. Relat.,* 1955, **8,** 251–273.

63. BENNIS, W. G. Leadership theory and administrative behavior: the problem of authority. *Admin. Sci. Quart.,* 1959, **4,** 259–301.

64. BENNIS, W. G. Revisionist theory of leadership. *Harvard Bus. Rev.,* 1961, **40**(2), 26–36, 146–150.

65. BESCO, R. O., & LAWSHE, C. H. Foreman leadership as perceived by supervisors and subordinates. *Personnel Psychol.*, 1959, **12**, 573–582.

66. BILLS, M. A. Relation of mental alertness to position and permanency in company. *J. appl. Psychol.*, 1923, **7**, 154–156.

67. BLAKE, R. R., & MOUTON, J. S. *Group dynamics—Key to decision-making.* Houston: Gulf Publishing, 1961.

68. BLAKE, R. R., & MOUTON, J. S. The intergroup dynamics of win-lose conflict and problem-solving collaboration in union-management relations. In M. Sherif (ed.), *Intergroup Relations and Leadership.* New York: Wiley, 1962, 94–140.

69. BLAKE, R. R., & MOUTON, J. S. Union-management relations: from conflict to collaboration. *Personnel*, 1961, **38**, 38–51.

70. BLAU, P. M. Patterns of interaction among a group of officials in a government agency. *Hum. Relat.*, 1954, **7**, 337–348.

71. BLAU, P. M., & SCOTT, W. R. *Formal organizations.* San Francisco: Chandler, 1962.

72. BLAUNER, R. Work satisfaction and industrial trends in modern society. In W. Galenson & S. M. Lipset (eds.), *Labor and trade unionism.* New York: 1960.

73. BLOOM, B. S., & BRODER, L. S. Problem-solving processes of college students. *Suppl. Educ. Monog.*, 1950, No. 73.

74. BLUESTONE, A. Major studies of workers' reasons for job choice. *Monthly Labor Rev.*, 1955, **78**, 301–306.

75. BLUM, A. A. Collective bargaining: ritual or reality? *Harvard Bus. Rev.*, 1961, **39**(6), 63–69.

76. BLUM, M. *Readings in experimental industrial psychology.* Englewood Cliffs, N.J.: Prentice-Hall, 1952.

77. BLUM, M. L., & RUSS, J. A study of employee attitudes toward various incentives. *Personnel*, 1942, **19**, 438–444.

78. BOCK, R. H. A new method for teaching linear programming. *J. Acad. Mgmt.* 1962, **5**, 82–86.

79. BRADFORD, L. P., & LIPPITT, R. Building a democratic work group. *Personnel*, 1945, **22**, 142–148.

80. BRAYFIELD, A. H., & CROCKETT, W. H. Employee attitudes and employee performance. *Psychol. Bull.*, 1955, **52**, 396–424.

81. BRAYFIELD, A. H., WELLS, R. V., & STRATE, M. W. Interrelationships among measures of job satisfaction and general satisfaction. *J. appl. Psychol.*, 1957, **41**, 201–205.

82. BRODE, W. R. The growth of science and a national science program. *Amer. Sci.*, 1962, **50**(1), 1–28.

83. BROOKS, E. What successful executives do. *Personnel*, 1955, **32**, 210–225.

84. BROWN, C. W., & GHISELLI, E. E. Prediction of labor turnover by aptitude tests. *J. app. Psychol.*, 1953, **37**, 9–12.

85. BROWN, W. *Exploration in management.* New York: Wiley, 1960.

86. BROWNE, C. G. Study of executive leadership in business. I. The R, A, and D scales. *J. appl. Psychol.*, 1949, **33**, 521–526.

87. BRUNER, D. Has success spoiled the unions? *Harvard Bus. Rev.*, 1960, **38**(3), 73–78.

88. BRUNER, J. S., GOODNOW, J. J., & AUSTIN, G. A. *A study of thinking.* New York: Wiley, 1956.

89. BURNS, T. The direction of activity and communication in a depart-

mental executive group: a quantitative study in British engineering factory with a self-recording technique. *Hum. Relat.*, 1954, **7**, 73 – 97.

90. BURNS, T. Micropolitics: mechanisms of institutional change. *Adm. Sci. Quart.*, 1961 – 1962, **6**, 257 – 281.

91. BURNS, T., & STALKER, G. M. *The management of innovation.* Chicago: Quadrangle, 1961.

92. BURTT, H. B. *Psychology and industrial efficiency.* New York: Appleton-Century, 1929.

93. BURWEN, L. S., & CAMPBELL, D. T. The generality of attitudes toward authority and nonauthority figures. *J. abnorm. soc. Psychol.*, 1957, **54**, 24 – 31.

94. CAMPBELL, D. T. Enhancement of contrast as composite habit. *J. abnorm. soc. Psychol.*, 1956, **53**, 350 – 355.

95. CAMPBELL, D. T. Systematic error on the part of human links in communication systems. *Information and Control*, 1958, **1**, 334 – 369.

96. CAMPBELL, D. T., & CHAPMAN, J. P. Testing for stimulus equivalence among authority figures by similarity in trait description. *J. consult. Psychol.*, 1957, **21**, 253 – 256.

97. CAMPBELL, H. Group incentive payment schemes: the effects of talk, of understanding and of group size. *Occup. Psychol.*, 1952, **26**, 15 – 21.

98. CAMPBELL, J. D. Subjective aspects of occupational status. *Amer. Psychol.*, 1954, **7**, 308(a).

99. CAMPBELL, R. E. The prestige of industries. *J. appl. Psychol.*, 1960, **44**, 1 – 5.

100. CARLSON, R. E., DAWIS, R. V., ENGLAND, G. W., & LOFQUIST, L. H. *The measurement of employment satisfaction.* Minnesota Studies in Vocational Rehabilitation. XIII. Bulletin 35, p. 49. Minneapolis: Industrial Relations Center, Univ. of Minnesota, 1962.

101. CARLUCCI, C., & CRISSY, W. J. E. How readable are employee handbooks? *Personnel Psychol.*, 1951, **4**, 383 – 395.

102. CARTWRIGHT, D. Social psychology and group processes. *Annual rev. Psychol.*, 1957, **8**, 211 – 236.

103. CARTWRIGHT, D., & ZANDER, A. F. (eds.) *Group dynamics: research and theory.* Evanston, Ill.: Row, Peterson, 1953, 1962.

104. CATTELL, R. B. *Factor analysis.* New York: Harper, 1952.

105. CATTELL, R. B. On the theory of group learning. *J. soc. Psychol.*, 1953, **37**, 27 – 52.

106. CENTERS, R. *The psychology of social classes: a study of class consciousness.* Princeton, N.J.: Princeton Univ., 1949.

107. CENTERS, R., & CANTRIL, H. Income satisfaction and income aspiration. *J. abnorm. soc. Psychol.*, 1946, **41**, 64 – 69.

108. CHALFEN, L. Psychological effects of unionism on the member. *J. soc. Psychol.*, 1947, **25**, 133 – 137.

109. CHAMBERLAIN, C. J. Coming era in engineering management. *Harvard Bus. Rev.*, 1961, **39**(5), 87 – 94.

110. CHAPANIS, A., GARNER, W. R., & MORGAN, C. T. *Applied experimental psychology.* New York: Wiley, 1949.

111. CHAPMAN, R. L., & KENNEDY, J. L. *The background and implications of the Rand Corporation Systems Research Laboratory studies.* RAND Paper P-740, 1955.

112. CHAPMAN, R. L., KENNEDY, J. L., NEWALL, A., & BIEL, W. C. The Systems

Research Laboratory's air-defense experiments. In H. Guetzkow (ed.), *Simulation in social science: readings.* Englewood Cliffs, N.J.: Prentice-Hall, 1962.

113.   CHORUS, A. The basic law of rumor. *J. abnorm. soc. Psychol.*, 1953, **48**, 313–314.

114.   CHURCHILL, N. C., COOPER, W. W., & SAINSBURY, T. *Auditing and audits per se in field and laboratory contexts.* ONR Research Memo 108. Contract Nonr 760(01). Pittsburgh: Carnegie Institute of Technology, 1963.

115.   CHURCHMAN, C. W., ACKOFF, R., & ARNOFF, E. L. *Introduction to operations research.* New York: Wiley, 1957.

116.   CLARK, C. H. *Brainstorming.* New York: Doubleday, 1958.

117.   CLARK, D. F., & ACKOFF, R. L. A report on some organizational experiments. *Operations Research*, 1959, **7**(3), 279–293.

118.   CLARKSON, G. *Portfolio selection: a simulation of trust investment.* Englewood Cliffs, N.J.: Prentice-Hall, 1962.

119.   CLELAND, S. *The influence of plant size on industrial relations.* Princeton, N.J.: Princeton Univ., 1955.

120.   CLOUGH, D. J. *Concepts in management science.* Englewood Cliffs, N.J.: Prentice-Hall, 1963.

121.   COCH, L., & FRENCH, J. R. P. Overcoming resistance to change. *Hum. Relat.*, 1948, **1**, 512–532.

122.   COFER, C. N. Motivation. *Annual rev. Psychol.*, 1959, **10**, 173–202.

123.   COHEN, A. R. Upward communication in experimentally created hierarchies. *Hum. Relat.*, 1958, **11**, 41–53.

124.   COHEN, D., WHITMYRE, J. W., & FUNK, W. H. Effect of group cohesiveness and training upon creative thinking. *J. appl. Psychol.*, 1964, **44**, 319–322.

125.   COHEN, K. J., CYERT, R. M., *et al.* The Carnegie Tech management game. *J. Bus.*, 1960, **33**, 303-321.

126.   COHEN, K. J., & RHENMAN, E. The role of management games in education and research. *Mgmt. Sci.*, 1961, **7**, 131–166.

127.   COLBY, A. N., & TIFFIN, J. The reading ability of industrial supervisors. *Personnel*, 1950, **27**, 156–158.

128.   COMREY, A. L., HIGH, W., & WILSON, R. C. Factors influencing organizational effectiveness. VI. A survey of aircraft workers. *Personnel Psychol.*, 1955, **8**, 79–100.

129.   COMREY, A. L., HIGH, W. S., & WILSON, R. C. Factors influencing organizational effectiveness. VII. A survey of aircraft supervisors. *Personnel Psychol.*, 1955, **8**, 245–257.

130.   COMREY, A. L., PFIFFNER, J. J., & BEEM, H. P. Factors influencing organizational effectiveness. II. The Department of Employment survey. *Personnel Psychol.*, 1953, **6**, 65–79.

131.   CONNER, F. G. Shelf help. *Civil service J.*, 1961, **1**, 30–31.

132.   CORSON, J. J. Innovation challenges conformity. *Harvard Bus. Rev.*, 1962, **40**(3), 67–74.

133.   COX, D. *Attitudes toward repetitive work.* London: N.I.I.P. Report No. 9, 1953.

134.   COX, D., & SHARP, K. M. D. Research on the unit of work. *Occup. Psychol.*, 1951, **25**, 90–108.

135.   CRAIG, H. F. *Administering a conversion to electronic accounting: a case study.* Boston: Div. of Res., Harvard Bus. Sch., 1955.

136. CRANDALL, R. E. De-emphasized wage incentives. *Harvard Bus. Rev.*, 1960, **40**(2), 113–116.

137. CRITES, J. O. Factor analytic definitions of vocational motivation. *J. appl. Psychol.*, 1961, **45**, 330–337.

138. CYERT, R. M., DILL, W. R., & MARCH, J. G. The role of expectations in business decision-making. *Admin. Sci. Quart.*, 1958, **3**, 307–340.

139. CYERT, R. M., & MARCH, J. G. A behavioral theory of organizational objectives. In M. Haire (ed.), *Modern organization theory.* New York: Wiley, 1959.

140. CYERT, R. M., & MARCH, J. G. *A behavioral theory of the firm.* Englewood Cliffs, N. J.: Prentice-Hall, 1963.

141. CYERT, R. M., SIMON, H. A., & TROW, D. B. Observation of a business decision. *J. Bus.*, 1956, **29**, 237–248.

142. DAHLE, T. L. Transmitting information to employees: a study of five methods. *Personnel*, 1954, **31**, 243–246.

143. DALE, E. Management must be made accountable. *Harvard Bus. Rev.*, 1960, **38**(2), 49–59.

144. DALE, E. New perspectives in managerial decision-making. *J. Bus.*, 1953, **26**, 1–8.

145. DALTON, M. Conflicts between staff and line managerial officers. *Amer. sociol. Rev.*, 1950, **15**, 342–351.

146. DALTON, M. Unofficial union-management relations. *Amer. sociol. Rev.*, 1950, **15**, 611–619.

147. DALTON, M. Managing the managers. In A. H. Rubenstein and C. J. Haverstroh, (eds.) *Some theories of organization.* Homewood, Ill.: Irwin, 1960.

148. DAVIS, K. A method of studying communication patterns in organizations. *Personnel Psychol.*, 1953, **6**, 301–312.

149. DAVIS, K. Management communication and the grapevine. *Harvard Bus. Rev.*, 1953, **31**, 43–49.

150. DAVIS, K., & ST. GERMAIN, E. E. An opinion survey of a regional union group. *J. appl. Psychol.*, 1952, **36**, 285–290.

151. DAVIS, L. E., & WERLING, R. Job design factors. *Occup. Psychol.*, 1960, **34**, 109–132.

152. DAVIS, N. M. Attitudes to work among building operatives. *Occup. Psychol.*, 1948, **22**, 56–62.

153. DAVIS, N. M. Some psychology conflicts caused by group bonus methods of payment. *Brit. J. Industr. Med.*, 1953, **10**, 18–26.

154. DAWSON, D. H. Management techniques and personnel development. *Management International*, 1961, **3**, 5–12.

155. DAY, R. C., & HAMBLIN, R. L. *Some effects of close and punitive styles of supervision.* Tech. Rept. 8, Contract Nonr 816(11). St. Louis: Washington Univ., 1961.

156. DEAN, L. R. Union activity and dual loyalty. *Industr. labor relat. Rev.*, 1954, **7**, 449–460.

157. DEARBORN, D. C., & SIMON, H. A. Selective perception: a note on the departmental identifications of executives. *Sociometry*, 1958, **21**, 140–144.

158. DEARDEN, J. Interdivisional pricing. *Harvard Bus. Rev.*, 1960, **38**(1), 117–125.

159. DE CHARMS, R., & BRIDGEMAN, W. *Leadership compliance and group behavior.* Tech. Rept. 9, Contract Nonr 816(11). St. Louis: Washington Univ., 1961.

160. DE CHARMS, R., & HAMBLIN, R. L. *Structural factors and individual needs in group behavior.* Annual Rept. Contract Nonr 816(11). St. Louis: Washington Univ., 1960.

161. DEEG, M. E., & PATERSON, D. G. Changes in social status of occupations. *Occupations*, 1947, **25**, 205–208.

162. DENT, J. K. Organizational correlates of the goals of business managements. *Personnel Psychol.*, 1959, **12**, 365–396.

163. DEUTSCH, M. An experimental study of the effects of cooperation and competition upon group processes. *Hum. Relat.*, 1949, **2**, 199–231.

164. DEUTSCH, M. The effects of past experience of success or failure, the perceived attitudes of other members and the probability of goal attainment upon member attitudes and group performance. *Amer. Psychol.*, 1954, **9**, 355 (Abstract).

164a. DEUTSCH, M. Conditions affecting cooperation I. Factors related to the initiation of cooperation. II. Trust and cooperation. Final Tech. Rept. Nonr 285(10). Research Center for Human Relations, New York Univ., 1957.

165. DEUTSCH, M. Some factors affecting membership motivation and achievement motivation in a group. *Hum. Relat.*, 1959, **12**, 81–95.

166. DEUTSCH, M. Trust and suspicion. *J. Conflict Resolution*, 1959, **2**, 265–279.

167. DICKINSON, Z. C. *Compensatory industrial effort.* New York: Ronald, 1937.

168. DILL, W. R. Environment as an influence on managerial autonomy. *Admin. Sci. Quart.*, 1958, **2**, 409–443.

169. DILL, W. R. What management games do best. *Bus. Horizons*, 1961, **4**, 55–64.

170. DOBBINS, D. A., & BASS, B. M. Differential effects of unemployment on white and Negro prison admissions in Louisiana. *J. crim. law crim. pol. Sci.*, 1958, **48**, 522–525.

171. DODD, S. C. Diffusion is predictable: testing probability models for laws of interaction. *Amer. sociol. Rev.*, 1955, **20**, 392–401.

172. DOUGLAS, A. *Industrial peace making.* New York: Columbia Univ., 1962.

173. DREWES, D. W., & BLANCHARD, R. E. A factorial study of labor arbitration cases. *Personnel Psychol.*, 1959, **12**, 303–310.

174. DRUCKER, P. F. *Concept of the corporation.* New York: John Day, 1946.

175. DUBIN, R. The efficiency of bureaucratic administration. In R. Dubin (ed.), *Human relations in administration.* Englewood Cliffs, N. J.: Prentice-Hall, 1951.

176. DUBIN, R. Technical characteristics of a bureaucracy. In R. Dubin (ed.), *Human relations in administration.* Englewood Cliffs, N. J.: Prentice-Hall, 1951.

177. DUBIN, R. Upward orientation toward superiors. In R. Dubin (ed.), *Human relations in administration.* Englewood Cliffs, N. J.: Prentice-Hall, 1951.

178. DUBIN, R. Stability of human organizations. In M. Haire (ed.), *Modern organization theory.* New York: Wiley, 1959.

179. DUBOS, R. Can man keep up with history? *Horizon*, 1962, **5**, 4–9.

180. DUNLAP, J. W. The management of morale. *Personnel Psychol.*, 1950, **3**, 353–359.

181. DUNLAP, J. W. Professional relations with clients. Symposium: Improving professional relationships. *Amer. Psychol.*, 1961, **16**, 439(a).

182. DUNNETTE, M. D. Personnel management. *Annual rev. Psychol.*, 1962, **13**, 285–314.

183. DUNNETTE, M. D., & BASS, B. M. Behavioral scientists and personnel management. *Industr. Relat.*, 1963, **2**(3), 115–130.

184. DUNNETTE, M. D., CAMPBELL, J., & JAASTAD, K. The effect of group participation on brainstorming effectiveness for two industrial samples. *J. appl. Psychol.*, 1963, **47**, 30–37.

185. DUNNETTE, M. D., & HENEMAN, H. G., JR. Influence of scale administrator on employe attitude responses. *J. appl. Psychol.*, 1956, **40**, 73–77.

186. EATON, J. W. Social processes of professional teamwork. *Amer. sociol. Rev.*, 1951, **16**, 706–713.

187. ECKERMAN, A. C. An analysis of grievance and aggrieved employes in a machine shop and foundry. *J. appl. Psychol.*, 1948, **32**, 255–269.

188. ECONOMIC RESEARCH DEPARTMENT. *Fringe benefits 1959.* Washington: U.S. Chamber of Commerce, 1960.

189. EDITORIAL STAFF. *Successful employe benefit plans.* Englewood Cliffs, N. J.: Hall, 1952.

190. EDWARDS, W. The theory of decision making. *Psychol. Bull.*, 1954, **51**, 380–417.

191. EDWARDS, W. Men and computers. In R. Gagne (ed.), *Psychological principles in system development.* New York: Holt, Rinehart & Winston, 1962.

192. EHRLICH, D., GUTTMAN, I., & SCHÖNBACH, P. Postdecision exposure to relevant information *J. abnorm. soc. Psychol.*, 1957, **54**, 98–102.

193. EMPLOYE RELATIONS DEPARTMENT. *The human problems in a merger.* Esso Standard Oil Company, 1959.

194. EMPLOYE RELATIONS DEPARTMENT, INTERSTATE OIL PIPELINE COMPANY. A readership survey of "the liner." *Soc. Sci. Res. Repts.* IV. *Surveys and inventories.* Standard Oil of N. J., 1962.

195. EVANS, C. E. & LASEAU, L. N. My job contest—an experiment in new employe relations methods. *Personnel Psychol.*, 1949, **2**, 1–16, 185–228, 311–367, 461–490.

196. FALK, B. G. The mutation of organizational principles in large companies. *Management International.*, 1961, **3**, 21–29.

197. FAUNCE, W. A. Automation in the automobile industry: some consequences for in-plant social structure. *Amer. sociol. Rev.*, 1958, **23**, 401–407.

198. FEIERBEND, R. L., & JANIS, I. L. An experimental comparison of two ways of organizing positive and negative arguments in persuasive communications. *Amer. Psychol.*, 1954, **8**, 362(a).

199. FEINBERG, M. R. Performance review . . . threat or promise? *Supervisory Mgmt.*, 1961, **6**(5), 2–12.

200. FESHBACH, S. The consequences of fear-arousal in public health education. *Proceedings of the XIV Int. Congr. of Appl. Psychol.* Copenhagen: Munksgaard, 1961,

201. FESHBACH, S., & SINGER, R. The effects of personal and shared threats upon social prejudice. *J. abnorm. soc. Psychol.*, 1957, **54**, 411–416.

202. FESHBACH, S., & SINGER, R. The effects of fear-arousal and suppression of fear upon social perception. *J. abnorm. soc. Psychol.*, 1957, **55**, 283–288.

203. FESTINGER, L. Studies in decision. I. Decision time, relative frequency of judgment and subjective confidence as related to physical stimulus difference. *J. exper. Psychol.*, 1943, **32**, 291–306.

204. FESTINGER, L. *A theory of cognitive dissonance.* Evanston, Ill.: Row, Peterson, 1957,

205. FESTINGER, L. The psychological effects of insufficient rewards. *Amer. Psychol.*, 1961, **16**, 1 – 11.
206. FIEDLER, F. E. *Social perception and group effectiveness.* Annual tech. Rept. Contract N6ori – 07135. Urbana: Univ. of Illinois, 1956.
207. FINE, B. J., & WEISS, W. *Conclusion-drawing, communicator credibility and anxiety as factors in opinion change.* Tech. Rept. 5, Contract Nonr 492(04). Boston: Boston Univ., 1956.
208. FISCH, G. G. Line-staff is obsolete. *Harvard Bus. Rev.*, 1961, **39**(5), 67 – 79.
209. FISHMAN, L. Limitations of the business executive as government administrators. *J. Bus.*, 1952, **25**, 89 – 95.
210. FISKE, D. W. Values, theory and the criterion problem. *Personnel Psychol.*, 1951, **4**, 93 – 98.
211. FLEISHMAN, E. A. Leadership climate, human relations training, and supervisory behavior. *Personnel Psychol.*, 1953, **6**, 205 – 222.
212. FLEISHMAN, E. A. The description of supervisory behavior. *J. appl. Psychol.*, 1953, **36**, 1 – 6.
213. FLEISHMAN, E. A. The measurement of leadership attitudes in industry. *J. appl. Psychol.*, 1953, **36**, 153 – 158.
214. FLEISHMAN, E. A., & HARRIS, E. F. Patterns of leadership behavior related to employe grievances and turnover. *Personnel Psychol.*, 1962, **15**, 43 – 56.
215. FLESH, R. A new readability yardstick. *J. appl. Psychol.*, 1948, **32**, 221 – 233.
216. FOA, U. G. Relation of workers' expectation to satisfaction with supervisor. *Personnel Psychol.*, 1957, **10**, 161 – 168.
217. FORM, W. H., & MILLER, D. C. *Industry, labor and community.* New York: Harper, 1960.
218. FREDERIKSON, N. In-basket tests and factors in administrative performance. In H. Guetzkow (ed.), *Simulation in social science: readings.* Englewood Cliffs; N. J.: Prentice-Hall, 1962.
219. FREEMAN, G. L., & TAYLOR, E. K. *How to pick leaders.* New York: Funk, 1950.
220. FRENCH, E. G. Motivation as a variable in work-partner selection. *J. abnorm. soc. Psychol.*, 1956, **53**, 96 – 99.
221. FRENCH, J. R. P., JR. An experimental study of resistance to influence. In *Annual Rept.*, Task Order Nonr 1224(11). Ann Arbor: Res. Center for Group Dynamics, Univ. of Michigan, 1957.
222. FRENCH, J. R. P., JR. The effects of the industrial environment on mental health: a theoretical approach. *Amer. Psychol.*, 1960, **15**, 453(a).
223. FRENCH, J. R. P., JR., ISRAEL, J., & ÅS, D. An experiment on participation in a Norwegian factory: interpersonal dimensions of decision-making. *Hum. Relat.*, 1960, **13**, 3 – 19.
224. FRYE, R., CASSENS, F. P., & VEGAS, O. V. Learning set as a determinant of perceived cooperation and competition. *Amer. Psychol.*, 1964, **19**, 482(a).
225. FRYE, R. L., & STRITCH, T. M. *Effect of group size on public and private coalescence.* Tech. Rept. 24, Contract N7onr 35609. Hattiesburg: Mississippi Southern College, 1960.
226. GAIENNIE, L. R. An approach to supervisory organizational control in industry. *Personnel Psychol.*, 1950, **3**, 41 – 52.
227. GAIENNIE, L. R. Organizational control in business. *J. appl. Psychol.*, 1954, **38**, 289 – 292.

228. GALBRAITH, J. K. *The affluent society.* Boston: Houghton Mifflin, 1958.

229. GARDNER, B. B. *Human relations in industry.* Homewood, Ill.: Irwin, 1947.

230. GEISLER, M. A. The simulation of a large scale military activity. *Mgmt. Sci.*, 1959, **5**(4), 359–368.

231. GEISLER, M. A., & STEGER, W. A. How to plan for management in new systems. *Harvard Bus. Rev.*, 1962, **5,** 103–110.

232. GELLERMAN, S. W. The company personality. *Mgmt. Rev.*, 1959, **48,** 4–8, 69–76.

233. GENNERO, E. Notes on the subject of business administration as a science. *Management International,* 1961, **3,** 83–89.

234. GERARD, H. B. Some effects of involvement upon evaluation. *J. abnorm. soc. Psychol.*, 1958, **57,** 118–119.

235. GIBB, J. R. The effects of group size and of threat reduction upon creativity in a problem-solving situation. Tech. Rept. 7, Contract Nonr-3088 (00). La Jolla: Western Behavioral Sciences Institute, 1964.

236. GIBB, J. R. *Factors producing defensive behavior within groups.* Final Tech. Rept. Contract Nonr 1147(03). Boulder: Univ. of Colorado, 1956.

237. GIBB, J. R. The T-group as a climate for trust formation. In BRADFORD, L. P., GIBB, J. R., & BENNE, K. D. *T-group theory and laboratory method: innovation in re-education.* New York: Wiley, 1964.

238. GIBBONS, G. C. *Stabilization of employment is good management.* Chicago: Amer. Mgmt. Assoc., Personnel Conf., February, 1953.

239. GIESE, W. J., & RUTER, H. W. An objective analysis of morale. *J. appl. Psychol.*, 1949, **33,** 421–427.

240. GILCHRIST, J. C., SHAW, M. E., & WALKER, L. C. Some effects of unequal distribution of information in a wheel group structure. *J. abnorm. soc. Psychol.*, 1954, **49,** 554–556

241. GILMER, B. V. H. Psychological aspects of women in industry. *Personnel Psychol.*, 1957, **10,** 439–452.

242. GILMER, B. V. H. *Industrial psychology.* New York: McGraw-Hill, 1961.

243. GLANZER, M., & GLASER, R. Techniques for the study of group structure and behavior. II. Empirical studies of the effects of structure in small groups. *Psychol. Bull.*, 1961, **58,** 1–27.

244. GLEASON, J. G. Attitude vs. information on the Taft–Hartley law. *Personnel Psychol.*, 1949, **2,** 293–299.

245. GOLD, R. Janitors vs. tenants: a status-income dilemma. *Amer. J. Sociol.*, 1951–1952, **57,** 486–493.

246. GOLDEN, C. S., & RUTTENBERG, H. J. *Motives for union membership. The dynamics of industrial democracy.* New York: Harper, 1942.

247. GOLDMAN, M., HORWITZ, M., & LEE, F. J. *Alternative classroom standards concerning management of hostility and effects on student learning.* Preliminary Rept. Contract N6ori07144, Bur. Educ. Res. Urbana: Univ. of Illinois, 1955.

248. GOMBERG, W. The use of psychology in industry: a trade union point of view. *Mgmt. Sci.*, 1957, **3,** 348–370.

249. GOODCHILDS, J., SCHONFIELD, J., & GIBB, J. R. *Some effects of group problem-solving of an enforced separation of problem-solving stages.* Tech. Rept. 8, Contract Nonr 1147(03). Washington. Nat'l. Training Laboratories, 1961.

250. GORDON, R. A. *Business leadership in the large corporation.* Washington: Brookings Institution, 1945.

251. GOULDNER, A. W. *Patterns of industrial bureaucracy.* Glencoe, Ill.: Free Press, 1954.
252. GRAHAM, S. *American culture.* New York: Harper, 1957.
253. GRANICK, D. *The Red executive.* New York: Doubleday, 1961.
254. GRANT, D. L. A factor analysis of managers' ratings. *J. appl. Psychol.,* 1955, **39,** 283–286.
255. GRAY, A. P. Afterthoughts on Fawley. *Occup. Psychol.,* 1955, **29,** 117–124.
256. GRAYSON, C. J., JR. *Decisions under uncertainty: drilling decisions by oil and gas operators.* Boston: Harvard Grad. Sch. Bus. Admin., 1960.
257. GREER, F. L. *Leader indulgence and group performance.* Washington. General Electric, 1960.
258. GRIFFITH, J. W., KERR, W. A., *et al.* Changes in subjective fatigue and readiness for work during the eight-hour shift. *J. appl. Psychol.,* 1950, **34,** 163–166.
259. GUETZKOW, H. Inter-agency committee usage. *Publ. admin. Rev.,* 1950, **10,** 190–196.
260. GUETZKOW, H. Isolation and collaboration: a partial theory of international relations. *J. Conflict Resolution,* 1957, **1,** 48–68.
261. GUETZKOW, H., & DILL, W. R. Factors in the organizational development of task-oriented groups. *Sociometry,* 1957, **20,** 175–204.
262. GUETZKOW, H., & GYR, J. An analysis of conflict in decision-making groups. *Hum. Relat.,* 1954, **7,** 367–382.
263. GUETZKOW, H., & KRIESBERG, M. *Executive use of the administrative conference.* New York: Amer. Mgmt. Assoc., 1950.
264. GUETZKOW, H., & SIMON, H. A. The impact of certain communication nets upon organization and performance in task-oriented groups. *Mgmt. Sci.,* 1955, **1,** 233–250.
265. GUILFORD, J. P. *A revised structure of intellect.* Reports from the Psychological Laboratory, No. 19. Los Angeles: Univ. of Southern Calif., 1957.
266. GUION, R. M. The employee load of first line supervisors. *Personnel Psychol.,* 1953, **6,** 223–244.
267. GUION, R. M. Industrial morale: the problem of terminology. *Personnel Psychol.,* 1958, **11,** 59–64.
268. GURIN, G., VEROFF, J., & FELD, S. *Americans view their mental health: A nationwide interview study.* New York: Basic Books, 1960.
269. GURMAN, E. B. The effect of self, task and interaction orientation on brainstorming. Unpublished doctoral dissertation. Baton Rouge: Louisiana State Univ., 1962.
270. GUTTMAN, L. The third component of scalable attitudes. *Int. J. opin. att. Res.,* 1950, **4,** 285–287.
271. HABBE, S. Does communication make a difference? *Mgmt. Rec.,* 1952, **14,** 414–416, 442–444.
272. HABERSTROH, C. J. Goals, programs and the training function. *Seminar on basic research on management controls.* Palo Alto, Calif.: Stanford Univ., 1963.
273. HAINES, G., HEIDER, F., & REMINGTON, D. The computer as a small group member. *Adm. Sci. Quart.,* 1961–1962, **6,** 360–374.
274. HAIRE, M. Role-perceptions in labor-management relations: an experimental approach. *Industr. labor relat. Rev.,* 1955, **8,** 204–216.
275. HAIRE, M. Psychological problems relevant to business and industry. *Psychol. Bull.,* 1959, **56,** 169–194.

276. HAIRE, M. Biological models and empirical theories of the growth of organizations. In M. Haire (ed.), *Modern organization theory*. New York: Wiley, 1959.

277. HAIRE, M. Business is too important to be studied only by economists. *Amer. Psychol.*, 1960, **15**, 271–273.

278. HAIRE, M. What is organized in an organization. In M. Haire (ed.), *Organization theory in industrial practice*. New York: Wiley, 1962.

279. HAIRE, M., GHISELLI, E. E., & PORTER, L. W. Psychological research on pay: an overview. *Industr. Relat.*, 1963, **3**, 1–8.

280. HAIRE, M., & GOTTSDANKER, J. S. Factors influencing industrial morale. *Personnel*, 1950–51, **27**(6), 445–454.

281. HAIRE, M., & MORRISON, F. School children's perceptions of labor and management. *J. soc. Psychol.*, 1957, **46**, 179–197.

282. HALPERN, R. S. Employee unionization and foreman's attitudes. *Admin-Sci. Quart.*, 1961–1962, **6**, 73–88.

283. HAMBLIN, R. L., & MILLER, L. K. Variations in interaction profiles and group size. *Sociological Quart.*, 19, 105–117.

284. HAMBLIN R. L., & WIGGINS, J. A. *Ambiguity and the rate of social adaptation*. Tech. Rept. 1, Contract onr 811(16). St. Louis: Washington Univ., 1959.

285. HAMMOND, K. R. Measuring attitudes by error-choice: an indirect method. *J. abnorm. soc. Psychol.*, 1948, **43**, 38–48.

286. HANDYSIDE, J. D. An estimate of the size of primary working groups in British industry. In National Institute of Industrial Psychology (ed.), *The Foreman: a study of supervision in British industry*. London: Staples Press, 1951.

287. HARBISON, F. H., & COLEMAN, J. R. *Goals and strategy in collective bargaining*. New York: Harper, 1951.

288. HARE, A. P. A study of interaction and consensus in different sized groups. *Amer. soc. Rev.*, 1952, **17**, 261–267.

289. HARRELL, T. W. *Industrial psychology*. New York: Rinehart, 1949; rev. 1958.

290. HARRISON, R. L. Workers' perceptions and job success. *Personnel Psychol.*, 1959, **12**, 619–625.

291. HARVEY, O. J. *Reciprocal influence of group and three types of leaders in an unstructured situation*. Contract Nonr 2149(02). Nashville, Tenn: Vanderbilt Univ.

292. HEISE, G. A., & MILLER, G. A. Problem-solving by small groups using various communication nets. *J. abnorm. soc. Psychol.*, 1951, **46**, 327–335.

293. HEMPHILL, J. K. Relations between the size of the group and the behavior of "superior" leaders. *J. soc. Psychol.*, 1950, **32**, 11–22.

294. HEMPHILL, J. K. *Situation factors in leadership*. Bur. of Educ. Res. Monogr. No. 32. Columbus: Ohio State Univ., 1950.

295. HEMPHILL, J. K., & PEPINSKY, P. N. *Leadership acts*. Report 8, Contract N6ORI 17 T.D. III. NR 171 123. Columbus: Personnel Research Board, Ohio State Univ., 1955.

296. HEMPHILL, J. K., SEIGEL, A., & WESTIE, C. W. An exploratory study of relations between perception of leader behavior, group characteristics and expectations concerning the behavior of ideal leaders. Unpublished manuscript.

297. HENRIKSSON, E. *Frånvaro från arbetet*. Stockholm: Norstedt, 1954.

298. HERBST, P. G. The analysis of social flow systems. *Hum. Relat.*, 1954, **7**, 327–336.

299.   HERSEY, R. Psychology of workers. *Personnel*, 1936, **14**, 291–296.
300.   HERSEY, R. *Zest for work*. New York: Harper, 1955.
301.   HERZBERG, F. MAUSNER, B., & SYNDERMAN, B. B. *The motivation to work*. New York: Wiley, 1959.
302.   HEYNS, R. W. Effects of variation in leadership on participant behavior in group discussions. *Process of Admin. Conf.* Ann Arbor: Univ. of Michigan, 1950.
302a. HILL, J. M. M., & TRIST, E. L. A consideration of industrial accidents as a means of withdrawal from the work situation. Tavistock Pamphlet No. 4. London, 1962.
303.   HITES, R. W. A questionnaire for measuring leader-identification. *Amer. Psychol.*, 1953, **8**, 368(a).
304.   HOFFMAN, L. R. Similarity of personality: a basis for interpersonal attraction? *Sociometry*, 1958, **21**, 300–308.
305.   HOFFMAN, L. R. Homogeneity of member personality and its effect on group problem-solving. *J. abnorm. soc. Psychol.*, 1959, **58**, 27–32.
306.   HOFFMAN, L. R. Conditions for creative problem-solving. *J. Psychol.*, 1961, **52**, 429–444.
307.   HOFFMAN, L. R., & MAIER, N. R. F. The use of group decision to resolve a problem of fairness. *Personnel Psychol.*, 1959, **12**, 545–559.
308.   HOFFMAN, L. R., & SMITH, C. G. Some factors affecting the behavior of members of problem-solving groups. *Sociometry*, 1960, **23**, 273–291.
309.   HOLMBERG, A. R. The research-and-development approach to change: participant intervention in the field. In R. N. ADAMS & J. J. PREISS (eds.), *Human organization research*. Homewood, Ill.: Dorsey, 1960.
310.   HOOD, R. C. Business organization as a cross product of its purposes and of its environment. In M. Haire (ed.), *Organization theory and industrial practice*. New York: Wiley, 1962.
311.   HOOS, I. R. When the computer takes over the office. *Harvard Bus. Rev.*, 1960, **38**, 102–112.
312.   HOPPOCK, R. *Job satisfaction*. New York: Harper, 1935.
313.   HOPPOCK, R., & SHAFFER, R. J. Job satisfaction researches and opinions of 1940–1941. *Occupations*, 1943, **21**, 457–463.
314.   HORSFALL, A. B., & ARENSBERG, C. M. Teamwork and productivity in a shoe factory. *Hum. Organ.*, 1949, **8**(2), 13–26.
315.   HORWITZ, M., GOLDMAN, M., & LEE, F. J. *Effects of two methods of changing a frustrating agent on reduction of hostility*. Preliminary Rept., Contract N6ori 07144. Bur. of Educ. Res. Urbana: Univ. of Illinois, 1955.
316.   HOUSEHOLDER, F. J. A railroad checks on its communications. *Personnel*, *1954*, **32**, 413–415.
317.   HOVLAND, C. I., HARVEY, O. J., & SHERIF, M. Assimilation and contrast effects in reactions to communication and attitude change. *J. abnorm. soc. Psychol.*, 1957, **55**, 244–252.
318.   HOVLAND, C. I., & MANDELL, W. An experimental comparison of conclusion-drawing by the communicator and by the audience. *J. abnorm. soc. Psychol.*, 1952, **47**, 581–588.
319.   HOVLAND, C. I., & WEISS, W. The influence of source credibility on communication effectiveness. *Public opin. Quart.*, 1951–1952, **15**, 635–650.
319a. HULL, R. L., & HOLSTAD, A. Morale on the job. In Watson, G., *Civilian Morale*. New York: Reynal & Hitchcock, 1942, 362–364.
320.   HUMAN RELATIONS RESEARCH OFFICE. *What HumRRO is doing, 1955*. HumRRO Bull. 3. Washington: George Washington Univ., 1956.

321. HURNI, M. L. Decision-making in the age of automation. *Harvard Bus. Rev.*, 1955, **33**, 49–58.

322. HUSBAND, R. W. Cooperative vs. solitary problem solution. *J. soc. Psychol.*, 1940. **11**, 405–409.

323. HYMAN, R. Creativity and the prepared mind: the role of information and induced attitudes. In Taylor, C. (ed.), *Widening horizons in creativity.* New York: Wiley, 1964.

324. INDIK, B. P., GEORGOPOULOS, B. S., & SEASHORE, S. E. Superior-subordinate relationships and performance. *Personnel Psychol.*, 1961, **14**, 357–374.

325. INDUSTRIAL RELATIONS DEPARTMENT. *Communication in United States Steel.* Pittsburgh: U.S. Steel, 1953. Out of print.

326. INSTITUTE OF LABOR AND INDUSTRIAL RELATIONS. *Labor-management relations in Illini City.* Vol. 1: *The case studies.* Champaign, Ill., 1953.

327. IRWIN, F., & SMITH, W. Value, cost and information as determiners of decision. *J. exp. Psychol.*, 1957, **54**, 229–232.

328. IRWIN, F., SMITH, W., & MAYFIELD, J. F. Tests of *two* theories of decision in an expanded judgment situation. *J. exp. Psychol.*, 1956, **51**, 261–268.

329. JACKSON, J. M. Analysis of interpersonal relations in a formal organization. Unpublished doctoral dissertation. Ann Arbor: Univ. of Michigan, 1953.

330. JACOBSON, E., CHARTERS, W. W., JR., & LIEBERMAN, S. The use of the role concept in the study of complex organizations. *J. soc. Issues.*, 1951, **7**, 18–27.

331. JACOBSON, E., TRUMBO, D., CHEEK, G., & NANGLE, J. Employee attitudes toward technological change in a medium-sized insurance company. *J. appl. Psychol.*, 1959, **43**, 349–354.

332. JACOBSON, H. B., & ROUCEK, J. S. (eds.). *Automation and society.* New York: Philosophical Library, 1959.

333. JAMBOR, H. *Discrepancies in role expectations for the supervisory position.* Doctoral dissertation. Minneapolis: Univ. of Minnesota, 1954.

334. JANIS, I. L., & FESHBACH, S. Effects of fear-arousing communications. *J. abnorm. soc. Psychol.*, 1953, **48**, 78–92.

335. JAQUES, E. *The changing culture of a factory.* New York: Dryden, 1952.

336. JAQUES, E. Objective measures for pay differentials. *Harvard Bus. Rev.*, 1962, **40**(1), 133–138.

337. JARMAN, W. M., & WILLINGHAM, B. H. The decentralized organization of a diversified manufacturer and retailer—Genesco. In M. Haire (ed.), *Organization theory in industrial practice.* New York: Wiley, 1962.

338. JARRARD, L. E. Empathy: the concept and industrial applications. *Personnel Psychol.*, 1956, **9**, 157–167.

339. JARRETT, R. F., & SHERRIFFS, A. C. Propaganda, debate, and impartial presentation as determiners of attitude change. *J. abnorm. soc. Psychol.*, 1953, **48**, 33–41.

340. JASINSKI, F. J. Foreman relationships outside the work group. *Personnel*, 1956, **33**, 130–135.

341. JENKINS, W. O. A review of leadership studies with particular reference to military problems. *Psychol. Bull.*, 1947, **44**, 54–79.

342. JOHNSON, R. E. Results of the 1958 C.Y.I. opinion survey. *Soc. Sci. Res. Repts.* IV. *Surveys and inventories.* Standard Oil of N.J., 1962.

343. JONES, E. E., & KOHLER, R. The effects of plausibility on the learning of controversial statements. *J. abnorm. soc. Psychol.*, 1958, **57**, 315–320.

344.   JONES, J. P. People—the independent variable. In M. Haire (ed.). *Organization theory in industrial practice.* New York: Wiley, 1962.

345.   JURGENSEN, C. E. Selected factors which influence job preferences. *J. appl. Psychol.,* 1947, **31,** 553–564.

346.   JURGENSON, C. E. What job applicants look for in a company. *Personnel Psychol.,* 1948, **1,** 433–445.

347.   KAHN, R. L. An analysis of supervisory practices and components of morale. In H. Guetzkow (ed.), *Groups, leadership and men.* Pittsburgh: Carnegie Press, 1951.

348.   KAHN, R. L. Human relations on the shop floor. In E. M. Hugh-Jones (ed.), *Human relations and modern management.* Amsterdam: North-Holland, 1958.

349.   KAHN, R. L. Productivity and job satisfaction. *Personnel Psychol.,* 1960, **13,** 275–287.

349a. KAHN, R. L., WOLFE, D. M., QUINN, R. P., SNOEK, J. D., & ROSENTHAL, R. A. *Organizational stress: studies in role conflict and ambiguity.* New York: Wiley, 1964.

350.   KANGAN, M. Are good foremen all we need? *Bull. Industr. Psychol. Personnel Pract.,* 1951, **7**(2), 38–44.

351.   KAPLAN, N. Research administration and the administrator, USSR and U.S. *Admin. Sci. Quart.,* 1961–1962, **6,** 51–72.

352.   KAPONYA, P. G. Salaries for all workers. *Harvard Bus. Rev.,* 1962, **40**(3), 49–57.

353.   KARSH, B., & LEVINE, S. B., Industrial relations for the next generation. *Quart. Rev. of Bus. and Ec.,* February 1961, **1**(1), 18–29.

354.   KATZ, D. Morale and motivation in industry. In W. Dennis (ed.), *Current trends in industrial psychology.* Pittsburgh: Univ. of Pittsburgh, 1949.

355.   KATZ, D. Survey research center: an overview of the human relations program. In H. Guetzkow (ed.), *Groups, leadership and men.* Pittsburgh: Carnegie Press, 1951.

356.   KATZ, D., & KAHN, R. L. Some recent findings in human relations research. In G. E. Swanson, T. M. Newcomb, and E. L. Hartley (eds.), *Readings in social psychology.* New York: Holt, 1952.

357.   KATZ, D., MACCOBY, N., & MORSE, N. C. *Productivity, supervision and morale in an office situation.* Ann Arbor: Institute for Social Research, Univ. of Michigan, 1950.

358.   KATZELL, R. A., BARRETT, R. S., & PARKWAY, T. C. Job satisfaction, job performance, and situational characteristics. *J. appl. Psychol.,* 1961, **45,** 65–72.

359.   KELLEY, H. H. Communication in experimentally created hierarchies. *Hum. Relat.,* 1951, **4,** 39–56.

360.   KENDALL, W. E. Industrial psychology. *Annual rev. Psychol.,* 1956, **7,** 197–232.

361.   KENNEDY, J. E., & O'NEILL, H. E. Job content and workers' opinions. *J. appl. Psychol.,* 1958, **42,** 372–375.

369.   KEOWN, W. H. *Some dimensions of company-union downward communication.* Bur. Bus. Res. Madison: Univ. of Wisconsin, 1955.

363.   KERR, C., DUNLOP, J. T., HARBISON, F. H., AND MYERS, C. A. *Industrialism and industrial man: the problems of labor and management in economic growth.* Cambridge, Mass.: Harvard Univ. 1960.

364.   KERR, C., & SIEGEL, A. The interindustry propensity to strike—an in-

ternational comparison. In A. Kornhauser, R. Dubin, and A. M. Ross (eds.), *Industrial conflict.* New York: McGraw-Hill, 1954.

365. KERR, W. A. Labor turnover and its correlates. *J. appl. Psychol.,* 1947, **31,** 366 – 371.

366. KIRCHNER, W., & BELENKER, J. What employes want to know. *Personnel,* 1955, **33,** 378 – 379.

367. KLARE, G. R., MABRY, J. E., & GUSTAFSON, L. M. The relationship of human interest to immediate retention and to acceptability of technical material. *J. appl. Psychol.,* 1955, **39,** 92 – 95.

368. KLAUS, D. J., & GLASER, R. Team learning as a function of member learning characteristics. Eastern Psychological Association Meeting. New York, 1963.

369. KNAUFT, E. B. Measured changes in acceptance of an employee publication. *J. appl. Psychol.,* 1951, **35,** 151 – 156.

370. KNIGHT, G. F., BRIDGMAN, J. J., & WENDT, E. R. Fair play fairly arrived at: the Burroughs exempt program. *Personnel,* 1961, **38**(1), 62 – 70.

371. KNOWLES, K. *Strikes: a study in industrial conflict.* New York: Philosophical Library, 1952.

372. KNOWLES, W. H. Human relations in industry: research and concepts. *Calif. mgmt. Rev.,* 1958, **1,** 87 – 105.

373. KORNHAUSER, A. Observations on the psychological study of labor-management relations. *Personnel Psychol.,* 1961, **14,** 241 – 249.

374. KRECH, D., CRUTCHFIELD, R. S., & BALLACHEY, E. L. *Individual in society.* New York: McGraw-Hill, 1962.

375. KRIEDT, P. H., & GADEL, M. S. Prediction of turnover among clerical workers. *J. appl. Psychol.,* 1953, **37,** 338 – 340.

376. KRUGMAN, H. E. Top-sacred scientists? *Personnel,* 1955, **32,** 44 – 46.

377. KUNNATH, J. G., & KERR, W. A. Function analysis of thirty-two American corporate boards. *J. appl. Psychol.,* 1953, **37,** 65 – 68.

378. KURILOFF, A. H. Management by integration and self-control. *Proceedings of the Industrial Engineering Institute,* February, 1963.

379. LAFITTE, P. *Social structure and personality in the factory.* New York: Macmillan, 1958.

380. LANDSBERGER, H. A. Interaction process analysis of the mediation of labor-management disputes. *J. abnorm. soc. Psychol.,* 1955, **51,** 552 – 558.

381. LANDSBERGER, H. A. The horizontal dimension in bureaucracy. *Admin. Sci. Quart.,* 1961 – 1962, **6,** 299 – 332.

382. LANIER, L. H. An evaluation of the annual review of psychology (volumes I – IV). *Psychol. Bull.,* 1954, **51,** 180 – 190.

383. LANZETTA, J. T., & ROBY, T. B. Effects of work-group structure and certain task variables on group performance. *J. abnorm. soc. Psychol.,* 1956, **53,** 307 – 314.

384. LAURENT, H. Incentives study. *Soc. Sci. Res. Repts. IV. Surveys and inventories.* Standard Oil of N.J., 1962.

385. LAWLER, E. E., 3d, & PORTER, L. W. Perceptions regarding management compensation. *Industrial Relations,* 1963, **3,** 41 – 49.

386. LAWRENCE, L. C., & SMITH, P. C. Group decision and employe participation. *J. appl. Psychol.,* 1955, **39,** 334 – 337.

387. LAWSHE, C. H., DUNLAP, J. W., KAAN, R. L., SHARTLE, C. L., & KATZELL, R. A. Blueprinting the next ten years of industrial psychology. *Personnel Psychol.,* 1959, **12,** 29 – 48.

388.   LAWSHE, C. H., & GUION, R. M. A comparison of management-labor atti-
       tudes toward grievance procedures. *Personnel Psychol.*, 1951, **4,** 3 – 17.
389.   LEARNED, E. P., ULRICH, D. N., & BOOZ, D. R. *Executive action.* Cambridge,
       Mass.: Harvard Univ., 1951.
390.   LEAVITT, H. J. Some effects of certain communication patterns on group
       performance. *J. abnorm. soc. Psychol.*, 1951, **46,** 38 – 50.
391.   LEAVITT, H. J. *Managerial psychology.* Chicago: Univ. of Chicago, 1958.
392.   LEAVITT, H. J. Recent concepts in administration. *Personnel Psychol.*, 1960,
       13, 287 – 294.
393.   LEAVITT, H. J. Task ordering and organizational performance in the
       common target game. *Behav. Sci.*, 1960, **5,** 233 – 239.
393a   LEAVITT, H. J. Recent concepts in administration. *Personnel Psychol.*, 1960,
       13, 287 – 294.
394.   LEAVITT, H. J. Toward organizational psychology. Address for Walter V.
       Bingham Day. Pittsburgh: Carnegie Institute of Technology, 1961.
395.   LEAVITT, H. J. Unhuman organizations. *Harvard Bus. Rev.*, 1962, **40**(4),
       90 – 98.
396.   LEAVITT, H. J., & BASS, B. M. Organizational psychology. *Annual rev.
       Psychol.*, 1964, **15,** 371 – 398.
397.   LEAVITT, H. J., & MUELLER, A. H. Some effects of feedback on communi-
       cations. *Hum. Relat.*, 1951, **4,** 401 – 410.
398.   LEAVITT, H. J., & WHISLER, T. L. Management in the 1980's. *Harvard
       Bus. Rev.*, 1958, **36,** 41 – 48.
399.   LEE, F. J., HORWITZ, M., & GOLDMAN, M. Power over decision-making
       and the response to frustration in group members. *Amer. Psychol.*, 1954, **8,**
       413 – 414 (Abstract).
400.   LEEPER, R. Cognitive processes. In S. S. Stevens (ed.), *Handbook of experi-
       mental psychology.* New York: Wiley, 1951.
401.   LESIEUR, F. (ed.) *The Scanlon plan.* New York: Wiley, 1958.
402.   LESTER, R. A. *Hiring practices and labor competition.* Princeton, N.J.: Prince-
       ton Univ., 1954.
403.   LEVENSTEIN, A. The psychologist joins the labor conflict. *Personnel Psy-
       chol.*, 1961, **14,** 250 – 259.
404.   LEVINE, J., & BUTLER, J. Lecture vs. group decision in changing behavior.
       J. appl. Psychol., 1952, **36,** 29 – 33.
405.   LEWIN, K. Frontiers in group dynamics: concept, method and reality in
       social science, social equilibria and social change. *Hum. Relat.*, 1947, **1,** 5 – 41.
406.   LEWIN, K., LIPPITT, R., & WHITE, R. K. Patterns of aggressive behavior in
       experimentally created social climates. *J. soc. Psychol.*, 1939, **10,** 271 – 299.
407.   LEWIS, D. J., & DUNCAN, C. P. Expectation and resistance to extinction of
       a lever-pulling response as functions of percentage of reinforcement and
       amount of reward. *J. exp. Psychol.*, 1957, **54,** 115 – 120.
408.   LICHTENBERG, P., & DEUTSCH, M. *A descriptive review of research on the
       staff process of decision-making.* AFPTRC-TR-54-129. San Antonio, Texas,
       1954.
409.   LIKERT, R. A technique for the measurement of attitudes. *Arch. Psychol.*,
       1932, No. 140.
410.   LIKERT, R. Effective supervision: an adaptive and relative process. *Per-
       sonnel Psychol.*, 1958, **11,** 317 – 332.
411.   LIKERT, R. Measuring organizational performance. *Harvard Bus. Rev.*,
       1958, **36,** 41 – 50.

412. LIKERT, R. *New patterns of management.* New York: McGraw-Hill, 1961.
413. LINCOLN, J. F. *Incentive management.* Cleveland: Lincoln Electric, 1951.
414. LLOYD, L. E. Origins and objectives of organizations. In M. Haire (ed.), *Organization theory in industrial practice.* New York: Wiley, 1962.
415. LODAHL, T. M., & PORTER, L. W. Psychometric score patterns, social characteristics, and productivity of small industrial work groups. *J. appl. Psychol.,* 1961, **45,** 73–79.
416. LOOMIS, J. L. Communication, the development of trust, and cooperative behavior. *Hum. Relat.,* 1959, **12,** 305–315.
417. LORENZ, E. Zur psychologie der industriellen gruppen arbeit. *Zeitschrift für angewandte Psychol.,* 1933, **45,** 1–45.
418. LORGE, I., FOX, D., & BRENNER, M. A survey of studies contrasting the quality of group performance and individual performance, 1920–1957. *Psychol., Bull.,* 1958, **53,** 337–372.
419. LORGE, I., WELTZ, P., FOX, D., & HERROLD, K. Evaluation of decisions written by *ad hoc* groups and simulated commanders. In A. H. Rubenstein & C. J. Haverstroh (eds.), *Some theories of organization.* Homewood, Ill.: Irwin, 1960.
420. LOTSOF, E. Expectancy for success and decision-time. *Amer. J. Psychol.,* 1958, **71,** 416–419.
421. LUBIN, J. F. The research program on business games at the Wharton School. In W. R. Dill, *et al., Proceedings of the conference on business games.* New Orleans: Tulane Univ., 1962.
422. LUCE, R. D., & RAIFFA, H. *Games and decisions: introduction and critical survey.* New York: Wiley, 1957.
423. MACE, C. A. Advances in the theory and practice of incentives. *Occup. Psychol.,* 1950, **24,** 239–244.
423a. MACK, R. W., & SNYDER, R. C. The analysis of social conflict—toward an overview and synthesis. *J. conflict Resolution,* 1957, **1,** 212–248.
424. MACKINNEY, A. C., & JENKINS, J. J. Readability of employee's letters in relation to occupational level. *J. appl. Psychol.,* 1954, **38,** 26–30.
425. MAHONEY, G. M. *Supervisory and administrative practices associated with worker attitudes toward an incentive system.* Ann Arbor: Institute for Social Research, Univ. of Michigan, 1953.
426. MAIER, N. R. F. Screening solutions to upgrade quality: a new approach to problem-solving under conditions of uncertainty. *J. Psychol.,* 1960, **49,** 217–231.
427. MAIER, N. R. F. *Problem-solving discussions and conferences.* New York: McGraw-Hill, 1963.
428. MAIER, N. R. F., & DANIELSON, L. E. An evaluation of two approaches to discipline in industry. *J. appl. Psychol.,* 1956, **40,** 319–323.
429. MAIER, N. R. F., & HOFFMAN, L. R. Quality of first and second solutions to group problem-solving. *J. appl. Psychol.,* 1960, **44,** 278–283.
430. MAIER, N. R. F., HOFFMAN, L. R., HOOVEN, J. G., & READ, W. H. *Superior-subordinate communication in management.* AMA Res. Study 52, New York, 1961.
431. MAIER, N. R. F., & MAIER, R. A. An experimental test of the effects of "developmental" vs. "free" discussions on the quality of group decisions. *J. appl. Psychol.,* 1957, **41,** 320–323.
432. MAIER, N. R. F., & SOLEM, A. R. Improving solutions by turning choice situations into problems. *Personnel Psychol.,* 1962, **15,** 151–157.

433. MALONEY, P. W. Why professional-technical candidates accept or decline job offers. *Social Sci. Res. Repts.* IV. *Surveys and inventories.* Standard Oil of New Jersey, 1962.

434. MALTZMAN, I., BOGARTZ, W., & BREGER, L. A procedure for increasing word association originality and its transfer effects. *J. exper. Psychol.*, 1958, **56**, 392–398.

435. MALTZMAN, I., BROOKS, L. O., *et al.* The facilitation of problem-solving by prior exposure to uncommon responses. *J. exper. Psychol.*, 1958, **56**, 399–406.

436. MALTZMAN, I., SIMON, S., *et al. Effects of different amounts of training on originality.* Tech. Rept. 3, Contract Nonr 233(50). Los Angeles: Univ. of California, 1959.

437. MANDELL, M. M., & DUCKWORTH, P. The supervisor's job: a survey. *Personnel*, 1955, **31**, 456–462.

438. MANN, F. C. Changing superior subordinate relationships. *J. soc. Issues*, 1951, **7–8**, 56–63.

439. MANN, F. C., & HOFFMAN, L. R. *Automation and the worker: a study of social change in power plants.* New York: Holt, 1960.

440. MANN, F. C., & SPARLING, J. E. Changing absence rates. *Personnel*, 1956, **32**, 392–408.

441. MANN, F. C., & WILLIAMS, L. K. Observations on the dynamics of a change to electronic data processing equipment. *Admin. Sci. Quart.*, 1960, **5**, 217–256.

442. MARCH, J. G., & SIMON, H. A. *Organizations.* New York: Wiley, 1958.

443. MARCHETTI, P. V. Some aspects of the manager-employee relationship in the retail grocery. *Amer. Psychol.*, 1953, **8**, 402(a).

444. MARKS, A. R. N. An investigation of modifications of job design in an industrial situation and their effects on some measures of economic productivity. Unpublished doctoral dissertation. Berkeley: Univ. of California, 1954.

445. MARQUIS, D. G., GUETZKOW, H., & HEYNS, R. W. A social psychological study of the decision-making conference. In H. Guetzkow (ed.), *Groups, leadership and men.* Pittsburgh: Carnegie Press, 1951.

446. MARQUIS, L., & GOLDHAMMER, K. American values. In E. S. Wengert, D. S. Harwood, *et al., The study of administration.* Eugene: Univ. of Oregon, 1961.

447. MARRIOTT, R. Size of working group and output. *Occup. Psychol.*, 1949, **23**, 47–57.

448. MARRIOTT, R. Sociopsychological factors in productivity. *Occup. Psychol.*, 1951, **25**, 15–24.

449. MARRIOTT, R., & DENERLEY, R. A. A method of interviewing used in studies of workers' attitudes. II. Validity of the method and discussion of the results. *Occup. Psychol.*, 1955, **29**, 69–81.

450. MARROW, A. J., & DAVID, G. The turnover problem—why do they "really" quit? *Personnel Admin.*, 1951, **14**(6), 1–6.

451. MARROW, A. J., & FRENCH, J. R. P., JR. Changing a stereotype in industry. *J. soc. Issues*, 1945, **1**, 33–37.

452. MARSCHAK, J. Lecture presented at the Seminar on the Social Science of Organizations. Pittsburgh: Univ. of Pittsburgh, 1962.

453. MARSTON, W. M. Studies in testimony. *J. crim. law Criminol.*, 1924, **15**, 5–31.

454. MARTIN, N. H., & SIMS, J. H. Thinking ahead: power tactics. *Harvard Bus. Rev.*, 1956, **34**(6), 25.

455. MASLOW, A. H. *Motivation and personality.* New York: Harper, 1954.

456. MASSARIK, F., TANNENBAUM, R., KAHANE, M., & WESCHLER, J. R. Sociometric choice and organizational effectiveness: a multi-relational approach. *Sociometry*, 1954, **16**, 211–238.

457. MATHEWSON, S. B. *Restriction of output among unorganized workers.* New York: Viking, 1931.

458. MAYO, E., & LOMBARD, G. F. F. Teamwork and labor turnover in the aircraft industry of Southern California. No. 32. Boston: Harvard Bus. Sch., 1944.

459. MCBAIN, W. N. Noise, the "arousal hypothesis," and monotonous work. *J. appl Psychol.*, 1961, **45**, 309–317.

460. MCCLELLAND, D. C. Risk-taking in children with high and low need for achievement. In J. W. Atkinson (ed.), *Motives in fantasy, action and society.* Princeton, N.J.: Van Nostrand, 1958.

461. MCCURDY, H., & LAMBERT, W. E. The efficiency of small human groups in the solution of problems requiring genuine cooperation. *J. Personality*, 1952, **20**, 478–494.

462. MCDONALD, J. Applications of game theory in business and industry. Games symposium. St. Louis: Amer. Assoc. for the Advancement of Sci., 1952.

463. MCGEHEE, W., & GARDNER, J. E. Music in a complex industrial job. *Personnel Psychol.*, 1949, **2**, 405–418.

464. MCGRATH, J. E. A summary of small group research studies. Arlington, Va.: Human Sciences Research, Inc., 1962.

465. MCGREGOR, D. M. Conditions of effective leadership in the industrial organization. *J. consult. Psychol.*, 1944, **8**, 55–63.

466. MCGREGOR, D. M. *The human side of enterprise.* New York: McGraw-Hill, 1960.

467. MCNULTY, J. E. Organizational change in growing enterprises. *Admin. Sci. Quart.*, 1962, **7**, 1–21.

468. MEAD, M. *Male and female.* New York: Morrow, 1949.

469. MEADOW, A., PARNES, S. J., & REESE, H. Influence of brainstorming instructions and problem sequence on a creative problem-solving test. *J. appl. Psychol.*, 1959, **43**, 413–416.

470. MEIER, R. L. Explorations in the realm of organization theory. IV. The simulation of social organization. *Behavioral Sci.*, 1961, **6**, 232–248.

471. MELLINGER, G. Interpersonal trust as a factor in communication. *J. abnorm. soc. Psychol.*, 1956, **52**, 304–309.

472. MELMAN, S. *Dynamic factors in industrial productivity.* Oxford: Basil Blackwell, 1956.

473. MEREI, F. Group leadership and institutionalization. *Hum. Relat.*, 1949, **2**, 23–39.

474. MERRIHUE, H. F., & KATZELL, R. A. ERI—Yardstick of employee relations. *Harvard Bus. Rev.*, 1955, **33**, 91–99.

475. MERTON, R. K. Bureaucratic structure and personality. *Social Forces*, 1939–1940, **18**, 560–568.

476. METCALF, H. C., & URWICK, L. (eds.). *Dynamic administration. The collected papers of Mary Parker Follett.* Bath, England: Mgmt. Public Trust, 1941.

477. METZNER, H., & MANN, F. Employee attitudes and absences. *Personnel Psychol.*, 1953, **6**, 467–485.

478. MEYER, H. H., & WALKER, W. B. A study of factors relating to the effec-
      tiveness of a performance appraisal program. *Personnel Psychol.*, 1961, **14,**
      291–298.
479. MEYER, H. H., & WALKER, W. B. Need for achievement and risk prefer-
      ences as they relate to attitudes toward reward systems and performance
      appraisal in an industrial setting. *J. appl. Psychol.*, 1961, **45,** 251–256.
480. MILLER, F. G., & REMMERS, H. H. Studies in industrial empathy. II. Man-
      agements' attitudes toward industrial supervision and their estimates of
      labor attitudes. *Personnel Psychol.*, 1950, **3,** 33–40.
481. MILLER, J. G. Toward a general theory for the behavior sciences. *Amer.
      Psychol.*, 1955, **10,** 513–531.
482. MILLER, L. K., & HAMBLIN, R. L. *An evaluation of some assumptions of the
      Davis-Moore theory of stratification.* Contract Nonr 816(11). St. Louis: Wash-
      ington Univ., 1961.
483. MILLER, N. E. Effects of group size on group process and member satis-
      faction. *Process of Admin. Conf.* Ann Arbor: Univ. of Michigan, 1950. (Ab-
      stract)
484. MILLER, R. B. The newer roles of the industrial psychologist. In B. V. H.
      Gilmer (ed.), *Industrial psychology.* New York: McGraw-Hill, 1960.
485. MILLS, C. W., & ATKINSON, M. The trade union leader: a collective por-
      trait. *Pub. opin. Quart.*, 1945, **9,** 158–175.
486. MILLS, J. Changes in moral attitudes following temptation. *J. Personality,*
      1958, **26,** 517–531.
487. MINER, J. B., & CULVER, J. E. Some aspects of the executive personality
      J. appl. Psychol., 1955, **39,** 348–353.
488. MINTZ, A. Non-adaptive group behavior. *J. abnorm. soc. Psychol.*, 1951, **46,**
      150–159.
489. MOORE, H. T. The comparative influence of majority and expert opin-
      ion. *Amer. J. Psychol.*, 1921, **32,** 16–20.
490. MORSE, N. C. *Satisfactions in the white-collar job.* Ann Arbor: Institute for
      Social Research, Univ. of Michigan, 1953.
491. MORSE, N. C., & REIMER, E. The experimental change of a major organ-
      izational variable. *J. abnorm. soc. Psychol.*, 1956, **52,** 120–129.
492. MUESER, R. E. The weather and other factors influencing employee
      punctuality. *J. appl. Psychol.*, 1953, **37,** 329–337.
493. MULDER, M. Communication structure, decision structure and group
      performance. *Sociometry*, 1960, **23,** 1–14.
494. MURASKIN, J., & IVERSON, M. A. Social expectancy as a function of judged
      social distance. *J. soc. Psychol.*, 1958, **48,** 11–14.
495. NATIONAL INDUSTRIAL CONFERENCE BOARD. *Factors affecting employee
      morale.* Studies in Personnel Policy, No. 85, 1947.
496. NATIONAL INSTITUTE OF INDUSTRIAL PSYCHOLOGY. *Joint consultation in
      British industry.* London: Staples Press, 1952.
497. NEALEY, S. M. Pay and benefit preference. *Industr. Relat.*, 1963, **3,** 17–28.
498. NEWALL, A. N., SHAW, J. C., & SIMON, H. A. *Elements of a theory of human
      problem-solving.* P-971. Santa Monica, Calif.: The Rand Corp., 1957.
499. NEW YORK TIMES. The automation picture and the effects on the Ameri-
      can economy. July 14, 1963, IV, p. 3E. © 1963 by the New York Times
      Company. Reprinted by permission.
500. NICHOLSON, P. J. An experimental investigation of the effects of training
      upon creativity. Unpublished doctoral dissertation. Houston, Tex.: Univ.
      of Houston, 1959.

501. Nissen, H. W. The nature of drive as innate determinant of behavioral organization. In M. R. Jones (ed.), *Nebraska symposium on motivation*. Lincoln: Univ. of Nebraska, 1954.

502. Odiorne, G. S. Some effects of poor equipment maintenance on morale. *Personnel Psychol.*, 1955, **8**, 195–200.

503. Olds, J. Physiological mechanisms of reward. In M. R. Jones (ed.), *Nebraska symposium on motivation*. Lincoln: Univ. of Nebraska, 1955.

504. Opinion Research Corporation. *Public opinion index for industry*. October, 1953.

505. Osborn, A. F. *Applied imagination; principles and procedures of creative thinking*. New York: Scribner, 1953.

506. Osgood, C. E. *An alternative to war or surrender*. Urbana: Univ. of Illinois, 1963.

507. Page, R. H., & McGinnies, E. Comparison of two styles of leadership in small group discussion. *J. appl. Psychol.*, 1959, **43**, 240–245.

508. Palmer, F. H., & Myers, T. I. Sociometric choices and group productivity among radar crews. *Amer. Psychol.*, 1955, **10**, 441–442. (Abstract)

509. Palmer, G. *Second annual report*. Contract Nonr 1575(05). Baton Rouge: Louisiana State Univ., 1961.

510. Parkinson, C. N. *Parkinson's law, and other studies in administration*. Boston: Houghton Mifflin, 1957.

511. Parnes, S. J. Effects of extended effort in creative problem solving. *J. educ. Psychol.*, 1961, **52**, 117–122.

512. Parnes, S. J., & Meadow, A. Effects of 'brainstorming' instructions on creative problem-solving by trained and untrained subjects. *J. educ. Psychol.*, 1959, **50**, 171–176.

513. Patchen, M. *The choice of wage comparisons*. Englewood Cliffs, N.J.: Prentice-Hall, 1961.

514. Paton, W. A., & Dixon, R. L. *Make-or-buy decisions in tooling for mass production*. Bur. Bus. Res. Ann Arbor: Univ. of Michigan, 1961.

515. Payne, S. L. *The art of asking questions*. Princeton, N.J.: Princeton Univ., 1951.

516. Peak, H., & Morrison, H. W. The acceptance of information into attitude structure. *J. abnorm. soc. Psychol.*, 1958, **57**, 127–135.

517. Pearson, R. G. Scale analysis of a fatigue check list. *J. appl. Psychol.*, 1957, **41**, 186–191.

518. Pelz, D. C. Leadership within a hierarchial organization. *J. soc. Issues*, 1951, **7**, 49–55.

519. Pelz, D. C. *Motivation of the engineering and research specialist*. General Mgmt. Series No. 186. New York: Amer. Mgmt. Assoc., 1957.

520. Pennington, D. F., Jr., Harvey, F., & Bass, B. M. Some effects of decision and discussion on coalescence, change and effectiveness. *J. appl. Psychol.*, 1958, **42**, 404–408.

521. Pepinsky, H. B., Pepinsky, P. N., Minor, F. J., et al. Team productivity and contradiction of management policy commitments. *J. appl. Psychol.*, 1959, **43**, 264–268.

522. Pepinsky, H. B., Pepinsky, P. N., & Pavlik, W. P. *Motivational factors in individual and group productivity. I. Successful task accomplishment as related to task relevant personal beliefs*. Columbus: Ohio State Univ. Found., 1956.

523. Perry, D., & Mahoney, T. A. In-plant communications and employee morale. *Personnel Psychol.*, 1955, **8**, 339–346.

524. PETRULLO, L., & BASS, B. M. *Leadership and interpersonal behavior.* New York: Holt, Rinehart & Winston, 1961.

525. PFIFFNER, J. M. *The supervision of personnel: human relations in the management of men.* Englewood Cliffs, N.J.: Prentice-Hall, 1951.

526. PHELAN, J. L. Authority and flexibility in the Spanish Imperial bureaucracy. *Admin. Sci. Quart.,* 1960–1961, **5,** 47–65.

527. PODUSKA, JEANNE. *A study of the nature and stability of value patterns found among Sears retail executives.* Psychol. Serv. Sec., Nat'l. Personnel Dept., Sears, Roebuck & Company.

528. PORTER, J. M., JR. The arbitration of industrial disputes arising from disciplinary action. Proceedings of the Second Annual Meeting, Industrial Relations Research Association. In H. W. Karn & B. V. H. Gilmer. *Readings in industrial and business psychology.* New York: McGraw-Hill, 1952.

529. PORTER, L. W. Differential self-perceptions of management personnel and line workers. *J. appl. Psychol.,* 1958, **42,** 105–108.

530. PORTER, L. W. Self-perceptions of first-level supervisors compared with upper management personnel and with operative line workers. *J. appl. Psychol.,* 1959, **43,** 183–186.

531. PORTER, L. W. A study of perceived need satisfactions in bottom and middle management jobs. *J. appl. Psychol.,* 1961, **45,** 1–10.

532. PORTER, L. W. Job attitudes in management. I. Perceived deficiencies in need fulfillment as a function of job level. *J. appl. Psychol.,* 1962, **46,** 375–384.

533. PORTER, L. W., & GHISELLI, E. E. The self-perceptions of top and middle management personnel. *Personnel Psychol.,* 1957, **10,** 397–406.

534. PORTER, L. W., HAIRE, M., & GHISELLI, E. E. A cross-cultural study of management attitudes. Paper presented at the XVII International Congress of Psychology, Washington, 1963.

535. PORTER, L. W., & LAWLER, E. E. The effects of "tall" versus "flat" organization structures on managerial job satisfaction. *Personnel Psychol.,* 1964, **17,** 135–148.

536. POSTMAN, L., & ZIMMERMAN, C. Intensity of attitude as a determinant of decision-time. *Amer. J. Psychol.,* 1945, **58,** 510–518.

537. PRYER, M. W., & BASS, B. M. Some effects of feedback on behavior in groups. *Sociometry,* 1959, **22,** 56–63.

538. PSYCHOLOGICAL SERVICE OF PITTSBURGH. *Job attitudes: review of research and opinion.* Pittsburgh, 1955.

539. PUBLIC AND EMPLOYEE RELATIONS RESEARCH SERVICE. *Leadership style and employee morale.* New York: General Electric, 1958.

540. PURCELL, T. V. *The worker speaks his mind.* Cambridge, Mass.: Harvard Univ., 1953.

541. PURCELL, T. V. Dual allegiance to company and union. *Personnel Psychol.,* 1954, **7,** 48–58.

542. PURCELL, T. V. *Blue collar man: patterns of dual allegiance in industry.* Cambridge, Mass.: Harvard Univ., 1960.

543. RAMBO, W. W. The construction and analysis of a leadership behavior rating form. *J. appl. Psychol.,* 1958, **42,** 409–415.

544. RANEY, E. T. How readable is your employee publication? *Personnel Psychol.,* 1949, **2,** 437–459.

545. RAVEN, B. H., & FRENCH, J. R. P. Legitimate power, coercive power, and observability in social influence. *Sociometry,* 1958, **21,** 83–97.

546. RAVEN, B. H., & RIETSEMA, J. The effects of varied clarity of group goal and group path upon the individual and his relation to the group. *Hum. Relat.*, 1957, **10**, 29–45.

547. RAVEN, J. C. The comparative assessment of intellectual ability. *Brit. J. Psychol.*, 1949, **36**, 12–19.

548. READ, W. H. Some factors affecting the accuracy of upward communication at middle management levels in industrial organizations. Unpublished doctoral dissertation. Ann Arbor: Univ. of Michigan, 1960.

549. REILLEY, E. W. Sound organization—keystone of management development. In M. J. Dooher and V. Marquis (eds.), *The development of executive talent.* New York: Amer. Mgmt. Assoc., 1952.

550. REMITZ, U. *Professional satisfaction among Swedish bank employees.* Copenhagen: Munksqaard, 1960.

551. RESEARCH GROUP IN PSYCHOLOGY AND THE SOCIAL SCIENCES. *The technology of human behavior.* Washington: Smithsonian Institution, 1960.

552. REVANS, R. W. Human relations, management and size. In E. M. Hugh-Jones (ed.), *Human relations and modern management.* Amsterdam: North-Holland, 1958.

553. RICE, A. K. Productivity and social organization in an Indian weaving shed. *Hum. Relat.*, 1953, **6**, 297–329.

554. RICE, A. K. *Productivity and social organization: the Ahmedabad experiment.* London: Tavistock Publications, 1958.

555. RICHARDSON, F. L. W., JR., & WALKER, C. R. *Human relations in an expanding company.* New Haven: Yale Labor and Management Center, 1948.

556. RICHMOND, A. H. Conflict and authority in industry. *Occup. Psychol.*, 1954, **28**, 24–33.

557. RIECKEN, H. W. The effect of talkativeness on ability to influence group solutions to a problem. *Sociometry*, 1958, **21**, 309–321.

558. ROACH, D. E. Factor analysis of rated supervisory behavior. *Personnel Psychol.*, 1956, **9**, 487–498.

559. ROBERTS, A. H., & JESSOR, R. Authoritarianism, primitiveness, and perceived social status. *J. abnorm. soc. Psychol.*, 1958, **56**, 311–314.

560. RODGERS, D. A. Personality correlates of successful role behavior. *J. soc. Psychol.*, 1957, **46**, 111–117.

561. ROETHLESBERGER, F. J. The foreman: master and victim of double talk. *Harvard Bus. Rev.*, 1945, **23**, 283–298.

562. ROETHLESBERGER, F. J., & DICKSON, W. J. *Management and the worker.* Cambridge, Mass.: Harvard Univ., 1938.

563. ROFF, M. E. A study of combat leadership in the Air Force by means of a rating scale: group differences. *J. Psychol.*, 1950, **30**, 229–239.

564. ROGERS, M. S., FORD, J. D., & TASSONE, J. A. The effects of personnel replacement on an information-processing crew. *J. appl. Psychol.*, 1961, **45**, 91–96.

565. RONAN, W. W. Work group attributes and grievance activity. *J. appl. Psychol.*, 1963, **47**, 38–41.

566. ROSE, A. M. Needed research on the mediation of labor disputes. *Personnel Psychol.*, 1952, **5**, 187–200.

567. ROSE, A. M. *Union solidarity.* Minneapolis: Univ. of Minnesota, 1952.

568. Rose, A. M. Conditions for irrational choices. *Soc. Res.* 1963, **30**, 143–156.

569. ROSEN, H., & ROSEN, R. A. H. *The union member speaks.* Englewood Cliffs, N.J.: Prentice-Hall, 1955.

570. ROSEN, H., & ROSEN, R. A. H. The union business agent's perspective of his job. *J. personnel admin. industr. Relat.*, 1957, **3**, 49–58.

571. ROSENBAUM, M. E. Social perception and the motivational structure of interpersonal relations. *J. abnorm. soc. Psychol.*, 1959, **59**, 130–133.

572. ROSS, A. M., & HARTMAN, P. T. *Changing patterns of industrial conflict.* New York: Wiley, 1960.

573. ROSS, I. C., & Zander, A. Need satisfactions and employee turnover. *Personnel Psychol.*, 1957, **10**, 327–338.

574. ROSS, R. J. For LRP-rotating planners and doers. *Harvard Bus. Rev.*, 1962, **40**(1), 105–115.

575. ROTHE, H. F., & NYE, C. T. Output rates among machine operators. III. A non-incentive situation in two levels of business activity. *J. appl. Psychol.*, 1961, **45**, 50–54.

576. ROY, D. Quota restrictions and gold bricking in a machine shop. *Amer. J. Sociol.*, 1952, **57**, 427–442.

577. Roy, R. H. Do wage incentives reduce costs? *Industr. lab. relat. Rev.*, 1952, **5**, 195–208.

578. SANFORD, F. H. Leadership identification and acceptance. In H. Guetzkow (ed.), *Groups, leadership and men.* Pittsburgh: Carnegie Press, 1951.

579. SAPOLSKY, A. Effect of interpersonal relationships upon verbal conditioning. *J. abnorm. soc. Psychol.*, 1960, **60**, 241–246.

580. SARGENT, S. S. Emotional stereotypes in the Chicago Tribune. *Sociometry*, 1939, **2**, 74. J. L. Moreno, M.D. (ed.), Beacon House Inc., Publishers.

581. SAWATSKY, J. C. Psychological factors in industrial organization affecting employee stability. *Canad. J. Psychol.*, 1951, **5**, 29–38.

582. SAYLES, L. R. *Behavior of industrial work groups: prediction and control.* New York: Wiley, 1958.

583. SCHACHTER, S. Deviation, rejection, and communication. *J. abnorm. soc. Psychol.*, 1951, **46**, 190–207.

584. SCHACHTER, S., ELLERTSON, N., McBRIDE, D., & GREGORY, D. An experimental study of cohesiveness and productivity. *Hum. Relat.*, 1951, **4**, 229–238.

585. SCHACHTER, S., FESTINGER, L., WILLERMAN, B., & HYMAN, R. Emotional disruption and industrial productivity. *J. appl. Psychol.*, 1961, **45**, 201–213.

586. SCHMIDT, W. H., & TANNENBAUM, R. Management of differences. *Harvard Bus. Rev.*, 1960, **38**(6), 107–115.

587. SCHRAMM, W. Mass communication. *Annual rev. Psychol.*, 1962, **13**, 251–284.

588. SCHRODER, H. M., & HUNT, D. E. *The role of three processes in determining responses to interpersonal agreement.* Tech. Rept. 5, Project Nonr 171–055. Department of Psychology: Princeton, N.J.

589. SCHUTZ, W. C. What makes groups productive? *Hum. Relat.*, 1955, **8**, 429–465.

590. SCHUTZ, W. C. *FIRO: a three dimensional theory of interpersonal behavior.* New York: Rinehart, 1958.

591. SCOTT, W. D., CLOTHIER, R. C., et al. *Personnel management* (3d ed.). New York: McGraw-Hill, 1941.

592. SCOTT, W. H., et al. *Technical change and industrial relations: a study of the relations between technical change and social structure in a large steelworks.* Liverpool: Liverpool Univ., 1956.

593. SEASHORE, S. E. Group cohesiveness as a factor in industrial morale and productivity. *Amer. Psychol.*, 1954, **8**, 468(a).
594. SEIDMAN, J., LONDON, J., & KARSH, B. Why workers join unions. *Ann. Amer. acad. pol. soc. Sci.*, 1951, **274**, 75–84.
595. SELEKMAN, B. M. *Labor relations and human relations.* New York: McGraw-Hill, 1947.
596. SELLTIZ, C., JAHODA, M., DEUTSCH, M., & COOK, S. W. *Research methods in social relations.* New York: Holt, 1959.
597. SELZICK, P. Foundations of the theory of organization. *Amer. sociol. Rev.*, 1948, **13**, 25–35.
598. SEXTON, R., & STAUDT, V. Business communication: a survey of the literature. *J. soc. Psychol.*, 1959, **50**, 101–118.
599. SHARTLE, C. L. Leadership aspects of administrative behavior. *Amer. Psychol.*, 1950, **5**, 337(a).
600. SHARTLE, C. L. *Executive performance and leadership.* Englewood Cliffs, N.J.: Prentice-Hall, 1956.
601. SHARTLE, C. L. Value dimensions and situational dimensions in organizational behavior. *Proceedings of the Tenth Annual Meeting.* Industr. Relat. Assoc.
602. SHAW, M. E. Some effects of unequal distribution of information upon group performance in various communication nets. *J. abnorm. soc. Psychol.*, 1954, **49**, 547–553.
603. SHAW, M. E. A comparison of two types of leadership in various communication nets. *J. abnorm. soc. Psychol.*, 1955, **50**, 127–134.
604. SHEPARD, H. A. Superiors and subordinates in research. *J. Bus.*, 1956, **29**, 261–267.
604a. SHERIF, M., HARVEY, O. J. *et al.* Intergroup conflict and cooperation. The Robber's Cave Experiment. Norman: University of Oklahoma Press, 1961.
605. SHEPARD, H. A. The psychologist's role in union-management relations. *Personnel Psychol.*, 1961, **14**, 270–279.
606. SHIMMIN, S. Workers' understanding of incentive payment systems. *Occup. Psychol.*, 1958, **32**, 106–110.
607. SHISTER, J., & REYNOLDS, L. G. *Job horizons: a study of job satisfaction and labor mobility.* New York: Harper, 1949.
608. SHYCON, H. N., & MAFFEI, R. B. Simulation-tool for better distribution. *Harvard Bus. Rev.*, 1960, **6**, 65–75.
609. SIMBERG, A. L., & SHANNON, T. E. The effect of AC creativity training on the AC suggestion program. Flint, Michigan: AC Spark Plug Division, General Motors, 1959.
610. SIMON, H. A. Theories of decision-making in economics and behavioral science. *Amer. econ. Rev.*, 1959, **69**, 253–283.
611. SIMON, H. A. *The new science of management decision.* New York: Harper, 1960.
612. SIMPSON, R. L. Vertical and horizontal communication in organizations. *Admin. Sci. Quart.*, 1959, **4**, 188–196.
613. SINHA, D. Behavior in a castastrophic situation: a psychological study of reports and rumors. *Brit. J. Psychol.*, (Gen. Sec.), 1952, **43**, 200–209.
614. SIROTA, D. Some effects of promotional frustration on employees' understanding of, and attitudes toward, management. *Sociometry*, 1959, **22**, 273–278.

615. SKINNER, B. F. *Science and human behavior.* New York: Macmillan, 1953.

616. SLATER, C. W. Some factors associated with internalization of motivation towards occupational role performance. Unpublished doctoral dissertation. Ann Arbor: Univ. of Michigan, 1959.

617. SLICHTER, S. H., HEALY, J. J., & LIVERNASH, E. R. *The impact of collective bargaining on management.* Washington: Brookings Institution, 1960.

618. SMITH, E. E. The effects of clear and unclear role expectations on group productivity and defensiveness. *J. abnorm. soc. Psychol.,* 1957, **55,** 213–217.

619. SMITH, E. E., & KIGHT, S. S. Effects of feedback on insight and problem-solving efficiency in training groups. *J. appl. Psychol.,* 1959, **43,** 209–211.

620. SMITH, F. J., & KERR, W. A. Turnover factors as assessed by the exit interview. *J. appl. Psychol.,* 1953, **37,** 352–355.

621. SMITH, H. C. Music in relation to employee attitudes, piece work production, and industrial accidents. *Appl. Psychol., Monogr.,* 1947, No. 14.

622. SMITH, M. Control interaction. *J. soc. Psychol.,* 1948, **28,** 263–273.

623. SMITH, M. B. Recent developments in the field of social psychology. *Ann. Amer. acad. pol. soc. Sci.,* 1961, **338,** 137–143.

624. SMITH, P. C. The curve of output as a criterion of boredom. *J. appl. Psychol.,* 1953, **37,** 69–74.

625. SMITH, P. C. The prediction of individual differences in susceptibility to industrial monotony. *J. appl. Psychol.,* 1955, **39,** 322–329.

626. SMITH, P. C., & LEM, C. Positive aspects of motivation in repetitive work: effects of lot size upon spacing of voluntary work stoppages. *J. appl. Psychol.,* 1955, **39,** 330–333.

627. SMUTS, R. W. *European impressions of the American workers.* New York: King's Crown Press, 1953.

628. SOLEM, A. R., ONACHILLA, V. J., & HELLER, K. Z. The posting problems technique as a basis for training. *Personnel Admin.,* 1961, **24,** 22–31.

629. SPRINGER, D. Ratings of candidates for promotion by co-workers and supervisors. *J. appl. Psychol.,* 1953, **37,** 347–351.

630. STAGNER, R. Psychological aspects of industrial conflict. II. Motivation. *Personnel Psychol.,* 1950, **3,** 1–16.

631. STAGNER, R. Dual allegiance as a problem in modern society. *Personnel Psychol.,* 1954, **7,** 41–47.

632. STAGNER, R. *Psychology of industrial conflict.* New York: Wiley, 1956.

633. STAGNER, R. Motivational aspects of industrial morale. *Personnel Psychol.,* 1958, **11,** 64–70.

634. STAGNER, R. The gullibility of personnel managers. *Personnel Psychol.,* 1958, **11,** 347–352.

635. STAGNER, R., DERBER, M., & CHALMERS, W. E. The dimensionality of union-management relations at the local level. *J. appl. Psychol.,* 1959, **43,** 1–7.

636. STAGNER, R., FLEBBE, D. R., & WOOD, E. V. Working on the railroad: a study of job satisfaction. *Personnel Psychol.,* 1952, **5,** 293–306.

637. STANTON, E. S. Company policies and supervisors' attitudes toward supervision. *J. appl. Psychol.,* 1960, **44,** 22–26.

638. STARBUCK, W. H. *Organizational growth and development.* Paper No. 67. Lafayette, Ind.: Institute for Quantitative Research in Economics and Management, Purdue Univ., 1964.

639. STEDMAN, G. E. An appreciation index. *Personnel,* 1945, **24,** 64–72.

640. STENNETT, R. G. The relationship of performance level to level of arousal. *J. exp. Psychol.*, 1957, **54**, 54–61.

641. STEWART, L. Games today. In J. M. Kibbee, C. J. Craft, & B. Nanus (eds.), *Management games.* New York: Reinhold, 1961.

642. STINCHCOMBE, A. L. Bureaucratic and craft administration of production. *Admin. Sci. Quart.*, 1959, **4**, 168–187.

643. STOCKFORD, L. O., & KUNZE, K. R. Psychology and the pay check. *Personnel*, 1950, **27**, 129–143.

644. STOGDILL, R. M. Personal factors associated with leadership. A survey of the literature. *J. Psychol.*, 1948, **25**, 35–71.

645. STOGDILL, R. M. The sociometry of working relationships in formal organizations. *Sociometry*, 1949, **12**, 282.

646. STOGDILL, R. M. Studies in naval leadership. Part II. In H. Guetzkow (ed.), *Groups, leadership and men.* Pittsburgh: Carnegie Press, 1951.

647. STOGDILL, R. M. Dimensions of organization theory. Unpublished manuscript, 1964.

648. STONE, C. H., & KENDALL, W. E. *Effective personnel selection procedures.* Englewood Cliffs, N.J.: Prentice-Hall, 1956.

649. STONE, P., & KAMIYA, J. Judgments of consensus during group discussion. *J. abnorm. soc. Psychol.*, 1957, **55**, 171–175.

650. STOTLAND, E. Peer groups and reactions to power figures. *Amer. Psychol.*, 1954, **8**, 478(a).

651. STOUFFER, S. A. An analysis of conflicting social norms. *Amer. sociol. Rev.*, 1949, **14**, 707–717.

652. STRICKLAND, L. H. Surveillance and trust. *J. Personality*, 1958, **26**, 200–215.

653. STRODTBECK, F. L. Husband-wife interaction over revealed differences. *Amer. J. Soc.*, 1951, **16**, 468–473.

654. STRODTBECK, F. L., & HOOK, L. H. The social dimensions of a twelve-man jury table. *Sociometry*, 1961, **24**, 397–415.

655. STRONG, E. K., JR., *Vocational interests of men and women.* Palo Alto, Calif.: Stanford Univ., 1943.

656. STRONG, L. Everyday is doomsday: ordeal of executive decision. *Mgmt. Rev.*, 1955, **44**, 746–755.

657. STRYKER, P. A slight case of overcommunication. *Fortune*, 1954, **49**, 116–117, 150–155.

658. STUHR, A. W. Some outcomes of the New York employee survey. *Soc. Sci. Res. Repts.* IV. *Surveys and inventories.* Standard Oil of N.J., 1962.

659. STUHR, A. W. The reward system and general morale. *Soc. Sci. Res. Repts.* IV. *Surveys and inventories.* Standard Oil of N.J., 1962.

660. SUPER, D. Occupational level and job satisfaction. *J. appl. Psychol.*, 1939, **23**, 547–564.

661. SURVEY RESEARCH CENTER. *Productivity, supervision and employee morale.* Hum. Relat. Series 1, Rept. 1. Ann Arbor: Univ. of Michigan, 1948.

662. SUTHERLAND, E. H. *White-collar crime.* New York: Dryden, 1949.

663. SUTTELL, B. J. *Research on the specific leader behavior patterns most effective in influencing group performance.* Annual Tech. Rept. Contract Nonr 890(03). Washington: *Amer. Inst. Res.*, 1955.

664. SYSTEM DEVELOPMENT CORPORATION. *1959 national salary survey of human factors professional personnel.* Santa Monica, Calif., 1959.

665. TANNENBAUM, A. S. Control in organizations: individual adjustment and organizational performance. *Seminar on Basic Research in Management Controls.* Palo Alto, Calif.: Stanford Univ., 1963.

666. TANNENBAUM, R. Managerial decision-making. *J. Bus.,* 1950, **23,** 33–37.

667. TANNENBAUM, R., & MASSARIK, F. *Participation by subordinates in the managerial decision-making process.* No. 14. Los Angeles: *Inst. Industr. Relat.,* Univ. of California, 1950.

668. TANNENBAUM, R., WESCHLER, I. R., & MASSARIK, F. *Leadership and organization.* New York: McGraw-Hill, 1961.

669. TAYLOR, D. W., BERRY, P. C., & BLOCK, C. H. Does group participation when using brainstorming facilitate or inhibit creative thinking? *Admin. Sci. Quart.,* 1958, **3,** 23–47.

670. TEAD, O. *The art of leadership.* New York: McGraw-Hill, 1935.

671. TERRIEN, F. W. *The effect of changing size upon organizations.* First Annual Rept. Contract Nonr 6346(00) NR177-253. San Francisco: Institute of Social Science Research, San Francisco State College, 1963.

672. THEIL, H. Economic forecasts and policy (2d rev. ed.). Amsterdam: North-Holland, 1961.

673. THISTLETHWAITE, D. L., DE HAAN, H., & KAMENETZKY, J. The effects of "directive" and "non-directive" communication procedures on attitudes. *J. abnorm. soc. Psychol.,* 1955, **51,** 107–113.

674. THISTLETHWAITE, D. L., & KAMENETZKY, J. Attitude change through refutation and elaboration of audience counter-arguments. *J. abnorm. soc. Psychol.,* 1955, **51,** 3–12.

675. THOMPSON, V. A. *Modern organization: a general theory.* New York: Knopf, 1961.

676. THORNDIKE, R. L. How children learn the principles and techniques of problem-solving. *Forty-ninth Yearbook.* Part I. Nat. Soc. Stud. Educ. Chicago: Univ. of Chicago, 1950.

677. THURSTONE, L. L. The intelligence of policemen. *J. Personnel Res.,* 1922, **1,** 64–74.

678. THURSTONE, L. L. AND CHAVE, E. J. *The measurement of attitude.* Chicago: Univ. of Chicago, 1929.

679. TIFFIN, J. AND LAWSHE, C. H., JR. War Labor Board decision trends. *Personnel,* 1945, **22,** 78–83.

680. TILLMAN, R., JR. Problems in review: committees on trial. *Harvard Bus. Rev.,* 1960, **38**(2), 7–12, 162–172.

681. TIME. Broadening the job: an answer to specialization and boredom. 1954, **63,** No. 15, April 12, 1954, p. 100.

682. TITUS, C. H. *The process of leadership, human relations in the making.* Dubuque, Iowa: W. C. Brown, 1950.

683. TORRANCE, E. P. The behavior of small groups under the stress conditions of survival. *Amer. sociol. Rev.,* 1954, **19,** 751–755.

684. TORRANCE, E. P. Group decision-making and disagreement. *Soc. Forces,* 1956–57, **35,** 314–318.

685. TORRANCE, E. P. Leadership in the survival of small isolated groups. In *Symposium on Preventive and soc. Psychiat.* Washington: Superintendent of Documents, U.S. Government Printing Office, 1958, 309–327.

686. TORRANCE, E. P., & ZILLER, R. C. Crew decisions under conditions of uncertainty. Paper presented to National Research Council-Air Force

Symposium on Personnel, Training, and Human engineering research. Washington, 1956.

687. TROW, D. B. Autonomy and job satisfaction in task-oriented groups. *J. abnorm. soc. Psychol.*, 1957, **54**, 204–209.

688. TRUMBO, D. A. Individual and group correlates of attitudes toward work-related change. *J. appl. Psychol.*, 1961, **45**, 338–344.

689. TUDDENHAM, R. D. *Some correlates of yielding to a distorted group norm.* Tech. Rept. 8, Contract NR 170–159. Berkeley: Univ. of California, 1958.

690. TURNER, A. N. Management and the assembly line. *Harvard Bus. Rev.*, 1955, **33**(5), 40–48.

691. UDY, S. H., JR. Bureaucratic elements in organizations. *Amer. sociol. Rev.* 1958, **23**, 415–418.

692. UDY, S. H., JR. "Bureaucracy" and "rationality" in Weber's organization theory. *Amer. sociol. Rev.*, 1959, **24**, 791–795.

693. UHRBROCK, R. S. Attitudes of 4,430 employees. *J. soc. Psychol.*, 1934, **5**, 365–377.

694. UHRBROCK, R. S. Music on the job: its influence on worker morale and production. *Personnel Psychol.*, 1961, **14**, 9–38.

695. UPHOFF, W. H., & DUNNETTE, M. D. Understanding the union member. Minneapolis: Industrial Relations Center, Univ. of Minnesota, 1956.

696. VAIL, S. Alternative calculi of subjective probabilities. In R. M. Thrall, *et al., Decision processes.* New York: Wiley, 1954.

697. VAN ZELST, R. H. Worker popularity and job satisfaction. *Personnel Psychol.*, 1951, **4**, 405–412.

698. VAN ZELST, R. H. Sociometrically selected work teams increase production. *Personnel Psychol.*, 1952, **5**, 175–185.

699. VAUGHAN, J. A. Surveying the man-in-the-middle of an industrial organization. Unpublished doctoral dissertation. Baton Rouge: Louisiana State Univ., 1963.

700. VAUGHAN, J. A., & BASS, B. M. Simulating the man-in-the-middle. *Amer. Psychol.*, 1963, **18**, 432(a).

701. VERNON, H. M. *Industrial fatigue and efficiency.* London: Dutton, 1921.

702. VINACKE, W. E. *The psychology of thinking.* New York: McGraw-Hill, 1952.

703. VITELES, M. S. Selection of cashiers and predicting length of service. *J. Personnel Res.*, 1924, **2**, 467–473.

704. VITELES, M. S. *Industrial psychology.* New York: Norton, 1932.

705. VROOM, V. H. Some personality determinants of the effects of participation. *J. abnorm. soc. Psychol.*, 1959, **59**, 322–327.

706. VROOM, V. H. Ego involvement, job satisfaction and job performance. *Personnel Psychol.*, 1962, **15**, 159–177.

707. VROOM, V. H. The effects of attitudes on perception of organizational goals. *Hum. Relat.*, 1960, **13**, 229–240.

708. VROOM, V. H., & MAIER, N. R. F. Industrial social psychology. *Annual rev. Psychol.*, 1961, **12**, 413–446.

709. WALD, A. *Statistical decision functions.* New York: Wiley, 1950.

710. WALKER, C. R. *Steeltown.* New York: Harper, 1950.

711. WALKER, C. R. *Toward the automatic factory: a case study of men and machines.* New Haven, Conn.: Yale Univ., 1957.

712. WALKER, C. R. Life in the automatic factory. In R. Gray (ed.), *Frontiers of industrial relations.* Pasadena: California Institute of Technology, 1959.

713. WALKER, C. R., & GUEST, R. H. The man on the assembly line. Cambridge, Mass.: Harvard Univ., 1952.

714. WALKER, J., & MARRIOTT, D. R. A study of some attitudes to factory work. *Occup. Psychol.*, 1951, **25**, 181–191.

715. WALLACH, A., KOGAN, N., & BEM, D. J. Diffusion of responsibility and level of risk-taking in groups. Eastern Psychological Association Meeting, April, 1963.

716. WARNER, L. W., & ABEGGLEN, J. C. Occupational mobility in American business and industry 1928–1952. Minneapolis: Univ. of Minnesota, 1955.

717. WARREN, J. R. Vocational interests and the occupational adjustment of college women. *J. Counsel. Psychol.*, 1959, **6**, 140–147.

718. WATSON, A. K. Electronic Frankenstein's monster? *Forbes*, 1962, **90**, Oct. 15, 1962, 40.

719. WEAVER, C. H. The quantification of the frame of reference in labor-management communication. *J. appl. Psychol.*, 1958, **42**, 1–9.

720. WEBER, M. *The theory of social and economic organization.* Glencoe, Ill.: Free Press, 1947.

721. WEINBER, M. G. Observations on the growth of information-processing centers. In A. H. Rubenstein & C. J. Haverstroh (eds.), *Some theories of organization.* Homewood, Ill.: Irwin, 1960.

722. WEINLAND, J. D. An objective method of determining credit. *J. appl. Psychol.*, 1957, **41**, 354–357.

723. WEISS, E. C. Relation of personnel statistics to organizational structure. *Personnel Psychol.*, 1957, **10**, 27–42.

724. WEISS, W. The relationship between judgments of a communicator's position and extent of opinion change. *J. abnorm. soc. Psychol.*, 1958, **56**, 380–384.

725. WEISS, W., & FINE, B. J. *The effect of induced aggressiveness on opinion change.* Tech. Rept. No. 2, Contract Nonr 492–04. Boston: Boston Univ.

726. WEISS, W., & LIEBERMAN, B. *The effects of "emotional" language on the induction and change of opinions.* Tech. Rept. No. 6, Contract Nonr 492(04). Boston: Boston Univ., 1956.

727. WEISSKOPF-JOELSON, E., & ELISEO, T. S. An experimental study of the effectiveness of brainstorming. *J. appl. Psychol.*, 1961, **45**, 45–49.

728. WEITZ, J. A neglected concept in the study of job satisfaction. *Personnel Psychol.*, 1952, **5**, 201–205.

729. WEITZ, J. Job expectancy and survival. *J. appl. Psychol.*, 1956, **40**, 245–247.

730. WEITZ, J., ANTOINETTI, J., & WALLACE, S. R. The effect of home office contact on sales performance. *Personnel Psychol.*, 1954, **7**, 381–384.

731. WEITZ, J., & NUCKOLS, R. C. Job satisfaction and job survival. *J. appl. Psychol.*, 1955, **4**, 294–300.

732. WELCH, M. K. The ranking of occupations on the basis of social status. *Occupations*, 1949, **27**, 237–241.

732a. WENDLEND, L. V. Employment prognosis of the post-poliomyelitic. *J. appl. Psychol.*, 1952, **36**, 328–332.

733. WERTHEIMER, M. *Productive thinking.* New York: Harper, 1945.

734. WESCHLER, I. R. The personal factor in labor mediation. *Personnel Psychol.*, 1950, **3**, 113–132.

735. WHEELER, D., & JORDAN, H. Change of individual opinion to accord with group opinion. *J. abnorm. soc. Psychol.*, 1929, **24**, 203–206.

736. WHERRY, R. J. What coordination is necessary? *Personnel Psychol.*, 1948, **1,** 7–20.
737. WHERRY, R. J. An orthogonal re-rotation of the Baehr and Ash studies of the SRA employee inventory. *Personnel Psychol.*, 1954, **7,** 365–380.
738. WHERRY, R. J. Factor analysis of morale data: reliability and validity. *Personnel Psychol.*, 1958, **11,** 78–89.
739. WHISLER, T. L. The "assistant-to" in four administrative settings. *Admin. Sci. Quart.*, 1960–1961, **5,** 181–216.
740. WHYTE, W. F. *Human relations in the restaurant industry.* New York: McGraw-Hill, 1948.
741. WHYTE, W. F. The social structure of the restaurant. *Amer. J. Sociol.*, 1949, **54,** 302–308.
742. WHYTE, W. F. *Money and motivation.* New York: Harper, 1955.
743. WICKERT, F. R. Turnover, and employees' feelings of ego-involvement in the day-to-day operations of a company. *Personnel Psychol.*, 1951, **4,** 185–197.
744. WICKESBERG, A. K., & CRONIN, T. C. Management by task force. *Harvard Bus. Rev.*, 1962, **5,** 111–118.
745. WIEST, W. M., PORTER, L. W., & GHISELLI, E. E. Relationships between individual proficiency and team performance and efficiency. *J. appl. Psychol.*, 1961, **45,** 435–440.
746. WILKINS, L. T. Incentives and the young male worker. *Int. J. opin. att. Res.*, 1950–1951, **4,** 540–561.
747. WILLERMAN, B. Group identification in industry. Unpublished doctoral dissertation. Cambridge: Massachusetts Institute of Technology, 1949.
748. WILSON, A. T. M. Some aspects of social process. *J. soc. Issues,* 1951, **5,** 5–22.
749. WILSON, R. C., BEEM, H. P., & COMREY, A. L. Factors influencing organizational effectiveness. III. A survey of skilled tradesmen. *Personnel Psychol.*, 1953, **6,** 313–325.
750. WISPE, L. G., & THAYER, P. W. Role ambiguity and anxiety in an occupational group. *J. soc. Psychol.*, 1957, **46,** 41–48.
751. WOODWARD, J. *Management and technology.* Problems of Progress in Industry, No. 3. London: Dept. of Sci. and Industr. Res., Charles House, 1958.
752. WOODWORTH, R. S. *Experimental psychology.* New York: Holt, 1938.
753. WORTHY, J. C. Organizational structure and employee morale, *Amer. soc. Rev.*, 1950, **15,** 169–179.
754. WRAY, D. E. Marginal men of industry: the foremen. *Amer. J. Sociol.*, 1949, **54,** 298–301.
755. WYATT, S. *The effect of change in activity.* No. 26. Industrial Fatigue Research Board. London: H. M. Stationery Office, 1924.
756. WYATT, S. *Incentives in repetitive work.* No. 69. Industrial Health Research Board. London: H. M. Stationery Office, 1934.
757. WYATT, S., & MARRIOTT, R. *A study of attitudes to factory work.* No. 292. Medical Research Council. London: H. M. Stationery Office, 1956.
758. YOUNGBERG, C. F. X., HEDBERG, R., & BAXTER, B. Management action recommendations based on one vs. two dimensions of a job satisfaction questionnaire. *Personnel Psychol.*, 1962, **15,** 145–150.
759. ZAJONC, R. B. *The effects of feedback and group task difficulty on individual*

and group performance. Tech. Rept. No. 15. Contract Nonr 1224(34). Ann Arbor: Univ. of Michigan, 1961.

760.   ZALEZNIK, A. Review of "A Polish factory." *Admin. Sci. Quart.,* 1961 – 1962, **6,** 119 – 121.

761.   ZALEZNIK, A., CHRISTENSEN, C. R., & ROETHLESBERGER, F. J. *The motivation, productivity, and satisfaction of workers: a prediction study.* Boston: Harvard Bus. Sch., 1958.

762.   ZANDER, A. F. *Effects of group goals upon personal goals.* Contract Nonr 1147(03), Tech. Rept. No. 12. Washington: National Training Laboratories.

763.   ZILLER, R. C. Four techniques of decision-making under uncertainty. *Amer. Psychol.,* 1954, **8,** 498(a).

764.   ZILLER, R. C. Leader acceptance of responsibility for group action under conditions of uncertainty and risk. *Amer. Psychol.,* 1955, **10,** 475 – 476(a).

765.   ZILLER, R. C., & BEHRINGER, R. D. Group persuasion by the most knowledgeable member under conditions of incubation and varying group size. *J. appl. Psychol.,* 1959, **43,** 402 – 406.

766.   ZILLER, R. C., BEHRINGER, R. D., & GOODCHILDS, J. D. Group creativity under conditions of success or failure and variations in group stability. *J. appl. Psychol.,* 1962, **46,** 43 – 49.

767.   ZILLER, R. C., & EXLINE, R. V. Some consequences of age heterogeneity in decision-making groups. *Sociometry,* 1958, **21,** 198 – 211.

AUTHOR INDEX

444

SUBJECT INDEX